VOGUE KNITTING

Classic Patterns from the
World's Most Celebrated Knitting Magazine

VOGUE KNITTING

Classic Patterns from the
World's Most Celebrated Knitting Magazine

From the Editors at *Vogue Knitting*

Introduction by Trisha Malcolm

Foreword by Anna Sui

RIZZOLI
NEW YORK

New York · Paris · London · Milan

First published in the United States of America in 2011
by Rizzoli International Publications, Inc.
300 Park Avenue South, New York, NY 10010
www.rizzoliusa.com

Vogue Knitting
Copyright Texts © 2011 Trisha Malcolm, Anna Sui, SoHo Publishing

For Rizzoli International Publications:
Editors: Julie Schumacher & Mandy DeLucia
Managing Editor: Lynn Scrabis
Editorial Assistants: Kayleigh Jankowski & Ashleigh Allen
Photography of magazine interiors: Andrea Thompson
Photography of magazine covers: Pete Deevakul
Production: Jessica O'Neil
Designer: Celina Carvalho

For *Vogue Knitting*:
Authors: Martha Moran, Cheryl Krementz, Erin Slonaker
Project Managers: Erin Slonaker, Alexandra Joinnides
Copy Editor: Faith Hale

Front cover image by Rose Callahan
Case image by Marcus Tullis

Printed in China

2011 2012 2013 2014 / 10 9 8 7 6 5 4 3 2 1
Library of Congress Control Number: 2011932816
ISBN - 13: 978-0-8478-3680-2

Contents

Anna Sui

I'll always associate knitting with my mother. She loves to knit, and as a little girl, I learned everything from her. Although I never achieved her skill and speed, I soon learned how to make slippers (and later, gloves and sweaters). One Christmas, everyone who knew us received hand-knitted slippers! My cousins even remember me making knit outfits for their Barbies.

My mother often corrected my knitting boo-boos. I'll never figure out how she could go back to almost the beginning and re-knit overnight what took me days to finish. She always maintained perfect tension, completely even stitches and rows. For the more challenging projects, I would normally ask my mom to just make them for me!

One of my favorite things to do with my mom was to go to J.L. Hudson, the big department store in downtown Detroit, to look for yarns. I think my forte was more in the selection of yarns and patterns. I always loved exotic combinations like mixing mohair, angora, space dye, and Lurex. I remember during my glove mania period, I created a pair using black iridescent Lurex with pink angora cuffs. I also made sweaters mixing fuchsia mohair yarn with stripes and twists of Lurex, space dye nubby yarns, and orange angora!

Beginning with my first fashion show, I have been fortunate to work with James Coviello for all my knitted garments, hats, and accessories. James is a talent of unparalleled skill and keen sensibility. I'm very proud that our collaborations have been featured numerous times within the pages of *Vogue Knitting*.

Vogue Knitting represents the unlimited possibilities of knitwear. Paging through every issue helped me develop my love for hand-made things and introduced me to the work of many of my favorite designers. *Vogue Knitting* inspired me and fostered my own dream of becoming a fashion designer.

Trisha Malcolm

Like many knitters, I have always been fascinated by the history of knitting. While we know relatively little about the very first knitters, I imagine them being as mesmerized by their stitching as we are. I see them sitting for long hours making those familiar, repetitive motions or caring for their tools and the thread with which they were working. And I know they did not knit in isolation, but rather with their families and peers. They passed their knowledge from generation to generation, and eventually, as people traveled, knitting was passed from land to land. These knitters were the original keepers of the art. In fact, most of the cool climates on the planet have a distinct knitting heritage and culture that has evolved over centuries—and lasted regardless of war, famine, disease, and persecution. I would suggest that the evolution of knitting has sped up considerably in the last decade or two, as has much of the world's activities. Never before have there been such radical changes in such a short amount of time.

The realities of modern life have had an impact on the culture of knitting, to be sure. Whereas in the past local people assembled to knit, we now commune with knitters from all over the world via the Internet. We meet "our own kind" at specific knitting events, the number of which grows every year, drawing knitters from the far corners of the globe. Needles have gone from simple to high tech. What was once private knowledge passed from generation to generation is now available to all in the wealth of knitting books on every knitting topic imaginable, a huge number of which were published relatively recently. The number of patterns available on the Internet, for purchase or free, is in the millions. The few apps and tablet downloads available are just the tip of the iceberg, and we will only become more mobile with our computers and smart phones. That which is yet to come is, I am sure, going to be even more exciting!

But even as we have moved knitting into the twenty-first century, some things have not changed. We are still in tune with its farmyard beginnings, for instance. Knitters long ago were no doubt connected to the animals they herded—they cared for them daily, used their fleece or fiber to create yarn, and eventually were sustained by them as food. Knitting is the ultimate "green" endeavor, using that which is in the local environment, not doing harm, and often recycling. No animals are killed for fiber, and plant-based fibers come from quick-growing plants, making yarn a totally renewable resource.

Modern knitters, then, are still the caretakers of the art of knitting. We incorporate it into our daily lives, reinvent it, create new ideas and techniques, dream up new yarns and tools. We pass our knitting knowledge on to others, watching with delight as those we teach take to our craft. Centuries from now, people will still be knitting because of our stewardship at this time in history.

Vogue Knitting is both a part of the earlier knitting evolution and moving forward with the future of knitting. In terms of the world's knitting heritage, our story is a mere blip, but in the lifetimes of the past several generations of knitters, we have played an active part. The concept of taking knitting patterns and publishing them in magazines probably only started in the late nineteenth century, and *Vogue Knitting*

"And in the act of making things, just by living their daily lives, they also make history. . . . It's something to celebrate–clothes made in love and service, something women have always done."
–Anne Bartlett, *Knitting: A Novel*

In its thirty years, *Vogue Knitting* has been helmed by just twelve women. Left to right: Nancy J. Thomas (1992–1995), Adina Klein (2007–2008), Carla Scott (1995–1996), Lola Ehrlich (1986–1988), Margery Winter (1995–1996), Trisha Malcolm (1997–2007; 2008–present), Sonja Dagress (1991–1992), Gay Bryant (1996–1997). Not pictured: Polly Roberts (1982–1985), Marilyn Cooperman (1985–1986), Margaret Korn (1989–1990), Meredith Gray Harris (1990–1991).

has the longest history of publishing solely knitting pattern collections. We see no sign of stopping, either, digitally connecting to knitters the world over as the nature of craft publishing changes.

Our reality is that the myriad people who have created the pages that are honored in this book are but modern caretakers of the art of knitting, and at special and specific moments in the knitting continuum they have given themselves over to this publication. No one can ever truly own *Vogue Knitting*—we can only nurture it as it makes its way into the future. The first editor and her team who "birthed" the first issue into existence were no more or less excited than our current staff is when an issue arrives fully bound and ready for distribution. And every person who has contributed in any way between then and now feels the same way. Just as there is an unimaginable sense of pride when a knitting project is completed, there is a feeling of accomplishment when a magazine is published. I think the fact that we are a publication that has been "resuscitated" gives us a special sense of our history, and we take special care with that. Being a part of the Condé Nast history also instills a unique sense of pride in us all.

There are many creators and caretakers to thank: To those with the vision and foresight to test *Vogue Knitting* in the 1930s—though there are none of you alive today—we honor you for creating this publication and sustaining it. To all who worked on *Vogue Knitting* from then until 1969, we thank you for your dedication, your recording of knitting and fashion history, and your inspiration.

In my mind, the greatest caretaker of all has been the president of SoHo Publishing, our company, the man who had the idea to republish *Vogue Knitting*: Art Joinnides. Art is a visionary, and the mentor I have learned most from in my publishing career and twenty years at *Vogue Knitting*. His ability to think creatively and to recognize and honor the passion that keeps knitting alive has led this magazine on a unique path over the past thirty years.

Since the 1982 re-launch, each of the editors in chief who came before me have added their personalities to the pages: Polly Roberts, Marilyn F. Cooperman, Lola Ehrlich, Margaret C. Korn, Meredith Gray Harris, Sonja Bjorklund Dagress, Nancy J. Thomas, Margery Winter, Carla Scott, Gay Bryant, and Adina Klein.

Those who have given the most to the pages over the years are undoubtedly Executive Editor Carla Scott and Creative Director Joe Vior, who have a combined forty-five years of service to the magazine between them. Carla's technical acumen and leadership and Joe's brilliant creative vision and talent are priceless—I honor and am eternally grateful for them every day.

Many other staff and contributors have enriched the magazine over the years—as they do today. To name them would be to miss many, and I would hate to miss anyone. Thank you all for being a part of the heritage that is *Vogue Knitting* and making it the amazing publication it is.

Our greatest recognition is to you, our reader. Without your passion for knitting from our pages, we would not carry on this legacy. Thanks for collecting our magazines, saving every issue, for knitting our designs, for sharing your efforts with us and your friends and family, and for always coming back to us with your loyalty and dedication. And to those who have passed on the art of knitting to others, thank you for caretaking what could have become a lost art, like so many other specialist forms of needlework.

The pages of this beautiful book take us back in time as we look at not just the history of *Vogue Knitting*, but at the history of knitting, style, fashion, and the people who influence our world. Of the hundreds of patterns we've printed, we've selected the most striking, the favorites, the interesting, and those that were a sign of the time they were published. They describe an amazing evolution. We hope you enjoy this historical perspective and join us in celebrating the milestone that is our thirtieth anniversary.

Trisha Malcolm, Editor in Chief

A Brief History
of *Vogue Knitting*

For thirty years, *Vogue Knitting* has arguably been the world's premier knitting magazine. Like the craft of knitting itself, *Vogue Knitting* has endured the ups and downs of a cyclical industry, the advent of new technologies, and the whims of all of those who find creative outlet in yarn and needles. So, what is it that distinguishes *Vogue Knitting* from its competitors, allowing it to thrive even during periods when the popularity of knitting waned? The answer to this question actually begins not thirty years ago, but eighty years ago, under the auspices of Condé Nast.

Winter 2010–2011

CASTING ON

Vogue Knitting first appeared on magazine stands in the 1930s, an era when knitting enjoyed great popularity as a practical, as well as pleasurable, endeavor. Published by Condé Nast and known then as *Vogue's Book of Knitting and Crochet*, the magazine was a direct response to readers' enthusiasm for the high-fashion knitwear sometimes featured on the pages of that ultimate arbiter of fashion and style (and the prize horse in the Condé Nast stable), *Vogue* magazine.

Vogue's Book of Knitting and Crochet debuted in 1932 at the modest price of 35 cents (the same price as *Vogue* magazine at the time; about 5 dollars in 2011). Over the next twelve years, three more editions were released (the 2nd, 3rd, and 4th) but it wasn't until 1944 that annual publication began, sporting a new title, *Vogue's Knitting Book, 5th Edition.* Annual editions continued until 1949, when output was increased to two issues a year (Spring/Summer and Fall/Winter), a schedule that sustained itself until 1969, when the magazine ceased publication. Along the way, special editions on children's knitwear (1964) and men's fashions (1965) were released; in the 1960s, the magazine received yet another title, *Vogue Knitting.*

From the beginning, the *Vogue* standards of quality, high-style high-fashion were evident in *Vogue Knitting*'s pages. Helmed by Ruth Seder (Cook), who also edited the Condé Nast sewing title *Vogue Patterns*, and the legendary Alexander Lieberman, who held senior artistic and editorial positions in his thirty-two-year tenure at *Vogue* (including Editorial Director from 1962–1994), *Vogue Knitting* showcased original designs photographed by the same high-caliber fashion photographers who shot for *Vogue:* Constantin Joffe, Frances McLaughlin-Gill, Clifford Coffin, Serge Balkin, Haanel Cassidy, Luis Lemus, William

Grisby and Fred Baker in the 1940s (Baker continued into the 1950s); Paul Himmel, Ted Croner, Sante Forlano, and Roger Prigentsuch in the 1950s; and Lionel Kazan, Andrei Punsuh, Ian MacWeeney, Tom Palumbo, Gianni Penati, and Jerry Savlati in the 1960s.

Throughout the '40s, '50s, and '60s, the magazine featured the ultimate in chic knitwear fashions and accessories—sweaters, dresses, jackets, suits, shawls, scarves, hats, gloves, and mitts, along with home décor items and even sandals and jewelry—each accompanied by how-to instructions. (The style of the instructions bears little resemblance to those on the pages of *Vogue Knitting* today.) The designs were worn by top models of the day and often shot on location. Florida, the Bahamas, Morocco, Bermuda, Cape Cod, Jamaica, Panama, and Cuba were just a few of the backdrops. Each issue also included a photo-illustrated technical and how-to section, along with advertisements from knitting-related businesses. Much like today, the early *Vogue Knitting*'s primary advertisers were yarn companies. The ads ran in full color, in contrast to *Vogue Knitting*'s black-and-white editorial pages. (Though the first four editions of *Vogue Knitting* included some hand-colored fashion spreads, in 1944 the magazine went to an all black-and-white editorial format. Color wasn't reintroduced until the tenth edition in 1947.) Knitting was a popular pastime, and American women were delighted with the means to re-create high-fashion pieces at home.

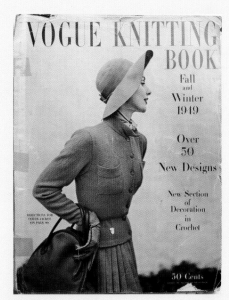

Fall/Winter 1949

But knitting's popularity (and *Vogue Knitting*) would not endure. By 1969, knitting was no longer a necessity, nor even a prized leisure activity. Women were entering the work force in increasing numbers, leaving little time for handcrafts, and technological advances in garment manufacturing and distribution resulted in an abundance of inexpensive ready-to-wear in everyone's local stores. Emerging feminism also encouraged a backlash against so-called "women's work." As a result, knitting and *Vogue Knitting* became casualties of a cultural revolution, and Condé Nast ceased publishing the magazine with the Fall/Winter 1969 issue.

Knitting went quietly underground for more than a decade, considered dated and dowdy by many. But in the early 1980s handknits began showing up on the fashion runways, and American women began pulling their needles out of the closet and looking for patterns that would help them re-create the styles they saw in the stores. And thanks to a few forward-thinking editors and publishers at another *Vogue*-branded magazine, *Vogue Knitting* again ventured onto the newsstands, taking a similar path to the one that brought it there in the 1930s.

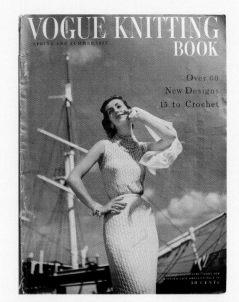

Spring/Summer 1955

In 1961, Condé Nast sold their Vogue Patterns line and companion magazine, *Vogue Patterns,* to the Butterick Company, who also licensed the Vogue name. By then Condé Nast had become advertising-driven, and these niche businesses no longer fit their model. "My sense of it is that they changed their DNA and didn't want to be in the instruction business anymore. So, they sold the pattern line and sewing magazine to us [Butterick], and eventually let *Vogue Knitting* go under," says current *Vogue Knitting* President Art Joinnides.

By 1980, the fashion industry was again focusing on knitwear on the runways, and *Vogue Patterns* decided to test the crafting waters by including a knitting pattern on its pages. (Future Editor Nancy Thomas designed, knit, and wrote instructions for the first designs—mother/daughter cabled pullover sweaters.) Readers were entranced and began asking for more.

Encouraged by the positive response, *Vogue Patterns* published more knitwear patterns and made the rounds of the yarn company showrooms in New York, learning more about the business with each visit. After the staff attended its first yarn industry trade show, Butterick's executives immediately recognized an opportunity and Joinnides began negotiations with Condé Nast to secure the rights to *Vogue Knitting*. "I looked at what we were at Butterick and realized we weren't just a sewing company, we were a content company, a DIY company. Our asset was teaching, and I was looking for other topics we could teach. In 1980–81, the knitting market was strong and well resourced, ripe for a high-quality knitting magazine. I called Bob Lapham [President of Condé Nast] and *Vogue Knitting* was re-launched on our handshake," recalls Art.

Vogue Knitting returned to the newsstands in the fall of 1982. Pulled together by Polly Roberts (then Editor in Chief of *Vogue Patterns)* and a team of talented art and editorial staff that included Nancy Thomas and Margaret Korn, it was filled with both beautiful knits and inspiring photography. The *Vogue Knitting* staff reached out to the top talents in the hand-knitting industry from designers to technical editors to yarn companies to cobble together the first issue. At the showroom of the Dutch yarn company Neveda, the editors discovered a lovely, romantic soft-yellow cardigan that manifested the high style and impeccable craftsmanship that would be the hallmark of *Vogue Knitting* and asked to use it in the premiere issue. That particular piece was designed and knit by Mari Lynn Patrick (who would go on to be the most prolific of all *Vogue Knitting*'s designers and technical contributors). The person who delivered the happy news that the magazine could indeed use the sweater was none other than Carla Scott (née Patrick), Mari Lynn's sister and *Vogue Knitting*'s resident technical genius and current Executive Editor.

The *Vogue Knitting* staff continued to harness the top talent of the hand-knitting industry, eventually producing two issues a year. Both Carla and Mari Lynn became regular contributors, Carla as an

From Swatch to Print the Old-Fashioned Way

Getting those first sweaters from swatch to printed page wasn't easy. Electronic publishing hadn't established itself in 1982, and aside from basic word processing, no part of the magazine was executed by computer. Charts and schematics were drawn by hand with every line of text sent off to an outside typesetter. Once set, the type was handed over to graphic designers who used X-acto blades, tape, and rubber cement to create "paste-ups" of each and every page. The advent of desktop publishing and digital photography has radically changed the way *Vogue Knitting* pages go to press today, but the attention to quality and detail fostered in those early years still remains.

instruction writer and Mari Lynn as a designer and technical expert. *Vogue Patterns'* long-term relationships with top Seventh Avenue designers meant that *Vogue Knitting*'s pages also included the work of leading designers of the time, including Perry Ellis, Calvin Klein, and Donna Karan. Contributions also flowed from the crème de la crème of hand-knitting design, with Anne Mieke, Nancy Marchant, Deborah Newton, and Kaffe Fassett supplying sweaters. And the magazine had plenty of technical substance to back up the style. Knitting legend Elizabeth Zimmermann began contributing technical articles in the Spring/Summer 1984 issue (she'd written for the original magazine from the 1950s until 1969 when it ceased publication) and icon Barbara Walker published her first *Vogue Knitting* piece in 1984.

Spring/Summer 1961

Carla joined the *Vogue Knitting* staff as a technical expert and editor in 1984, leaving her job as Showroom Manager at Neveda where she worked for yarn industry legend Irving Nacht. "I had to think long and hard about it," says Carla, "I had a great job I was very happy with. But I thought '*Vogue Knitting*, my gosh, what a great opportunity; and one that might not come again.' My gut told me to take the job; I just had to do it."

For the next couple of years, Carla, Nancy, and Lola Ehrlich, who joined the staff the same day as Carla, were the resident knitting experts. The magazine's Editors in Chief (first Polly Roberts, then Marilyn F. Cooperman) were pulled from the *Vogue Patterns* ranks, and didn't knit. It wasn't until 1986 that a knitting expert moved into the Editor in Chief chair, and that expert was Lola Ehrlich.

Lola (who served as Editor in Chief from 1986 to 1989) was born in the Netherlands, grew up in Paris, and lived in London before moving to New York, where she embarked on a successful career both as a craft magazine editor and a knitwear designer. She was on staff at *McCall's Needlework* when *Vogue Knitting* hired her as Senior Editor in 1984. When Marilyn left in 1986, Lola stepped in as Editor in Chief.

In 1986, *Vogue Knitting* began publishing three times a year, adding a Holiday issue to the schedule. Lola's team (Nancy, Carla, and technical expert Joni Coniglio, who joined the staff in 1987 as a technical instruction writer) not only put out a fabulous magazine, they also undertook the mammoth job of creating *Vogue Knitting: The Ultimate Knitting Book*, an encyclopedic knitting reference that's remained in print since 1989. The book was a herculean undertaking and an international effort as well. The illustrations drawn by Chapman Bounford Associates in the U.K. were based on painstakingly prepared references from the *Vogue Knitting* staff. (Joni knit a swatch for every illustration in the book, mounted them on boards, and drew the technical details, then shipped everything off to the U.K. to be rendered.) These illustrations proved to be seminal and unprecedented—lush, realistic, and nearly three-dimensional; every twist of the yarn is crystal clear. They set a new standard for the magazine, and for other knitting publishers. Photographer Jack Deutsch was discovered because of this book; he shot all the swatches and technical how-to images, and he has been *Vogue Knitting*'s go-to technical photographer ever since.

Fall/Winter 1985

Lola left *Vogue Knitting* in 1989 and in December of that year opened her eponymous millinery shop, Lola, in New York's East Village. Since then, she's become one of the world's premier milliners designing for the likes of Ralph Lauren, Donna Karan, Michael Kors, and Kate Spade. She still maintains a connection to the *Vogue* brand, designing hats for the pattern line. *Vogue Knitting's* next two Editors in Chief, Margaret C. Korn (1989) and Meredith Gray Harris (1990) were culled from *Vogue Patterns.* In 1991, Sonja Dagress (former Editor in Chief of *Simplicity Knitting,* which had closed) took the post, and Carla Scott left *Vogue Knitting* to pursue a freelance career (she'd return to the magazine in 1995). With Sonja's departure in 1992, Nancy Thomas was named Editor in Chief, a post she'd hold until 1995. It was during Nancy's tenure that Trisha Malcolm was first hired as associate managing editor. It was also in 1992 that Butterick took on what would prove to be a decades-long, custom-publishing venture for Gruner & Jahr: *Family Circle Easy Knitting.*

By 1995, the knitting times were changing again. Interest in the craft was fading, and Publisher Art Joinnides made the difficult decision to cut costs by letting the *Vogue Knitting* staff go and taking the magazine out of house. Nancy Thomas became the Editor of *Knitter's Magazine,* then moved to Lion Brand as Editorial Director, and then was named Vice President of Creative Services at Tahki•Stacy Charles and is now Creative Director at Coats North America.

Proof that Good Collaborations . . . Like Good Marriages . . . Can Stand the Test of Time: SoHo Publishing and *Family Circle* Magazine.

By Barbara Winkler, former Executive Editor, *Family Circle*

Family Circle and Butterick first teamed up in the late 1980s when *Family Circle* ran some fashion spreads featuring clothes made from Butterick Patterns, offering a free pattern to readers as a bonus. Butterick benefited because 8 million *Family Circle* readers saw its designs, and *Family Circle* had a wonderful freebie for its audience.

Butterick morphed into SoHo, sewing lost its clout, and this project was phased out—but not the partnership. In the early 1990s, the two companies joined forces to produce *Family Circle Easy Knitting*, an annual magazine that soon blossomed into a quarterly.

Family Circle Easy Knitting proved very successful thanks to the editorial direction of SoHo's Trisha Malcolm, who worked closely with *Family Circle* Executive Editor Barbara Winkler. The two also partnered to produce *HomeCrafts*, a quarterly promoting all kinds of DIY projects, from pillows to paint projects to paper crafts.

Says Barbara, "Our association with SoHo was a way to satisfy readers we wouldn't normally reach, but the best part of the alliance was the people: Trisha is an expert on knitting trends, yet she knew how to translate the high-style of *Vogue Knitting* to the more middle-of-the-road *Family Circle* reader. She's an editor who is flexible and always open to other ideas, a quality that made her a joy to work with. As for Art, he's a true visionary; he was the mastermind behind the original Butterick/*Family Circle* partnership and the guy who pushed through everything else. I have enormous respect for them both." Susan Ungaro was editor at *Family Circle* then and adds, "I loved our editorial sessions with Barbara and Trisha, and I have fond memories of watching our editorial staff bond over lunchtime knitting projects, helping each other from beginner to advanced. Even more special for me is the fact that as a young girl, my Irish mother taught me the basics of knitting, but I had somehow dropped it. Editing the *Family Circle Knitting* series inspired me to pick it up again and even teach my daughter Christina how to knit a simple scarf when she was nine. We still have our mom and daughter scarves."

With Nancy's departure, the magazine was outsourced to a freelance production company headed by Margery Winter (who'd worked part-time for *Vogue Knitting* in the past) and Carla Scott. They kept *Vogue Knitting* running from 1995 to 1996 before shifting the mantle to Gay Bryant, who juggled the job of *Vogue Knitting*'s Editor in Chief along with her post as the editor of *Working Woman* magazine. Gay's tenure ended with the Spring 1997 issue, and she eventually took the helm at *Mirabella*, where she won a National Magazine Award for General Excellence. By early 1997, Art had decided that outsourcing *Vogue Knitting* wasn't working as well as he'd anticipated, and he began wooing *Vogue Knitting*'s current editor, Trisha Malcolm, to run it in-house. Trisha, who had worked as the magazine's managing editor from 1992 to 1993, had also served as the editor of *Make It!*, Butterick's short-lived craft magazine, and had worked tirelessly on Butterick's PBS series *Sewing Today*. She took a break in 1994 to return to her homeland of Australia, where she did a stint as craft editor at Australian *Family Circle*, but returned to Butterick in 1996 to work on a sewing and craft business project. "Art came into my office and said, 'I'd like you to be Editor in Chief of *Vogue Knitting*,'" Trisha recalls. "I just laughed because it was the ultimate job, and I just didn't think it was possible that he was offering it to me. I thought 'I'm too young, I don't know enough, this is too much.' But Art kept coming in every day, offering me the job, until one afternoon he managed to alleviate the last of my doubts. That was it. I was in as Editor in Chief."

Winter 1991–1992

Art had a special challenge for every *Vogue Knitting* editor—to see it as not just a magazine, but as something much broader. "Trisha is the one who made that happen, the one who took a magazine and expanded it into many areas, leveraging the *Vogue Knitting* brand, reputation, and expertise to do other magazines, books, custom publishing, and conferences. She just took the ball and ran with it."

Trisha's name is now so synonymous with *Vogue Knitting* (aside from brief break in 2007, when Adina Klein took over editing responsibilities, Trisha's headed the magazine since 1997) that it's hard to believe she didn't see it until 1990, when she was working for another ("not very highbrow") magazine in New York. (She was just a little girl in Australia when the original *Vogue Knitting* folded in 1969.) "I remember seeing [*Vogue Knitting*] and thinking, 'This is fabulous. I'd love to work on a magazine like this—it's a dream job.'" Trisha's first assignment when she landed that dream job was to present the Spring/Summer 1997 issue (on which she'd not worked at all) at the annual TNNA market, a trade show for those in the knitting industry. The first issue that was all hers was Fall 1997. "It's funny," she notes. "The first issue I ever worked on [back with Nancy in 1992] was the tenth anniversary issue, and this [Fall 1997] was the fifteenth anniversary issue."

Fall 2002

Under Trisha's steady guidance, *Vogue Knitting* expanded to four issues a year. Readership was steadily growing, along with a resurgence of interest in the craft. The fashion world was again spotlighting handknits, and *Vogue Knitting*'s pages were filled with the work of the industry's best—both from within the hand-knitting world and

Fall 2003

Winter 2005–2006

the Seventh Avenue showrooms. Knitting was gaining ground (and respect) as a handcraft and new yarns were flooding the market. *Vogue Knitting* was gaining ground (and respect), even outside the knitting world—in 2006, the *Chigago Tribune* named *Vogue Knitting* one of the 50 Best Magazines in America, the only craft magazine so honored.

Things were also changing at Butterick. In the early 1990s, the company exploited its DIY capabilities to create product for other companies, including books for the Time Life series, sewing and craft continuity programs, and custom publishing. The SoHo publishing division was created in 1994 (initially to publish the lifestyle glossy, *Soho Magazine),* and in 1999 they founded their book distribution operation, West Broadway Books. In 2001, the pattern company was sold to the McCall Pattern Company, a deal that included the *Vogue* and Butterick pattern lines and *Vogue Patterns* magazine. Rather than merge with McCall's, Joinnides and Jay Stein, Butterick's president, formed their own company, bringing along SoHo Publishing, West Broadway Books, and *Vogue Knitting* (and its entire staff) as their flagship publication. The new company grew by leaps and bounds over the next decade, establishing a book publishing company (Sixth&Spring Books in 2003) and adding more craft and knitting magazine titles to the mix—all of it hinging on the stellar reputation of *Vogue Knitting*.

DETAILS MAKE THE DIFFERENCE

Save for a few bumpy issues during its outsourced days, *Vogue Knitting* has been heralded for its unparalleled technical expertise and its impeccable standards for pattern instructions and charts. Carla Scott was instrumental in establishing many of those, creating a uniform instruction writing style and setting standards and procedures for ensuring that those instructions were correct. When *Vogue Knitting* premiered in 1982, stitch charts, schematics, symbolcraft, and metric measures were not a standard part of American knitting instructions (outside the U.S., particularly in Europe and Japan, knitting patterns routinely included them). Fluent in German, French, Spanish, and Italian, Carla had been knitting from European patterns ever since being introduced to them as a teen by her sister, Mari Lynn. Carla knew firsthand the benefits and clarity that charts and metrics could provide. She introduced those standards to *Vogue Knitting*, and other American magazines and knitting patterns eventually followed suit. Years later, in the early 2000s, the Craft Yarn Council (CYC) recruited the top knitting-pattern writers and editors in the business (Carla and Joni among them) to draw up a set of universal standards, which were adopted industry-wide and internationally.

"The same emphasis we put on fashion we put on technical expertise, and Carla is the point person, the continuum on this," relates Art. "She is enormously respected in the industry." That opinion is shared by Deborah Newton, "In the early 1980s, *Vogue Knitting* editors Sally Harding and Nancy Thomas invited me to work in the magazine's New York office for a few days each week, helping the amazing technical whiz Carla Patrick with instructions and sizing. I had a penchant for this work too, even as I continued to submit designs to the magazine. It was a very creative time for me, as a designer and as a technical person as well. I learned so much working with Carla that to this day when I visit the office, I always say, 'Carla taught me everything I know!'"

Vogue Knitting's pattern checking is rigorous, but even with the most meticulous standards, mistakes sometimes happen. When they do, corrections are quickly issued. In the old days, that meant a section for errata printed in the subsequent issue. Today, corrections are posted on *Vogue Knitting*'s website as soon as the error is identified. Most problems are caught and fixed before the magazine goes to press, thanks to the eagle eyes and creative resourcefulness of *Vogue Knitting*'s technical staff.

The Pattern Evolution

"If you compare *Vogue Knitting*'s instructions today to those in the Condé Nast years, there are some differences, as well as similarities," explains Carla Scott. "The style of the basic written instructions is what's changed the least. The abbreviations they used are the same ones we use today, and the description of the process is very close to ours now. But there are some significant differences. The one that stands out the most is that, prior to 1982, there were no schematic drawings or stitch charts. They also didn't provide finished measurements, so determining the size of the garment meant that knitters had to read through the entire instruction and along with the gauge, figure out what the final measurements would be."

"In the premier issue [1982] schematics accompanied some patterns, and within two years, all the patterns had them. Basic finished measurements (bust/chest, length, width at upper arm) were placed at the beginning of each instruction so that the knitter could gauge what size to make. Metric measurements were included in all the instructions because *Vogue Knitting* was sold around the world. Stitch charts were introduced early on as well, with articles on how to use them. While many readers initially balked at them, today we get complaints if we don't use charts."

EXPERT ADVICE

Knitting technique luminaries like Elizabeth Zimmermann and Meg Swansen have also contributed to *Vogue Knitting*'s stellar reputation, along with experts like Mari Lynn Patrick, Nicky Epstein, Barbara Walker, and Deborah Newton. Elizabeth Zimmermann started writing for the magazine in 1984; when she was no longer able to contribute, her daughter Meg continued the tradition, writing a piece for every issue since 1997. (Meg had been contributing articles to *Vogue Knitting* since 1990). "I wish I'd been around to work with Elizabeth Zimmermann," says Trisha. "My biggest regret is that I never got to meet her. Luckily, I finally got to meet Meg Swansen at *Vogue Knitting* LIVE in 2011." One of Nancy Thomas' most treasured possessions is a handwritten letter she got from Elizabeth Zimmermann.

Another integral part of *Vogue Knitting*'s stature and success are the incredible designers whose sweaters, scarves, and other treasures grace the magazine's pages. The names read like a who's who of the knitterati: Nicky Epstein, perhaps the most creative (and most prolific) mind in knitting; Debbie Bliss, with her incredible eye for shape and very English sense of style; Deborah Newton, with her impeccable finishing; the incredibly innovative Lily Chin; Kristin Nichols, whose

Spring/Summer 2005

Holiday 2005

incredible colorwork never ceases to inspire; Margaret Stove and her gorgeous laces; and Norah Gaughan, whose mathematical approach results in the most stunning of cables. Teva Durham of Loop-d-Loop fame launched her design career as an associate editor for *Vogue Knitting*, and many of the staff past and present also contribute to the styles in each issue. "Watching new designers we discover develop, publishing them for the first time, and seeing the joy they get from seeing their designs in print is so satisfying," says Trisha.

Names familiar from Seventh Avenue and the fashion runways also make their way into *Vogue Knitting*. James Coviello, Twinkle, Pierrot, and Tom Scott are just a few of the cutting-edge designers who've shared their singular senses of style with *Vogue Knitting* readers, joining a long list of more established names like Adrienne Vittadini, Perry Ellis, Calvin Klein, Anne Klein, Isaac Mizrahi, Michael Kors, Donna Karan, Anna Sui, Missoni, Rebecca Moses, Oscar de la Renta, Nanette Lepore, Cynthia Rowley, Rebecca Taylor, Joan Vass, Marc Jacobs, and more. (Jacobs was a regular visitor at Butterick's offices in the mid-1980s, when he was a design student. He spent many days looking through the archives and extensive fabric library for inspiration. His first sweater design for Perry Ellis appeared in *Vogue Knitting*'s Fall 1989 issue.)

FROM SWATCH TO SWEATER

Each issue of *Vogue Knitting* is design-driven, and Trisha and her staff keep their fingers on the pulse of international fashion, taking careful note of the silhouettes, shapes, styles, and colors that will eventually be available to consumers. Any one of these can be a jumping off point for next year's knitwear designs. Sometimes it's a new yarn that starts things off, other times it's a particular garment or detail (say a twinset or cowl) that inspires a story.

In the days before the Internet (and when *Vogue Knitting* offered just two issues a year), the editors invited knitwear designers to meetings where they were presented with mood boards filled with magazine swipes and swatches illustrating where fashion was headed two issues down the road. The increase in the number of issues and time and budget constraints put an end to these meetings; instead photos of the boards were simply mailed to those who requested them. These days, e-mailed pdf files instantly connect designers around the globe with the vision for each issue, which is sent to a large list of designers both well known and not. (One of the magazine's best-kept secrets is that anyone can submit a design, provided they follow the guidelines presented on the *Vogue Knitting* website, www.vogueknitting.com.)

Designers submit sketches and a swatch (often via e-mail), and Trisha and her team start sorting through them (hundreds per issue) to decide which will make the final cut. Some designs are handled a little differently. "With some designers we'll send them a swipe of a particular silhouette or an idea and say, 'We want something like this,' then wait for what they come up with," explains Trisha. "Sometimes we give yarn to designers and see where inspiration takes them." Final yarn choices for the selected designs are based on color trends, the popularity, and the availability of certain yarns. "We want knitters around the world to easily be able to make the designs," explains Trisha. "If a yarn is selling well, it's an indication that people like knitting with it."

Each issue also includes designs from the most recent runway shows. *Vogue Knitting* has long-standing ties to Seventh Avenue, relationships that began with *Vogue Patterns*. Trisha and her crew regularly visit designer showrooms to select styles that will best appeal to *Vogue Knitting* readers. Once selected the styles are brought back to *Vogue Knitting*'s offices to begin the long process of adapting them to hand-knitting instructions. "We basically have to start from scratch, because these [Seventh Avenue] designs are usually machine-knit, often in yarns exclusive to the designer," explains Trisha. "The instructions used for production knitting are nothing like those used in handknitting. We have to write instructions for handknitters, using yarn that's available in most yarn shops." *Vogue Knitting*'s knitters then re-create the styles devising the hand stitches to execute it. Carla loves this facet of the magazine's production. "It's like a puzzle," she explains. "Study the structure, research stitch books to find the stitch (and if you can't find one, you have to experiment to create it), and then start swatching."

Instructions need to be written and sized in multiple sizes for submitted designs as well. When a sweater arrives at *Vogue Knitting*, the editors first measure all the pieces and examine the construction. Is it knit in one piece, in several pieces? Measurements are taken and schematics are drawn. Swatches are made to check the gauge, needle size, and pattern stitches. As many sizes as possible are calculated, from X-Small to 3X. It's a lot of painstaking effort, but necessary to provide readers what they need to successfully complete a project.

While the fashion mood of the moment certainly plays a role in the designs selected for *Vogue Knitting*, there are other issues to consider, including the season, industry trends, and the yarns available. To appeal to the magazine's varied readership, each issue needs to offer a balanced mix of styles. Some appeal to the younger, trendier crowd, while others have a more classic, sophisticated sensibility; all need to have a compelling reason to be knit—be that a fabulous yarn, stitch, or interesting construction technique.

PICTURE PERFECT

From its inception, *Vogue Knitting* has always stood out from the crowd in terms of the overall look of the magazine. Careful attention to design, layout, and photography define it as a fashion as well as a knitting magazine. Steve Isoz was the art director first responsible for creating *Vogue Knitting*'s signature blend of high-end photography and story-oriented page design; since 1990 Joe Vior (now creative director of SoHo Publishing) has been responsible for crafting the magazine's stunning visual impact. Before joining *Vogue Knitting*, Joe art directed Spanish-language editions of several Hearst magazines, including *Harper's Bazaar* and *Good Housekeeping*. He moved to

Fall 2007

Holiday 2007

Butterick in 1984 as a graphic designer in the promotion division, working with various editors on special promotions before becoming the art director for *Vogue Knitting*.

"Luckily I have spent much of my career working with Joe," says Trisha. "I trust him completely. He has an amazing vision and I have learnt so much from him over the years."

Joe has a deep understanding that, in the eyes of knitters, *Vogue Knitting* is synonymous with style. "I think what sets *Vogue Knitting* apart from all other knitting magazines is that we just don't think about the knitting, we also think about the bigger picture, a way of life, an aspirational way of life," he says. "We consider color, fashion—everything that takes a sweater from being something you wear to an actual piece of art that considers structure, silhouette, and fit." Model selection, hairstyle and make-up, and the accessories and styling of the designs are also critical to capturing the look. "You have to fall in love with what you are shooting," says Joe. "It takes a village, a lot of people and a lot of improvising. I've even bought fabric and wrapped it around a model to create a skirt to best set off the sweater design. I want people to get excited not just about the knitting, but about the whole look. We have sophisticated and outspoken readers, and we have to use all of these things to meet our readers' standards."

Shooting fashion for *Vogue Knitting* presents a few challenges with which fashion magazines like *Vogue* and *Harper's Bazaar* don't have to contend. *Vogue Knitting* photographs not only have to be artful, masterfully shot, and perfectly lit, they also have to show the design, construction, and stitching details of each garment so that readers can understand how to make the styles. While Joe and Trisha give their photographers a certain amount of freedom of artistic expression, they sometimes have to rein in that creativity to make sure the essential details of each design are clear.

Though dozens of photographers have contributed to *Vogue Knitting*'s signature look, today all the magazine's photography is done by two acclaimed masters of the camera: Paul Amato and Rose Callahan. Paul, a former assistant to both Patrick Demarchelier and Helmut Newton, got his big break from *Vogue*'s Alexander Leibermann. Rose is an accomplished fashion, portrait, and reportage photographer. Both have mastered the fine art of delivering spectacular fashion photographs that meticulously capture the details of what's being shot.

For its more technical photographs, *Vogue Knitting* turns to photographer Jack Deutsch, a master of the art, and the original photographer for *Vogue Knitting: The Ultimate Knitting Book*. (Photographers Brian Krause and Marcus Tullis have also contributed their skills.) Shooting swatches, stitches, and techniques is a tricky business, so the knitting editor serves as the art director for these shoots, selecting yarns and colors that will allow the camera to capture details of stitches.

Location shooting is another key component of *Vogue Knitting*. While filled with beautiful locales, the magazine's home base of New York City doesn't have the ideal weather for shooting summer sweaters in December. Over the last thirty years, *Vogue Knitting* has traveled to Puerto Vallarta, Puerto Rico, Los Angeles, St. Thomas, Mexico, and

Miami for warm-weather backdrops; fall and winter issues have been photographed everywhere from romantic cityscapes in Paris, New York, and other metropolitan areas to less plush (but no less lovely) farms and country trails of New York, Connecticut, and New Jersey.

The final step in presenting the designs to the reader is the layout of the pages, and Joe Vior works hand in hand with Trisha on these. They have to create the right balance between the various stories in any given issue. This has been made much easier with the advent of digital photography. Joe can actually begin editing photos on his way home from the shoot, and turn up at the office the next day with rough layouts.

Color and clarity is also a key factor once the pictures make it to the printed page. Knitters need to know the exact color of the yarns being used, so accuracy is important. In the pre-digital days, snips of yarns were sent along with layouts of the ad or editorial pages so the production department could match colors exactly. The same snips were attached to the proofs sent back to the editorial offices allowing the art department to double check the match. Digital photography has made color rendering easier and even more accurate—now colors can be checked as the sweaters are shot. "We still take the time to check every color to make sure it's absolutely right," says Joe.

Photo Legends

Over the years, *Vogue Knitting* has showcased the work of a virtual who's who of fashion photographers. Here are just a few:

• PATRICK DEMARCHELIER (*Vogue, Harper's Bazaar, Rolling Stone, Life, Newsweek, Mademoiselle, Glamour, Elle, Marie Claire*; Dior, Louis Vuitton, Celine, TAG Hauer, Chanel, Yves Saint Laurent, Lacoste, Calvin Klein, Ralph Lauren, Revlon, Lancome, Armani, Chanel, GAP, Versace, and L'Oreal)

• MARIO TESTINO (*Vogue, Vanity Fair*; Diana, Princess of Wales and her sons, the British Royal family, pop stars like Madonna and Michael Jackson, movie stars; Burberry, Gucci, Zara, Michael Kors, Dolce & Gabbana, Estee Lauder, Valentino, and Versace)

• ERIC BOMAN (*Vogue, Vanity Fair*; Manolo Blahnik, Duran Duran)

• DIEGO UCHITEL (*Elle, Vanity Fair, Harper's Bazaar, Vogue (Hommes, Germany, Spain), New York Times Sunday Magazine, Premier, Rolling Stone*)

• DEWEY NICKS (*Vogue, GQ*; Tommy Hilfiger, Guess, and Polo; directed TV commercials for Tommy Hilfiger, Hugo Boss, Quicksilver, and Union Bay)

• TORKIL GUDNASON (*Vogue, Harper's Bazaar, Elle, Allure, Marie Claire, Paper, Vanity Fair*; Estee Lauder, Guerlain, Elizabeth Arden, L'Oreal, Lancome, Piaget, Bergdorf Goodman, Montblanc, and Rolex; Catherine Zeta-Jones, Milos Forman, Isaac Mizrahi, and Bjork)

• JOSÉ PICAYO (*Harper's Bazaar, Rolling Stone, LA Times Magazine, Esquire, New York Magazine, House & Garden, Elle Décor, House Beautiful, Martha Stewart, New York Times Sunday Magazine*; Anne Klein, Neiman Marcus, Nine West, Nordstrom, West Elm, and Williams-Sonoma)

• ROBERT TRACHTENBERG (*New York Times Sunday Magazine, Rolling Stone, O, Esquire, Vanity Fair*; Neiman Marcus, Marshall Fields, Warner Brothers, NBC, Universal, Disney, ABC, and Turner Broadcasting)

Other acclaimed photographers who have shot for *Vogue Knitting*: Jim Varriale, Rudi Molacek, Benoît Malphettes, Paul Sunday, Jim Jordan, Dick Nystrom, Carlo Dalla Chiesa, Alberto Tolot, Marco Santelli, Barry Hollywood, Philip Newton, Elisabeth Novick, Peter Augustin, Bob Hiemstra, and Richard Pierce.

Fall/Winter 1993

SELLING STYLE

All magazines have ties to advertisers, but in the case of *Vogue Knitting*, the connection is more intertwined than most. "Advertisers are the reason we're here. Our ads are about things our readers find useful—materials and supplies they want to use in their own work," says Trisha. "A yarn company runs an ad with a beautiful garment or stitch pattern, and the reader says 'Here's a great new yarn I want to use.' Or, 'Wow, another new design I can make.'" That *Vogue Knitting* is the number one knitting magazine in the world provides value for those doing the advertising; the magazine provides what Art calls the "halo effect." As Doreen Connors, *Vogue Knitting*'s director of advertising explains, "We run an editorial featuring a yarn, the readers fall in love with the design and make it, buying that company's yarn in the process. And the yarn company's ad in that same issue reinforces that experience."

Diane Friedman of Tahki•Stacy Charles concurs, "*Vogue Knitting* has been a fashion inspiration to handknitters and the quintessential marketing vehicle for distributors for the past thirty years. Whether it be advertising, editorials, or reaching out to teach new techniques to knitters, *Vogue Knitting* has always been the leader."

Many of *Vogue Knitting*'s advertisers have been with the magazine from the start. Massachusetts-based Classic Elite has had the back cover of every issue since the Fall/Winter 1988 issue. "[Owner] Pat Chew (who passed away in 2008) always wanted the best, and since she couldn't have the front cover, she'd take the back," says Trisha. Berroco Yarns (with *Vogue Knitting* since 1982), Brown Sheep, Cascade, Clemens, JCA/Reynolds Yarns, Knitting Fever, Lion Brand, Patons, Plymouth Yarn, Skacel, Tahki•Stacy Charles, Trendsetter (formerly Fantasia), and Westminster Fibers/Rowan Yarns also have a long history with the magazine. Ads and editorial coverage in *Vogue Knitting* also helped to launch companies like Be Sweet, Blue Sky Alpacas, Namaste, Art Yarns, and many more.

HAVE NEEDLES, WILL TRAVEL

In 1997, *Vogue Knitting* decided to take its knitting expertise on the road, rounding up an adventurous band of more than sixty knitters, meeting a select group of instructors on the trail for a fiber-fueled tour of Scandinavia. In the years since, *Vogue Knitting* has been to Australia and New Zealand (1998); an Alaska cruise and train tour to Denali and Fairbanks (1999); the United Kingdom and Ireland (2000); an Amsterdam and Baltic/Russia cruise (2001); Ireland and the Scottish Isle of Lewis (2002); Italy (2003); an Alaska cruise and train tour to Denali and Fairbanks (2004); England (2005); Iceland and Scandinavia (2006); Australia and New Zealand (2007); Toronto, Ottawa, and Quebec City (2008); a Caribbean cruise (2009); Italy (2010); and France and Germany (2011). The 30th anniversary year, 2012, will see them touring to Iceland and Scotland.

The trips are a treat for both readers and *Vogue Knitting* staff. "Our trips are all about knitting and yarn. Everyone knits, and we exchange ideas and expertise," explains Carla Scott. "We give presentations and visit mills, yarn shops, and local designers. We show the new issue,

It's All in the Family

"I always remember as a young boy that my Aunt Irma would be knitting, and she always had a copy of *Vogue Knitting* magazine next to her," Stacy Charles reminisces. "Many years later as an adult, my aunt began importing and selling Anny Blatt yarns in the United States. When *Vogue Knitting* magazine re-launched in 1982 we were a proud advertiser and received some great editorials. It was an exciting moment for our entire family: 'We made it into the pages of *Vogue!*' It is a relationship I still value and continue to this very day. The standards, the quality, and the consistency have made *Vogue Knitting* a must for any fashion knitting enthusiast."

answer questions, and run workshops on techniques and design. We hand out projects on the bus and give them yarn to knit with."

Many lasting friendships have been made on these journeys. "On our first trip to Scandinavia in 1997 I established friendships with two teachers there whom I am still very close to today," recounts Trisha. "And I would never had met them any other way." Trisha and Carla have also discovered incredible knitting talent on the trips. In Denmark, Trisha was able to connect with Hanne Falkenberg; in New Zealand she was introduced to Margaret Stove. "Margaret does the most incredible knitted lace I've ever seen, all based on the flora of New Zealand," says Trisha. "When Prince William was born, New Zealand's official gift to the new heir was a shawl knit by Margaret." Some designers are even discovered among the ranks of the travelers. After one of the Australia trips, those who'd joined the excursion were invited to submit a sketch of a design inspired by the experience. The winners had their designs showcased in *Vogue Knitting*. "One of the winners, Cheryl Murray, is still designing for *Vogue Knitting*, and she's not the only one," says Carla.

KNITTING ON

Under Trisha's leadership, *Vogue Knitting* has grown to five issues a year. Two special editions were also published, one for kids in 2001, which was very successful (a previous kids' edition had been published in 1993), and another for men (in 2002), which didn't do quite as well, despite readers saying they wanted more men's sweaters. *Vogue Knitting* has also initiated and supported other knitting endeavors.

Beginning in 1992, the *Vogue Knitting* staff had been putting out two (then four) issues a year of *Family Circle Knitting* for owner Grunar & Jahr. In 2007, at the height of the knitting boom, output increased to four. A year later, Meredith Publishing purchased *Family Circle* from G&J, however, without SoHo's specialty-distribution chops, the magazine soon folded. To fill this niche SoHo created *KnitSimple*, a less challenging but still inspiring complement to *Vogue Knitting* that releases four issues a year to this day—Carla Scott is the Editor in Chief. "*KnitSimple* is geared toward both new knitters and experienced knitters who just don't have a lot of time for a lot of detailed knitting projects," says Trisha. "And it's the only knitting magazine on the market that includes designs for men, women, kids, and plus sizes in every issue."

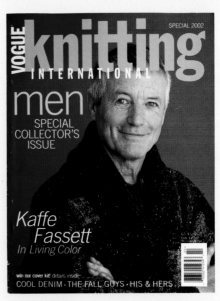

Special 2002

Winter 2008–2009

As knitting gained ground with a younger, edgier customer base, *Vogue Knitting* began exploring new ways to reach them. Chatting at JoAnn Fabric's 60th anniversary party in 2003, Art, Trisha, and Lion Brand Yarn CEO David Blumenthal came up with the concept for a cutting-edge knitting magazine that would target the fashion sense and emerging knitting skills of a younger consumer. The result was *knit.1,* a playful magazine that spent five years (2004–2009) on the newsstands.

In 2005, *Vogue Knitting* turned its attention to the yarn industry itself, reviving *Yarn Market News,* a trade magazine that had a successful run during the knitting boom years of the 1980s. The new era of knitting had ushered in a new kind of yarn shop owner eager for information and strategies for building business and Trisha and Art saw a great opportunity to provide that insight by reviving the magazine. Helmed by Karin Strom, a respected industry veteran, *Yarn Market News* was an instant hit; the news and advice on its pages eagerly awaited for by shop owners and yarn industry execs alike. In 2008, *Yarn Market News* expanded its services by hosting what was dubbed the Smart Business Conference, a three-day workshop, presentation, and networking event for shop owners. *Yarn Market News* conferences feature experts in social media, merchandising, display, and distribution from outside the yarn business. Erin Slonaker took over the magazine in 2010.

REQUIRED READING

Magazines aren't the only media outlet for *Vogue Knitting*'s vast wealth of knitting knowledge. Under SoHo's publishing arm, Sixth&Spring Books, *Vogue Knitting* creates books, patterns, leaflets, booklets, and pamphlets for themselves, yarn companies, and other knitting businesses.

Perhaps one of *Vogue Knitting*/SoHo's most successful ancillary businesses is its book publishing operation. *Vogue Knitting*'s first book, *Vogue Knitting: The Ultimate Knitting Book* hit bookstores in 1989 when *Vogue Knitting* was still owned by the Butterick Company. An updated version was released in 2002, followed by a compendium volume in 2004. Since 1989, the book has sold more than one million copies, solidifying it as *the* definitive knitting reference. As this book goes to press, *Vogue Knitting*'s team is working on a completely revised and updated edition.

Vogue Knitting's successful *Knitting on the Go* series also got its start during the Butterick years (1999 to be exact), and the series has more than thirty titles and sales of hundreds of thousands. The award-winning *Stitchionary* series, now six titles strong, is also a bookstore favorite, and Trisha and the editors often pull the best designs from the magazine and package them into hardcover books. *Vogue Knitting* also supports dozens of designers in their writing efforts, publishing books under their Sixth&Spring Books imprint from Nicky Epstein, Debbie Bliss, Rosemary Drysdale, Cathy Carron, Deborah Newton, and more.

MAKING CONNECTIONS

Like the knitters who look forward to each issue, *Vogue Knitting* has embraced the electronic age. The magazine's website, vogueknitting. com, launched in the Butterick days, got a complete redesign in 2007, and its features are routinely improved and updated. Perhaps the most exciting innovation is VK360, a digital tool that showcases the sweaters from each issue from every conceivable perspective and angle. "It's fantastic," says Trisha "You can see all the techniques, construction, and stitching details with the zoom function, and you can look at the garment from the front, back, side, top, bottom— anywhere. Readers can see exactly what the design looks like: 'Oh, the sweater is supposed to look like that in the back.' 'Ah, the stitch pattern changes here.' We can have the high-fashion photography on the magazine pages and show all the details at VK360. It's really the best of both worlds." *Vogue Knitting* also posts outtakes from magazine photo shoots on its website, so readers can get a multitude of views of a single design.

Holiday 2008

In 2005, *Vogue Knitting* began digitizing its pattern library and offering patterns for sale online; new designs are being added all the time. "The patterns are our biggest asset; it's what we do, and our pattern sales help support other ventures," says Trisha. *Vogue Knitting* sells back issues online as well.

Aware that today's knitters rely more and more on electronic aids, *Vogue Knitting* introduced its first iPhone app in 2010. It includes information on gauge and needle size, a row counter, stitch glossary, project pages, a directory of types of yarn, and photo storage. *Vogue Knitting*'s first all-digital issue for the iPad was introduced in January 2011.

Social media like Facebook and Twitter has been another phenomenally successful forum for *Vogue Knitting*, and its readers and its fan base are growing by leaps and bounds. It's a great way to address the needs and concerns of readers, to make sure the magazine is giving them what they want and need. And readers often give *Vogue Knitting* something they need, too. "Let's say we're in a meeting discussing something like the difference between knitting with bamboo and metal needles, who likes what, and what do most people prefer. We can post the question on Facebook or Twitter and get hundreds of responses in minutes. Nine out of ten times, there's a clear majority opinion," say Trisha. "Social media also gives us an opportunity to keep our readers up to date about the knitting world on a daily basis."

Fall 2009

Not that the magazine is adverse to face-to-face communication. Inspired in part by the success of the Smart Business conferences, in 2011 *Vogue Knitting* embarked on what is perhaps the most ambitious consumer knitting show in North America—*Vogue Knitting* LIVE—a multiple-day event that features classes, lectures, and workshops from the knitting world's best and brightest. Thousands of teachers, knitters and vendors come from every corner of the globe to attend demonstrations, live fashion shows, receptions, and book signings. For *Vogue Knitting*, the highlight is that so many of the magazine's designers and advertisers get to connect with *Vogue Knitting* readers under one roof.

Vogue Knitting's next venture is to launch an exclusive club for top-tier readers, giving them subscriptions, early access to books, advertiser samples, and various discounts.

Spring/Summer 2011

YARN FORWARD

Both knitting and *Vogue Knitting* have come a long way in thirty years, but don't expect the magazine to rest on its laurels. With an ever-growing pool of designers supplying wonderful projects and innovative techniques and ever-evolving outlets in which to showcase and share them, the magazine will continue to inspire and educate. As the magazine explores everything that digital media has to offer, it will eventually take even more advantage of video technology, creating moving views of the fashions on its pages.

The *Vogue* name, high style, top designers, technical acumen, incredible photography, loyal advertisers, books, and dedicated readers have all contributed to *Vogue Knitting*'s incredible success over the last thirty years, but credit is also owed to the tireless staff. "It's lots of work putting out the magazine," says Carla, "But we're like a little family. Everyone is willing to do things outside their job description and work for the team. We all love what we do—each one of us thinks ours is the dream job."

Vintage Patterns

1980s

Irish Sweater-Coat

This Irish sweater-coat is emblematic of the traditional yet of-their-time projects in the premier issue of the new *Vogue Knitting*. Using the latest in current fibers—striated, "color-misted" *Dji-Dji*, a wool/viscose blend by Stanley Berroco—as well as a flowing 1980s bubble shape and a modern ribbed-yoke detail (visible in the center inset photo), designer Sheila Bradshaw let readers know that the new *Vogue Knitting* would nod to its ancestry while making history on its own.

Legacy—it's a word that looms large in the relaunch issue. It had been thirteen years since the original had ceased publication, yet the magazine had never ceased to exist in the mind of its many fans. Knitters saved and collected old issues as a matter of pride, and their vocal enthusiasm for the title helped resuscitate it: In her first editor's note, Polly Roberts credited avid readers of *Vogue Patterns* who had been "pleading for a comeback" with bringing about the renaissance of *Vogue Knitting*.

But times and fashion had changed during the magazine's hiatus, forcing the editorial "heirs apparent" to rise to the challenge of honoring *Vogue Knitting*'s storied past while forging ahead into the craft's future. To do that, hand-knitting patterns were commissioned from mainstream ready-to-wear designers known for their knitwear, including Adrienne Vittadini, Kansai Yamamoto, and Joan Vass. Exclusive *Vogue Knitting* pattern/yarn kits were assembled and offered via the magazine. How-tos on gauge and blocking taught technical basics to a new generation of readers. And the introduction of a "Then and Now" feature cast back into the archives, updating a classic piece from the old days, starting with a sweater dress (it was the early '80s, after all).

FALL/WINTER 1982 • Instructions Page 186

8

PLAYING THE HEAVY ROLES WITH PANACHE

IDYLLIC TEXTURAL RELATIONSHIP characterizes the handsome couple, opposite. Her rugged turtleneck by Andree Rubin combines an interesting variety of stitch patterns in a donegal tweed yarn by Tahki Imports, Ltd. His hefty turtle shows its fashion muscle in a bold trinity stitch with striping pattern. By Lynn Schroeder; Yarn by Columbia-Minerva. Her Very Easy Vogue culottes, 8398. His Calvin Klein trousers, 2256.

IRISH CHARM IN TWEEDY YARN in facile Irish designer Sheila Bradshaw's hip-flowing sweatercoat, above. A grand fluidity with deftly ribbed yoke (close-up on that detail, center, left). A color-misted beauty in striated yarn by Stanley Berroco. Very Easy Vogue skirt, 8285. Ralph Lauren blouse, 2881.

EASY TO KNIT BOMBER JACKET, top left, is easily one of the niftiest shapes around! Mari Lynn Patrick gives it a unique collaring and an asymmetrical closing with crochet buttons and loop buttonhole niceties. A reverse stockinette stitch in an astrakhan-type yarn for the body; easy garter stitch collar and bandings. Yarn by Neveda. Knickers, 8406. Ralph Lauren cape, 2616; blouse, 8189.

STRIPES & A RUFFLED SURPRISE for an out-of-the-rut pullover by Arlene Mintzer, left. Her ruffled yoke gives a jaunty touch to a much-loved classic. A zesty sweater in an extra warm alpaca yarn by Plymouth, crocheted in a textury popcorn stitch. Very Easy Vogue skirt, 8208.

Romantic Rosebud Cardigan

Styling has always been a hallmark of *Vogue Knitting*. This feminine sweater, for instance, was paired with a more masculine tie-front blouse and pleated checkerboard pants. If you were inclined to make the entire outfit, pattern and fabric yardage information for the sewn pieces could be found in a special guide after the knit instructions—a further acknowledgement of the cross-crafting of *Vogue Pattern* readers who were so integral to *Vogue Knitting*'s resurrection.

Mari Lynn Patrick's career as a *Vogue Knitting* designer began with the very first issue—and she's made her mark in nearly every edition since, a feat no other designer can claim. In this issue, Patrick was represented by no less than six patterns, including an asymmetrical "bomber jacket" in *Astrakhan* yarn and a floppy-collared Fair Isle sweater in vivid neons, primarily Pepto-Bismol pink. But it's her textured "New Romantics" cardigan—with its bobbled rosebuds, standup collar, and crocheted buttons, originally knit in *Sirene Double* wool from Neveda—that best epitomizes the magazine's early output.

FALL/WINTER 1982 • Instructions Page 187

THE NEW ROMANTICS

Pointelle Pullover

This elegant lace pullover by Zara Zsido, originally knit in Wendy's *Darling* yarn, juxtaposes the subtle peekaboo effect of pointelle openwork with a demure collar and peplum, further enhanced by pearl button accents. The intent to embrace warm-weather knitting is apparent throughout this issue, but the looks on its pages bear little resemblance to the breezy collections readers of current *Vogue Knitting* issues have come to expect from a Spring/Summer edition. Here are al fresco settings and arm-baring designs, to be sure—including several shells that pair with Chanel-inspired suit jackets and skirts—but there are even more full-fledged, long-sleeved sweaters better suited for brisker months.

Instead, the editors focused on yarns, colors, and techniques that speak to knitting's off-season. Silk, cotton, and linen were explored in a primer on cool-to-the-touch natural fibers. Smoky pales and vivid brights were pegged as the perfect farewell-to-winter palettes. And a how-to on yarn overs prepped readers for projects calling for lace—then as now, a mainstay of May-through-August stitching.

A quick historical note: This issue also included the first of what would be many *VK* interviews with celebrities passionate about knitting—in this case, newscaster and television personality Betty Furness, who claimed to never be without needles and states, "Obviously, knitting is a necessity to me."

SPRING/SUMMER 1983 • Instructions Page 189

29

...ardigan coup that
...ols the virtues of
...e prettiness! Left:
...ictorian air in the
...g, hip-tied cardigan
...h soft-turn collar,
...adened shoulder. A
...ri Lynn Civelek de-
...h. Yarn by Colum-
...-Minerva. Skirt,
... Easy Vogue 8528.
...ht: Cream of the
... cardigan with an
...n-work stitch for
...attached collar and
...lum...very effec-
... contrast with the
...ntelle. Zara Zsido
...igns it with Wendy
...n. Skirt from Vogue
...tern 8525. Note the
...fect pearl button
...ches in both!

COLD CHIC
THE GREAT OUTDOOR KNITS

1

2

Leafy Lace Poncho

This poncho, a collaborative design by Barbara Nudelman and Susan Prince, put to use principles taught earlier in the issue, in an article about the necessities of careful seaming: The garment is assembled from rectangular panels knit in a leafy-lace pattern with one of the tweed blends so popular at the time, Phildar's *Show 251*. It was accompanied by an equally innovative project, a dramatic crocheted Berber hat (see page 192 for instructions). While it has never been a focus, crochet remains a skill *VK* encourages readers to know, as hook work comes in handy in finishing or embellishing special pieces.

This issue also featured "Introducing Perry Ellis!" emblazoned on the cover. With this emphatic cover line, *Vogue Knitting* proudly welcomed one of the biggest names on Seventh Avenue to its cadre of "prestige designers." Credited as the creative mind who "more than any other American designer has been responsible for the resurgence in popularity of handknits," Ellis debuted in these pages with an intarsia zebra-striped number and two cropped sweaters marked by his signature cables and tweed.

Ellis's entry wasn't the only first in this issue, billed prominently as the magazine's "first anniversary." The edition also boasted the first time "full-color, life-size" photos of the yarn used in each project in case readers wanted to find a suitable substitute to make each pattern. (It's a feature that continues to this day.) It was also the first time *VK* ran a Yarn Buying Guide for international readers in the United Kingdom and Australia, and the first time the magazine featured a sock pattern, a child's pattern (a girl's cabled vest, part of a mom-and-me duo) and a pattern for a poncho.

FALL/WINTER 1983 · Instructions Page 191, Hat 192

THE MONTE CARLO SPIRIT

1. AARLAN/ULLTEX Soie-Silk

Fitzgerald Pullover

C alvin Klein. Betty White. Celebrities were prominent in *VK*'s second Spring/Summer issue, though neither had quite the long-lasting impact on the knitting community as the now-legendary members of the early knitterati, Elizabeth Zimmermann and Barbara G. Walker; both of their first of *Vogue Knitting* columns appeared in this edition. It's apropos, then, that the representative pattern was inspired by another influential celebrity—F. Scott Fitzgerald, whose 1930s bestseller *Tender Is the Night* served as a template for "soigne sweaterings that are the very spirit of the '80s." Mari Lynn Patrick (credited as Mari Lynn Civelek) designed this graceful top with ruffled-edge eyelet flanges that wing over a fitted bodice, anchored by sleek hip ribbing. It was shown in Aarlan/Ulltex's *Soie-Silk*, a silk/wool blend.

Zimmermann, the beloved icon behind classic texts such as *Knitting Without Tears* and *The Knitter's Almanac*, waxed philosophic about grafting with Kitchener stitch. (Her *VK* legacy continues to this day, in a regular column penned by her daughter and flame-keeper, Meg Swansen.) Walker, author of the seminal *Treasuries of Knitting Patterns*, delved into her own personal history, explaining "How I Discovered Knitting . . . and Why."

As for the other previously mentioned klieg-light names: The ultra-hot Klein made his first hand-knitting patterns available in this issue (a short-sleeved argyle pullover and a white cardi vest with patch pockets on the chest and hipline, for the record). And avid stitcher White checked in between A-list TV gigs on *The Mary Tyler Moore Show* and *The Golden Girls* to say "I can't remember when I didn't have yarn in my hands."

SPRING/SUMMER 1984 · Instructions Page 192

27

27. BERGER DU NORD Prodiges

Classic Cable Sweater

With several issues under their belt, *VK*'s editors were beginning to stretch the magazine's range, mixing stylish-yet-wearable staples with more avant-garde techniques and fashions. This scarlet Calvin Klein–designed sweater, stitched in Berger du Nord's *Prodiges* wool, is an ideal example of the former. It's got all the makings of a wardrobe perennial—crisp lines, bravura texturing (vertical eyelets separate columns of pristine cables) and timeless detailing (especially that miniature shawl collar).

Just a few pages later, though, were garments of a decidedly trendier nature—the equivalent of intarsia graffiti by a single-monikered "fashion artist" known as Antonio. These pieces were bold, brash, and meant for the nightclub. One sweater even had a canvas tabard piece that unfurled from suspenders at the shoulders, veiling the knitted graphics at the wearer's whim. Novelty yarns—an array of tubes, ribbons, fabric, feathers, leather, and fur—were highlighted as an *au courant* way to embellish. One notable ad touted *Mme Defarge* yarn, a so-wrong-it's-right fiber named for the sinister stitcher of *A Tale of Two Cities*. Other techniques introduced in this issue include slip-stitch mosaic knitting as well as condo knitting, a speedy approach to stitching on two drastically different sized needles, pairing, for example, a size 35 with a size 7.

Mock Plaid Sweater

Marc Jacobs was only twenty-two years old and a rising fashion star when he submitted his first hand-knitting design to *Vogue Knitting*. This sophisticated faux-plaid charmer in Reynolds' *Lopi*—one of the few venerable fibers seen in the magazine's early editions that's still available today—fit right in with the three main themes of this packed-to-the-gills issue: easy-wear simple-stitch knits, ski-slope chic, and drama, drama, drama (as evidenced by an exaggerated bubble rib at the cuffs and hemline). Jacobs used a crochet hook to stripe knitted blocks of color to achieve the main body's mock-plaid effect.

Though these shoulders slope insouciantly, prominently defined shoulders were a hallmark of women's fashion in the 1980s. To help readers transform their knits to conform with this trend, Nancy J. Thomas wrote a techniques article Joan Collins would have approved of, about knitting your own shoulder pads—preferably in the same color and at the same gauge as your sweater. For times when that proved impossible, a handy yarn substitution guide—the reborn magazine's first—helped readers select suitable yarn alternatives.

FALL/WINTER 1985 · Instructions Page 195

elax into the easy knitting of splendid patternings, striking color combos. Opposite: Focus on the finesse of funnel collaring; a ribbed V-shape yoke; set-in pockets. Designed by B.J. Berti in yarn by Noro/ Knitting Fever. Pants, 1445. This page: The easy technique of striping blocks of color with a crochet chain produces this mock plaid drama! Designed by Marc Jacobs. Reynolds yarns. Pants, 9160.

6

6. REYNOLDS Lopi

For his initial design with us...Valentino shapes this soigné little cardigan, with attached ascot embroidered with status initialling. A delicate fine-weight knitting for the dedicated pro. Welcome, Valentino... you're worth every dedicated moment! Mohair blend yarn by Valentino/Stacy Charles Collection.

31

31. VALENTINO/STACY CHARLES COLLECTION "132"

valentino

Monogrammed Cardigan

Monograms made a big comeback in the '80s, spurred on by the popularity of *The Official Preppy Handbook*. Mainstream designer fashions were flush with fancy initialing, so it's only fitting that the first of many *VK* appearances by the estimable Valentino included "status initialing." A VG—for Valentino Garavani, of course—was prettily embroidered on an ascot attached to the designer's tony crossover cardigan with a pleated yoke detail. The fiber used was a fine-gauge mohair from Valentino's namesake yarn line in the Stacy Charles Collection.

Style-setters like Valentino inside the issue were balanced by a style icon on the back cover: actress Angie Dickinson. Wearing a *Dynasty*–worthy draped-rib sweater, hair teased high and arms akimbo, Dickinson stares off the page fiercely and all but dares the reader not to want to knit with the advertised yarn, *Fashionella*, "a new concept" from the Melrose Designer's Choice Cravenella line. With the yarn market changing so greatly over the decades, archival ads like this serve as a potent reminder of long-forgotten fibers and brands.

$\mathcal{L}$ace Leaf Sweater

One Sweater, Three Ways. It's a concept that's lasted through the years in the pages of *Vogue Knitting*: demonstrate how the mood and look of a single pattern changes depending on the type of yarn used. For the initial outing of the format, editors showcased Justine Wolferseder's verstaile lace pullover, dressed up with a split turtleneck and dolman sleeves. The fashion spread displays the garment in three different fibers, modeled by three distinct types of women—a silky rayon for the "social butterfly," a tweedy alpaca/wool blend for the "good sport," and an elegant mohair for the style-setter looking to get "down to business."

SOCIAL BUTTERFLY IN A RICH SILKEN RAYON

GOOD SPORT IN A TWEEDY ALPACA/WOOL

104

FALL/WINTER 1985 • Instructions Page 197

17

r pride...this lovely
-patterned sweater
t shapes up into 3
icing personalities.
marvelous, magical
over is designed by
ine Wolferseder
she interprets it in
ood-changing yarns
steal the scene,
ht and day. Chic
agger in a deep
man sleeve drifting
o a shapely waist.
h versatility in the
rific split turtleneck.
de with easy-to-fol-
stitch chart. Yarn
ources from far left:
lrose rayon; Tahki's
edy, alpaca/wool;
er/Merino mohair
nd. The Vogue skirt,
8; pants, 1445.

TAHKI Tweedy Alpaca

TIBER/MERINO Le Doux Mohair

MELROSE Satina

1 SWEATER
3 WAYS

105

Ballerina-Style Pullover

Breaking out of its initial biannual publishing schedule, *Vogue Knitting* added an extra issue during prime knitting season: Holiday.

The premiere of this seasonal edition leaned heavily on glitz and glamour, becoming an expected style staple. Metallic yarns sparkled and smoldered in a collection of evening sweaters just right for making merry. A tutorial on beading allowed ambitious knitters to add their own shimmer to their projects (the secret, then and now, is pre-threading yarns). The magazine's first gift guide included whimsical knits like a baby jester suit complete with pointed pompom hat and intarsia cat sweaters for the whole family—appealing, no doubt, to the time-tested connection between stitcher and feline. Also just right for gift-giving: Elizabeth Zimmermann's fabled mittens with "afterthought thumbs," the topic of the legend's Holiday column. Soon-to-be supermodel Stephanie Seymour even made an appearance, wearing a Calvin Klein twinset and sleeveless polo. All of it reflected the edition's declaration that "Simple elegance is back, at long last."

That can certainly be said for this ballerina-style raglan-sleeve pullover by Florence Vidal, chic in Reynolds' *Tipperary Tweed*. With its "dancer's de rigueur shoulder-top shaping" and three-quarter-length sleeves, the silhouette is "best worn tucked in and belted." It's accessorized by a knitted textured headband with a cable and garter-stitch knot at the center.

HOLIDAY 1986 · Instructions Page 202

Knitting savant Barbara Walker created a positive-negative stitch technique—turquoise on one side, vibrant blue on the other—for a truly

Fast moving, these three flashes of blue— for gifts or to keep to whiz right through.

reversible muffler, *left,* Florence Vidal's ballerina-style raglan-sleeve pullover, *right,* has a dancer's *de rigueur* shoulder-top shaping and three-quarter length sleeves. It looks marvelous in this Reynolds wool tweed. Best worn: tucked in, belted. The deeply textured cabled headband with garter stitch knot at center front, is by Emily Kaufman, in Berger du Nord wool. Skirt, 9055.

5

Very Easy
Very Vogue

6

37

Deep Rib Cardigan

Revisiting patterns from the original *Vogue Knitting* was a regular feature right from the relaunch. This deeply ribbed cardigan appeared as part of an expansion of the popular "Then & Now" feature, showcasing four gorgeous vintage projects instead of just one. Lithe and lean in Crystal Palace's silk/wool *Creme*, this sweater was updated with golden buttons but still called for the ribbon-backed buttonholes specified in the original 1949 pattern.

Also updated: *VK*'s editorial team. Lola Ehrlich, who now sat in the editor's seat, widened the type of article found in the magazine's pages. Along with a bevy of important tutorials—on sleeve caps, short row shaping, bobbles, and popcorn stitches—this issue also included the precursor to the current Library book reviews and a culture piece about literary characters who knit. (Miss Marple, we're looking at you.) For more knitting culture, readers got a peek at the stunning knit collection at London's Victoria & Albert Museum, still viewable today.

FALL/WINTER 1986-1987 · Instructions Page 204

With a new pulled together attitude, our THEN sweaters have all it takes NOW. Far left: The pull that makes a point of broad shoulders ... today's fashion focus. Textural beauty in the handsome ribbing at hi-neck inset, hem and cuffs. From *Vogue Knitting*, Winter 1953. Yarn by Emu/Plymouth. This page: a slim deep-rib gives this longline, raglan sleeve cardigan great sleekness. Our only change: golden buttons. But those fastidious grosgrain ribbon-back buttonholes are as they were in *Vogue Knitting*, Summer 1949. Luxurious silk and wool blend yarn from Crystal Palace.

15. Emu/Plymouth, *Superwash DK*

16. Crystal Palace, *Crème*

16

81

Giant Cable Sweater

Think chunky knits speeding off huge needles is a recent phenomenon? Think again. Oversized sweaters were everywhere in the '80s, putting fashion-forwardness squarely in the hands of knitters—who, like everyone else, paired the massive garments with the skinniest of leggings.

The gargantuan cables on this magnum opus by designer Margaret Bruzelius are deceptive. Though they look intricate, as with all garments bearing the time-saving "Very Easy Very Vogue" imprimatur, these twists could be successfully tackled and tamed by even knitting newbies, who might then saunter around town giving off an air of "fabulous turtled nonchalance." (The sweater was originally shown in wool/mohair Tahki *Jumbo Tweed*.) Stitchers looking for more of a challenge had plenty to feast on in this issue, though. Colorwork geometrics, lushly textured Arans, and traditional "gentry knits" made up the rest of the collection.

FALL/WINTER 1986–1987 · Instructions Page 205

G K N I T S !

simple shapes plus the enticement of rich, colorful, textural yarns set the pace

Very Easy
Very Vogue
20

Butterfly-Stitch Cardigan

A paean to the individualist, this issue of *VK* celebrates the freedom knitters find in going off-pattern. Explained editor Lola Ehrlich: "The sweaters inside, as always, reflect the season's fashion trends. But our aim is not to inhibit your creativity. We recognize that, as a knitter, you are the final arbiter of fashion: just by changing a color or adding a design detail, you make the sweater truly your own." To that end, the magazine launched a series of articles on the design process—this one focusing on the "dialogue between designer and yarn"— backed up by a tutorial on alterations, all the better to achieve a custom fit.

Fit was especially key to the garments in the "Vienna Airs" feature. Shot within a setting that evoked the romance of the Vienna Woods at the turn of the last century, these designs carried more than a dash of Old World charm, with "small, allover texture and dressmaker details." Sylvia Jorrin's butterfly-stitch cardigan, shown in wool *Aerobic* from Baruffa/ Lane Borgosesia, gets its formal flair from a detachable velvet collar-and-cuff set, echoed by the velvet-covered buttons.

FALL/WINTER 1987 • Instructions Page 206

15

65

Purple Takes to Texture and Stripes Go Racing

29

The chevron stitch pattern on Norah Gaughan's all-violet high-neck pull, this page, creates an embossed effect. Note, the left shoulder buttons, the reverse stockinette stitch ridges at neck, rib, and squared armholes. In a Melrose cotton-stretch fiber blend that's completely resilient. Skirt: Perry Ellis, 1775. Color blocks (including a solid red back) and racing stripes on Anne Mieke's drop shoulder, hemmed-edge pull, opposite, evoke the line of the tight-fitting bicycling maillots. In a mercerized Filatura di Crosa/Stacy Charles cotton.

High-Neck Pullover

Anne Macdonald's *No Idle Hands: A Social History of American Knitting* remains one of the essential resources knitters should have in their personal reference libraries. *Vogue Knitting* recognized the importance of this text right out of the gate, excerpting the book prior to its publication in autumn 1988. The chosen chapter is particularly fascinating, focusing on American knitting efforts during wartime—reaching back as far as the Revolution and extending through World War II.

Also of historical importance was the magazine's ability to hone in on designers who would prove to have lasting influence. A series on master knitters starts here with a provocative interview with "rock star of handknitting" Kaffe Fassett, who claimed to be "sensually involved" with color and made readers a promise he's more than fulfilled in the intervening years: "I just want to get more and more intricate—and I want to drag all of you along with me."

Speaking of master knitters, Norah Gaughan was not the industry force she would soon become when this violet pullover was originally published (knit in a resilient Melrose cotton-stretch blend called *Memory Eight*). But the lush texture and unexpected detailing that continues to epitomize her design ethos was evident even then. An allover chevron stitch pattern and ribbing keep the knitting interesting; buttons along the left shoulder add a touch of the asymmetry Gaughan so loves.

SPRING/SUMMER 1988 · Instructions Page 208

22

ANNE KLEIN

debuts on these pages w
two vibrant pulls. Black ve
bows, slipped into cable-t
openings, dress up a fuc
angora crop-top, this pe
Edges and cuffs are encase
thick cotton/poly cording
a rounded effect. In a Melr
angora blend with a
strand of rayon. A highm
tunic, opposite, in a Juni
Yarns/Scheepjeswool woo
decked with an intarsia fl
motif in an Anny Blatt ang
blend and a Melrose ray
Hair and makeup: Susan Hous

| 22. Melrose, 70/30 Angora |
| 22. & 23. Rayonette |
| 23. Anny Blatt, Angora Sup |
| Scheepjeswool/Junipe Superwash Zermatt |

54

Bow Beauty

Much of this Holiday issue was tied up with a bow—literally, in the case of this angora sweater that marked the *VK* designer debut of Louis Dell'Olio for Anne Klein II. The velvet bows are slipped into cable-type openings, while a cotton/poly cording is encased within the neckline, cuffs, and hemline, lending a rounded effect to the edges. The piece itself was originally shown in fuchsia *70/30 Angora* yarn by Melrose, plied with a thin strand of *Rayonette* for shape.

Other gift-wrapped packages in this issue: a tutorial on stitching bows into knit fabric via techniques like the butterfly stitch; classic Christmas picture sweaters, complete with intarsia fairy lights and partridges in pear trees; and an afghan with a Currier & Ives–worthy sleigh scene stitched around the perimeter. A particularly important present to readers was the introduction of patterns meant specifically for larger women, a size range the magazine strives to include whenever possible. The feature focused on sweaters that visually slim with vertical and diagonal stripes, mixing black with red and navy with periwinkle to show the ways color play can enhance plus-sized garments.

Polo Club Sweater

Only one aspect of the cabled "Thoroughbred" on the cover of *Vogue Knitting*'s Fall 1989 issue gave away the sweater's birthdate: In the late '80s, when smoking pervaded the culture in a more potent way than it currently does, it was not yet taboo to describe the variegated skein of Froehlich-Wolle *Renaissance* in which the sweater was originally knit as "tobacco" toned. Otherwise, the multi-twist, polo-collared pullover, credited to the *VK* staff, is timeless as can be.

That *VK* staff now included Margaret Korn as the new editor in chief and Margery Winter as senior editor. Winter would go on to great heights in the knitting world, eventually taking the helm at *Vogue Knitting* and acting as the creative force at several influential yarn companies, including Berroco. Another important name in these pages: Fair Isle guru Alice Starmore, whose first *VK* article spoke to a subject she knew well—steeking, the act of cutting into a tube of stranded knitting to insert sleeves, a neckline and, for a cardigan, a button band. Though many knitters balk at the thought of taking scissors to their handknits, Starmore's matter-of-fact expertise removed the worry from the process.

FALL 1989 · Instructions Page 211

4

wing Coat

The daring young designer of this striking trapeze coat is none other than Deborah Newton, a name well known to *VK* readers. Creating "a supple swing with the greatest of ease," she gave the main trapeze panel an asymmetrical rolled hem with contrast piping and chose an extremely drapey yarn—the wool/rayon *Cablenella* by Melrose. The effect is effortless movement, a stunning counterbalance to the second-skin miniskirts and leggings of the era.

This piece appeared in a feature called "Novel Knits in a Modern Minimal Mood," the only patterns in the Fall '89 issue to be photographed in a studio. Everything else had been shot al fresco—in a picturesque wood, an urban cityscape, or, most notably, on the grounds and Atlantic Ocean beaches of Gurney's International Health and Beauty Spa in Montauk, New York. In her editor's letter, Margaret Korn gushed over the gorgeous setting and discussed a bit about the still-thriving spa's unusual "marinotherapeutic services." Today, with so much made of the therapeutic nature of knitting itself, Gurney's spa seems a prescient choice of background for a relaxing collection of weekend handknits.

FALL 1989 · Instructions Page 212

23

IN THE SWING OF THINGS
Deborah Newton lets loose with a
trapeze paneled coat that has an
asymmetrical hem, set-in sleeves,
curvy collar and single button
closure. Contrast rolled trim puts
an edge on it. Melrose's wool/
rayon yarn gives it supple swing
with the greatest of ease.

22. Classic Elite, *Boston*

Sharon

23. Melrose, *Cablenella*

Bubble Sweater

Getting in just under the gun, before the 1980s turned into the 1990s, Marc Jacobs designed not just "the sweater of the season" but, arguably, the sweater of the decade. Jacobs, named design director of the Perry Ellis label after Ellis's death in 1986, created the unique shape of his bubble-style sweater by exponentially expanding widthwise down from the funnel neck and deeply ribbed yoke, until the roomy body hit thigh length. The momentous piece, shot on location in Manhattan's Meatpacking District, is worked in two variegated strands of Classic Elite's perennially popular *La Gran* mohair.

Just as this singular garment provides a bookend to the fashion of the '80s, this issue gives a sneak peek at what knitting in the '90s might look like: A feature about the latest in novelty yarns showcased all sorts of fur and fluff, ombres and color-shifters, tweeds and blends—all of which had a major role to play in the craft's future evolution.

FALL 1989 • Instructions Page 214

34

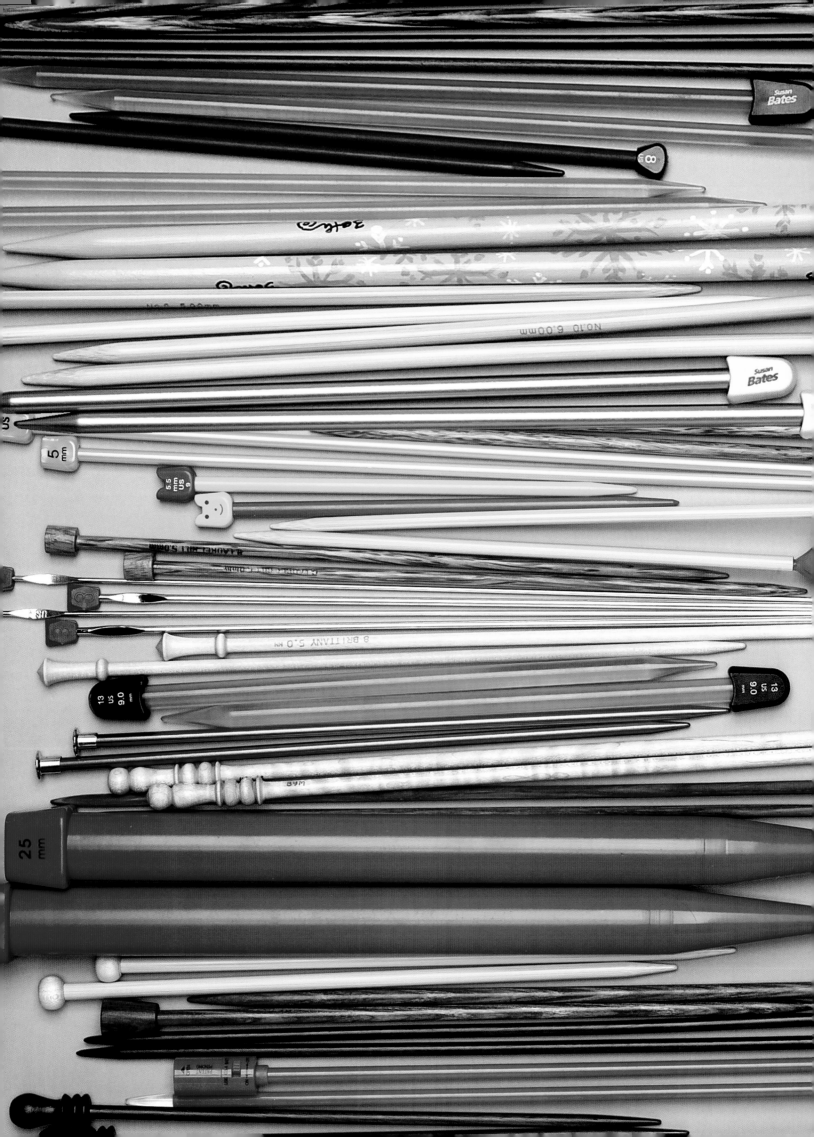

Favorite Styles

Zigzag Stitch Sweater

Missoni Jacket

Sinuous Sweater

Trapeze Dress

Sparkly Sweater

Desert Garden Pullover

Blue Waves Sweater

Cabled Sweater

Red Hot Sweater

Garter Ridge Cardigan

Turtleneck Tunic

Trellis Cardigan

Striped Sweater

Tape Tee

Diagonal-Ridge Turtleneck

Seed Stitch Poncho

Cabled Twinset

Retro Coat

Reversible Rib Shawl

1990s

PATRICIA BROWN
REWORKS PROFESSOR
HIGGIN'S PREFERRED
GARB. RIGHT, CARVING
A FEMININE SHAPE
WITH CABLED DARTS A
THE WAISTLINE . . . AN
A SHAPELY SHAWL CO
LAR THAT BUTTONS
HIGH; IN ANNY BLATT
WOOL. OPPOSITE, A
VOGUE ORIGINAL
INSPIRED BY ARMY
SURPLUS PULLOVERS I
OLIVE DRAB IS
ANYTHING BUT . . .
CLOSE FITTING, IT HAS
A ZIGZAG STITCH
BODICE AND POOR-BO
RIBBED SLEEVES, IN
CHRISTIAN DE
FALBE/CASCADE WOO

Borrowed
FROM THE
Boys

Christian de
Falbe/Cascade,
Chandos

12

Zigzag Stitch Sweater

The curse of the boyfriend sweater is the phenomenon of knitting a sweater for a beau, only to subsequently find yourself on the short end of a breakup. One way to get around the fabled curse is to take some of the best elements of men's wear and put a feminine spin on them. That was the gist of "Borrowed from the Boys," a feature that infused aspects of tailored, military clothing (epaulets and olive drab) into bespoke sweaters for her. This *Vogue Knitting* original, with its crisp columns of zigzag stitch and ribbed poor-boy sleeves, was specifically inspired by army surplus pullovers and originally knit in *Chandos* wool from Christian de Falbe/Cascade.

Army togs weren't the only bit of Americana to inspire garments in this issue. There was also a story on folk art colorwork, a genre that experienced a renaissance in the early '90s, thanks to mainstream designers like Ralph Lauren who mined the motifs of the American Southwest and Pacific Northwest.

This first edition of the new decade also welcomed the first *VK* baby—Michela Coniglio, daughter of longtime *Vogue Knitting* technical expert Joni Coniglio, was ushered into the world with "the best baby sweater," a timeless lace cardigan by the irrepressible mother/daughter team of Elizabeth Zimmermann and Meg Swansen.

FALL 1990 · Instructions Page 216

Missoni Jacket

The Missoni cover garment for Fall 1991 is such a *VK* touchstone, it was one of only ten archival patterns reimagined for the magazine's silver anniversary issue in 2006. The husband-and-wife team of Ottavio and Rosita Missoni—whose namesake fashion label was "synonymous with a distinctive use of color and pattern"—came by their stylish ski-slope aesthetic naturally, living and working in the picturesque foothills of the Italian Alps. This roomy hooded cardigan mixes stripes and tilted triangles with bright solids offsetting softer tweeds, showing the range of yarns from Filatura di Crosa/Stacy Charles.

The riot of colorwork in this sweater set the scene for the rest of the issue, chockablock with ethnic motifs from the Baltics, Turkey, the pueblo, even Amish country. Other palette pleasers included a tutorial about multicolored ribbing and an acorn hat with circus-bright bobbles knit on the bias by Lily Chin, introduced in this issue as a Master Knitter of the '90s. Showing the cheek and chic that would become her hallmark, Chin recalled a conversation she had while knitting on a park bench in New York City, when a man came up to her and said, "You're too young to be doing that." Chin replied simply, "Obviously, you're too ignorant to be doing this."

Bright solids, muted tweeds and bold patter-ning...the winning in-gredients for the Mis-sonis' hooded, color-blocked jacket, large photo at left; in Filatura di Crosa/Stacy Charles yarns. Small photos: Runway shots from Missonis' triumphant Fall showing in Milan.

14

$\mathcal{S}$inuous Sweater

The flip side to all that color in the Fall '91 issue was a neutral palette selected to show off uncommon texture. The "blister-stitch" effect Norah Gaughan created in this singular sweater is a good example of the groundbreaking techniques with which *VK* designers were encouraged to experiment. The soft puckering, achieved by knitting certain stitches into the row below, is flanked by sinuous ribbing that adds a curvaceous quality to the boxy sweater, stitched originally in a wool/mohair/acrylic blend called *Sympathie* from Filatura di Crosa/Stacy Charles.

Also plying more natural tones in this issue was Donna Karan New York, the brand that defined casual chic in the 1990s. The very next issue of *VK* would register that the label's name had been abbreviated to the now-revered acronym of DKNY.

Quick historical note: This issue marks the first time Joe Vior was listed as creative director on the magazine's masthead. Vior's visual panache remains a major reason the magazine continues to be worthy of the "vogue" in its name.

FALL 1991 · Instructions Page 219

**NEUTRAL SHADES,
NATURAL TEXTURES
PLAY AGAINST THE
GLEAM OF NEW-AGE
METALLICS** A blister
stitch effect is achieved
with sinuous ribs by
Norah Gaughan, right,
for a soft pullover with a
deep round neck and
loose, cropped shape;
in blend of wool, mohair
and acrylic from Filatura
di Crosa/Stacy Charles.

**INNOVATIVE STITCH-
ES ADD TEXTURAL
DRAMA AND DEFINE
SHAPE...** Left, Helene
Rush crafts a refined
jacket in a travelling diagonal stitch. An I-cord
draws in the waist; bell
stitch edging gives vol-
ume to the peplum; in
Reynold's natural wool.

19

relaxed Shapes

ladylike whimsy...

31

FROM A SWINGY, FLARED DRESS...TO A GENTLY
WRAPPED COAT.. SOFTNESS IN LIGHT-AS-AIR MOHAIR.

LEFT: LAURIE MACMILLAN REFINES A TRAPEZE DRESS
WITH PRECISELY SHAPED RAGLAN ARMHOLES, CON-
TRASTING CUFFS AND RIBBED TIE COLLAR; IN A TIBER/
CLASSIC ELITE MOHAIR BLEND. RIGHT: ANITA OLIVERIA
WHIPS UP A CLUTCH COAT WITH A DEEPLY ROMANTIC
CAPELET COLLAR; IN HAYFIELD/CASCADE'S LUSH MO-
HAIR BLEND. PANTS, 2726.

Trapeze Dress

Call it retro, call it vintage—*VK* called it "ladylike whimsy." Always eager to hark back to the styles it championed in decades past, 1990s-era *Vogue Knitting* infused a bit of the modern day into its pastiche patterns. That's what works so well in Laurie Macmillan's raglan-sleeve trapeze dress with a contrasting ribbed tie collar. The 1960s swing silhouette is brought up to date by its fiber, *Mohair Doux* by Tiber/Classic Elite.

This look also displayed many of the hallmarks of *VK* sweaters of the early 1990s, when "fashion" equaled "casual": an oversized, relaxed fit. Jeans and leggings were the preferred pants of choice, and editors curated tops that both looked stylish in the magazine yet worked as a wearable piece of clothing out in the real world.

FALL 1991 • Instructions Page 221

$\mathcal{S}$parkly Sweater

"All that glitters. All that glows," this theme was epitomized by this evening sweater by Lily Chin, who used a sequined yarn, Tiber *Ecailles*, along with Classic Elite's *Paisley* for a sparkly effect. The feather trim—actually a feather boa cut to fit around the scoop neck—is applied separately.

"Go for the Glamour!" crowed the cover of this party-hearty issue of *Vogue Knitting*. But before all the shimmer, the magazine shined a light on its readers' interests, publishing a sampling of responses from a questionnaire that asked for pointed feedback about the magazine. Their responses were fascinating—proof that knitters held strong opinions they were happy to voice well before the Internet age gave everyone instant access to the *VK* staff. Missives ranged from "I'm spoiled by *Vogue*'s style" to "You have way too many avant-garde sweaters. No one wants to look like something from another planet." One particular letter sums up the consensus of thought, however: "Whenever I make a *VK* sweater, people stop me on the street to comment that they've never seen anything so nice in the stores. That's why I knit."

A LITTLE NIGHT MAGIC

simply dazz

All that glitters. All that glows. Evenings of incandescent charm. Sweaters with dramatic impact. It's never been so easy to create this much style!

19
Very Easy
Very Vogue

LILY CHIN KNOWS HOW TO IGNITE THE NIGHT WITH A TRIM, JET BLACK PULLOVER. Knit-in sequin yarn gives it extra sparkle and applied feather trim supplies the ultimate touch of fantasy around the scoop neck. Made with Classic Elite's "Paisley," a wool/rayon blend and Tiber "Ecailles" a carry along yarn with sequins. Very Easy Very Vogue. Vogue skirt, 9813. Instructions, page 84. Makeup by Ariella, hair by Terry Foster. Photographed at Cafe Des Artistes restaurant, 1 W. 67 St., N.Y., N.Y.

WINTER 1991–1992 • Instructions Page 222

g!

sunbaked

DKNY leads the way with trailblazing desert tones

3
DKNY

neutrals

$\mathcal{D}$esert Garden Pullover

The concept behind *VK*'s "Desert Neutral" feature is that fashion chameleons should never blend into the background. DKNY's desert-inspired sweater, in Classic Elite's cotton/silk blend *Willough*, employs clever construction techniques to achieve the central nesting mosaic effect of four diagonally knit squares.

This project and many of the others in this issue were shot on location in Palm Springs, California. The *VK* staff set up shop at the historic Orchid Tree Inn, in the foothills of the "dazzling" San Jacinto Mountains and mere miles from the area's famous hot springs.

In addition to introducing readers to such a picturesque resort location, this issue also marked the premier of a section that's become a major element of the magazine: Very New Very Vogue. VNVV was designed to "keep you updated on the knitty gritty," with news about the knitting world and quick takes on yarn and accessories stitchers need to know about. The first VNVV checked in with former editor Lola Ehrlich, who had opened a millinery shop in Manhatttan, highlighted a new Anny Blatt yarn and some decorative buttons, and ran a picture of a quartet of *VK* editors (including editor in chief Nancy J. Thomas and then–associate managing editor Trisha Malcolm) linking arms, modeling their own versions of the DKNY "tree sweater" from the Winter '92 edition. Then just a single page, Very New Very Vogue now spans dozens in each issue, incorporating new yarn updates, knitterly news from the U.K. and Canada, and singing the praises of an Inspirational Yarn Shop.

Blue Waves Sweater

This issue traveled from desert to sea-scape. "They Call It the Blues" explored "aquatic shades of turquoise," from aquamarine to azure and everything in between. Norah Gaughan took the watery motif literally, knitting waves into her roomy scoop-necked tee, stitched side-to-side and originally shown in Reynolds *Saucy Sport* mercerized cotton.

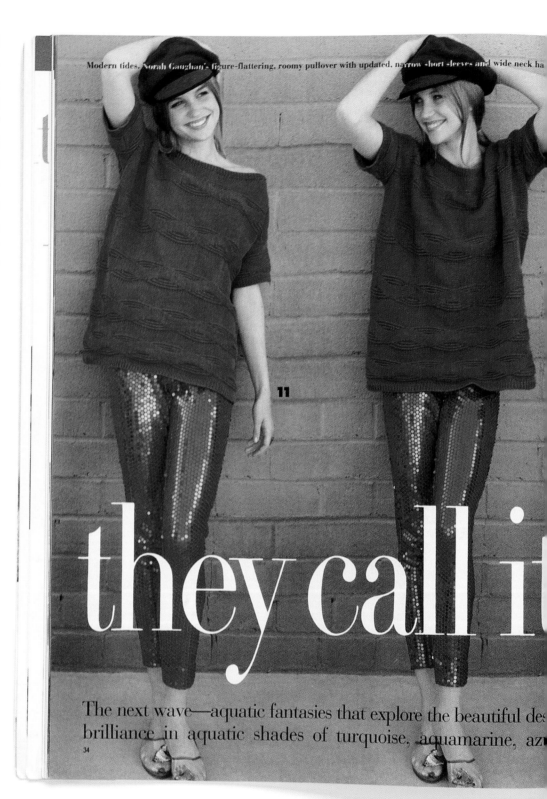

Modern tides. Norah Gaughan's figure-flattering, roomy pullover with updated, narrow short sleeves and wide neck ha...

11

they call it

The next wave—aquatic fantasies that explore the beautiful des... brilliance in aquatic shades of turquoise, aquamarine, az...

34

tif knit side to side. Reynolds "Saucy Sport" mercerized cotton. Intermediate. Pants, Vogue 7680. Instructions on page 69.

the blues!

ossibilities under the sea. Blues have a cool otherworldly
oyal, and navy. Wear them to be leagues ahead of the times.

35

Cabled Sweater

Pam Allen's cropped cabled sweater, in an "old-fashioned" oatmeal *Yukon* wool from Lang/Berroco, is a textured treat and palette cleanser of sorts, as the vast majority of this issue was dedicated to the color burst that is Fair Isle knitting. And to celebrate, *VK* went on location for two glorious weeks to the source of all things Fair Isle, the Shetland Islands.

The Shetlands are a "modern-day mecca for knitters," reported editor in chief Nancy J. Thomas from the historic (and reportedly haunted) Busta Inn, nestled amid many sheep crofts (farms) during lambing season. "Yarn shops can be found along the narrow cobblestone streets of Lerwick. Children learn to knit in elementary school, and the women are the fastest knitters I've ever seen. And yes, they really do use the traditional knitting belts and long double-pointed needles." Along with a dozen-plus Fair Isle patterns, the issue featured instruction on the technique from preeminent Fair Isle expert and Shetland native Alice Starmore, who also narrated *VK*'s instructional video on the time-honored technique shot during Thomas's visit—a way for all readers to experience this singular "knitter's fantasy" for themselves.

FALL 1994 • Instructions Page 226

The ragg-time revival: great old fashioned yarn gets a whole new look in these very modern classics. Left: Patchwork let's you showcase the enticing texture that the right stitches create from simpler wools, enhanced here by alternating solid and ragg yarns. The perfect fall jacket, it guarantees style with built-in coziness. Designed by Nan Hadden in Mahopac "Katonah" wool yarn. Expert. Jumper, Vogue 1389. Hat by Brenda Lynn in Lang/Berroco "Yukon" wool. Intermediate. Right: The pullover for all occasions. Shown cropped here, it can very easily be lengthened. Pam Allen designed it with all-over cabling and a body-hugging fit to prove that warm doesn't have to mean bulky. Lang/Berroco "Yukon" wool. Very Easy Very Vogue. Skirt, Vogue 1403.

18
Very Easy
Very Vogue

From
raggs to...rich,
new designs

59

Red Hot f

Red Hot Sweater

Pointing to poinsettia red for the holidays, new co-editors Margery Winter and Carla Scott led off a collection of "red-hot" classics. Their collaboration, an oversized seed-stitch cowlneck, exudes a luxurious comfort. The yarns used for this sweater, the woolen *Color Kid* and the mohair-blended *Iceland* from Cascade, were the types of high-end fiber found not in chain craft stores but at the independent local yarn shop—now widely known by the acronym LYS.

To celebrate the importance of the LYS in the knitting community, *VK* launched "Inspirational Yarn Shop," a running feature in which the magazine checks in with an influential, inspiring North American yarn shop. For the premiere, a trio of shops were selected from around the country: Colorful Stitches in Lenox, Massachusetts, and La Lana Wools in Taos, New Mexico, both still going strong, and Denver's now-shuttered Skyloom Fibres. The "roving reporter" (pun intended) who visited these shops in the mid-1990s was none other than Melanie Falick, the designer/editor/author who went on to write the much-admired *Knitting in America,* which visited dozens of the knitting world's most creative designers in their own studios, and to eventually establish her own craft-book imprint.

WINTER 1995–1996 • Instructions Page 228

Garter Ridge Cardigan

This cardigan by Mari Lynn Patrick comes from a collection of perfect knits for a work wardrobe: Garter ridges give the piece a crocheted look, offset nicely by stockinette patch pockets. It was shown in *Pima Natural* cotton from Creative Yarns International; the pattern for the linen-stitch tote bag was included, too, as part of an entire ensemble. As for the other patterns for this issue, it was back to Palm Springs to show off warm-weather staples like jaunty nautical stripes and lacy tops, which joined newer entries, including a whole feature on home decor (throws and pillows worked with natural yarns and plenty of texture).

By the mid-1990s, with high-tech devices increasingly demanding attention in people's daily lives, carpal tunnel syndrome and other repetitive stress injuries were on the upswing. This type of malady wasn't new to knitters, though, and *Vogue Knitting* educated its readers about how to deal with sore stitching muscles in an article in this issue. Photos of hand exercises to soothe and strengthen illustrated the approach to continued knitting comfort. (Good advice, then and now: Stretch your back, neck, arms, and hands often when knitting to keep limber.)

SPRING/SUMMER 1996 • Instructions Page 229

15
Very Easy
Very Vogue

16

45

87 1990s

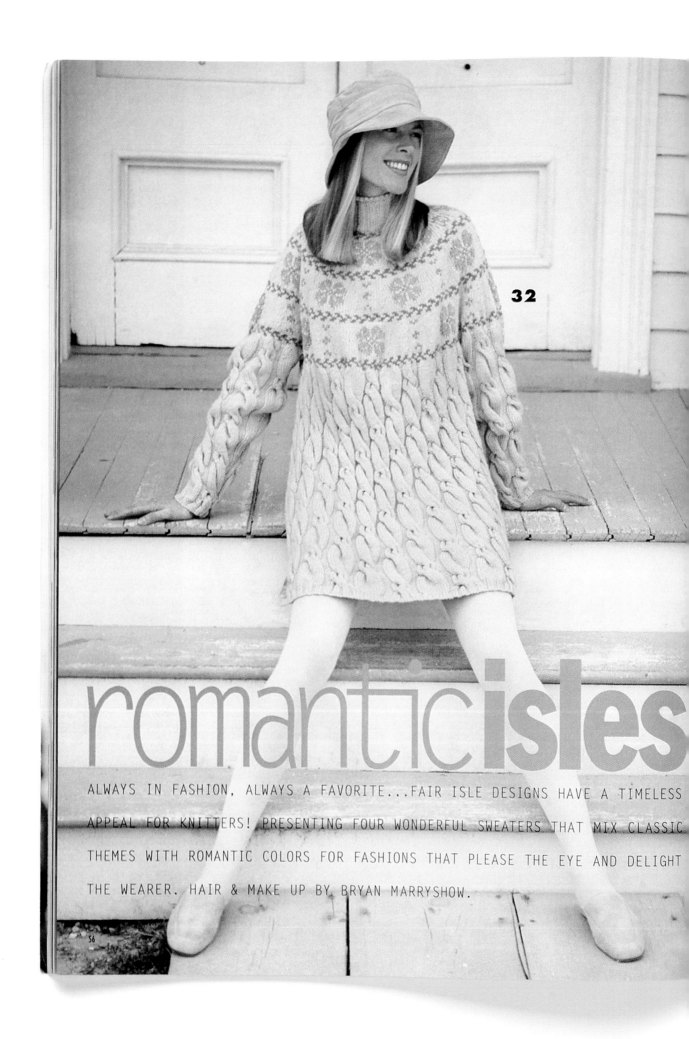

32

romantic isles

ALWAYS IN FASHION, ALWAYS A FAVORITE...FAIR ISLE DESIGNS HAVE A TIMELESS

APPEAL FOR KNITTERS! PRESENTING FOUR WONDERFUL SWEATERS THAT MIX CLASSIC

THEMES WITH ROMANTIC COLORS FOR FASHIONS THAT PLEASE THE EYE AND DELIGHT

THE WEARER. HAIR & MAKE UP BY BRYAN MARRYSHOW.

56

Turtleneck Tunic

omen's Wear Daily proclaimed winter 1996-97 to be "The Year of the Turtle"—and *Vogue Knitting* agreed. This particular issue featured tons of gorgeous turtleneck sweaters, including this one by Jacqueline Jewett combining colorwork and wide, deep cables (worn as a minidress here over tights, but equally suitable as a tunic over pants or a longer skirt). It was knit in Cascade *220,* a staple wool in hundreds of colors that remains to this day a yarn shop best-seller.

In keeping with the trend, seven of the other turtlenecks shown in this issue came from *VK*'s prestige-designer ranks, with '90s favorites Cynthia Rowley, Todd Oldham, and Kenneth Richard joining veteran stalwarts like Donna Karan, Adrienne Vittadini, Missoni, and Joan Vass. In fact, it was Rowley who summed up the edition's theme perfectly: "I think you can't go wrong with a big comfy sweater to keep you warm on the crisp days of the season."

WINTER 1996-1997 · Instructions Page 230

Trellis Cardigan

This intricate sweater by Norah Gaughan, casually wearable yet exquisitely rendered, was part of a feature that took a "new twist" on cabled knitting. Its trellis pattern consists of traveling cables in a lattice scheme that intertwines just below the yoke, with a contrasting cabled collar framing the piece. The Skacel Collection distributed the yarn it was originally knit in, *Setana* by Ilse Wolle.

This issue of *Vogue Knitting* welcomed Trisha Malcolm back to the masthead, this time as editor in chief, a position she holds to this day. She put her own fashion-forward imprint on the magazine right from the get-go and has displayed an unerring eye for talent and beauty ever since.

An additional note about Malcolm's taking the helm: It's only fitting that this issue announced the launch of the magazine's website, VogueKnitting.com: Malcolm's been a huge supporter of technological advances in the Internet age. In 2010 and 2011, she oversaw the creation of *Vogue Knitting* apps for Apple's iPhone and iPad, respectively, devices she has unapologetically heralded as being a great boon to designers and knitters alike.

FALL 1997 · Instructions Page 232

...or the cable lover. ...A lattice pattern of ...ing cables forms a ...trellis on Norah ...aughan's cardigan, ...twining in delicate ...ts at the chest and ...pper back. Cabled ...lar and cuffs are a ...lever frame to this ...nctive design. Knit ...n "Setana" by Ilse ...olle, distributed by ...Skacel Collection. ...Experienced.

8

Striped Sweater

saac Mizrahi was one of the biggest names in 1990s fashion. A specialist in stirring the pot of sportswear, his first piece of many for *Vogue Knitting*—this paintbox of an oversized ribbed turtleneck—proved to be a fan favorite. It was knit in randomly broken stripes using nearly two dozen shades of Classic Elite's lofty *Mini Mohair*.

VK introduces:

ISAAC MIZR

THIS AWARD-WINNING DESIGNER IS WORLD-RENOWNED FOR CREATING CLOTHING WITH A PARED DOWN, PRACTICAL KIND OF LUXURY. NOW, ISAAC MIZRAHI BRINGS HIS BRAND OF CLEAN-CUT MODERNISM TO VOGUE KNITTING!

He is known as the "Whiz Kid" of the fashion world, and in ten short years Isaac Mizrahi has risen to international stardom as a result of his bold and innovative interpretations of American sportswear, as well as his witty, often irreverent, and always refreshing personal style. He is a quintessential New Yorker, and his collections, which blend the unexpected with the traditional, consistently reflect a clean, modern romanticism which the designer sees as the essence of his favorite city. This simple sweater—his first-ever design featured in Vogue Knitting—is signature Mizrahi: elegantly casual and generously cut for comfort, in a whimsical mix of colors that is an intrinsic part of everything he designs. It's the kind of contemporary classic you'll take pleasure in knitting as well as wearing—a warm and welcome addition to your weekend wardrobe this season, and destined to become a well-worn favorite in the seasons to come!

46

WINTER 1997-1998 • Instructions Page 235

Isaac Mizrahi puts a
new twist on stripes.
Oversized ribbed
turtleneck uses
twenty-four shades
of lofty mohair in
randomly broken
stripes. The yarn is
"Mini Mohair" from
Classic Elite.

15

Tape Tee

Sheen and sheer were the watchwords for Spring/Summer '98, as *VK* took the show back on the road to Miami Beach's Eden Roc Resort, where much of this breezy issue was photographed. The "sheen" came from a designer showcase of the summery new batch of ribbon yarns, featuring this form-fitted cabled tee by Joan Vass. A slight roll neck and tiny trim pockets complete the look, originally stitched in the sleek tape yarn *Melbourne* by Sesia.

The "sheer" came from a collection of peekaboo lace, warm-weather staples designed to heat up the style quotient without being stifling. A primer on ways to create opaque fabrics punctuated by barely there sections contributed to the translucent trend. And a guide on how to wear these see-through fashions while remaining covered in the right places encouraged more modest readers to dare to bare a little more skin.

Additionally, knitters were introduced to figure-flattering hand-knitting patterns courtesy of *Designing Women* star Delta Burke, who spearheaded her own plus-sized fashion collection. Duffers got their due, too: A seasonally appropriate golf-centered article displayed links-worthy club sweaters and tops for guys and gals, topped off by a caddy's bag full of club cozies.

SPRING/SUMMER 1998 • Instructions Page 236

SLEEK SHAPING WITH AN URBAN EDGE

Joan Vass

Fit for city life. Lean lines shape up in a creamy "tape" yarn— "Melbourne" by Sesia. Streamlined cables, body-conscious fit, trim pockets and a slight rollneck add a smart, sophisticated edge to the ever-essential tee. Intermediate.

14

OSCAR
BY OSCAR
DE LA RENTA

16

Explore the comfort factor. *This page and on our cover:* Natural wonder. The raw appeal of a silk and wool blend, Tahki "Chelsea Silk," pays off in this softly-draped Oscar by Oscar de la Renta design. Diagonal-ridged body, ribbed raglan sleeves and a face-framing turtleneck all in a wonderfully-relaxed silhouette.

Diagonal-Ridge Turtleneck

A winning Oscar by Oscar de la Renta turtleneck graced the cover of the Fall '98 issue. Along with an exquisite drape—due in part to Tahki's *Chelsea Silk*, the silk/wool blend it was knit in—the oatmeal pullover also featured a furrowed diagonal-ridge body and relaxed raglan sleeves.

As all-American as this look is, the edition spent a great deal of time Down Under, via a reminiscence of a recent *VK* trip to Australia and New Zealand. *Vogue Knitting* began organizing skein-centric excursions in the early '90s, inviting readers bursting with wanderlust to join editors, designers, and yarny experts to explore far-flung locales with robust knitting cultures. Among the locales the magazine's groups have explored over the years: Scandinavia, the United Kingdom, Bolivia, Peru, the Caribbean, Germany, France, Italy, Canada, and Alaska. These trips continue to integrate dedicated stitching workshops into lots of touring, balancing visits to local yarn shops, fiber mills, and farms with more general sightseeing and, lore has it, plenty of great food.

FALL 1998 · Instructions Page 237

Under wraps. *Opposite:*
Turn heads with a generous
hooded cape in lush, plush
bouclé—"Muschio" from
Gringnasco/JCA. Designed
by Diane Zangl. *This page:*
Make your escape in style.
Generous face-framing
turtleneck poncho, finished
with twisted edging and
knitted tassel trim. See
Stitch Glossary for details.
Designed by Nicky Epstein in
Lion Brand "AL•PA•KA."

30

Seed Stitch Poncho

P early gray was Nicky Epstein's color of choice for this oversized poncho, stitched originally in Lion Brand's *AL PA KA*. With its dramatic standup turtleneck, finished twisted edges, and knitted tassel trim, the cloak no doubt lived up to its lofty billing: "There's nothing like a cape to create an air of glamour and mystery." Credit the prolific Epstein for being ahead of the times with this garment: The full-on poncho craze that helped to reinvigorate the knitting industry in the early 2000s was still several years away.

Color-trend forecasting is a crucial but largely cryptic aspect of fashion design. Yet it shouldn't be, which is why *Vogue Knitting* has revisited the topic several times since introducing the concept to readers in the Fall '98 issue. As the article "Forecast: Color" pointed out, color-trend experts divine the next hot palettes by analyzing popular culture and current events. For example, "Growing eco-consciousness is the inspiration for natural textures and colors; movies like *Titanic* set the stage for a romantic revival." At the time this issue was published, the "spa mentality" elevated healing shades of blue into public consciousness, sun-baked desert tones combined for a sophisticated paintbox, and grays represented "a growing yin-and-yang sensibility—less of a black-and-white view of life."

FALL 1998 · Instructions Page 238

Cabled Twinset

In the minds of many fashion watchers, the twinset is the quintessential knit. Isaac Mizrahi elevates that dynamic duo here by reinterpreting an array of traditional Guernsey patterns in a sleek, modern way. The sculpted cardigan features twisted ribs amid its diamond-cabled columns, while the body-skimming shell picks up the texturing in a subtle way, sending embossed triangles tripping down the center front. Both garments have back pieces knit in seed stitch and were originally shown in *Super Lambswool* by Lane Borgosesia.

It's a virtuoso performance, to be sure, but a quieter moment amid a host of more dramatic garments. Anna Sui rang in with a diamond eyelet sweater embellished with shimmering crimson paillettes. An evening-wear feature pulled out all the stops, with faux fur, theatrical asymmetry (a particularly memorable tunic dipped down on one side to a knee-length point), and even a sexy one-shouldered halter top.

isaac mizrahi

15

WINTER 1998-1999 • Instructions Page 239

This page and opposite: Retro revival. Isaac Mizrahi appreciates the beauty of classic handwork and has a knack for re-interpreting it with a modern sensibility. Case in point, this exquisite twinset. Worked in an array of traditional Guernsey patterns, the cardigan front is a masterpiece of twisted ribs and sculpted stitches. Underneath, a perfectly-fitted shell that picks up the diamond pattern from the cardigan-sleeves, reinter-preting it as a center-front band. The backs of both pieces are knit in seed stitch; the yarn is "Super Lambswool" by Lane Borgosesia.

15

The sweater set is front-page fashion news... sleek, chic and ever so sophisticated

Retro Coat

"Big needles are back!" blared the cover, and this trend was further explored through updates of patterns originally printed in 1968, the last time bulky knits were so in vogue, so to speak. This retro charcoal coat was worked identically to its forebear, with a stockinette-stitch body and wide garter-stitch border. This time, however, it was knit with a whopping five strands of yarn held together on U.S. size 35 needles (that's not a typo—size 35!). A cluster of fibers from Filatura di Crosa/ Stacy Charles was used in the revamp: two strands of *Muschio,* two strands of *Ultralight,* and one of *Sympathie Tweed.*

There was good reason for the return of the superchunky knit. In the autumn of 1999, "The resurgence of this oversized-stitch trend is in keeping with the 'home craft' theme that is showing up in everything from fashion to decorating—a comforting balance to the many hard-edge predictions for the new millennium," designer Mari Lynn Patrick explained in an article accompanying large-and-in-charge sweaters. "The larger the stitch and the more naive the style and pattern, the more the sweater speaks as a project made by hand, and the greater the appeal to the first-time or novice knitter as a project within their reach." Eloquently stated.

FALL 1999 · Instructions Page 242

Built for comfort *and* for speed.
Opposite: There's nothing slow and steady about this turtle. We added full fashioning to the raglan sleeves, altered the size and shape of the turtleneck, and loosened up the fit. A combination of two tweed and two plain strands creates the tweedy texture.
THE NEEDLE: Size 19/16mm.
THE YARN: Four strands of "AL•PA•KA" from Lion Brand.

This page: Take fashion into the fast lane. Worked in the same stockinette and wonderfully textural garter-stitch border as the original (the only change we made was to the yarn and color), this cozy coat is ready to move.
THE NEEDLE: Size 35/19mm.
THE YARN: Two strands of "Muschio," one strand of "Sympathie Tweed," and two strands of "Ultralight" from Filatura Di Crosa/Stacy Charles Collection.

For the inside story on big-needle knits see page 54.

15
Very Easy
Very Vogue

53

Reversible Rib Shawl

The millennium approaches and to celebrate the turn of the century, *VK* turned to its master knitters of the '90s for predictions on stitching in the 2000s. Looking back, we can report that their gut instincts were eerily on target. Norah Gaughan was correct in her assumption that the craft would become "increasingly important as a tool for self-enrichment." Mari Lynn Patrick foresaw the proliferation of deconstructed sweaters, plenty of accessories (from bags to bikinis) and "complex structures balanced against easy knits." But it was Lily Chin who got it most right: "The Internet has profoundly influenced knitting," she said. "Knowledge and supplies that were previously hard to find are now a mere mouseclick away. As a result, knitting techniques that were somewhat obscure will become commonplace."

Though Chin didn't completely predict the vibrant knitting community that would emerge online, she did design the perfect accent piece for the cusp of the millennium: Her ethereal cable-rib shawl has been a favorite since this issue's publication. Its original incarnation was dubbed "the ultimate indulgence," knit in supersoft *Butterfly* by Filatura di Crosa/ Stacy Charles Collection.

&

'Tis the season of
enchanted evenings. Work
a little knit magic
into your party plans

THE NIGHT LIGHTS

*M*odern Classics

Waffle-Knit Coat	Whip-Stitch Tunic
Ribbed Yoke Sweater	Fitted Jacket
Diamond-Lace Top	Rainbow Shawl
Cotton Tunic	Fair Isle Cardigan
Coral Cables	Forestry Cardigan
Wrap Star Cardigan	Bulky Coat
Fine Lines Cowlneck	Peplum Cardigan
Aran Attitude Pullover	Dolman Pullover
Shawl Collar Sweater	Striped Cardigan
Take Two Twinset	Lace Capelet
Shaped Camisole	Cabled Cardigan
Woven Cable Twinset	Cabled Swing Poncho
Lace Cape	Lace Jacket
Striped Kimono	Multitextured Cardigan
Belted Lace Pullover	Cabled Pullover
Wrap Front Pullover	Fisherman's Cardigan
Seed Stitch Suit	Hooded Lace Cardigan
Striped Tunic	Medallion Coverup
Loop Stitch Cardigan	Gold-Tone Bikini

2000s

Waffle-Knit Coat

A feature on knitted coats included this elegant number by Mari Lynn Patrick, stitched in *Alaska* from Garnstudio/Aurora Yarns. The piece's interior shaping and doubled collar give it a timeless style edge over the boxy and puffy mass-market coat designs of the time—"sensible chic," it was called. And that red? Too perfect.

The saturated solid set up a nice contrast to a large story about yet another burgeoning trend for the new century: hand-painted yarn. Small hand-dyers, hand-painters, and hand-dippers had been treating fiber as a canvas for a while, but there's no doubt that the 2000s ushered in the grand era of independent artisanal yarn companies. Kit Hutchin, soon-to-be owner of Churchmouse Yarns & Teas, the influential yarn shop on Bainbridge Island, Washington, formally introduced *VK* readers to the bounty of beautiful artistry available on one-of-a-kind skeins by the likes of Colinette, Cherry Tree Hill, Prism, Great Adirondack, Mountain Colors, Fiesta, Hanah Silk, and, of course, Koigu. Accompanying the article was a quartet of patterns—two sweaters, a scarf, and a poncho—designed to best display the unique qualities and color repeats found in hand-painted yarns.

FALL 2000 • Instructions Page 245

34
Very Easy
Very Vogue

Keep
cozy
without
losing
your cool

Ribbed Yoke Sweater

With a yarn as artfully opulent as 100 percent cashmere (Trendsetter's *Dali* was used here), minimalism is the right design approach. That's why Mari Lynn Patrick kept the lines on her short-sleeved pullover lithe and refined. The rib-yoked top has a rolled neck and a touch-me factor that's off the charts.

At the onset of 2001, *VK* added a fourth issue each year. This special collector's issue, printed each May, gave readers more patterns per annum. For this particular issue, though, a wide-ranging spectrum of yarn provided the main skein attraction: Cushy chunkies hit the "express lane." Mohair blends made for ethereal evening wear (turn the page for an example). Nubby tweed merinos staked their claim as the go-to choice for textured classics. A new breed of eyelash yarns allowed readers to "walk on the wild side with fabulous fakes." And then there was cashmere, representing the ultimate in luxury fibers.

WINTER 2000-2001 · Instructions Page 246

16

the caché of cashmere

s the ultimate expression in fine fiber art

18

The season of subtle, sexy finesse. Luxe

Diamond-Lace Top

Over the years, Shirley Paden has proved herself a maestro of gossamer lace. Her prodigious way with a yarn over renders this barely there lace button-up the perfect formal cardi. (*VK* recommended pairing the piece with a nude cami, to create an ensemble that's "revealing without being risqué.") Paden used a fine mohair, *Baby Kid Extra* by Filatura di Crosa/Tahki•Stacy Charles, in navy, an unexpectedly deep color choice for such an airy fabric.

This issue also featured a fascinating collaboration between two of our favorite designers: king of colorwork Kaffe Fassett teamed up with the empress of embellishment, Nicky Epstein, to create a garment that paired each artist's signature aesthetic. This cardi of many colors had a multihued fabric by Fassett— florals up top, stripes from the yoke down—with Epstein providing I-cord frog closures and embroidering, beading and bobbling the blossoms for a dimensional petal effect.

Though Fassett was at the forefront of successful male hand-knitting designers, he wasn't the only guy represented in this issue. According to a *VK* survey, the ranks of men knitters were increasing in the early 2000s—and they wanted patterns. The result was an article highlighting the differences between knitting for women and knitting for men, complete with a "Collar Class" listing half a dozen necklines (from polo to placket inset) that a man's sweater wardrobe couldn't do without.

WINTER 2000-2001 • Instructions Page 247

Cotton Tunic

This cotton cabled tunic from Norah Gaughan, in *Miranda* by Adrienne Vittadini/JCA, slips right into the resort-wear vibe. It fit with the whites versus brights dichotomy set up in this issue and also epitomizes the retro '80s silhouettes so in season—tweaked by "a new emphasis on easy fit with a slightly sexy feel," according to Trisha Malcolm's editor's letter.

For the warm-weather issue of 2001, *Vogue Knitting* flew south to Puerto Rico. Much of the issue was shot by the ocean and in historic Old Town in and around San Juan.

Puerto Rico wasn't the only exotic locale in this issue. Editors Carla Scott and Rosemary Drysdale recounted their epic *VK* in the U.K. adventure with a photo-filled trip diary. The sixteen-day excursion to England, Wales, Ireland, and Scotland was chock-full of fantasy fiber events, including visits with knitting royalty Sasha Kagan, Brandon Mably, Debbie Bliss, Colinette Sainsbury, Alice Starmore, Jean Moss, Louisa Harding, and Maggie Jackson, with stops at Rowan Yarns headquarters, the majestic Victoria & Albert Museum, the historic Woolen Mills in Blarney, and the Edinburgh home of Yesterknits, the world's largest repository of knitting patterns.

SPRING/SUMMER 2001 • Instructions Page 249

Summer sizzles
in bold shades
of coral, pink,
turquoise, and
tangerine, cooled
down with a
splash of white.

Opposite: Tangerine dream.
Classic cables take a new
turn interspersed with eyelets
and worked in a featherweight
ribbon yarn, Trendsetter Yarns
"Dolcino." Interpreted by
Mari Lynn Patrick. *This page:*
The light idea. A cool, cabled
cotton tunic is the perfect
partner for bright bottoms.
Designed by Norah Gaughan
and knit all in one piece
in Adrienne Vittadini/JCA
"Miranda."

14

light

Opposite: Fringe bene
Colorwork stripes bri
up a full-fashioned te
Tasseled trim adds a
touch of attitude.
Designed by Gitta
Schrade in Berroco, I
"Pronto." *This page:*
Sunny side up. Chunk
cables in cool coral (c
of the hottest shades
the season) work thei
way into decreasing n
at the neckline. Desig
by Gabrielle Hamil in
Karabella Yarns "Soft

15

Coral Cables

The flip side to all the whites in the Spring/Summer 2001 edition were the brights, of course. Fuchsia, lemon, turquoise, and coral brought a tropical punch to the magazine's pages. Flush with the freshest shade of the season, this fun cabled number by Gabrielle Hamill echoes the vividness surrounding San Juan sites. Knit originally in Karabella Yarns' *Softig*, the piece has chunky cables that work upward into decreasing ribs at the yoke.

There was plenty of texture in this issue, comprising nearly forty sweaters, tops, tanks, and coverups for women. Not a bag or a scarf or a hat to be seen. Even the tutorials and workshops—on shoulder joining, yarn overs, and dropped stitches—revolved around full-size garments. That's why a decor piece on sleek knitted slipcovers was so refreshing. Written by Teva Durham—a former *VK* editor soon to be a breakout design star with her Loop-D-Loop collection—"Preferred Seating" walked readers through the surprisingly simple process of stitching up a well-fitting armchair slipcover in mohair. It was the right story at the right time, published just as the notion of DIY home improvement started to catch on in a big way.

SPRING/SUMMER 2001 · Instructions Page 250

Wrap Star Cardigan

Straight off the runway, this design from Oscar by Oscar de la Renta is gorgeous proof that in the early aughts, "dressing down is looking a lot more like dressing up." The exquisite cardi, in taupe wool *Modigliani* by Needful Yarns and Things, boasts one of the most figure-flattering silhouettes in knitdom—the front wrap. The sweater's texture comes from diagonal ribbing that meets at a slimming V at the back and a perpendicular panel of cables, knit separately and sewn around the neckline to form the collar.

With a marquis name like Oscar setting the stage, this issue was the perfect place to check in with the burgeoning group of confessed celebrity knitters—Julia Roberts being the brightest of the superstars who unapologetically knit on set. Check-ins at Hollywood-area yarn shops revealed an A-list clientele that ranged from Julianne Moore and Brooke Shields to Debra Messing and Jane Krakowski. Actress Camryn Mannheim, an Emmy winner for *The Practice*, even had her baby shower at La Knitterie Parisienne, where friends like Calista Flockhart and Marlee Matlin stitched a square for a nursery-bound blanket. Former *Family Ties* star Justine Bateman took to the craft to such an extent that she launched her own design line, creating chenille halters, mohair bikinis, fur-trimmed scarves, and merino pullovers.

FALL 2001 · Instructions Page 251

2

OSCAR by Oscar de la Renta

$\mathcal{F}$ine Lines Cowlneck

The cover for this autumn edition promised "Cowls, Coats & Cables," and Mari Lynn Patrick was one of many designers to deliver the goods on the cowl—the season's chicest neck treatment. Her body-hugging pullover with slightly flared sleeves carries striping created by a two-row slip-stitch pattern. A deep U neckline allows for the low drape of the oversized cowl.

This sweater was knit in a wool/mohair/acrylic blend, *Christine* by Dive/Lane Borgosesia. But alpaca was the fiber that made the biggest splash in the issue. As luxury-yarn shoppers enjoyed the renaissance of alpaca fiber—once reserved for Andean royalty—*VK* let its readers in on the animal's fascinating history and ably described the outstanding qualities of yarn spun from alpaca fleece, increasingly available from homegrown North American companies like Blue Sky Alpacas.

Another sign of the times: This issue marked the discontinuation of the Vogue Sewing guide that had been included in *Vogue Knitting* since the magazine's relaunch. The end of one era marked the beginning of the next—in which knitting becomes an even stronger cultural force with a vocal and growing fan base, online and off.

FALL 2001 · Instructions Page 253

Aran Attitude Pullover

"Creating Hope." That was the title of Trisha Malcolm's editor's letter in this issue, the first published after the terrorist attacks of September 11, 2001. For twenty years, the *Vogue Knitting* office in downtown Manhattan had a perfect view of the Twin Towers, located but a mile away. That fateful morning, the staff watched as the landscape of New York City—and, indeed, the country—changed irrevocably. The office was closed for a full week, and when the editors returned, it was to a new, unsure reality. Knitting, of course, was one method of coping.

"Many people have told me how knitting helped them through this difficult time, providing a calming activity as they watched the constant television coverage or reflected on the events," Trisha wrote, thanking the readers who called or e-mailed to make sure the *VK* team was safe. "We have always known knitting to be therapeutic."

This cropped Debbie Bliss design, sporting plenty of cables to get lost in, is emblematic of the casual tenor of the issue's collection, curated well before world events took such a turn for the unknown. And the relaxed tone of the issue acted as balm to the unsure times.

4

Shawl Collar Sweater

*V*K celebrated its twentieth anniversary in 2002 with a special collector's issue featuring "enduring classics"—selected yarns that had been around since the magazine's relaunch. By singling out these time-tested skeins, *Vogue Knitting* feted not just its own birthday but also the longevity of the knitting industry as a whole. Without the yarn companies—it goes without saying—there would be no patterns, no *VK*, no yarn shops, no knitting.

Another venerable yarn commemorated in the special twentieth-anniversary issue for being a mainstay: *Donegal Tweed* wool from Tahki Yarns/Tahki•Stacy Charles. "Spun in the small Irish village of Kilcar, with wonderful flecks of saturated color woven in," *Donegal Tweed* is still going strong to this day. It was knit up into this dramatic pullover by Irina Poludnenko, a design that maximizes the fiber's "earthy, homespun look, rugged textural interest and easy hand." The sweater boasts a shawl collar inset into a square neckline and slant ribs that accentuate a central ribbed panel.

FALL 2002 · Instructions Page 257

"Donegal Tweed"
Tahki Yarns/Tahki•Stacy Charles, Inc.

Debut: 1970
Fiber content: 100 percent pure new wool
Best-selling colors: Neutrals, followed by autumnal shades
Lasting impact: Donegal tweed is a plain or twill weave dotted with colored stubs throughout. Like its fabric cousin, Tahki's durable "Donegal Tweed" yarn—spun in the small Irish village of Kilcar—has wonderful flecks of saturated color woven in. Boasting an earthy, homespun look, rugged textural interest and an easy hand, the yarn offers an array of applications for both garments and home design. It is available in fifty-nine traditional and fashion colors; four to five new hues are introduced each season.
New this season: Denims, Cool Greens, Gold, Charcoal

Slanted ribs accent the center panel of Irina Poludnenko's dramatic pullover. A square neck, shawl collar and set-in sleeves offer flattering detail.

7

*T*ake Two Twinset

A mix of classic and current designs infused the twentieth-anniversary edition with a taste of knitting's past, present, and future. One of the best era-spanning examples was this twinset from the prolific Debbie Bliss, as renowned for her vintage/modern baby knits as for her gorgeous women's garments. Knit in *Merino Aran* from Debbie Bliss/KFI, it consists of a sleeveless cabled turtleneck and matching cardi with a short-row shaped shawl collar.

Also straddling the decades: Kay Niederlitz's famed Map of the World sweater, one of the most popular knits ever presented in *Vogue Knitting*. Since its original publication in the Spring/Summer 1991 issue, "wars have been fought, borders have shifted—so we decided it was time to once again circumvent the globe." Niederlitz reimagined her intarsia map sweater into afghan form, shifting the original 360-degree patterning that wrapped around the pullover's front and back into more of a flat-map format. The result: a vibrant atlas in fiber, every bit as groundbreaking as the sweater on which it was modeled.

FALL 2002 • Instructions Page 258

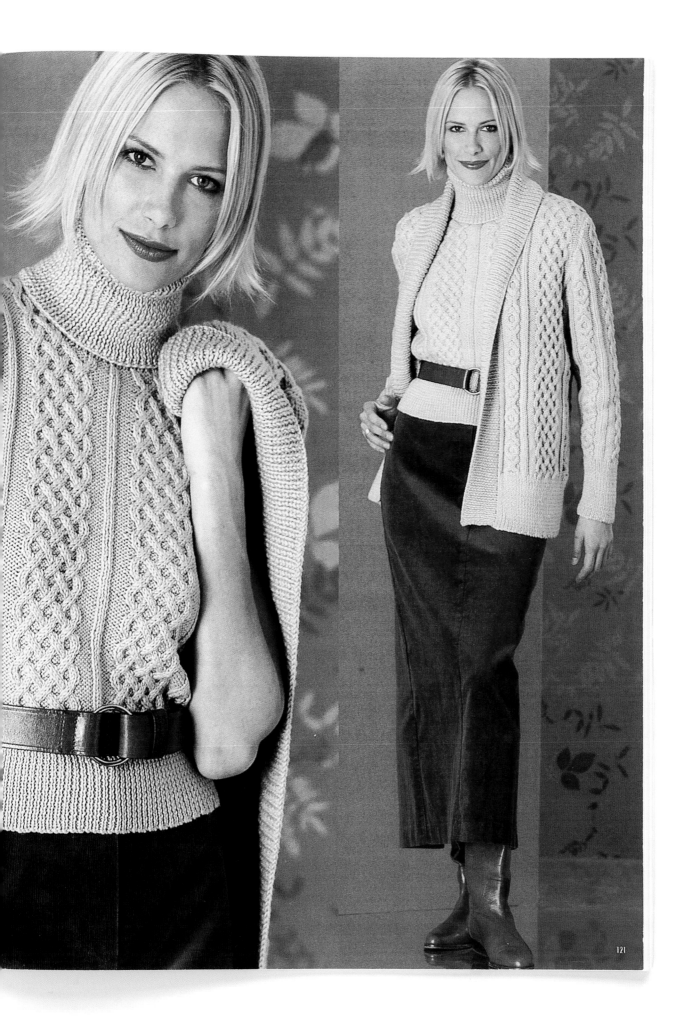

3

Shaped Camisole

I n the warm-weather issue of 2003, Trisha Malcolm announced that *VK* would no longer print special issues each summer. Instead, the fourth issue each year would be devoted to holiday knitting. But with that first seasonal edition still months away, the staff was free to focus on sun-drenched knits for a heat wave. It's a collection that benefited those with toned shoulders and midriffs, heavily showcasing cropped tops, peekaboo pullovers, and plenty of lace, like this lovely cami, with an allover eyelet-leaf pattern and plunging back. It was designed by Larissa Bulakh and shown in Dale of Norway's *Svale*.

This issue also included a trip diary from *VK*'s tour of Ireland and the Outer Hebrides. Rosaleen Hegarty, the founder of the Irish National Knitting Center in Buncrana, gave the group a charming poem by an unknown Irish poet. Its verses are near irresistible, as this excerpt attests:

"In the middle of problems, the big ones and small
It's always proper and fittin'
To trust and to pray
Til the lord shows the way
And go right ahead with your knittin'"

SPRING/SUMMER 2003 · Instructions Page 260

Woven Cable Twinset

VK's "Sweaters & the City" paid homage to urban style-setting with such chic pieces as Oscar de la Renta's runway-ready sweater/cape twinset. The fitted turtleneck sweater and collared cape is knit in a multi-dimensional woven-cable pattern. It was originally shown in *Luna* from Filatura di Crosa/Tahki•Stacy Charles. (At the de la Renta fashion show, this ensemble included a matching hat, whose pattern was included alongside a workshop on cabling without a cable needle.)

COUTURE CLASSIC

DREAM WEAVER
Oscar de la Renta's sophisticated cape-and-pullover duet is instant drama. The woven cable pattern creates a brilliantly textured fabric for a multidimensional effect, while deeply ribbed edging makes for a simple, unobtrusive frame. A broad, shoulder-gracing collar on the cape and fitted waist on the turtleneck add a flourish of femininity. Worked in "Luna" from Filatura Di Crosa/Tahki•Stacy Charles, Inc. The matching cap is on the following pages.

12

66

WINTER 2003–2004 • Instructions Page 262

THIS SMASHING TWIST ON THE TWINSET FROM LEGENDARY DESIGNER OSCAR DE LA RENTA WAS THE RUNWAY KNIT HIT OF THE FALL/WINTER 2003 NEW YORK COLLECTIONS.

OSCAR DE LA RENTA

67

$\mathcal{L}$ace Cape

ierrot "never went to design school and often claims to know nothing about fashion." That didn't stop the artist formerly known as Pierre Carrilero from wowing celebs like Sarah Jessica Parker with his witty knits. Pierrot debuted in this issue of *Vogue Knitting* with an oversized lace cape, stitched in Knit One Crochet Too's alpaca-blend *Temptation*.

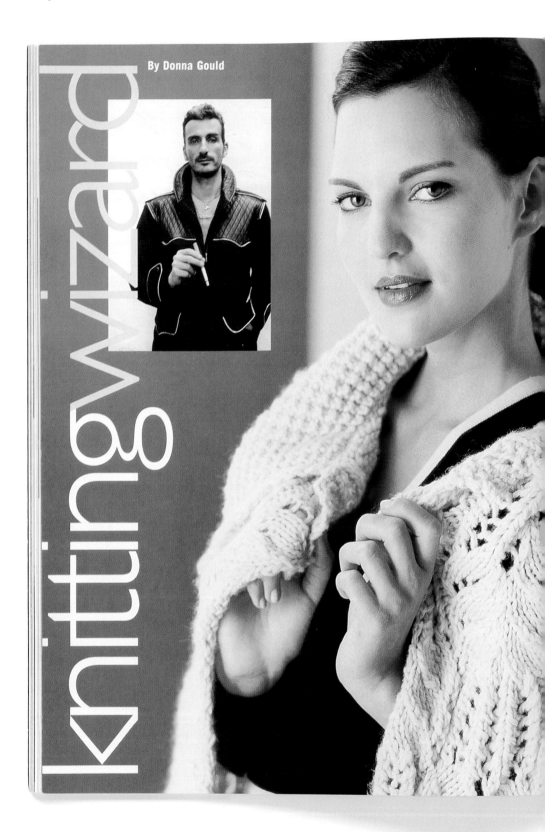

By Donna Gould

knittingwizard

FALL 2004 · Instructions Page 263

P

ierre Carrilero—known to the design world as Pierrot—never went to design school and often claims to know nothing about fashion. But his sharp wit and intricately crafted knits have made him a legend in knitting circles—and won raves from trendsetting stores and style icons like Sarah Jessica Parker (who donned his clothes in

Introducing Pierrot

Sex and the City) and Kim Basinger (who sported his pink cardigan in the film *The Door in the Floor*.)

(continued on page 140)

3

Pierrot credits the fabulously feminine styles his mother once wore as inspiration for the strict-but-sexy shapes he sent down the fall catwalk—including the lacy pink cape shown here. It is worked in K1C2's alpaca-blend "Temptation."

71

Striped Kimono

Trisha Malcolm reported in her editor's letter that in autumn 2004, there was a national knitting-needle shortage! Knitting was once again so popular, sticks were being snapped up faster than manufacturers could make them. What was behind this latest stitching surge? The scarf, of course.

A new breed of novelty yarns in rainbow-bright colorways allowed newer knitters to work up fashion scarves without knowing anything more than the knit stitch. And these new knitters found themselves getting hooked. So as they looked to increase their skills, *VK* was there to help. "Under Wraps" starred ponchos, wraps, and capes designed to help newbies "segue from scarf to sweater with ease." Lori Henry's sassily striped kimono is a prime example of the step-up-from-scarf projects. Its sideways construction—stitched cuff to cuff—alternates stripes of contrasting yarn (originally, Fiesta Yarns' *Kokopelli DK* and *La Boheme*), quickly finished with an edging of single crochet. Simple, yes, but also fashionable enough to appeal to more experienced readers who turn to *VK* for challenging patterns. And they got them in this issue, which also included articles on cables, colorwork, and Kors—the esteemed Seventh Avenue designer (and future *Project Runway* judge) Michael Kors made his *VK* debut with this issue.

FALL 2004 · Instructions Page 264

Belted Lace Pullover

"Channel your inner California Girl," urges the description for this belted diamond-and-lace pullover by Shirley Paden. Part of a story about lighter-weight winter knits for more temperate climes, it was stitched in *Cool Wool 2000* from Lana Grossa/Unicorn Books & Crafts. This issue also featured an interview with actress Karen Allen. The *Raiders of the Lost Ark* star proved to be quite the textile artist, creating her own line of boutique machine-knits: Monterey Fiber Arts.

Snow and sleet may be falling in the East, but on the left coast the forecast calls for plenty of sun—and some of the softest, sexiest sweaters of the season.

WEST COAST WINTER

WINTER 2004-2005 • Instructions Page 265

nnel your
California
with Shirley
en's pretty
erned V neck.
hed in an
er lace and
nond pattern
cinched with
atching belt,
a surefire way
anish the
er doldrums.
yarn is Lana
ssa/Unicorn
ks and Crafts'
ol Wool 2000."

17

75

The life
AQUATIC

This page: Norah Gaughan's wrap-front
hoodie captures the mystery of the
big blue with lacy cabled borders and
a cropped cut. It's knit in Trendsetter
Yarns' "Spiral."

Opposite: Cool stitch combinations of
easy lace shape up Mari Lynn Patrick's
figure-loving tunic, worked in "Mandarin"
from Sandnes/Norwegian Spirit. The
bodice is knit side to side, eyelet bands
separate stitch sections.

11

Wrap Front Pullover

This star garment by Norah Gaughan, a cropped wrap-front hoodie that's as interesting to look at as it is comfortable to wear, is both fun and stylish. Its fabric, a mix of lacy cabled bobbles and stockinette, was shown in Trendsetter Yarns' *Spiral*.

Knitting actress Courtney Thorne-Smith graced the cover of this issue, posing in a braided scarf in support of Knit for Her Cure, an initiative that benefited the Gynecologic Cancer Foundation through the sale of hand-knit scarf kits. Knitters who purchased the kits—designed by the likes of Nicky Epstein, Sally Melville, Melissa Leapman, and Jennifer Wenger, who created the tricolor wrapper Thorne-Smith modeled—were urged to knit two: one for themselves or a friend, another to warm the spirit of a woman going through chemotherapy treatment.

Thorne-Smith spoke to *VK* about her love of knitting, a craft she'd learned as a child and picked up again years later. "The yarns got so amazing," said the star of *According to Jim, Melrose Place,* and *Ally McBeal,* who's been known to stitch on set and handcraft Christmas presents for all her castmates. "There are great cashmere yarns I use to knit for myself and fuzzy, fun, multicolored yarns I use to knit for my niece. When I started knitting we'd go to a budget store and grab a skein of basic acrylic yarn; there weren't the options there are today. That's part of the fun."

$\mathcal{S}$eed Stitch Suit

Since the days of Coco Chanel, the knit suit has been the *ne plus ultra* of fashion. And it remained so in this design from autumn of the mid-aughts. Exhibit A: Anna Sui's ultrachic buttoned jacket/side-zip skirt set. The seed-stitch fabric received its tweedy effect by combining strands of nubbly black and ecru yarn (originally, Naturally's *Sensation*). A shot of color was injected at the collar and patch pockets with buzzy yellow-and-black trim and ties.

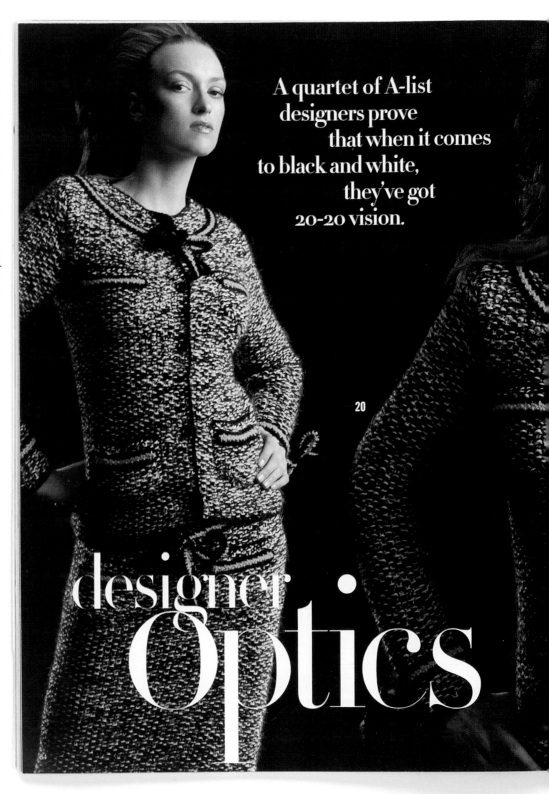

A quartet of A-list designers prove that when it comes to black and white, they've got 20-20 vision.

20

designer Optics

FALL 2005 • Instructions Page 269

anna sui

This edgy, elegant suit owes its tweedy texture to a seed-stitch design worked with one strand each of black and ecru "Sensation" by Naturally/S.R. Kertzer. The buttoned jacket and side-zip skirt both have round patch pockets at the front. All black-and-yellow trim and ties are worked in single crochet with one strand of Naturally's "Merino Finé 10 Ply."

85

$\mathcal{S}$triped Tunic

T winkle—née Wenlan Chia—emerged mid-decade as a shining star in knit fashion, marrying chunky yarns with contemporary style and witty color play in a way that's all her own. This vibrantly striped cowl-neck tunic is a signature Twinkle confection, its bold gradation of stripes worked with the "wrong side" as the outside, lending the fabric its "ticking" effect. The piece was triple-stranded for speed in already bulky *Black Forest Yarn* by Naturwolle/Muench Yarns. Twinkle now has her own yarn line with Classic Elite Yarns.

This being the Holiday issue, gifts and evening wear were much on the minds of the *VK* staff. Gorgeous sweaters—some shot through with metallics and ribbon—dressed up the night. Nine prominent designers dreamed up posh pillows as decorous presents for the home. And a special seasonal primer discussed the fine points of bestowing knit-themed gifts to fellow stitchers. Some of the best ideas: put together a beginner's starter kit, augment a library of knitting reference books, purchase iTunes songs and burn a CD of soothing music to stitch by, or donate a woolly animal to a Third World family in need through Heifer International.

HOLIDAY 2005 · Instructions Page 271

twinkle

3

67

143 2000s

1

Loop Stitch Cardigan

ily-gilding was a particular watchword in this issue of *VK*, in which many designers treated sweaters as a canvas for trims, appliqué, and other embellishments. Sandi Prosser took the idea a step further, incorporating her adornment into the fabric itself, forming small 3-D loops all over her divine little jacket, shown in Koigu Wool Designs' *Painter's Palette Premium Merino*. The loops are made by working eight extra rows over three stitches, then joining the strand back to the main piece.

It's somewhat of a complex technique—and likely a bit daunting to the ranks of newer knitters progressing past the scarf. To cater to these eager beginners, as well as to veterans looking for projects that finish fast, *Vogue Knitting* announced in this issue the debut of a brand-new sister magazine, *Knit Simple*.

kors light

**15
Very Easy
Very Vogue**

Want to really **shape up for summer?** Shed those heavy
wools for something a tad trimmer: skinny Michael Kors
sweaters stitched up in **light and luscious** yarns.

82

Whip-Stitch Tunic

A little whip stitch goes a long way in this simple but stunning tunic from Michael Kors. (*VK* dubbed it "Kors Light," as it was originally made in a lightweight luxury-yarn blend: Classic Elite Yarns' cashmere/silk *Posh*.) Its body-skimming silhouette is flattering to a wide range of figures: Oprah Winfrey chose to wear it in a fashion spread in *O* magazine, to dazzling effect. The tunic's thigh-brushing length opens up a plethora of styling choices. Wear it on its own, over a bathing suit, perhaps, or pair it with skinny jeans, a pencil skirt, or leggings for an all-seasons resort-wear look.

Elsewhere in this issue, the focus was on lace—"dominating fashion in ways not seen since the Seventies." Openwork infused pretty day pieces with European flair as well as lingerie-inspired camis and cardis, meant for more private moments; eyelets winked from a collection of farm-fresh tees and tops; and intricate cutouts enhanced the fabric of natural beauties knit with eco-friendly fibers. When better to play peekaboo than summer, after all?

SPRING/SUMMER 2006 · Instructions Page 273

9

newyorknoir

In this dirty, pretty city, where fashion meets fortune,
a dame's gotta dress to impress. So she does, in 1930s-flair
retro knits that'll knock the hardest-boiled palooka off his feet.

Fitted Jacket

"In this dirty, pretty city, where fashion meets fortune, a dame's gotta dress to impress," opened the "New York Noir" pictorial in this winter edition, and Shirley Paden captured the 1930s-flair retro vibe perfectly. Her fitted jacket with notched three-quarter-length sleeves—worked in a textured bee stitch with Baruffa's *Merinos Sei,* distributed by Lane Borgosesia/Trendsetter Yarns—was designed to stop traffic.

From the gritty streets of Manhattan, *VK* traveled to a true knitter's paradise—Scandinavia. A trip diary took readers along on a reminiscence of the magazine's latest tour, to Iceland, Norway, Sweden, and Denmark. Along the way, the group stopped at Iceland's Istex, home of Lopi yarn, as well as Dale of Norway headquarters, and enjoyed meet-and-greets with Danish stitching stars Hanne Falkenberg and Vivian Hoxbro, respectively the creator of the famed Mermaid sweater and the preeminent practitioner of domino and shadow knitting. Rounding out the theme, Danish designer Lipp Holmfeld contributed three jaunty caps to the fashion section, and Beth Brown Reinsel discussed the ins and outs of Scandinavian knitting, now taken to mean the act of stitching a tube, then steeking the openings.

Rainbow Shawl

"Summertime, and the knitting is breezy," was the idea behind the Very Easy Very Vogue feature for 2007's warm-weather issue. This luxurious wrap is knit from the top down in an easy increase pattern, with "10 stops on the color wheel along the way." Worked in a decadent 100 percent cashmere yarn, *Cashmere Breeze* from S. Charles Collezione/Tahki•Stacy Charles, the piece was designed by Linda Morse, a knitter who knows her way around a high-end fiber: The owner of Manhattan's luxe yarn boutique String also authored *Luxury Knitting: The Ultimate Guide to Exquisite Yarns*. So when Morse gives her seal of approval to a skein, knitters tend to listen.

Two other grande dames of knitting—Elizabeth Zimmermann and Maie Landra—also received attention in this issue. While going through her mother's journals, Meg Swansen came across a garter-stitch surplice baby jacket that makes a charming companion piece to Zimmermann's better-known Baby Surprise jacket. And on the eve of the publication of *Knits from a Painter's Palette*, *VK* spoke with Landra about her life in the knitting industry. The founder of Koigu Wool Designs, the influential hand-painted yarn company, let readers in on her painstaking method of using yarn as a canvas; her signature modular, mitered style; and finding inspiration in both her Estonian roots and the beauty of the Canadian countryside in which she lives.

SPRING/SUMMER 2007 • Instructions Page 278

**25
Very Easy
Very Vogue**

Luxury heats
up with pacific
bands of silk,
vivid panels of
cashmere.

A pot of gold's got nothing on
the rich vibrancy of Linda Morse's
rainbow cape. It's knit from the
top down in an easy increase
pattern with ten stops on the color
wheel of "Cashmere Breeze"
from S. Charles Collezione/Tahki•
Stacy Charles. A stockinette
border picked up after the fact
crisply edges the wrap.

85

Fair Isle Cardigan

From Russia to the United Kingdom in a half-dozen pages. *VK* celebrated knitting's British invasion in several ways. An in-depth article tracked the status of handknitting across the Pond, healthy thanks to the strong training up-and-comers receive at an array of British fashion colleges as well as through a robust design program at Rowan Yarns, the U.K.'s premier yarn company. "Stitch Degrees of Separation" mapped the nexus of connections among two dozen of the brightest names in Brit knits.

Several of these stars—including Sasha Kagan, Martin Storey, Louisa Harding, Marie Wallin, and Alice Starmore—joined Debbie Bliss as "lords and ladies of the knitting realm" in the fashion section. Bliss credited fellow British designer Marion Foale as her knitting inspiration, seeking the same "fresh timelessness" in her own pieces. She achieved just that with this form-fitting Fair Isle cardigan in her own *Cashmerino Baby* yarn, distributed by KFI.

Finishing this roundabout tour of the British Isles, American designer Tom Scott—who often draws on his Scottish heritage, injecting the family tartan into knits whenever possible—joined the ranks of *VK*'s Seventh Avenue partners with a quartet of sculpted knits, deconstructed to perfection.

HOLIDAY 2007 • Instructions Page 279

her designs for women, Lon-
mer Bliss—so well known
eside for her knits for babies
children—achieves the fresh
elessness she admires in the
k of Marion Foale, her own
rite Brit-knit designer, who
ilarly updated silhouettes
n the past to fit contemporary
es. Bliss's formfitting Fair Isle
digan, in "Cashmerino Baby"
Debbie Bliss/KFI, sports a V
kline and thin striping above
hip and cuff ribbing.

21
VK+

83

Forestry Cardigan

For the Fall issue of 2008, *Vogue Knitting* ventured to the "True North," highlighting the vibrant knitting culture coming from Canada. A knitcentric country if ever there was one, Canada is home to some of the most influential designers, yarn companies, yarn shops, and knit bloggers in the world. An in-depth article took readers from sea to sea, alerting them to Canadian knit spots and names from Nova Scotia to Montreal, Toronto to Vancouver.

"Northern Exposure" then asked nearly a dozen knit artisans based in Canada to create a design evocative of their home. Robin Melanson, Mags Kandis, Gayle Bunn, Fiona Ellis, and Lucy Neatby were among the knitterati who rose to the challenge. As did Montrealer Veronik Avery, whose Forestry Cardigan is the ultimate in Canada chic: "My intention was to design something a little rustic but appropriate to city life." The raglan-shaped sweater, flecked with *London Tweed* from Needful Yarns, has a shawl collar and coin cables down the front panels.

This issue also pays homage to the past and future of knitting, celebrating the golden anniversary of Schoolhouse Press, the publishing company founded by Elizabeth Zimmermann, and introducing *VK*'s readers to Ravelry.com, the game-changing social networking site for knitters and crocheters.

FALL 2008 · Instructions Page 281

11
VK+

ONIK AVERY
ESTRY

ntention was to design some-
a little rustic but appropriate
y life," says Montrealer Avery.
ccompli: The raglan-shaped
stry" cardigan merges an out-
y texture and hue of "London
d" from Needful Yarns with
ity in the form of coin-cabled
anels framed with ribbed
s and a shawl collar. Avery, the
ive director for JCA and author
itting Classic Style (STC Craft),
s instinctively how to mix the
nd the sheltering, as well as
ctile with the virtual. "For
cal knitting group, the Internet
een invaluable," Avery says.
lan our knit nights on our
te and Yahoo! Groups, so we
anage to get out in even the
inclement weather." Coat by
n Wang at Jeffrey Schwager;
by Pazuki at Sola; Hydra boots
rylrobin.

87

twinkle

Twinkle's Wenlan Chia once again demonstrates why she's a master at manipulating conventions of proportion, knitting her loose-fitting coat with a bubble-shaped back, a deep foldover collar and three-quarter sleeves. Oversized eyelets and giant buttons match the heavy fiber gauge; the coat's knit with "Soft Chunky" by Twinkle by Wenlan/Classic Elite Yarns. Dress by Twinkle.

17

With Wenlan Chia in your corner, it's easy to feel practically playful.

Bulky Coat

Joining Michael Kors in our designer spotlight was no less an authority on knits than Twinkle herself. Wenlan Chia posed with our model to show off her latest design—a bulky coat with a bubble-shaped back and deep foldover collar that demonstrates why Twinkle is "a master at manipulating conventions of proportion." (See how the huge eyelets and buttons play into the oversized perfection?) It was shown in *Soft Chunky* from Twinkle by Wenlan/Classic Elite Yarns. And, like every other pattern in this issue, could be viewed all the way around with VK 360, a new website feature announced in this issue. This online-only video allowed readers to study the garments from every angle, even those unseen in the magazine.

As gorgeous as the fashion was, Winter 2008 brought unpleasant news from the outside world. The United States was experiencing a difficult economic recession, and in her editor's letter Trisha Malcolm ruminated about the place of knitting during uncertain times. "While there is gloom and doom all around, there is still hope; there is still knitting," she wrote. "Like the financial world, we are slowing down and turning back to those elements of our heritage that ground us. Frugal living is suddenly a trend. And, of course, knitting sits perfectly in that place; making beauty from the chaos around us; using a tool of logic to keep us focused and centered; giving us so much pleasure in the simple task of making something beautiful by hand." All reasons that the knitting community came out of the recession stronger than ever.

WINTER 2008-2009 • Instructions Page 283

Peplum Cardigan

anette Lepore, the latest Seventh Avenue A-lister to join the *VK* designer ranks, loves the versatility of knits. "I like to have fun with texture and weight, yarns and stitches, crochet mixed with knit," she explained. Celebrity clients like Sarah Jessica Parker, Eva Longoria, and Mischa Barton like when Lepore has fun with knits, too, and her aesthetic is epitomized in this flouncy cardi: The back peplum is shaped with increases in the main lace pattern; the sleeves, lapel, and hemline are worked in a masculine fisherman's rib that contrasts the feminine flourishes handsomely. A custom fabric was created by combining one strand each of two Tahki•Stacy Charles yarns—Tahki Yarns' *Rio* and Filatura di Crosa's *Baby Kid Extra*.

talkingfashion
Nanette Lepore

"One of the beauties of knits is that you're not married to the lines and structure of woven fabric. That's what makes it a little more freeing and fun."

33

96

FALL 2009 • Instructions Page 286

Lepore's three-quarter-sleeve cardi embodies her signature femininity. The back lace flounce is shaped with increases that occur in the main lace pattern, while the sleeves, lapels and bottom border are worked in a fisherman's rib. The body of the sweater is knit in one piece from the top down in a variety of lace patterns in "Rio" by Tahki Yarns/Tahki• Stacy Charles and "Baby Kid Extra" by Filatura Di Crosa/ Tahki•Stacy-Charles held together. The lapels, worked from the bottom up, are knit separately and sewn on.

PHOTOGRAPHS BY PAUL AMATO
FOR LVAREPRESENTS.COM
HAIR AND MAKEUP STYLED
BY INGEBORG FOR BENEFIT
COSMETICS

Dolman Pullover

As the first decade of the aughts drew to a close, *VK* took a bold stance: "It's color that counts!" proclaimed the Holiday 2009 issue, and, as such, most of the features focused on a particular spectrum of the rainbow. Pales and plums and paintbox brights, in patterns "bold and bright, shaded and striped, ombre and ethnic," meant to make knitters—and their admirers—take notice.

Who better then Kaffe Fassett, then, to come up with a project that represents the kaleidoscope? But there's a trick to this dolman-sleeved pullover: Instead of the twenty-odd hues with which Fassett usually works, the piece is stitched in just two self-striping colorways of *Colourscape Chunky* by Rowan/Westminster Fibers. (The dye progression in the skein naturally produces the color changes in the fabric.) That diagonal stripe shift is a result of introducing a second skein intarsia-style, right below the shoulder drop.

The sweater—rated Very Easy Very Vogue and sized as a VK+ pattern—is constructed traditionally, with a front, a back, and two sleeves. This issue, however, included the second in a two-part series on the growing trend of seamless knitting by designer/photographer/Brooklyn Tweed blogger Jared Flood. Seamless knitting allows the knitter to construct a flat garment in the round in one piece, alleviating the (for some) dreaded need to sew the pieces together in finishing.

HOLIDAY 2009 • Instructions Page 285

4
Size +
Very Easy

51

Black & White

1
Size +

MAKE A GRAPH

Striped Cardigan

Brandon Mably usually plies a palette as crowded as that of his mentor, Kaffe Fassett. Here, he pared down his color wheel, instead using just black and gray to striking effect. His graphic statement is a true conversation piece, so oversized that one size fits all! It's worked from side to side with vertical intarsia stripes and corrugated ribbing, and was shown in Mission Falls' late, lamented *1824 Wool*.

Male designers were prominent in this Winter issue. Joining Mably was Josh Bennett, who provided a mini collection of men's sweaters and vests based on the type of understated knits he'd be comfortable wearing—no crazy-quilt Cosby sweaters here. And Cully Swansen became the third generation of Zimmermann/Swansens to write a column for *Vogue Knitting*, subbing for mom Meg to debut a bicolor cabled hat with twists that zig and zag.

Finally, there was exciting breaking news in the editor's letter: In response to readers' feedback about wanting "more patterns" and "more issues," Trisha Malcolm announced that *Vogue Knitting* was adding a fifth issue each year. "Early Fall" would now be published between Spring/Summer and traditional Fall, ringing in prime knitting season a bit earlier per annum.

WINTER 2009-2010 · Instructions Page 288

Lace Capelet

"Knits worthy of a Fitzgerald heroine" brought an air of Jazz Age romance to this issue. The three-part pictorial, shot at a Gatsby-esque manor in New York, concentrated on decorative details, mohair, and lace. A prime example: Tanis Gray's drapey capelet, shown in *Prima* by Debbie Bliss/KFI. It's knit in two traditional lace patterns, one for the main body, the other for the scalloped edging. These sections are joined with a three-needle bind-off, an effective way of seaming with knitting needles instead of a sewing needle. Elsewhere in the issue, "Beyond Kitchener" explored a plethora of charted grafting techniques, meant to produce invisible joins between separate pieces of knit fabric.

In this *VK* issue, Gordana Gehlhausen, who just missed going to Fashion Week on the sixth season of every fashionista's favorite show, *Project Runway*, memorably introduced herself to the world by telling the camera: "Give me a sheep and I'll make you a sweater." The zigzag lace tunic she shared in the magazine proves that she wasn't kidding.

SPRING/SUMMER 2010 • Instructions Page 290

3

1
Size +

The Dream Team

INTRODUCING THE DYNAMIC SEVENTH AVENUE DESIGN DUO
LUTZ & PATMOS

Before we met Lutz & Patmos, we had never encountered a Seve[...]
Avenue design team so simpatico with our style sensibilities. But [...]
knitwear specialists, who in 2006 were inducted into the prestigi[...]
Council of Fashion Designers of America, are simply not like any[...]
other design duo.

Tina Lutz and Marcia Patmos created their own line in 2000 [...]
five years of designing for luxury retailer Barneys New York. Bot[...]
are lifelong knitters: Lutz took up the craft in grade school in Ger[...]
her native country, while Patmos, an American, began stitching [...]
custom clothes for her Barbie dolls at the age of 5.

After studying at Esmond University in Paris, Lutz worked an[...]
lived in Tokyo and San Francisco before moving to New York in [...]
one year after Patmos migrated to Manhattan. There, the two com[...]
their fifteen-plus years of knitwear and pattern-making expertise [...]
develop their brand.

L&P eschew seasonal trends, choosing instead to explore the [...]
boundaries of knitwear through shape, texture, seaming and vol[...]
Women drawn to their style, the designers say, dress effortlessly, [...]
avoid fads and have an international, open-minded, ageless atti[...]
about fashion. Fashion editor Sarah Liebowitz met with the pair [...]
recently to learn more about their design process.

**It's not always easy working [...]
a partner. What's the secret to [...]
successful collaboration?**
We design and fit our two collectio[...]
[Lutz & Patmos; Leroy & Perry] toge[...]
beyond that, we split the responsibi[...]
Tina takes care of branding, specia[...]
projects, PR, guest-designer projects[...]
finances and accounting. Marcia ta[...]
care of production and sales.

**Your goal as a design team i[...]
to steer clear of the five-minu[...]
trend. Is it a challenge to con[...]
stantly deliver something fres[...]
and innovative that will also stand the test of time[...]
We love to work with volume, seams and graphic shapes and [...]

Cabled Cardigan

ashion moves quickly. In autumn 2010, Tina Lutz and Marcia Patmos were Seventh Avenue's hottest design duo. Their *VK* debut a few issues back proved that their machine-knit collection translated beautifully to handknitting, and the shades-of-gray sweater trio they created for this edition was a favorite of readers and staffers alike. Alas, just months later, the partners in fashion went their separate ways. But we'll always have these patterns to remind us of their finite but fabulous collaboration. This bulky cardigan carries an allover cable pattern—with especially large twists up the back—and knitted-in patch pockets. It was shown in *Montana* from Tahki Yarns/Tahki•Stacy Charles.

Warm pieces like this are great for cold weather, something Hannah Kearney knows an awful lot about. Kearney, the first American athlete to win gold at the Vancouver Winter Olympics earlier in the year—her event: women's freestyle skiing, widely known as moguls—knits to keep toasty on the slopes and stylish off of them. She spoke with *VK* about her stitching prowess and her life on skis as an Olympic champ.

Another issue, another big announcement from Trisha Malcolm: *Vogue Knitting* was launching *Vogue Knitting* LIVE, a three-day event at the New York Hilton filled with classes led by the biggest names in knitdom as well as a yarny marketplace of epic proportions. The inaugural event, held in January 2011, would prove such a rousing success, planning immediately began to take the show on the road to Los Angeles later in the year.

EARLY FALL 2010 • Instructions Page 292

Cabled Swing Poncho

The fashion in the Holiday 2010 edition centered on opulent details and traffic-stopping reds. Case in point: Michele Wang's multitextured poncho, exuberantly cabled and patterned, with a broken-rib hood and slit pockets knit into the front. The piece is essentially two large rectangles sewn together, with space left unstitched at the top to make armholes. It was stitched in Zealana's *Aspire Tui*, a unique blend of wool, fur, and sustainable possum fiber from New Zealand.

Normally, *VK*'s Holiday issue includes a guide to some type of stitchy essential. This time, it had a special section on what every knitter needs in her dream library. There were the classics, of course, including Elizabeth Zimmermann's *Knitting Without Tears*, Maggie Righetti's *Knitting in Plain English*, Montse Stanle's *Knitter's Handbook,* and Clara Parkes's *The Knitter's Book of Yarn*, a newer entry into the canon. How-tos and stitch guides like *Vogue Knitting's Ultimate Knitting Book* and the popular *Stitchionary* series joined Nicky Epstein's *Knitting on the Edge* titles and Sally Melville's *The Knit Stitch*. Beginners were pointed toward Debbie Stoller's seminal *Stitch 'N Bitch* and Sharon Turner's *Teach Yourself Visually: Knitting*. Recommendations ranged through titles about sock, toy, and gift knitting, baby and men's garments, and even knit lit—a growing trend of nonfiction stories set in a yarn shop milieu.

6
Size +

MICHELE WANG
Little Red would be so jealous.
Wang's multitextured poncho in
Zealana's "Aspire Tui"—essentially
two large rectangles sewn together,
with the top left open for armholes—
has knit-in slit pockets in front and a
broken-rib hood. See the hood and
closeup views of the texture patterns
on our website feature VK360.

65

$\mathcal{L}$ace Jacket

Brooke Nico's fantastic Edwardian-inspired lace jacket marries vintage style with modern construction: The shawl-collared piece, in *Baby Kid Extra* from Filatura di Crosa/Tahki•Stacy Charles, is knit from the center out, starting with the pentagon shape on the back. It's emblematic of the softer side of Fall 2010, an issue otherwise filled with powerful looks: prairie-wear in a Southwestern-desert palette; strong cables that take on a life of their own; a new collection of colorworked Brit knits, starring a boxy Union Jack cardigan; and sophisticated knee-high socks just begging to be paired with the season's breed of miniskirts.

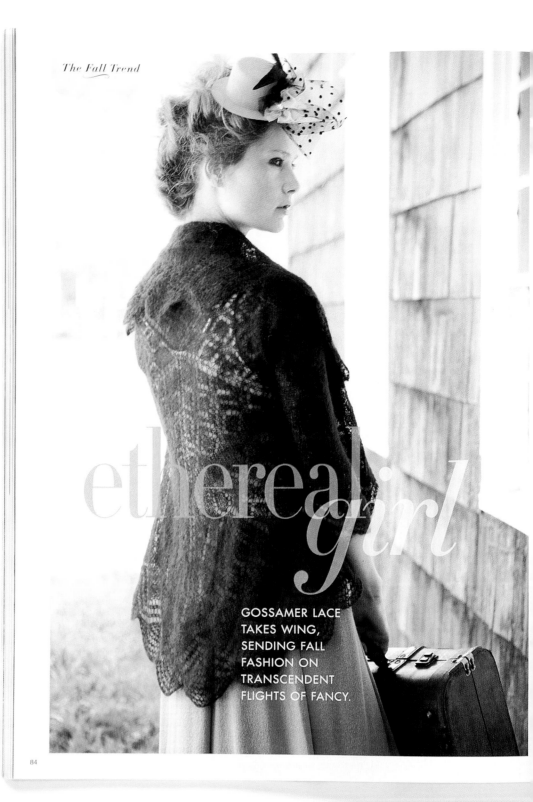

The Fall Trend

ethereal girl

GOSSAMER LACE TAKES WING, SENDING FALL FASHION ON TRANSCENDENT FLIGHTS OF FANCY.

84

FALL 2010 • Instructions Page 296

OKE NICO

beauty, modern
on. Nico's exquisite
ket, in "Baby Kid
y Filatura Di Crosa/
cy Charles, is a
n shape that's knit
center out; the
ece forms the shawl
nd curved body.
re jacket is bor-
ith a traditional
lace pattern.

intage apparel
n Landaeus;
ndaeus.com. For
al fashion credits,
ge 144.

RAPHS BY
LLAHAN.
MAKEUP
BY INGEBORG
A

*M*ultitextured Cardigan

"Taylor-made" to be a standout, Rebecca Taylor's oversized designer cardi achieves its aim. Knit in one huge rectangle, then shaped by the way it's sewn together, the piece is stitched in alternating bands of trinity stitch and elongated bobbles; cabled patch pockets add yet another texture to the mix. It was shown in a creamy tone of *Worsted Hand Dyes* from Blue Sky Alpacas.

Want to know the secret of Taylor's oversized cardi? It's knit in Blue Sky Alpacas' "Worsted Hand Dyes" in one large rectangle and shaped by the way it is sewn together. Cabled patch pockets (in alpaca "Royal") grace the body, which is knit in alternating bands of trinity stitch and elongated bobbles.

For fashion credits, see page 144.

PHOTOGRAPHS BY
PAUL AMATO
FOR LVAREPRESENTS.COM.
HAIR AND MAKEUP
STYLED BY STEPHEN RAMSEY
FOR TIMOTHY PRIANO

16
Size +

THIS CONVERSATION PIECE IS IMBUED WITH TAYLOR-MADE DETAILS: EXTREME TEXTURE AND SMART SEAMING.

88

FALL 2010 • Instructions Page 299

89

Cabled Pullover

Over the years, ski sweaters of one sort or another have played a large role in *VK*'s winter issues. Classic Nordic styles were showcased, with colorworked yokes and sturdy fibers; slinky ski-bunny numbers in angora and cashmere, just right for cocoa by the fire; and hearty woolen workhorses, perfectly pretty layering pieces for a day on the slopes. The retro "Chalet Chic" pieces in this edition—evocatively shot across the Hudson River from *VK* headquarters, in New Jersey's Watchung Reservation—were imbued with "ski-lodge esprit," a certain Old World élan epitomized by Josh Bennett's creamy Alpine-inspired sweater. Originally shown in Manos del Uruguay's *Silk Blend*, the piece was worked cuff to cuff in a rectangle cleverly divided so that horizontal cabling continues unbroken along the neckline.

One technique well suited to warm ski sweaters is brioche stitch, a method of slip-stitching that creates a cushy, reversible, rib-like fabric. Designer Nancy Marchant literally wrote the book on brioche knitting—called *Knitting Brioche*—and walked readers through the process in this issue, including a pattern for a jaunty crossover scarf worked with either end of one variegated fiber, for an interesting almost-ombre effect.

WINTER 2010-2011 · Instructions Page 300

...posite: Josh Bennett's
...-fitting cabled turtleneck
...a dashing figure. It's
...ked in the round in a loose-
...d cable with Cascade
...as' "Pastaza."

...s page: A little Alpine
...dresses up the weekend.
...Bennett's creamy cabled
...ater, in Manos del Uruguay's
...Blend," is worked in a
...ectangle from cuff to cuff
...is cleverly divided so that
...ables continue unbroken
...g the neckline edge.

...ct vintage apparel and
...essories courtesy of Malin
...daeus. For fashion credits
...ughout, see page 120.

...TOGRAPHS BY ROSE CALLAHAN.
... AND MAKEUP STYLED BY LENA
...G MAKE UP FOR EVER

2
Very Easy

CHALET CHIC

Fisherman's Cardigan

"Few designs have stood the test of time quite as beautifully as the ever-versatile, always-appropriate cardigan." That was the sentiment at the heart of "The Art of the Cardigan," five slip-on sweaters that harked back to past fashions yet keep current in style and fiber choice. Take John Brinegar's shawl-collared fisherman's rib cardigan as an example. Its professorial tone is softened by a fetching salmon shade of tonal *Tonos Chunky* by Misti Alpaca.

Other pieces in this cardigan collection included a verdant green stunner with a focal point ruffle draped diagonally along the button band, a dusty-pink wrap jacket that displayed deconstruction at its most chic, a plum swing jacket that brushes the thighs, and a teal take on the Mr. Roger's sweater, its masculine lines tweaked to play up a woman's silhouette. It all points to the fact that "the cardi's core DNA hasn't changed in centuries." Expect to see plenty more of the humble cardigan in future issues of *Vogue Knitting*—it's a designer's favorite for a reason.

WINTER 2010-2011 · Instructions Page 302

Collared

NORAH GAUGHAN
Opposite: Gaughan's flair for eye-catching drama remains true to type. This stunner, in Berroco's "Ultra Alpaca," showcases an exquisite draped ruffle worked in "Ultra Alpaca Light" from stitches picked up along the buttonhole band and tacked into place.

JOHN BRINEGAR
This page: Fans of Brinegar's contemporary classics will flip for this shawl-collared fisherman's rib cardigan, knit with the irresistible "Tonos Chunky" from Misti Alpaca.

For fashion credits, see page 120.

PHOTOGRAPHS BY PAUL AMATO
FOR LVAREPRESENTS.COM.
HAIR AND MAKEUP STYLED
BY LENA

11

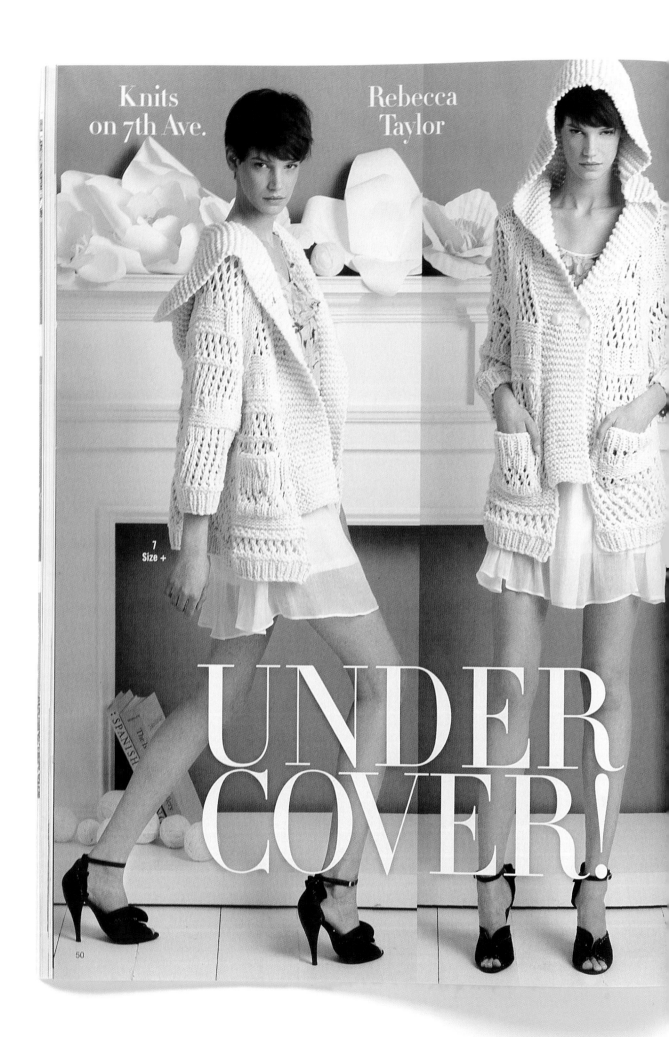

Knits on 7th Ave.

Rebecca Taylor

7
Size +

UNDER COVER!

50

Hooded Lace Cardigan

Rebecca Taylor's crisp yet feminine hooded cardi, knit with a double strand of *All Seasons Cotton* from Rowan/Westminster Fibers, proved a huge favorite of members of the *Vogue Knitting* group on Ravelry.com—and no wonder. It's a fun knit, with bands of lace and texture that change gradually on the back. The double-breasted garter-stitch front bands broaden upward to form the hood.

The Spring/Summer issue of 2011 brought *Vogue Knitting* thoroughly up-to-date, technology-wise. Upon its launch, the iPad became a favorite around the *VK* office, with the staff quickly finding many knitterly uses for the touch-screen format. Eager to extend their enthusiasm to their readers, *VK*'s creative minds developed an app that allows the magazine to be viewed page by page on the iPad. This was the first edition available in its entirety for tablet reading—and, boy, did it look great on the iPad's sharp, color-sensitive screen.

SPRING/SUMMER 2011 · Instructions Page 305

Medallion Coverup

The lace coverup is a mainstay of every *VK* Spring/Summer issue. Shiri Mor brings the runway to ocean's edge with this exquisite piece. Her poncho-style tunic is constructed from separately knit lace medallions that are assembled in finishing. The lapels are formed from partial squares that expand around the back to complete the neckline. It was shown in Patons' *Grace*.

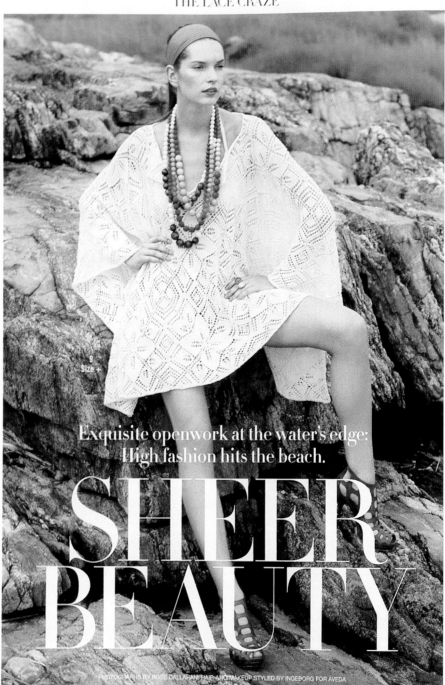

THE LACE CRAZE

9
Size +

Exquisite openwork at the water's edge:
High fashion hits the beach.

SHEER
BEAUTY

PHOTOGRAPHS BY ROSE CALLAHAN. HAIR AND MAKEUP STYLED BY INGEBORG FOR AVEDA

52

SPRING/SUMMER 2011 · Instructions Page 307

JRI MOR

...ate and inventive, Mor's
...eous poncho-style piece
...ists of lace medallions that
...nitted separately and
...mbled in finishing. Partial and
...quares form the "lapels" and
...ght back neck, respectively.
...ked in "Grace" from Patons.

...ashion credits throughout,
...age 112.

53

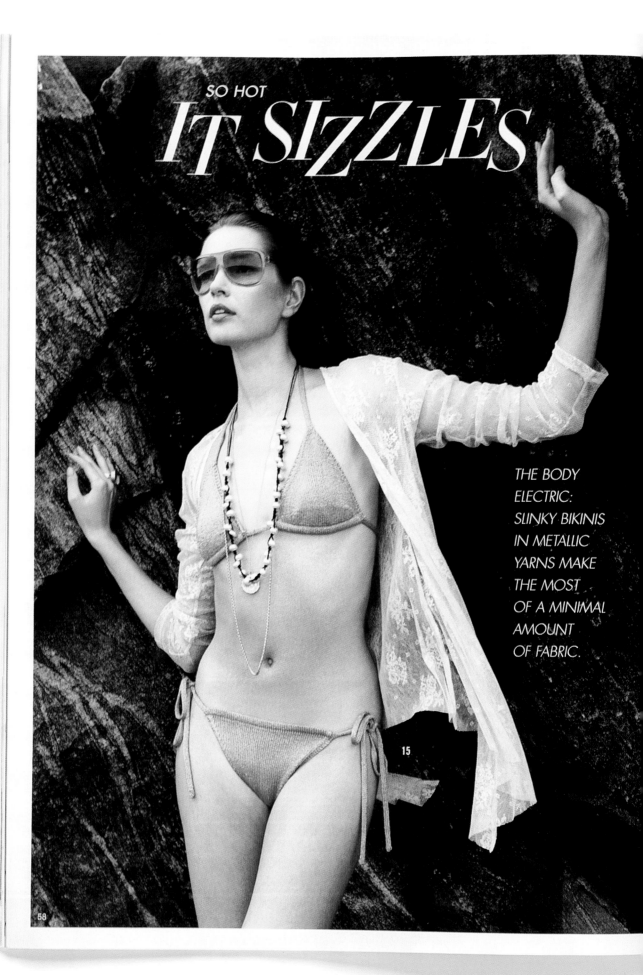

SO HOT
IT SIZZLES

THE BODY
ELECTRIC:
SLINKY BIKINIS
IN METALLIC
YARNS MAKE
THE MOST
OF A MINIMAL
AMOUNT
OF FABRIC.

15

58

Gold-Tone Bikini

With this teeny bikini, *VK* throws down the ultimate summer fashion gauntlet: Bare if you dare. Elizabeth Kosich's slinky two-piece suit was stitched in a smoldering golden tone of stretchy *Gatsby* by Katia/KFI. The top is shaped with short rows, with ribbing along the cup sides and a knit-in hem on the lower edge. The bottom is worked in one piece, from the top of the front to top of the back. It sports knitted-in hems, ribbing around the leg openings and hip ties on either side.

Not every reader would be tempted to knit a bikini. *Vogue Knitting* is a potent inspirational tool, imparting what is possible with knit fabric, then leaving readers to decide whether to make it or not. This marriage of high-fashion inspiration and DIY practicality is what has set *Vogue Knitting* apart for the past thirty years.

SPRING/SUMMER 2011 · Instructions Page 309

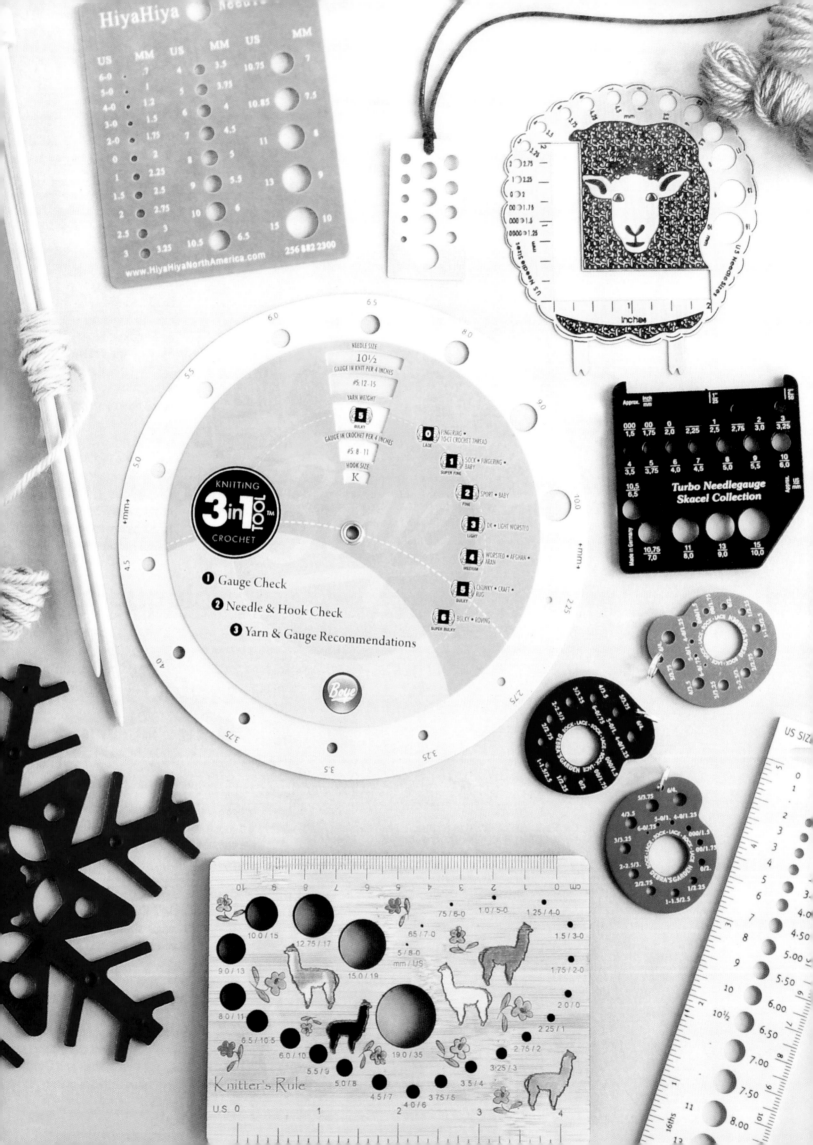

Instructions

Meg Swansen recalls, "Elizabeth Zimmermann always thought *Vogue Knitting* to be a superlative magazine, and she was bereft when publication stopped [in 1969]. It was through a knitting project, which originated with *British Vogue* in 1957, that the business now called Schoolhouse Press, was initiated.

"Years later, when Nancy Thomas was appointed Editor of the revived version of *Vogue Knitting*, she invited my mother to write a regular column—to which my ma said, 'Certainly.'

"EZ's first article was about Kitchener Stitch and, between the two of us, we have had a technical article or a garment in nearly every issue since. We were (and are) very pleased to remain associated with the magazine."

Irish Sweater-Coat

EXPERIENCED

Full-cut hip-length coat with ribbed yoke, tight cuffs, and full sleeves. Sized for Small, Medium, and Large. Directions are for smallest size with larger sizes in parentheses. If there is only one figure, it applies to all sizes.

KNITTED MEASUREMENTS
• Bust 40 (43, 45¾)"/101.5 (109, 116) cm
• Upper arm 14½"(15, 16) cm

MATERIALS 4
• 16 (18, 20) 1¾oz/50g balls (each approx 110yds/101m) of Berroco *Dji-Dji* (wool/viscose) in #8522 Brown Mist
• To substitute, seek a worsted-weight yarn with similar fiber content
• One each sizes 6, 10, and 11 (4, 6, and 8mm) circular needles OR SIZE TO OBTAIN GAUGE
• Size G/6 (4mm) crochet hook
• Three ⅝" (15mm) buttons

GAUGE
12 sts and 14½ rows = 4"/10 cm over Double Strand Twist St st using size 11 (8mm) needles. TAKE TIME TO CHECK GAUGE.

PATTERN GLOSSARY
Twisted Stockinette Stitch
Row 1 (RS) K1 through back loop (k1 tbl).
Row 2 (WS) P.

Twisted Rib Stitch
Row 1 (RS) K1tbl, ★p1, k1tbl; rep from ★ to end.
Row 2 (WS) P1, ★ k1, p1; rep from ★ to end.

NOTE
Yarn is held doubled throughout.

BACK
With larger needles and two strands of yarn, cast on 68 (72, 76) sts. Work in garter for 4 rows. Work in twisted St until piece measures 5"/12.5 cm from beg. **Next row (RS)** Dec 1 st each end. Continuing in twisted st rep dec row every 4"/10 cm 3 times more—60 (64, 68) sts. Work even in twisted St st until 20"/51 cm from beg, ending with a WS row.
Armhole shaping
Keeping in twisted St st, dec 1 st each end every row twice, every other row 3 times—50 (54, 58) sts. Sl rem sts to a holder for yoke.

LEFT FRONT
With larger needles and two strands of yarn, cast on 38 (40, 42) sts. K 4 rows.
Next Row (RS) Work twisted St st to last 4 sts, k 4 (front band). **Next Row (WS)** K 4, p to end. Rep these 2 rows for pat. Work as established 5"/12.5 cm from beg, ending with a WS row. Dec 1 st side edge, then every 4"/10 cm 3 times more—34 (36, 38) sts. Work to underarm as for back.
Armhole Shaping
Keeping in twisted st with garter front band, dec 1 st at armhole edge every row twice, every other row 3 times—29 (31, 33) sts. Sl rem sts to a holder for yoke.

RIGHT FRONT
Work to correspond to left front, reversing shaping.

SLEEVES
With size 10 (6mm) needles and two strands of yarn, cast on 29 (31, 33) sts. Beg with WS row, work in twisted rib for 3"/7.5 cm, ending with a WS row. **Next row (RS)** Work row 1 of twisted rib, increasing 27 sts evenly across—56 (58, 60) sts. Change to larger needles and work 8 rows even in twisted st. Dec 1 st each end of next row, then every 8th row 5 times more—44 (46, 48) sts. Work even until 18"/46 cm from beg.
Cap Shaping Work same as back armhole. Sl rem 34 (36, 38) sts to a holder for yoke.

YOKE JOINING ROW
Place the following sts on circular needle: 29 (31, 33) left front sts, 34 (36, 38) left sleeve sts, 50 (54, 58) back sts, 34 (36, 38) right sleeve sts, 29 (31, 33) right front sts—176 (188, 200) sts. DO NOT JOIN.
Row 1 (RS) K4 (front band), p2, k2tbl ★p4, k2tbl; rep from ★, end p2, k4 (front band). **Row 2 (WS)** K6 ★p4, k2; rep from ★, end k4. Rep these 2 rows once more. **Dec Row (RS)** K4, p2, k2tbl ★p1, p2tog, p1, k2tbl; rep from ★, end p2, k4. Keeping in rib pat as established, work 3 rows. **Dec Row (RS)** K4, p2, k2tbl ★ p1, p2 tog, k2tbl; rep from ★, end p2, k4—122 (130, 138) sts. Keeping in rib pat as established, work until yoke measures 4"/10 cm from beg, ending with a WS row. **Dec (RS)** K4, ★p2tog, k2tbl; rep from ★, end p2tog, k4—93 (99, 105) sts. Keeping in rib pat as established, work until yoke measures 6 (6½, 7)"/15 (16.5, 18) cm, end with a WS row. **Dec (RS)** K4, p1, ★k2tog tbl, p1; rep from ★, end p1, k4. Work 1 row. Change to size 6 needles. Work 4 rows in rib as established. Bind off in pat.

FINISHING
Sew side and sleeve seams. Sew lower edges of caps to front and back. Sew 3 buttons along left front edge, placing top button in center of neckband, bottom button at start of yoke and

center the third button. Make loop buttonholes opposite buttons as follows: Using double strand of yarn and G/6 (4mm) crochet hook, attach yarn with sl st, ch 4, sl st into 1st ch to

make loop. **Next Row** Work 8 sc into loop. Pull yarn through last st to finish off.

Romantic Rosebud Cardigan

EXPERIENCED

Close-fitting, rib-yoked cardigan with popcorn floral designs, set-in sleeves with puffed sleeve caps. Sized for Small, Medium, and Large. Directions are for smallest size with larger sizes in parentheses. If there is only one figure, it applies to all sizes.

KNITTED MEASUREMENTS
• Bust (buttoned) 33 (36½, 40)"/84 (93, 101.5) cm
• Upper arm 10½ (11½, 12½)"/26.5 (29, 32) cm

MATERIALS 🧶4🧶
• 14 (15, 16) 1¾oz balls (each approx

83yds/76m) of Neveda *Sirene Double* (wool) in #2317 Oatmeal
• To substitute, seek an aran-weight yarn with similar fiber content
• One each sizes 4 and 7 (3.5 and 4.5mm) needles OR SIZE TO OBTAIN GAUGE
• Size F/5 (3.75mm) crochet hook

GAUGE
20 sts and 28 rows = 4"/10 cm over St st using size 7 (4.5mm) needles. TAKE TIME TO CHECK GAUGE.

STITCH GLOSSARY
MB Make bobble as foll:
Row 1 (RS) Into next st, kfb twice, k1, turn—5sts.
Row 2 P5.
Row 3 K5.
Row 4 Sl 2nd, 3rd, 4th and 5th sts over 1st st—1st.

BACK
Starting at lower edge with smaller needles, cast on 75 (83, 91) sts. **Row 1 (RS)** *K1, p1, rep from *, end k1. **Row 2 (WS)** *P1, k1, rep from *, end p1. Rep these 2 rows for rib for 2"/5 cm, ending with a WS row. Change to larger needles and p across next row, inc 6 sts evenly across—81 (89, 97) sts. **Next Row (RS)** *K3, MB rep from * across, end k1. **Next Row (WS)** P across. **Next Row (RS)** K across. **Next Row (WS)** P across. **Next Row (RS)** K1, *MB, k3; rep from * across. Work in St st for 5 rows, beginning with p row.
Rosebud Pattern
Rows 1 and 3 K8 (12, 16), *k1tbl,

k15; rep from *, end last rep k8 (12, 16).
Rows 2 and 4 P8 (12, 16), *p1tbl, p15; rep from *, end last rep p8 (12, 16). **Row 5** K6 (10, 14), [insert crochet hook to back of work under horizontal bar before the 9th (13th, 17th) twisted st of Pat Row 1, draw up a long lp, yo hook, draw through lp] 3 times, leaving sts on hook, yo, draw through the 3 sts, put this st on right-hand needle (½ leaf made), * k2, k1tbl, k2, insert crochet hook under horizontal bar after the same twisted st, work ½ leaf as before (1 leaf completed), k11, work ½ leaf as before under horizontal bar before next twisted st; rep from *, end with 1 leaf pat, k6 (10, 14). **Row 6** P5 (9, 13), *p2tog, p2, p1 tbl, p2, p2tog, p9; rep from *4 times, end p2tog, p2, p tbl, p2, p2tog, p5 (9, 13). **Row 7** K8 (12, 16), *[kfb] twice, take the 4 sts on to crochet hook, yo, draw through lps, put this st onto left-hand needle and p it (Rosebud completed), k 15; rep from *, end 1 Rosebud in next st, k 8 (12, 16). **Row 8** Purl. **Row 9** K4 (8, 12), *k1tbl, k7; rep from *, end last rep k4 (8, 12). Follow chart, working Rosebud Pat as established through Row 48, then rep Rows 1 through 24. Should measure approx 13½"/34 cm from beg. Discontinue Rosebud Pat.
Armhole Shaping
Working St st, bind off 3 sts beg next 2 rows. Dec 1 st each end of next row, then every 4th row once more—71 (79, 87) sts. **Small** P1 row. **Medium** work 5 rows in St st. **Large** work 9 rows in St st.

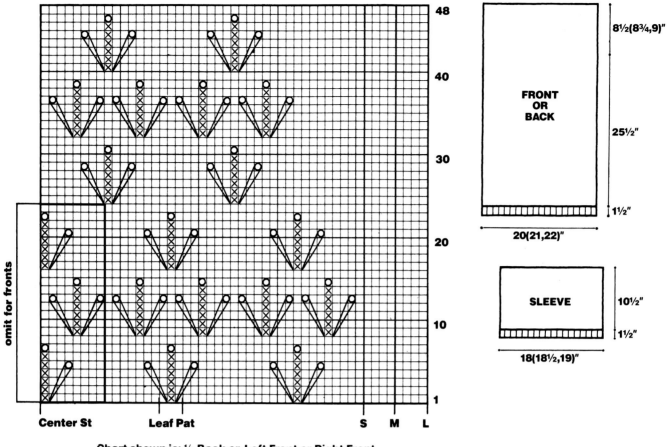

48

40

30

20

10

1

omit for fronts

Center St   Leaf Pat   S   M   L

Chart shown is: ½ Back or Left Front or Right Front

◘ — Rosebud
⊠ — Twisted k on right side
⊠ — Twisted p on wrong side
□ — St st (k on right side; p on wrong side)

FRONT OR BACK

8½(8¾,9)"

25½"

1½"

20(21,22)"

SLEEVE

10½"

1½"

18(18½,19)"

Yoke Shaping

Row 1 (RS) K 15, ★ MB in next st, k3; rep from ★9 (11, 13) times more, MB in next st, k15 (11 (13, 15) bobbles made. Work 3 rows in St st. **Row 5** K13, ★MB, k3; rep from ★10 (12, 14) times more, MB in next st, k13. **Row 6** Purl. **Row 7** K19, bind off center 33 (41, 49) sts, k19. **Row 8** Working both sides at the same time, purl. **Row 9** Left Side: K11, MB in next st, k3, MB in next st, k3tog—17 sts. Right Side: attach new ball of yarn, k3tog, MB, k3, MB, k11—17 sts. **Rows 10 through 12** Work even in St st. **Row 13** First Side: K9, MB, k3, MB, k3 tog—15 sts. Second Side: K3tog, MB, k3, MB, k9—15 sts. **Rows 14 through 16** Work even in St st. Continue to work 2 Bobbles each side every 4th row, having 2 sts less every Bobble row until 1 st remains before and after Bobbles—7 sts each side. Work 3 rows even. Bind off rem sts each side for shoulders.

LEFT FRONT

Starting at lower edge, with smaller needles, cast on 37 (41, 45) sts. Work rib as for back, ending with a RS row. Change to larger needles and p next row, inc 4 sts evenly spaced across—41 (45, 49) sts. **Next Row (RS)** ★K3, MB rep from ★ across, end k1. Work 5 rows St st. Beg Rosebud Pat, following chart, having 2 Rosebud pats across. **Note** It is indicated on chart what is left off on fronts. Work to underarm as back.

Armhole shaping

At armhole edge, bind off 3 sts once. Dec 1 st at arm edge, then every 4th row once—36 (40, 44) sts. Work to yoke shaping portion as back.

Yoke shaping

Row 1 (RS) K15 ★MB, k3; rep from ★ 4 (5, 6) times more, MB in last st. P 1 row, k 1 row, p 1 row. **Row 5** K 13, ★MB in next st, k 3; rep from ★4 (5, 6) times more, MB in next st, k2. **Row 6** Purl. **Row 7** K19, attach a 2nd ball, bind off 17 (21, 25) sts for

neck. Working on the 19 sts only, beg with Row 8 of back yoke shaping and work to correspond to one side.

RIGHT FRONT

Work to correspond to left front, reversing all shaping.

SLEEVES

With smaller needles, cast on 37 (41, 45) sts. Work in k1, p1 rib for 2"/5 cm. Change to larger needles. **Next Row (WS)** P 1 row, inc 4 sts evenly spaced—41 (45, 49) sts. **Next Row (RS)** ★K3, MB rep from ★ across, end k1. **Next Row (WS)** P across. **Next Row (RS)** Inc 1 st beg and end of row. Work St st and rep inc row every 2¼"/6 cm 6 times—55 (59, 63) sts. Work even until 17½"/44.5 cm.

Cap shaping

Bind off 3 sts beg next 2 rows. Dec 1 st each end every other row 5 times—39 (43, 47) sts. Work even until cap measures 6 (6¼, 6½)"/15 (16, 16.5) cm, ending with a p row.

Bind off 5 sts beg next 4 rows. Bind off rem sts.

FINISHING
Back ribbed yoke
From right side, using smaller needles, pick up and work k33 (41, 49) sts that were bound off. ★ Work 1 row in k1, p1 rib. **Next Row** With crochet hook, pick up 1 st from shaped neck edge and sl onto left-hand needle, work in rib as established to end, pick up 1 st from shaped neck edge and sl onto needle (2 sts added). Rep from ★ 21 times more—77 (85, 93) sts.

Shoulder shaping
Continuing in rib, bind off 6 (7, 7) sts beg next 4 rows, then 7 (7, 8) sts beg next 2 rows—39 (43, 49) sts. Bind off rem sts for back of neck in rib.

Left front ribbed yoke
With smaller needles, right side facing, pick up and k 17 (21, 25) bound-off neck sts. Work 1 row in k1, p1 rib. **Next row (RS)** Pick up and k 1 st from shaped neck edge, work in rib to end. **Next row (WS)** Work in rib as established. Rep last two rows until there are 31 (35, 39) sts on needle and

ribbed yoke measures approx 4¼"/11 cm along straight edge.

Neck shaping
At neck edge, bind off 6 sts once, then 4 (5, 6) sts every other row twice, then at same edge, dec 1 st every other row 2 (2, 3) times. AT THE SAME TIME, pick up and k 1 st at shaped neck edge 4 times more—19 (21, 22) sts. Work to shoulder as for back.

Shoulder shaping
At arm edge, bind off 6 (7, 7) sts every other row twice, 7 (7, 8) sts once.

Right front ribbed yoke
Work to correspond to left front, reversing shaping. Sew shoulder, side and sleeve seams. Sew in sleeves, easing in fullness at the top.

Front Bands
Attach, yarn at lower right front. **Row 1** Sc along right front, 3 sc in corner, sc around neck, taking in slightly to fit, 3 sc in corner, sc along left front (make sure to have same number of sc as right front). Ch 1, turn. Mark for 8 buttonholes evenly spaced along Right Front, placing top one at neck and last ½"/13mm from lower edge. **Row 2** Sc along left front,

3 sc in corner, sc around neck, 3 sc in corner ★ work to within 1 st of next buttonhole marker, ch 2, skip 2; rep from ★ until 8 buttonholes are made, sc to end. Ch 1, turn. **Rows 3, 4, 5:** Sc along fronts and around neck, working 3 sc at neck corners. **Row 6** Do not turn at end of Row 5. With right side facing, working backwards from left to right, ★ sc in next sc, ch 1, skip 1; rep from ★ along front edges and around neck. Fasten off.

Buttons
Make 8. Using F/5 (3.75mm) crochet hook, ch 3, join with a sl st to form a ring. **Rnd 1** 4 sc in ring. **Rnd 2** 2 sc in each sc—8 sc. **Rnd 3** ★Sk 1 sc, sc in next sc, rep from ★ around—4 sc. Fill opening with yarn to make button firm. Fasten off, leaving a 6"/15 cm strand. Sew opening tog with a tapestry needle. Sew on buttons.

Fall/Winter 1982 · No. 22

Pointelle Pullover

EXPERIENCED

Pointelle cardigan with a wide-set collar and matching peplum. Sized for Small, Medium, and Large. Directions are for smallest size with larger sizes in parentheses. If there is only one figure, it applies to all sizes.

KNITTED MEASUREMENTS
• Bust 36 (40, 44)"/91.5 (101.5, 112) cm
• Length (including peplum) 25 (26¼, 27¾)"/63.5 (66.5, 70.5) cm
• Upper arm 16 (16¼, 18)"/40.5 (42, 46) cm

MATERIALS
• 8 (9, 10) 1¾oz/50g balls (each approx 157yd/145m) of *Crepe DK* (acrylic/ nylon/wool) in #532 champagne (A)
• To substitute, seek DK-weight yarns with similar fiber content
• 4 (5, 5) ¾oz/20g balls (each approx 74yd/68m) of Wendy *Darling* (nylon/ acrylic) in color #810 cream (B)
• To substitute, seek fingering-weight yarn with similar fiber content
• One pair each sizes 2 and 4 needles OR SIZE TO OBTAIN GAUGE
• Fifteen ⅜"/1 cm buttons
• ¹⁄₁₆"/2mm elastic to fit around waist

GAUGES
• 26 sts and 36 rows to 4"/10 cm over pat st using A and size 4 needles.
• 32 sts and 40 rows to 4"/10 cm over peplum/collar pat st using B and size 2 needles. TAKE TIME TO CHECK GAUGE.

STITCH GLOSSARY
Pattern Stitch
(Multiple of 14 sts + 5)
Row 1 ★K5, yo, sl1, k1, pass sl st over k st (SKP), k2, p1, k2, k2tog, yo; rep from ★, end k5.
Rows 2 and 4 P9, ★k1, p13; rep from ★ end k1, p9.
Row 3 K6, ★yo, SKP, k1, p1, k1, k2tog,

yo, k7; rep from ★, end last rep k6.
Row 5 K7, ★yo, SKP, p1, k2tog, yo, k9; rep from ★, end last rep k7.
Row 6 As row 2.
Rep Rows 1-6 for pat st.

BACK
With larger needles and A, cast on 117 (131, 145) sts. **Row 1 (RS)** K9, ★p1, k13; rep from ★, end p1, k9. **Row 2 (WS)** P9, ★k1, p13; rep from ★ end k1, p9. **Row 3** Work row 1 of pat st. Cont in pat until back measures 12 (12½, 13)"/30.5 (32, 33) cm, end with a WS row.
Raglan Armhole shaping
Bind off 6 (7, 8) sts at beg of next 2 rows. **Next row** K2, k2tog, work pat to last 4 sts, k2tog, k2. **Next row** Work even in pat. Rep last 2 rows for raglan armhole shaping 36 (40, 44) times more—31 (35, 39) sts rem. Bind off.

LEFT FRONT
With larger needles and A, cast on 64 (70, 78) sts. **Next row (RS)** K9 (14, 9), ★p1, k13; rep from ★, end p1, k12 (13, 12). **Next row** K1, p11 (12, 11) ★k1, p13; rep from ★, end k1, p9 (14, 9). **Next row** K0 (5, 0), rep from ★ of row 1 of pat st, end k8 (9, 8) instead of k5. Cont in this way to work pat st

as established to correspond to back until same number of rows as back to armhole.
Armhole shaping
Next row (RS) Bind off 6 (7, 8) sts at beg of row, work pat to end. Work 1 row even. **Next row** K2, k2tog, work pat to end. **Next row** Work even in pat. Rep last 2 rows for armhole shaping 28 (32, 36) times more. **Next row** K2, k2tog, work pat to end.
Neck shaping
Next row (WS) Bind off 5 sts at beg of row (neck edge), work to end. Cont to work armhole shaping, at neck edge bind off 4 sts 4 (3, 0) times, 5 sts 0 (1, 4) times. Mark places on left front edge for 12 buttons evenly spaced.

RIGHT FRONT
Work to correspond to left front, reversing shaping and placement of pat and working buttonholes opposite button markers. **Buttonhole row (RS)** K2, yo, k2tog (buttonhole), cont in pat to end.

SLEEVES
With smaller needles and A, cast on 46 (50, 54) sts. **Row 1 (RS)** ★K1, p1; rep from ★ to end. Rep last row for 2½"/6.5 cm. Change to larger needles and B and k next row inc 43 (39, 49) sts evenly across row—89 (89, 103) sts. Work pat as for back inc 1 st at each end of row every 1½"/4 cm 8 (10, 8) times, working inc sts in pat. Work even on 105 (109, 119) sts until sleeve measures 17½ (18, 18½)"/44.5 (46, 47) cm, end with a WS row.
Cap shaping
Bind off 6 (7, 8) sts at beg of next 2 rows. Working raglan dec as for back, dec every k row until 19 (13, 13) sts rem. Bind off.

PEPLUM
With smaller needles and B cast on 31 sts. K one row. **Next row** P4, [yo, p2tog, p9] twice, yo, p2tog, p3 (3 buttonholes made). **Pat Row 1 (RS)** K8, p1, k7, p1, place marker, k5, place marker, yo, SKP, k3, yo, SKP, inc 1 st, k1 —32 sts. **Row 2** P16, k1, p5, k1,

p9. **Row 3** K8, p1, k7, p1, sl marker, k6, sl marker: yo, SKP, k3, yo, SKP, inc 1 st, k1—33 sts. **Row 4** P17, k1, p5, k1, p9. **Row 5** K8, p1, k7, p1, sl marker, k7, sl marker, yo, SKP, k3, yo, SKP, inc 1 st, k1— 34 sts. **Row 6** P18, k1, p5, k1, p9. **Rows 7-20** Cont in this way, working inc pat having 1 more k st between markers on each RS row and 1 more p st at beg of each WS row—41 sts. Beg dec as foll: **Row 21** K8, p1, k7, p1, sl marker, k12, sl marker, k2tog, yo, k3, k2tog, yo, k2, k2tog, k1—40 sts. **Row 22** P24, k1, p5, k1, p9. **Row 23** K8, p1, k7, p1, k11, k2tog, yo, k3, k2tog, yo, k2, k2tog, k1—39 sts. **Row 24** P23, k1, p5, k1, p9. **Row 25** K8, p1, k7, p1, k10, k2tog, yo, k3, k2tog, yo, k2, k2tog, k1—38 sts. **Row 26** P22, k1, p5, k1, p9. **Rows 27-38** Cont in this way working dec pat having 1 less k st between markers on each RS row and 1 less p st at beg of each WS row—32 sts. One point completed. Rep Rows 3-38 for pat until there are 10 (11, 12) points. **Last row** K8, p1, k7, p1, k3, k2tog, yo, k3, k2tog, yo, k2, k2tog, k1 —31 sts. Bind off.

COLLAR
Work as for peplum (omitting buttonholes) until there are 8 (8, 9) points.

FINISHING
Block. Sew side and sleeve seams. Set sleeves into raglan armholes. Sew peplum to lower edge of cardigan easing in extra fullness. Sew collar to neck edge, easing in fullness. Cut elastic to desired waist measurement and weave through peplum. Sew on buttons.

$\mathcal{L}$eafy Lace Poncho

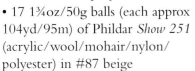

EXPERIENCED

Poncho of rectangular panels in lace stitch. One size.

KNITTED MEASUREMENTS
• Width across top 56½"/141 cm
• Length 36"/91 cm

MATERIALS
• 17 1¾oz/50g balls (each approx 104yd/95m) of Phildar *Show 251* (acrylic/wool/mohair/nylon/polyester) in #87 beige
• To substitute, seek a DK-weight yarn with similar fiber content
• One pair size 10 (6mm) needles OR SIZE TO OBTAIN GAUGE
• Size G (4.50mm) crochet hook

GAUGE
15 sts to 4"/10 cm over pat st using size 10 (6mm) needles. TAKE TIME TO CHECK GAUGE.

STITCH GLOSSARY
Pattern Stitch
(multiple of 15 sts + 1 extra)
Row 1 ⋆ K1, yo, k1, k2tog tbl, p1, k2tog k1, yo, p1, k2tog tbl, p1, k2tog, yo, k1, yo; rep from ⋆, end k1.
Row 2 P1, ⋆p4, k1 p1, k1, p3, k1, p4; rep from ⋆ to end.
Row 3 ⋆K1, yo, k1, k2tog tbl, p1, k2tog, k1, p1 sl1, k2tog, psso, yo, k3, yo; rep from ⋆, end k1.
Row 4 P1, ⋆p6, k1, p2, k1, p4; rep from ⋆, to end.
Row 5 ⋆[K1, yo] twice; k2tog tbl, p1 [k2tog] twice, yo, k5, yo; rep from ⋆, end k1.
Row 6 P1, ⋆p7, k1, p1, k1, p5; rep from ⋆ to end.
Row 7 ⋆K1, yo, k3, yo, sl1, k2tog, psso, p1, yo, k1, k2tog tbl, p1, k2tog, k1, yo; rep from ⋆, end k1.
Row 8 P1, ⋆[p3, k1] twice, p7; rep from ⋆ to end.
Row 9 ⋆k1, yo, k5, yo, k2tog tbl, k1, k2tog tbl, p1, k2tog, k1, yo; rep from ⋆, end k1.
Row 10 P1, ⋆p3, k1, p2, k1, p8; rep from ⋆ to end.
Rep rows 1-10 for pat.

NOTE
Back is worked in 2 sections and sewn together when finishing.

RIGHT BACK
With size 10 (6mm) needles, cast on 106 sts. Beg pat st and work even until piece measures 36"/91 cm from beg. Bind off loosely.

LEFT BACK
Work as for right back.

RIGHT FRONT
With size 10 (6mm) needles, cast on 106 sts. Work as for right back until front measures 34"/86 cm from beg, end with a WS row.

Neck shaping
Next row (RS) Bind off first 15 sts in k st, work across rem sts in pat st. Work even in pat for 2"/5 cm. Bind off loosely.

LEFT FRONT
Work as for right front until piece measures 34"/86 cm from beg, end with a RS row.
Neck shaping
Next row (WS) Bind off first 15 sts in p st, work across rem sts in pat st. Work even in pat for 2"/5 cm. Bind off loosely.

FINISHING
DO NOT BLOCK. Sew back sections tog along selvage edges. Sew back and fronts tog at shoulders. With RS facing and using size G (4.5mm) hook, work 1 row of sc up right front at center edge, along neck edge and down left front. Work a 2nd row of sc around neck edge only. Then with RS facing, work 1 row of sc along side edges of back and fronts.

Fall/Winter 1983 • No. 1

Crocheted "Berber" Hat

VERY EASY VERY VOGUE

Fits head sizes 21-23"/54-60 cm.

CROCHETED MEASUREMENTS
• Circumference of hat 23"/60 cm

MATERIALS
• One 3½oz/100g ball (approx 45yd/41m) of Scheepjeswol *Narvik* (wool) in color #7201 cream tweed
• To substitute, seek a DK-weight yarn with similar fiber content

• Size Q (16mm) crochet hook OR SIZE TO OBTAIN GAUGE

GAUGE
4 sc and 4 rows to 4"/10 cm using size Q (16mm) hook. TAKE TIME TO CHECK GAUGE.

NOTE
Hat is worked in rounds; do not turn at end of round.

DIRECTIONS
Ch 24 to measure approx 24"/60 cm. Join into a circle by working 1 sl st into first ch taking care not to twist chain **Rnd 1** Ch 1, 1 sc in same ch as sl st was worked, ★1 sc in next ch; rep from ★ to end—24 sc. **Rnd 2** 1 sc in each sc to end of rnd. **Rnd 3-5** Rep rnd 2 three times, marking beg of 5th rnd for ridge rnd. **Rnd 6** 1 sc in first sc, ★skip 1 sc, 1 sc in each of next 3 sc; rep from ★, end skip 1 sc, 1 sc in each of last 2 sc—18 sc. **Rnd 7** 1 sc in each of first 3 sc, skip 1 sc, ★1 sc in each of next 3 sc, skip 1 sc; rep from ★, end 1 sc in each of last 2 sc—14 sc. **Rnd 8** 1 sc in each of first 3 sc, skip 1 sc, ★1 sc in each of next 3 sc, skip 1 sc; rep from ★, end 1 sc in each of last 2 sc—11 sc. Close top as foll: **Rnd 9** Skip first sc, 1 sc in next sc, ★skip 1 sc, 1 sc in next sc; rep from ★, end skip last sc and join with a sl st to top of first sc of rnd. Fasten off leaving long loose end.

FINISHING
With WS facing and blunt-ended needle, run loose end through last rnd of sts, pull to gather sts tog and secure end. **Ridge rnd** Join yarn at marker at beg of rnd 5 with a sl st in top of rnd 4, ch 1, folding hat along rnd 5; work 1 sc in same st as sl st was worked, ★1 sc between next 2 sts of rnd 5 (working into top of rnd 4); rep from ★ around, join with a sl st in top of first sc of rnd. Fasten off.

Fall/Winter 1983 • No. 2

Fitzgerald Pullover

EXPERIENCED

Sleeveless pullover with ruffled eyelet flanges and deep hip ribbing. Sized for Small, Medium, Large, and X-Large. Directions are for smallest size with larger sizes in parentheses. If there is only one figure, it applies to all sizes.

KNITTED MEASUREMENTS
• Bust 34 (36, 38, 40)"/85 (90, 95, 100) cm
• Length 25½ (26, 26¼, 26½)"/64.5 (65.5, 66.5, 67) cm

MATERIALS
• 16 (17, 19, 21) ¾oz/20g balls (each approx 84yd/75m) of Aarlan *Silk* (silk, wool) in #1824 white
• To substitute, seek a fingering-weight yarn with similar fiber content
• One pair each sizes 2 and 4 (2.75 and 3.25mm) knitting needles OR SIZE TO OBTAIN GAUGE
• Size 3 (3.25mm) circular knitting needle 29"/80 cm long

GAUGE
28 sts and 36 rows to 4"/10 cm over St st using size 4 (3.5mm) needles. TAKE TIME TO CHECK GAUGE.

NOTE
Pullover is made in two pieces with ruffle eyelet picked up and knit along p-st ridge later.

BACK
With smaller needles, cast on 128 (134, 142, 148) sts. Work in k1, p1 rib for 6½"/16.5 cm, dec 9 (8, 9, 8) sts evenly across last WS row—119 (126, 133, 140) sts. Change to larger needles. **Row 1 (RS)** K15 (18, 21, 24), p1 and mark st (for p-st ridge), k87 (88, 89, 90), p1 and mark this st (for p-st ridge), k15 (18, 21, 24). **Row 2 (WS)** P15 (18, 21, 24), k1, p87 (88, 89, 90), k1, p15 (18, 21, 24). Rep last 2 rows for pat until back measures 18 ½ (19, 19, 19)"/47 (48, 48, 48) cm from beg, end with a WS row.

Armhole shaping
Bind off 5 (6, 7, 7) sts at beg of next 2 rows, 3 (3, 3, 4) sts at beg of next 2 rows, 2 sts at beg of next 2 rows. Dec 1 st at each end of every other row 3 (4, 5, 6) times—93 (96, 99, 102) sts. Cont p-st ridges as established, work even until armhole measures 6½ (6½, 6¾, 7)"/16.5 (16.5, 17, 17.5) cm, end with a WS row.

Neck shaping
Next row (RS) Work first 19 (20, 21, 22) sts and sl onto holder, join a 2nd ball of yarn and p center 55 (56, 57, 58) sts (for turning ridge), sl rem 19 (20, 21, 22) sts onto holder. Working on center sts only and beg with a p row, work in St st for 7 rows for facing. Bind off loosely.

Right shoulder band
Pick up yarn at inside neck edge of right shoulder (to work next row on WS), cast on 6 sts for facing, work to end. **Next row (RS)** Work 18 (19, 20, 21) sts, sl 1 st purlwise, k6. **Next row** P to marked p-st ridge, k1, p to end. Rep last 2 rows until armhole measures 7 (7, 7¼, 7½)"/17.5 (17.5, 18.5, 19) cm, end with a WS row.
Shoulder shaping Bind off 8 (8, 9, 9) sts at armhole edge twice, 9 (10, 9, 10) sts once.

Left shoulder band
Rejoin yarn at inside edge of left shoulder (to work next row on RS), cast on 6 sts for facing and complete to correspond to right shoulder band.

FRONT
Work as for back until armhole measures 4 (4, 4¼, 4½)"/10 (10, 10.5, 11.5) cm, end with a WS row. Work neck shaping, right and left shoulder bands and shoulder shaping as for back.

FINISHING
Press pieces on WS with a damp cloth and warm iron. Sew shoulder seams. Turn facings to inside of neck edge and sew in place.

Ruffle eyelet band
Note Be sure to place markers throughout as indicated, as they are integral to working pat correctly. With RS facing and circular needle, pick up and k176 (180, 182, 184) sts evenly along p-st ridge of one piece to shoulder, place marker for shoulder, pick up and k176 (180, 182, 184) sts along p-st ridge of other piece to lower band—352 (360, 364, 368) sts. **Row 1 (WS)** Purl, inc 1 st in every 4th st—88 (90, 91, 92) sts inc for 440 (450, 455, 460) sts. Beg short rows as foll: **Row 2 (RS)** K to last 8 sts, leave these sts uncorked, turn. **Row 3** Sl 1, p to last 8 sts, leave these sts unworked, turn. **Row 4** Sl 1 and dec 1 st at each side of shoulder marker, k to 8 sts before last unworked sts, leave these sts unworked, turn. **Row 5** Sl 1 and p to 8 sts before last unworked sts, leave these sts unworked, turn. **Row 6** (eyelet row 1) Sl 1, k14 (19, 21, 24), ★place marker, yo, ssk, k32★; rep between ★ and ★ to shoulder marker ending last rep k16 (16, 17, 16), (there are 6 eyelets) sl marker, k16; rep between ★ and ★ on other side leaving 8 sts unworked before last unworked sts. **Row 7** Rep row 5. **Row 8** (eyelet row 3) Sl 1, k to 2 sts before first marker, ★k2tog, yo, k1, yo, ssk, k29★; rep between ★ and ★ to shoulder, dec 1 st at each side of shoulder marker, k to 2 sts before next marker; rep between ★ and ★ on other side leaving 8 more sts unworked. **Row 9** Rep row 5. **Row 10** (eyelet row 5) Sl 1, k to first marker; rep between ★ and ★ of row 6 to shoulder marker then k to next marker and rep between ★ and ★ of row 6 leaving 8 more sts unworked. **Rows 11, 13, 15, and 17** Rep row 5. **Row 12** Rep row 4. **Row 14** Rep row 2. **Row 16** Rep row 4. **Row 18** Counting sts to center eyelet between first 2 markers (beg first eyelet 16 sts after first marker); rep between ★ and ★ of row 6, having one eyelet worked at shoulder, and leaving 8 more sts unworked. **Rnd 19** Rep row 5. **Row 20** Rep row 8 omitting shoulder decs. **Rows 21 and all foll WS rows** Rep row 5. **Row 22** Rep row 10. **Row 24** Rep row 4. **Row 26** Rep row 2. **Rows 28, 30, and 32** Counting sts to center eyelet between first 2 markers as before, work eyelet rows 1, 3, and 5. **Row 34** Rep row 2. **Row 36** Rep row 4. **Row 38** Rep row 2. **Row 40** K across all sts to end, closing holes at each 8-st interval as foll: k8, insert tip of LH needle from front to back into center of st 2 rows below last st on RH needle, sl st onto LH needle and k2tog, k in this way to end. **Row 41** Knit. Bind off loosely knitwise. Work 2nd ruffle eyelet band in same way. Turn last 2 rows of ruffle bands to WS and sew in place for facing at outside edge of ruffle. Press ruffles flat on WS with a damp cloth and warm iron. Sew side seams.

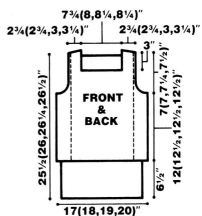

$\mathcal{C}$lassic Cable Sweater

EXPERIENCED

Cable and openwork pullover with small V-collar and set-in sleeves by Calvin Klein. Sized for Small, Medium, and Large. Directions are for smallest size with larger sizes in parentheses. If there is only one figure, it applies to all sizes.

KNITTED MEASUREMENTS
• Bust 37 (39, 41)"/93 (97, 103) cm
• Length 23 (23½, 24¼)"/58.5 (59.5, 61.5) cm
• Upper arm 14¼ (14½, 15)"/35.5 (36.5, 37.5) cm

MATERIALS
• 14 (14, 15, 15) 1¾oz/50g balls (each approx 90yd/85m) of Berger du Nord *Prodiges* #7202 red.
• To substitute, seek a worsted-weight yarn with similar fiber content
• One pair each sizes 4 and 6 (3½ and 4mm) knitting needles OR SIZE TO OBTAIN GAUGE
• Cable needle (cn)

GAUGE
• 20 sts and 26 rows to 4"/10 cm over St st using size 6 (4mm) needles. TAKE TIME TO CHECK GAUGE.
• 1 cable panel (34 sts) to approx 5"/12.5 cm.

STITCH GLOSSARY
Cable Pattern (8 sts)
Row 1 (RS) P1, k6, p1.
Row 2 and all WS rows K1, p6, k1.
Row 3 P1, sl next 3 sts to cn and hold at back of work, k3, k3 from cn, p1.
Rows 5 and 7 Rep row 1.
Row 8 Rep row 2.
Rep rows 1–8 for cable pat.

Openwork Pattern (5 sts)
Row 1 (RS) Knit.
Row 2 and all WS rows Purl.
Row 3 K2, yo, k2tog, k1.
Rows 5 and 7 Knit.
Row 8 Purl.
Rep rows 1–8 for openwork pat.

BACK
With smaller needles cast on 91 (95, 101) sts. Beg rib and cable pats. **Row 1 (RS)** K0 (0, 1), [p1, k1] 4 (5, 6) times, ★work row 1 of cable pat over next 8 sts, [k1, p1] twice, k1★; rep between ★'s once more, work row 1 of cable pat over next 8 sts, [k1, p1] 3 times, k1; rep between ★'s twice, work row 1 of cable pat over next 8 sts, [k1, p1] 4 (5, 6) times, k0 (0, 1). **Row 2** (P0), (0, 1) [k1, p1] 4 (5, 6) times, ★work row 2 of cable pat over next 8 sts, p1, [k1, p1] twice★; rep between ★'s once more, work row 2 of cable pat over next 8 sts, [p1, k1] 3 times, p1: rep between ★'s twice, work row 2 of cable pat over next 8 sts, [p1, k1] 4 (5, 6) times, p0 (0, 1). Cont in pats as established, work k1, p1 rib between cables until 32 rows have been worked from beg (4 cable pat reps) and back measures approx 3½"/9 cm from beg. Change to larger needles. **Beg cable and openwork pats: Row 1 (RS)** K8 (10, 13), ★work row 1 of cable pat over next 8 sts; row 1 of openwork pat over next 5 sts★; rep between ★'s once more, work row 1 of cable pat over next 8 sts, place marker, inc 1 st in next st, k5, inc 1 st in next st, place marker; rep between ★'s twice, work row 1 of cable pat over next 8 sts, k8 (10, 13)—93 (97, 103) sts.

Row 2 (WS) P8 (10, 13) ★work row 2 of cable pat over next 8 sts, row 2 of openwork pat over next 5 sts★; rep between ★'s once more, work row 2 of cable pat over next 8 sts, sl marker, p9, sl marker; rep between ★'s twice, work row 2 of cable pat over next 8 sts, p8 (10, 13). Cont in pats as established, working first and last sts in St st, sl markers every row and inc 1 st after first marker and 1 st before 2nd marker every pat row 1 (every 8th row), working inc sts in St st until back measures approx 15"/38 cm from beg, end with pat row 4 of 10th cable and openwork pat rep.
There are 111 (115, 121) sts.

Armhole shaping
Being sure to cont incs at markers every pat row 1 for 6 (6, 7) times more (a total of 16 (16, 17) inc rows), bind off 4 (5, 6) sts at beg of next 2 rows, 2 sts at beg of next 2 (2, 4) rows. Dec 1 st each end every other row 2 (3, 3) times. Cont incs, work in pats until armhole measures 8 (8½, 9¼)"/20.5 (21.5, 23.5) cm. Bind off all 107 (107, 109) sts.

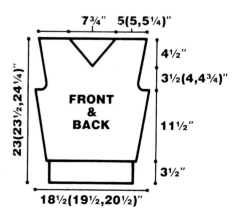

7¾" 5(5, 5¼)"
4½"
3½(4, 4¾)"
FRONT & BACK
23(23½, 24¼)"
11½"
3½"
18½(19½, 20½)"

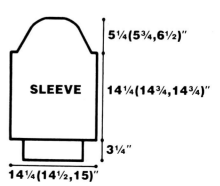

5¼(5¾, 6½)"
SLEEVE
14¼(14¾, 14¾)"
3¼"
14¼(14½, 15)"

FRONT

Work as for back until armhole measures 3½ (4, 4¾)"/9 (10, 12) cm, end with a WS row.

V-neck shaping

Note When working V-neck shaping, be sure to cont incs at markers every pat row 1 as before. **Next row (RS)** Work pat to center st, join 2nd ball of yarn and bind off center st, work pat to end. Working both sides at same time with separate balls of yarn, dec 1 st at each neck edge every row 13 times, then every other row 6 times. When there are same number of rows and incs as back to shoulder, bind off rem 34 (34, 35) sts each side for shoulders.

SLEEVES

With smaller needles cast on 44 (46, 48) sts. Work in k1, p1 rib for 3¼"/8.5 cm, inc 36 sts evenly spaced across last WS row—80 (82, 84) sts. Change to larger needles. **Beg cable and openwork pats: Row 1 (RS)** K23 (24, 25), ★work row 1 of cable pat over next 8 sts, row 1 of openwork pat over next 5 sts★; rep between ★'s once, work row 1 of cable pat over next 8 sts, k23 (24, 25). **Row 2 (WS)** P23 (24, 25), ★work row 2 of cable pat over next 8 sts, row 2 of openwork pat over next 5 sts★; rep between ★'s once, work row 2 of cable pat over next 8 sts, p23 (24, 25). Cont in pats as established (working first and last sts in St st) until sleeve measures 17½ (18, 18)"/44.5 (45.5, 45.5) cm from beg, end with a WS row.

Cap shaping

Bind off 4 (5, 6) sts at beg of next 2 rows, 2 sts at beg of next 2 rows. Dec 1 st each end every other row 10 (12, 14) times. Bind off 4 (2, 2) sts at beg of next 2 (2, 6) rows, 3 sts at beg of next 8 (8, 4) rows. Bind off rem 16 sts.

Collar

With smaller needles cast on 46 sts. Work in k1, p1 rib for 1 row. **Next row** Cast on 4 sts at beg of row, rib across all sts—50 sts. Rep this row 19 times more—126 sts. Bind off 4 sts at beg of next 20 rows—46 sts. Work even for 1 row. Bind off.

FINISHING

Block pieces to measurements. Sew shoulder, side and sleeve seams. Set in sleeves. Fold collar in half lengthwise and sew to neck edge through both thicknesses.

Fall/Winter 1984 · No. 27

*M*ock Plaid Sweater

VERY EASY VERY VOGUE

Oversized, mock plaid pullover with raglan sleeves and crewneck. Sized for Small, Medium, and Large. Directions are for smallest size with larger sizes in parentheses. If there is only one figure, it applies to all sizes.

KNITTED MEASUREMENTS

- Bust 44 (48, 56)"/111 (120, 140) cm
- Length 22½ (23, 24)"/56.5 (57.5, 60) cm
- Upper arm 19 (21¾, 23)"/47 (54.5, 57) cm

MATERIALS (5)

- 6 (6, 7) 3½oz/100g balls (each approx 110yd/108m) of Reynolds *Lopi* (wool) in #90 eggplant (MC)
- 2 balls each of color #84 plum (A) and #80 pink (E)
- 1 ball each of color #78 red (B), #103 orange-red (C) and #154 red heather (D)
- To substitute, seek a bulky-weight yarn with similar fiber content

- One pair size 10 (6mm) knitting needles OR SIZE TO OBTAIN GAUGE
- Size 9 (5.5mm) circular knitting needle 24" (60 cm) long
- Size 9/I (5.5mm) crochet hook
- Shoulder pads (optional)
- Split stitch markers
- Bobbins

GAUGE

- 14 sts and 18 rows to 4"/10 cm over St st using size 10 (6mm) needles. TAKE TIME TO CHECK GAUGE.

NOTE

1) Wind a large bobbin each of colors A-E to make blocks of color.
2) When changing colors for color blocks, on knit rows, take the 2nd color from under the first color and knit next st on needle. Drop first color and

cont with 2nd color. Rep across row for each color change. On purl rows, rep this process to avoid holes where two colors join.

3) Vertical lines are worked after pieces are complete by crocheting a chain with MC.

BACK

With size 10 (6mm) needles and MC, cast on 78 (84, 98) sts. **Rib row 1 (RS)** *K2, p2; rep from *, end k2 (0, 2). **Rib row 2 (WS)** P2 (0, 2), *k2, p2; rep from * to end. Rep last 2 rows for 6"/15 cm, end with a WS row. **Beg color block and stripe pat: Row 1 (RS)** K20 E; k20 (20, 24) D, k15 (18, 21) C, k14 (16, 20) B, k9, (10, 13) A. **Row 2 (WS)** P9 (10, 13) A, p14 (16, 20) B, p15 (18, 21) C, p20 (20, 24) D, P20 E. Rep color block pat rows 1 and 2 for a total of 12 rows. Do not cut bobbins. Work 2 rows of MC in St st (k 1 row, p 1 row). Rep color block pat rows 1 and 2 for 10 rows. Work 2 rows of MC in St st. Rep color block pat rows 1 and 2 for 8 rows. Work 2 rows of MC in St st. Work color block pat rows 1 and 2 for 6 rows. Piece measures approx 15½"/38.5 cm from beg.

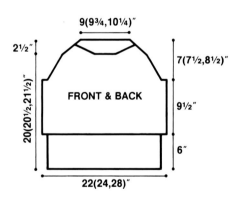

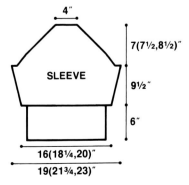

Raglan shaping

Work in MC, bind off 3 (3, 4) sts at beg of next 2 rows. Work color block pat rows 1 and 2 for 4 rows, then cut bobbins and cont in MC only and AT SAME TIME, dec 1 st each end every other row 10 times, then every row 10 (12, 17) times—32 (34, 36) sts. Bind off all sts.

FRONT

Work rib as for back for 6"/15 cm, end with a WS row. **Beg color block and stripe pat: Row 1 (RS)** K9 (10, 13) A, k14 (16, 20) B, k15 (18, 21) C, k20 (20, 24) D, k20 E. **Row 2 (WS)** P20 E, p20 (20, 24) D, p15 (18, 21) C, p14 (16, 20) B, p9 (10, 13) A. Cont in color block pat as established and work to correspond to back, including raglan shaping, until 54 (56, 60) sts rem, end with a WS row.

Neck shaping

Next row (RS) Dec 1 st, work across row until 19 sts are on RH needle, join a 2nd ball of yarn and bind off next 14 (16, 20) sts, work to last 2 sts, dec 1 st. Working both sides at once and cont raglan shaping as for back, bind off 2 sts from each neck edge every row 6 times. Fasten off last st each side.

RIGHT SLEEVE

With size 10 (6mm) needles and MC, cast on 56 (64, 70) sts. **Rib row 1** *K2, p2; rep from *, end k0 (0, 2). Work in k2, p2 rib as established until same length as back. Change to color E. Work in stripe pat only as for back using E and MC only, and AT SAME TIME, inc 1 st each and every 6th row 5 (6, 5) times—66 (76, 80) sts. Work even in stripe pat until there are same number of rows as back to armhole.

Cap shaping

With MC, bind off 3 (3, 4) sts at beg of next 2 rows. Work 4 rows with E, then cont with MC only, and AT SAME TIME dec 1 st each end every other row 7 (4, 7) times, then every row 16 (24, 22) times—14 sts. Bind off.

LEFT SLEEVE

Work as for right sleeve using color A and MC in stripe pat only.

FINISHING
Front vertical chain stripes

Note Not all blocks are evenly divided. It may be necessary to approximate spacing when placing markers and working stripes as described below. In first St st row above rib, place 14 markers as foll: **Marker 1** Place in last st of A block. **Marker 2** Place in center of B block. **Marker 3** Place in last st of B block. **Markers 4 and 5** Divide C block into thirds and place 2 markers. **Marker 6** Place in last st of C block. **Markers 7, 8 and 9** Divide D block into fourths and place 3 markers. **Marker 10** Place in last st of D block. **Markers 11, 12, 13 and 14** Divide E block into fifths and place 4 markers. With RS facing, crochet hook and MC, work a vertical chain in each color block marked row. To make stripes on back, reverse markers foll same color as for front. On right sleeve, make 12 (14, 15) evenly spaced vertical chains (approx 1 chain in every 4th st). Omit vertical stripes on left sleeve. Block pieces to measurements. Sew raglan sleeve caps to front and back raglan armholes.

Neckband

With RS facing, circular needle and MC, pick up and k24 (26, 28) sts evenly along back of neck, 10 sts along top of sleeve, 32 (34, 36) sts around front neck, 10 sts along top of right sleeve—76 (80, 84) sts. Join and place marker for beg of rnd. Work in rnds of k2, p2 rib for 4"/10 cm. Bind off loosely. Fold band in half inside and sew in place. Sew side and sleeve seams.

$\mathcal{L}$ace Leaf Sweater

EXPERIENCED

Oversized, leaf pattern pullover with raglan sleeves, split turtleneck and fitted waistband. Sized for Small, Medium, and Large. Directions are for smallest size with larger sizes in parentheses. If there is only one figure, it applies to all sizes.

KNITTED MEASUREMENTS
• Finished bust measurement 48½ (54, 60)"/121 (136, 150) cm
• Length 22 (23¼, 24)"/58 (60, 62) cm
• Upper arm 21½"/53.5 cm

MATERIALS ⓪4🔊
Version 1:
• 13 (14, 15) 1¾oz/50g balls (each approx 87yd/78m) of Melrose *Satina* (rayon ribbon) in color #21 cream
• To substitute, seek a worsted-weight yarn with fiber content similar to the original sweater of your choice
• One pair each sizes 5 and 7 (3.75 and 4.5mm) knitting needles OR SIZE TO OBTAIN GAUGE

Version 2:
• 7 (8, 9) 3½oz/100g balls (each approx 175yd/158m) of Tahki *Tweedy*

Alpaca (alpaca/wool) in #251 beige tweed
• One pair each sizes 5 and 8 (3.75 and 5mm) knitting needles OR SIZE TO OBTAIN GAUGE
Version 3:
• 7 (8, 9) 1¾oz/50g balls (each approx 154yd/140m) of Tiber/Merino *Le Doux Mohair* (mohair/nylon) in #49 beige
• One pair each sizes 5 and 8 (3.75 and 5mm) knitting needles OR SIZE TO OBTAIN GAUGE

GAUGE
25 sts to 6"/15 cm and 20 rows to 3½"/9 cm over leaf pat using size 7 or 8 (4.5 or 5mm) needles (See version for needle size). TAKE TIME TO CHECK GAUGE.

NOTES
1) To work chart for body, beg with first st of chart, work to 12-st rep, then work rep a total of 2 (3, 4) times, then beg with first st after rep, work to end of chart.
2) As this pattern is done completely by chart, it is essential to get the correct row gauge to obtain the proper sweater length.

BACK
With smaller needles, cast on 69 (79, 91) sts. **Rib row 1 (RS)** K1 tbl*p1, k1 tbl; rep from * to end. **Rib row 2 (WS)** P1, *k1 tbl, p1; rep from * to end. Rep rib rows 1 and 2 for 1¾ (2¼, 2¾)"/4.5 (6, 7) cm, end with a RS row. Change to larger needles. **Next row (WS)** P, inc 8 (10, 10) sts evenly spaced across—77 (89, 101) sts. **Beg leaf pat:** Foll chart for body, work row 1 of chart as foll: **Row 1 (RS)** K2, k2tog tbl, k4, yo, k1, yo, *k4, k3tog tbl, k4, yo, k1, yo; rep from * to last 8 sts on LH needle, k4, k2tog tbl, k2. There will be 5 (6, 7) full leaf pats with ½ pat each end. **Row 2 and all WS rows** Purl. **Row 3** K2, k2tog tbl, k3, yo, k3, *yo, k3, k3tog tbl, k3, yo, k3; rep from * to last 7 sts on LH needle, yo, k3, k2tog tbl, k2. **Row 5 (Inc row)** k1

m1 k1, k2tog tbl, k2, yo, k4, *k1, yo, k2, k3tog tbl, k2, yo, k4; rep from * to last 7 sts on LH needle, end k1, yo, k2, k2tog tbl, k1, m1, k1. Cont in this way, working chart through row 52 and inc 1 st each end of every 4th row 11 times more—101 (113, 125) sts. Piece measures approx 10¾ (11¼, 11¾)"/28 (29.5, 30.5) cm from beg.
Raglan shaping
Cont with chart, bind off 2 sts at beg of next 2 rows, then work k2tog tbl decs as indicated on chart through row 116 (120, 122)—23 (31, 39) sts. Piece measures approx 22 (23¼, 24)"/58 (60, 62) cm from beg. Place sts on holder.

FRONT
Work as for back.
SLEEVES
With smaller needles, cast on 39 sts. Work rib as for back for 2 (2½, 3)"/5 (6.5, 7.5) cm, end with a RS row. Change to larger needles. **Next row (WS)** P, inc 12 sts evenly spaced across—51 sts. **Beg leaf pats** Foll chart for sleeve, work chart through row 80, inc 1 st each end every 4th row 19 times as indicated on chart—89 sts. Piece measures approx 16 (16½, 17)"/41 (42.5, 43.5) cm from beg.
Raglan cap shaping
Cont with chart, bind off 2 sts at beg of next 2 rows, then work k2tog tbl decs as indicated on chart through row 144 (148, 150)—11 (7, 3) sts—approx 27¼ (28½, 29¼)"/71 (73, 75) cm from beg. Place sts on holder.

FINISHING
Block pieces to measurements. Sew raglan sleeve caps to raglan armholes, leaving left front raglan seam open. Sew side and sleeve seams.
Collar
Version 2:
With smaller needles, cast on 11 sts, with same strand and WS facing, p all sts from holder, beg with left sleeve—79 (87, 95) sts. **Next row**

(RS) Cast on 10 sts at beg of row, k1 tbl, *p1, k1 tbl; rep from * to end—89 (97, 105) sts. **Next row (WS)** P1, *k1 tbl, p1; rep from * to end. Cont in rib on all sts until piece measures 8"/20.5 cm from beg. Bind off in rib.

Versions 1 and 3:

With smaller needles, cast on 13 sts and with same strand and WS facing, beg with left sleeve p all sts around neck from holders, and inc 24 sts evenly spaced across—105 (113, 121) sts. **Next row (RS)** Cast on 14 sts at beg of row, work in rib as for version 2 to end—119 (127, 135) sts. Cont in rib on all sts until piece measures 8"/20.5 cm from beg. Bind off in rib. Sew left front raglan seam, overlapping collar, left over right, and sewing 4 cast-on sts at beg of rows down to neck edge.

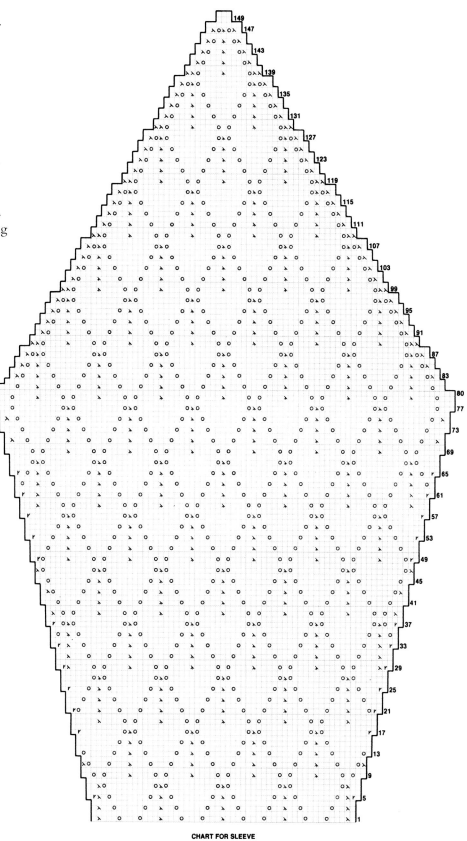

CHART FOR SLEEVE

FRONT & BACK

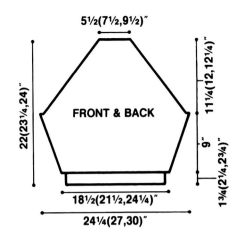

5½(7½,9½)"

22(23¼,24)"

11¼(12,12¼)"

9"

18½(21½,24¼)"

1¾(2¼,2¾)"

24¼(27,30)"

SLEEVE

21½"

2½(1½,½)"

11¼(12,12¼)"

14"

2(2½,3)"

12¼"

CHART FOR BODY

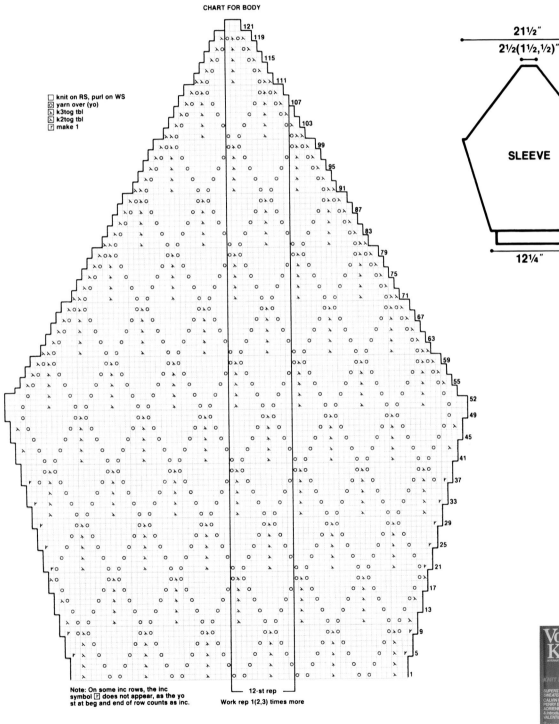

□ knit on RS, purl on WS
◎ yarn over (yo)
⋋ k3tog tbl
↘ k2tog tbl
r make 1

121
119
115
111
107
103
99
95
91
87
83
79
75
71
67
63
59
55
52
49
45
41
37
33
29
25
21
17
13
9
5
1

Note: On some inc rows, the inc
symbol r does not appear, as the yo
st at beg and end of row counts as inc.

— 12-st rep —

Work rep 1(2,3) times more

$\mathcal{M}$onogrammed Cardigan

EXPERIENCED

Loose-fitting cardigan with saddle shoulder, fitted waistband and attached scarf by Valentino. To fit sizes Small, Medium, Large, and X-Large. Directions are for smallest size with larger sizes in parentheses. If there is only one figure, it applies to all sizes.

KNITTED MEASUREMENTS
• Bust (buttoned) 41 (43, 45, 47)"/103 (107.5, 113, 117.5) cm
• Length 22 (23, 24, 25)"/56 (58, 61, 63) cm
• Upper arm 16 (16½, 17, 17½)"/40 (41.5, 42.5, 44) cm

MATERIALS 2
• 11 (12, 12, 23) 1¾oz/50g balls (each approx 273yd/250m) of Filatura di Crosa/Stacy Charles Collection *Valentino132* (mohair/acrylic/wool/polyester) in #208 gray tweed
• To substitute, seek a fingering-weight yarn with similar fiber content
• One pair each sizes 1 and 3 (2.25 and 3.25mm) knitting needles OR SIZE TO OBTAIN GAUGE
• Size 1 (2.25mm) circular needle 36"/90 cm long
• Six 1"/25mm buttons

• Small amount of gold embroidery floss
• 3" x 4" (7.5 cm x 10 cm) piece of interfacing for embroidery
• Shoulder pads
• Stitch markers

GAUGE
24 sts and 32 rows to 4"/10 cm over St st using size 3 (3.25mm) needles. TAKE TIME TO CHECK GAUGE.

BACK
With smaller needles, cast on 99 (105, 111, 115) sts. Work in k1, p1 rib for 3"/7.5 cm. Change to larger needles. **Next Row (RS)** K across, inc 13 (13, 13, 15) sts evenly spaced—112 (118, 124, 130) sts. **Next Row (WS)** P across. Cont in St st, inc 1st each end every 12th row 7 times—126 (132, 138, 144) sts. Work even until piece measures 13½ (14, 14½, 15)"/34.5 (35.5, 37, 38) cm from beg, end with a WS row.

Armhole shaping
Bind off 6 sts at beg of next 2 rows. Dec 1 st each end every other row 4 times, every 4th row 8 (9, 10, 11) times—90 (94, 98, 102) sts. Bind off 3 sts at beg of next 16 rows, 4 sts at beg of next 2 (2, 0, 0) rows, 5 sts at beg of next 2 (2, 4, 4) rows. Bind off rem 24 (28, 30, 34) sts.

RIGHT FRONT
With smaller needles, cast on 63 (65, 69, 71) sts. Work in k1, p1 rib for 1¼"/3 cm, end with a WS row.
Buttonhole row 1 (RS) Rib 3 sts, bind off next 6 sts for buttonhole, rib until there are 11 sts from last bound-off sts, bind off next 6 sts, rib to end.
Buttonhole row 2 Rib, casting on 6 sts over each set of bound-off sts. Cont in rib until piece measures 3"/7.5 cm from beg. Change to larger needles. K next row, inc 6 (7, 6, 7) sts evenly spaced across—69 (72, 75, 78) sts. Cont in St st, inc 1 st at underarm edge only (end of RS rows) 7 times, and AT SAME TIME, when piece measures 7 (8, 9, 10)"/17.5 cm

(20, 22.5, 25) cm from beg, end with a WS row and work 2 buttonholes as before. Cont inc at underarm edge, work until piece measures 7½ (8½, 9½, 10½)"/19 (21.5, 24, 26.5) cm from beg.

Neck shaping
Dec 1 st at neck edge (beg of RS row) on next row, then cont dec every 6th row 14 times more, and AT SAME TIME, when same length as back to armhole, end with a RS row and work as foll:

Armhole shaping
Next row (WS) Bind off 6 sts, work to end. Cont to dec at underarm edge every 4th row 9 (10, 9, 10) times, then every other row 0 (0, 4, 4) times, then bind off from underarm edge 3 sts 4 times, 4 sts 6 (4, 4, 2) times, 5 sts 2 (4, 4, 6) times.

Right front facing
With larger needles, cast on 27 sts. Work in St st for 4 (5, 6, 7)"/10 (12.5, 15, 17) cm, end with a WS row. Work one buttonhole at front edge over next 2 rows to correspond to first buttonhole in 2nd st of buttonholes on right front. Work even until piece measures 4½ (5½, 6½, 7½)"/11.5 (14, 16.5, 19) cm from beg. Work neck shaping as on right front at end of RS rows—12 sts. Work even for 3"/7.5 cm more. Bind off.

LEFT FRONT
Work to correspond to right front, reversing all shaping and omitting buttonholes.

Left front facing
Work to correspond to right front facing, reversing all shaping and omitting buttonhole.

LEFT SLEEVE
With smaller needles, cast on 50 (54, 56, 60) sts. Work in k1, p1 rib for 3"/7.5 cm. Change to larger needles. K next row, inc 6 sts evenly spaced across—56 (60, 62, 66) sts. Cont in St st, inc 1 st each end every 4th row 7 (5, 3, 1) times, then every 6th row 13 (15, 17, 19) times—96 (100, 102, 106)

sts. Work even until piece measures 17 (17½, 18, 18½)"/43 (44.5, 45.5, 47) cm from beg, end with a WS row.

Cap shaping

Bind off 6 sts at beg of next 2 rows. **Next row (RS)** Bind off 2 sts (back edge), k to end. **Next row (WS)** Bind off 4 sts (front edge), p to end. Cont to bind off at back edge only 2 sts 1 (1, 0, 0) times more, then dec 1 st at same edge every other row 14 (16, 19, 21) times, and AT SAME TIME, at front edge bind off 3 sts twice, 2 sts 1 (1, 0, 0) times, then dec 1 st every other row 12 (14, 17, 19) times—42 sts.

Shape back section

Next row (RS) K22, k2tog (dart edge), place rem 18 sts on holder. Cont to dec 1 st at inside dart edge every 4th row 10 times, then bind off at same edge 3 sts twice, 2 sts twice, and AT SAME TIME, dec 1 st at underarm edge every 4th row 3 times, then work edge even. Fasten off.

Shape front section

Sl 18 sts from holder to needle to work next row from RS. **Next row (RS)** K2tog (dart edge) k to last st, m1, k1. Cont to inc 1 st at underarm edge (end of RS rows) every other row 17 times more, and AT SAME TIME, dec 1 st at inside dart edge every row 3 times more, then every other row 17 times. Bind off rem 15 sts.

FINISHING

Sew center top of sleeve (dart edges) tog. Sew back edge of sleeve to back armhole and front edge of sleeve to front armhole, gathering bound-off sts at top of front to form pleats. Sew side and sleeve seams.

Front and neck band

With RS facing and circular needle, beg at lower right front edge, pick up and k120 (128, 136, 144) sts along right front edge, 20 sts along top of sleeve, 24 (28, 30, 34) sts along back of neck, 20 sts along top of sleeve, 120 (128, 136, 144) sts along left front edge—304 (324, 342, 362) sts. Work in k1, p1 rib for 1½"/4 cm. Bind off in rib. Fold band in half to WS and

sew in place. Sew 4 buttons opposite buttonholes. Sew one button on left front, 10 (11, 12, 13)"/25 (28, 30.5, 33) cm from front edge. Sew one button on right front to correspond.

SCARF

Note Edges of scarf will roll naturally to inside. With larger needles, cast on 60 sts. Work in St for 38"/96.5 cm. Bind off. Embroider monogram in center of scarf, 5"/12.5 cm from cast-on edge, as foll: Trace monogram onto interfacing and pin to scarf. Using satin st, embroider monogram over tracing. Cut away interfacing and discard. Place marker on side edge of scarf without monogram, 13"/33 cm from bound-off edge. Place 2nd marker 12"/30.5 cm from first marker. Sew scarf between markers to back of neck and top of sleeves inside ribbed edge so that monogram is on right side of cardigan.

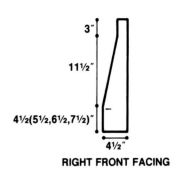

RIGHT FRONT FACING

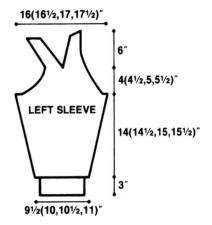

LEFT SLEEVE

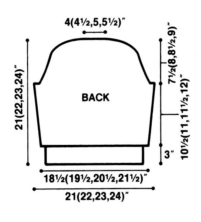

BACK

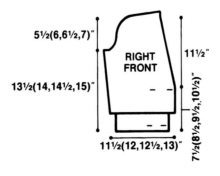

RIGHT FRONT

Cabled Headband to Match Ballerina-Style Pullover

INTERMEDIATE

Cabled headband with center front knot. One size.

KNITTED MEASUREMENTS
Circumference around band 23"/58.5 cm.

MATERIALS
• 1 3½oz/100g balls (each approx 140yd/130m) of Berger du Nord *Douceur No. 6*
(wool dl) in color #9136 blue.
• To substitute, seek a bulky-weight yarn with similar fiber content
• One pair size 7 (4.25mm) needles OR SIZE TO OBTAIN GAUGE
• Cable needle (cn)

GAUGE
26 sts and 24 rows to 4"/10 cm over 1 rep of cable pat using size 7 (4.5) needles. TAKE TIME TO CHECK GAUGE.

STITCH GLOSSARY
Front Cross (FC) (over 4 sts) Sl 3 sts to cn and hold to front of work, p1, k3 from cn.
Back Cross (BC) (over 4 sts) Sl 1 st to cn and hold to back of work, k3, p1 from cn.
Front Knit Cross (FKC) (over 6 sts) Sl 3 sts to cn, hold to front of work, k3, k3 from cn.
Back Knit Cross (BKC) (over 6 sts) Sl 3 sts to cn, hold to back, k3, k3 from cn.

Cable Panel
(panel of 26 sts)
Row 1 and 3 (WS) K5, p6, k4, p6, k5.
Row 2 (RS) P5, BKC, p4, FKC, p5.
Row 4 P4, BC, FC, p2, BC, FC, p4.
Row 5 and all WS rows K the knit sts and p the purl sts.
Row 6 P3, [BC, p2, FC] twice, p3.
Row 8 P3, k3, p4, BKC, p4, k3, p3.
Row 10 P3, k3, p4, k6, p4, k3, p3.
Row 12 Rep row 8.
Row 14 P3, [FC, p2, BC] twice, p3.
Row 16 P4, FC, BC, p2, FC, BC, p4.
Row 18 and 20 Rep rows 2 and 4.
Row 22 P4, [k3, p2] twice, k3, sl last 8 sts worked from RH needle to cn and wrap yarn 6 times counter-clockwise around these 8 sts, sl them back to RH needle, p2, k3, p4.
Row 24 Rep row 16.
Rep rows 1-24 for cable pat.

BAND
Cast on 32 sts. **Beg cable pat: Row 1** K3, place marker, work cable pat over 26 sts, place marker, k3. **Row 2** K3, work cable pat over 26 sts, k3. Cont in this way k first and last 3 sts on every row and working cable pat rep over 26 sts twice, then 4 rows once more. **Dec row (WS)** K3, ssk, work to last 5 sts in cable pat, k2tog, k3. Rep dec row every other row 5 times more—20 sts. Work through row 17 of pat—piece measures approx 10½"/26.5 cm. Work in garter st for 3½"/9 cm, end with a RS row. **Inc row** (Beg with row 1 of cable pat) K3, make 1, p5, k4, p5, make 1, k3. **Row 2** BKC, p4, FKC. Rep inc row every other row 5 times more and working sts into cable pat—32 sts. Work in cable pat until same length as opposite side of 3½"/9 cm garter st piece. Bind off. Tie knot in garter st area and sew ends of piece tog to form band.

Holiday 1986 · No. 5

Ballerina-Style Pullover

VERY EASY VERY VOGUE

Oversized, short pullover with raglan sleeves, tapered waist and two piece sleeve with buttoned cuff. Sized for Small, Medium, Large, and X-Large. Directions are for smallest size with larger sizes in parentheses. If there is only one figure, it applies to all sizes.

KNITTED MEASUREMENTS
• Bust 39 (41, 44, 47)"/97 (103, 110, 117) cm
• Length 19 (20, 21, 22)"/48 (50.5, 53, 55) cm
• Upper arm 20 (20½, 22, 22½)"/50 (52, 55, 57) cm

MATERIALS
• 5 (5, 6, 6) 3½oz/100g balls (each approx 145yd/132m) of Reynolds

Tipperary Tweed in #989 blue
• To substitute, seek a bulky-weight yarn with similar fiber content
• One pair each sizes 9 and 10½ (5.5 and 6.5mm) needles OR SIZE TO OBTAIN GAUGE
• Size 9 (5.5mm) circular needle 16"/40 cm
• Four ⅝"/15 mm buttons

GAUGE
12 sts and 16 rows to 4"/10 cm over St st using size 10½ (6.5mm) needles. TAKE TIME TO CHECK GAUGE.

BACK
With smaller needles, cast on 46 (48, 52, 54) sts. Work in k1, p1 rib for 4 rows. Change to larger needles. Work in St st, inc 1 st each end every 4th row 6 (7, 7, 8) times—58 (62, 66, 70) sts. Work even until piece measures 8 (8½, 9, 9½)"/20.5 (21.5, 23, 24) cm from beg.
Raglan shaping
Bind off 3 sts at beg of next 2 rows. Dec 1 st each end every other row 11 (12, 15, 16) times, every 4th row 5 (5, 4, 4) times. Bind off rem 20 (22, 22, 24) sts for back neck.

FRONT
Work as for back until armhole measures 8½ (9, 9½, 10)"/21 (22.5, 23.5, 24.5) cm and there are 26 (28, 30, 32) sts, end with a WS row.
Neck shaping
Next row (RS) Dec 1 st, work until

there are 8 (8, 9, 9) sts on RH needle, join 2nd ball of yarn and bind off center 8 (10, 10, 12) sts, work to last 2 sts, dec 1 st. Cont raglan dec and working both sides at once, bind off from each neck edge 2 st 3 times.

LEFT SLEEVE
Left Half
With smaller needles, cast on 22 (22, 24, 24) sts. Work in k1, p1 rib for 4 rows, end with a WS row. Change to larger needles. **Next row (RS)** K4 (button edge), k to end. **Next row (WS)** P to last 4 sts, k4. Cont in St st, working 4 sts at button edge in garter st (k every row) and AT SAME TIME, inc 1 st at underarm edge at end of next row and every other row until piece measures 3"/7.5 cm from beg, end with a WS row. **Next row (RS)** Bind off 4 sts, work to last st, inc 1 st. Cont in St st only and cont inc at underarm edge until there are 28 (28, 30, 30) sts, then inc at underarm edge every 4th row 2 (3, 3, 4) times—30 (31, 33, 34) sts. Work even until piece measures 9 (9½, 10, 10½)"/22.5 (24, 25, 26.5) cm from beg, end with a RS row. **Raglan cap shaping** Bind off 3 sts

2 buttons, first marker ½"/1.5 cm from lower edge, 2nd marker 4 rows below bind-off.
Right half
Work to correspond to left, reversing by working underarm inc and dec at beg of RS rows, center edge at end of RS rows and beg of WS rows and working buttonholes opposite markers by yo, k2tog for each buttonhole.

RIGHT SLEEVE
Work to correspond to left sleeve, reversing left and right halves.

FINISHING
Block pieces. Sew center sleeve seam using invisible seam leaving garter sts at center edge free. Sew raglan sleeve caps to raglan armholes. Sew side and sleeve seams.
Neckband
With RS facing and circular needle, pick up and k 20 (21, 22, 23) sts along back neck, 12 sts along top of left sleeve, 26 (27, 28, 29) sts along front neck and 12 sts along right sleeve—70 (72, 74, 76) sts. Join and work in k1, p1 rib for 2"/5 cm. Bind off in rib. Sew on buttons.

SCHEMATIC FOR SWEATER NUMBER 6

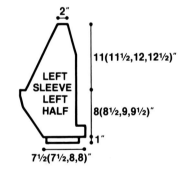

at beg of next row, then cont to dec 1 st at underarm edge as for back until there are 16 (16, 17, 17) sts, end with a WS row. **Next row (RS)** Dec 1 st (center edge), work to end. Cont raglan dec at underarm edge, dec 1 st at center edge every 4th row 4 times more. After all dec have been worked, bind off rem 6 sts. Place markers on button edge for

$\mathscr{D}$eep Rib Cardigan

INTERMEDIATE

Standard-fitting cardigan with deep rib, raglan sleeves and round neck initially published in *Vogue Knitting*, Summer 1949. Sized for Small, Medium, Large, and X-Large. Directions are for smallest size with larger sizes in parentheses. If there is only one figure, it applies to all sizes.

KNITTED MEASUREMENTS
• Bust (buttoned) 35 (37, 39, 41)"/88 (92.5, 98, 102.5) cm
• Length 22¼ (23, 23¾, 24½)"/56.5 (58.5, 60.5, 62.5) cm
• Upper arm 13½ (14, 15, 15½)"/34 (35, 37.5, 39) cm

MATERIALS 4
• 9 (10, 10, 11) 1¾oz/50g balls (each approx 135yd/123m) of Crystal Palace *Creme* (silk/wool) in #2260 jade
• To substitute, seek a worsted-weight yarn with similar fiber content
• One pair each sizes 3 and 5 (3.25 and 3.75mm) needles OR SIZE TO OBTAIN GAUGE

• Eight ⅝"/15mm buttons
• 2 yd/2m grosgrain ribbon to match

GAUGE
24 sts and 32 rows to 4"/10 cm over St st using size 5 (3.75mm) needles. TAKE TIME TO CHECK GAUGE.

BACK
With larger needles, cast on 90 (96, 102, 108) sts. Work in k2, p2 rib for 6"/15.5 cm. Change to smaller needles. Rib for 2½"/6.5 cm more. Change to larger needles. Rib until piece measures 10"/26 cm from beg. Cont in St st, inc 1 st each end every 4th row 4 (3, 2, 1) times, every 6th row 2 (3, 4, 5) times—102 (108, 114, 120) sts. Work even until piece measures 14¼ (14½, 14¾, 15)"/36.5 (37, 38, 38.5) cm from beg.

Raglan armhole shaping
Bind off 6 (6, 7, 7) sts at beg of next 2 rows. **Row 1 (RS)** K to last 6 sts, SKP, k4. **Row 2 (WS)** P to last 6 sts, sl 1, p1 psso, p4. Rep last 2 rows until there are 28 (30, 30, 32) sts. Bind off sts for back neck.

LEFT FRONT
With larger needles, cast on 53 (57, 60, 63) sts. **Next row (RS)** Work in k2, p2 rib to last 3 sts, sl 1 purlwise, wyib, k2 (garter st edge). **Next row** K2, p1, rib to end. Rep last 2 rows (changing needles as for back) for 10"/26 cm. Cont in St st, keeping 3 sts at front edge for hem, and working inc and raglan armhole shaping at side edge only (beg of RS rows) as for back until there are 31 (32, 32, 33) sts.

Neck shaping
Note The 6 raglan dec sts may not be available when shaping neck. Work dec into pat according to rem sts. Cont raglan dec, bind off from neck edge (beg of WS rows) 8 (10, 10, 9) sts once, 3 sts 2 (2, 2, 3) times, 2 sts 3 times, 1 st 1 (1, 1, 0) times. Fasten off last st. Place markers at front edge for 7 buttons, first marker ½"/1.5 cm from lower edge, last marker 1½"/4 cm below first neck dec, others spaced evenly between.

RIGHT FRONT
Work to correspond to left front, reversing all shaping and working buttonholes opposite manners as ton: **Next row (RS)** K2, sl 1, k2, bind off 3 sts, work to end. On next row, cast on 3 sts over bound-off sts.

SLEEVES
With smaller needles, cast on 50 (54, 54, 58) sts. Work in k2, p2 rib for 3"/7.5 cm. Change to larger needles. Work in St st, inc 1 st each end every 6th row 5 (5, 14, 14) times, every 8th row 10 (10, 4, 4) times—80 (84, 90, 94) sts. Work even until piece measures 18 (18½, 18½, 19)"/45 (46, 46, 47.5) cm from beg.

Raglan cap shaping
Bind off 6 (6, 7, 7) sts at beg of next 2 rows. Rep 2 rows of raglan shaping as for back until there are 6 sts. Bind off.

FINISHING
Block pieces. Sew raglan caps to front and back armholes. Sew side and sleeve seams.

Neckband
With RS facing and smaller needles,

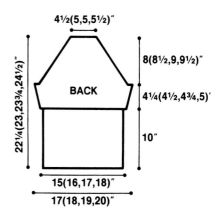

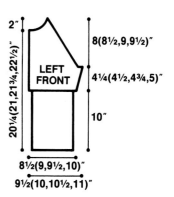

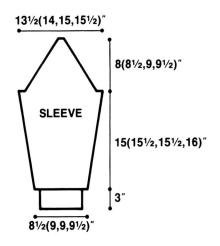

13½(14,15,15½)"

8(8½,9,9½)"

SLEEVE

15(15½,15½,16)"

3"

8½(9,9,9½)"

beg at right front neck edge, pick up and k26 (27, 27, 28) sts along right front edge, 6 sts along top of sleeve, 28 (30, 30, 32) sts along back neck, 6 sts along top of 2nd sleeve, 26 (27, 27, 28) sts along left front neck edge—92 (96, 96, 100) sts. Cont garter and sl st edge, work in k2, p2 rib for 2 rows. Work buttonhole 2 sts in from right front edge. Rib until band measures 1"/2.5 cm. Bind off in rib. Cut ribbon to fit front bands. Sew to facing sts of

fronts. Fold to WS and stitch in place. Cut buttonholes through ribbon. Reinforce buttonhole area. Sew on buttons.

Fall/Winter 1986-1987 · No. 16

Giant Cable Sweater

VERY EASY VERY VOGUE

Oversized, jumbo cable pullover with drop shoulders and loose turtleneck. Sized for Small, Medium, Large, and X-Large. Directions are for smallest size with larger sizes in parentheses. If there is only one figure, it applies to all sizes.

KNITTED MEASUREMENTS
• Bust 38 (41, 44, 47)"/96 (104; 111, 118) cm
• Length 26 (27, 27, 28)"/66 (68.5, 68.5, 71) cm
• Upper arm 21 (22, 22, 23)"/52 (56, 56, 57) cm

MATERIALS
• 9 (10, 10, 11) 3½oz/100g balls (each approx 108yd/99m) of Tahki *Jumbo Tweed* (wool/mohair) in color #562 purple/black tweed
• To substitute, seek a super bulky–weight yarn with similar fiber content
• One pair each sizes 9 and 11 (5.5 and 8mm) needles OR SIZE TO OBTAIN GAUGE
• Sizes 9 and 11 (5½ and 8mm) circular needles 24"/60 cm
• Stitch holders and stitch markers
• Cable needle (cn)

GAUGE
11 sts and 20 rows to 4"/10 cm over garter st using size 11 (8mm) needles. TAKE TIME TO CHECK GAUGE.

STITCH GLOSSARY
Jumbo Cable Pattern
(over 12 sts)
Rows 1, 3, 5 and 7 (RS) Knit.
Row 2 and all WS rows Purl.
Row 9 (cable row) Sl all 12 sts to double pointed needle (dpn). Turn dpn one half turn clockwise. Working loosely, k sts from dpn (cable made).
Rows 11, 13, 15 and 17 Knit.
Row 18 Purl.
Rep rows 1-18 for cable pat.

BACK
With smaller straight needles, cast on 60 (64, 68, 72) sts. **Rib row 1** ★K2, p2; rep from ★ to end. Rep rib row 1 for 7 (8, 8, 9)"/18 (20.5, 20.5, 23) cm, inc 8 sts evenly spaced across last row—68 (72, 76, 80) sts. Change to larger straight needles. **Beg cable pat: Next row (RS)** K8 (9, 10, 11), place marker, ★work row 1 of cable pat over next 12 sts, place marker, k8 (9, 10, 11); rep from ★ twice more. **Next row** K8 (9, 10, 11), sl marker, ★work row 2 of cable pat over next 12 sts, sl marker, k8 (9, 10, 11); rep from ★ twice more. Cont in pat, working sts between cables in garter st (k every row) until 18 rows of cable pat have been worked 5 times— piece measures approx 26 (27, 27, 28)"/66 (68.5, 68.5, 71) cm from beg. Bind off all sts.

FRONT
Work as for back until piece measures 23 (24, 24, 25)"/58.5 (61, 61, 63.5) cm, end with a WS row.
Neck shaping
Next row (RS) Work 26 (27, 28, 29) sts, join 2nd ball of yarn and bind off center 16 (18, 20, 22) sts, work to end. Working both sides at once, dec 1 st at each neck edge every other row 6 times—20 (21, 22, 23) sts each side. Work even until same length as back.

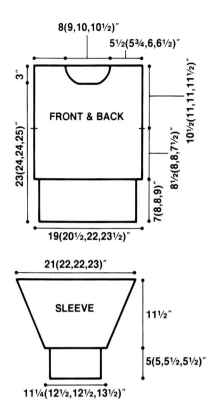

8(9,10,10½)"

5½(5¾,6,6½)"

3"

FRONT & BACK

23(24,24,25)"

10½(11,11,11½)"

8½(8,8,7½)"

7(8,8,9)"

19(20½,22,23½)"

21(22,22,23)"

SLEEVE

11½"

5(5,5½,5½)"

11¼(12½,12½,13½)"

Bind off sts each side.

SLEEVES

With smaller straight needles, cast on 24 sts. **Rib row 1** ★K2, p2; rep from ★ to end. Rep rib row 1 for 5 (5, 5½, 5½)"/12.5 (12.5, 14, 14) cm, inc 12 (16, 16, 18) sts evenly spaced across last row—36 (40, 40, 42) sts. Change to larger straight needles. **Beg cable pat: Next row (RS)** K12 (14, 14, 15), place marker, work row 1 of cable pat over next 12 sts, place marker, k12 (14, 14, 15). **Next row** K12 (14, 14, 15), sl marker, work row 2 of cable pat over next 12 sts, sl marker, k12 (14, 14, 15). Cont in pat, working sts each side of center cable in garter st, and AT SAME TIME inc 1 st each end every 4th row (working inc sts into garter st) 13 times—62 (66, 66, 68) sts. Work even until 18 rows of cable pat have been worked 3 times— piece measures approx I6½ (16½, 17, 17)"/41 (41, 42.5, 42.5) cm from beg. Bind off.

FINISHING

Block pieces. Sew shoulder seams. With RS facing and smaller circular needle, beg at right shoulder, pick up and k28 (30, 32, 34) sts along back neck, 36 (38, 40, 42) sts along front neck—64 (68, 72, 76) sts. Join and work in rnds of k2, p2 rib for 6"/15 cm. Change to larger circular needle. Rib for 6"/15 cm more. Bind off in rib. Place markers 10½ (11, 11, 11½)"/26 (28, 28, 28.5) cm down from shoulder seams on front and back for armhole. Sew top of sleeves to back and front between markers. Sew side and sleeve seams.

Butterfly-Stitch Cardigan

15

INTERMEDIATE

Close-fitting, butterfly stitch cardigan with set-in sleeves and round neck; optional sewn, detachable collar and cuffs. Sized for X-Small, Small, Medium, Large, X-Large. Directions are for smallest size with larger sizes in parentheses. If there is only one figure, it applies to all sizes.

KNITTED MEASUREMENTS

• Bust (buttoned) 31½ (34½, 37½, 40½, 42¾)"/79.5 (86, 93.5, 100, 107.5) cm
• Length 21¼ (22, 22½, 23¼, 24)"/52.5 (54.5, 56.5, 58.5, 60.5) cm
• Upper arm 12¾ (12¾, 14, 14, 15½)"/32 (32, 35.5, 35.5, 39) cm

MATERIALS ③

• 8 (8, 9, 9, 10) 1¾oz/50g balls (each approx 180yd/165m) of Baruffa/Lane Borgosesia *Aerobic* (wool) in #8541 fuchsia.
• To substitute, seek a DK-weight yarn with similar fiber content
• 13 (13, 14, 14, 15) ⅝"/15mm buttons
• One pair each sizes 2 and 4 (2.75 and 3.5mm) needles OR SIZE TO OBTAIN GAUGE
• Detachable sewn collar and cuffs

GAUGE

28 sts and 52 rows to 4"/10 cm over butterfly stitch using size 4 (3.5mm) needles. TAKE TIME TO CHECK GAUGE. **Note** Block swatch before measuring.

STITCH GLOSSARY
Butterfly Stitch
(multiple of 10 sts plus 9 extra)
Note On rows 10 and 20, work butterfly stitch loosely.
Rows 1, 3, 5, 7 and 9 (RS) K2, ★sl 5

wyif, k5; rep from ★, end sl 5 wyif, k2.

Rows 2, 4, 6 and 8 Purl.

Row 10 (WS) P4, ★insert LH needle down through the 5 loose strands below next st, p these 5 strands tog with next st on needle, p9; rep from ★, end last rep p4, instead of p9.

Rows 11, 13, 15, 17 and 19 K7, ★sl 5 wyif, k5; rep from ★, end sl 5 wyif, k7.

Rows 12, 14, 16, and 18 Purl.

Row 20 P9, ★insert LH needle down through the 5 loose strands below next st, p these 5 strands tog with next st on needle, p9; rep from ★ to end.

Rep rows 1–20 for butterfly stitch.

BACK

With smaller needles, cast on 109 (119, 129, 139, 149) sts. Work in k1, p1 rib for 4"/10 cm. Change to larger needles. Work in butterfly stitch until piece measures 13¼ (14, 14, 14¾, 14¾)"/33 (35, 35, 37, 37) cm from beg, end with pat row 20 (10, 10, 20, 20).

Armhole shaping

Note When working dec, if there are less than 5 sts to slip at edges, work these sts in St st. Bind off 5 sts at beg of next 2 rows. Dec 1 st each end every other row 5 times— 89 (99, 109, 119, 129) sts. Work even until armhole measures 8 (8, 8½, 8½, 9¼)"/19.5 (19.5, 21.5, 21.5, 23.5) cm, end with pat row 20 (10, 20, 10, 20). K1 row, p1 row. Bind off.

LEFT FRONT

Note Work 1 selvage st at front edge as foll: on RS rows, sl 1 wyib, on WS rows, p1. With smaller needles, cast on 58 (63, 68, 73, 78) sts. Work in k1, p1 rib for 4"/10 cm. Change to larger needles. Beg with row 11, work butterfly st as foll: **Beg pat: Row 11 (RS)** K7, ★sl 5 wyif, k5; rep from ★, end sl 0 (5, 0, 5, 0) wyif, sl 1 wyib (selvage st). Cont in pat until piece measures same length as back to armhole, ending with pat row 10 (20, 20, 10, 10). Shape armhole at underarm edge only as for back—48 (53, 58, 63, 68) sts. Work even until armhole measures 5½ (5½, 6, 6, 6¾)"/13.5 (13.5, 15.5, 15.5, 17.5) cm, end with pat row

19 (9, 19, 9, 19).

Neck shaping

Next row (WS) Bind off 7 (8, 9, 9, 9) sts (neck edge), work to end. Cont to bind off from neck edge 3 sts once, 2 sts once. Dec 1 st at neck edge every other row 10 (10, 11, 11, 12) times. When same length as back, bind off rem 26 (30, 33, 38, 42) sts. Place markers for buttons on left front edge, with 10 (10, 11, 11, 12) markers in center of St st rows between butterflies, and rem 3 markers evenly along rib band, with last marker ½"/1.5cm from lower edge.

RIGHT FRONT

Work as for left front, reversing all shaping by working neck shaping at beg of RS rows, and reversing placement of butterfly pat as foll: **Beg pat: Row 11 (RS)** Sl 1 wyib (selvage st), sl 0 (5, 0, 5, 0) wyif, ★k5, sl 5 wyif; rep from ★, end k7. Work buttonholes opposite markers as foll: **Next row (RS)** K2, bind off 3 sts, work to end. On next row, cast on 3 sts over bound-off sts.

SLEEVES

With smaller needles, cast on 43 (43, 49, 49, 51) sts. Work in k1, p1 rib for 1½"/4 cm, inc 6 (6, 10, 10, 8) sts evenly across last row—49 (49, 59, 59, 59) sts. Change to larger needles. Work in butterfly st, inc 1 st each end (working inc sts into pat) every 8th row 10 (7, 7, 3, 25) times, every 10th row 10 (13, 13, 17, 0) times—89 (89, 99, 99, 109) sts. Work even until piece measures 16 (17, 17, 17½, 17½)"/40.5 (42.5, 42.5, 44.5, 44.5) cm from beg, end with pat row 10 (20, 20, 10, 10).

Cap shaping

Bind off 5 sts at beg of next 2 rows, 3 sts at beg of next 2 rows, 2 sts at beg of next 2 rows. Dec 1 st each end every other row 18 (18, 23, 23, 28) times, every 4th row 6 (6, 5, 5, 4) times. Bind off rem 21 (21, 23, 23, 25) sts.

FINISHING

Block pieces. Sew shoulder seams. Set in sleeves. Sew side and sleeve seams.

Neckband

With RS facing and smaller needles, beg at right front neck edge, pick up and k131 (135, 143, 143, 147) sts evenly around neck edge. Work in k1, p1 rib for ¾"/2 cm. Bind off. Sew on buttons.

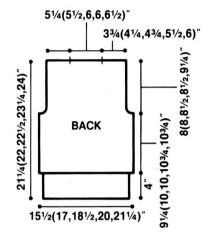

5¼(5½,6,6,6½)"
3¾(4¼,4¾,5½,6)"
8(8,8½,8½,9¼)"
BACK
21¼(22,22½,23¼,24)"
9¼(10,10,10¾,10¾)"
4"
15½(17,18½,20,21¼)"

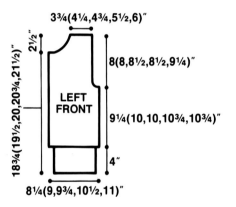

3¾(4¼,4¾,5½,6)"
2½"
8(8,8½,8½,9¼)"
LEFT FRONT
9¼(10,10,10¾,10¾)"
18¾(19½,20,20¾,21½)"
4"
8¼(9,9¾,10½,11)"

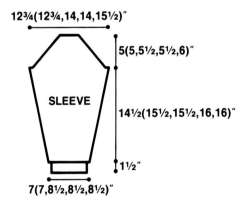

12¾(12¾,14,14,15½)"
5(5,5½,5½,6)"
SLEEVE
14½(15½,15½,16,16)"
1½"
7(7,8½,8½,8½)"

High-Neck Pullover

EXPERIENCED

Oversized, chevron pattern pullover with square armholes, left shoulder buttoned edge and high neck. Sized for X-Small, Small, Medium, Large, and X-Large. Directions are for smallest size with larger sizes in parentheses. If there is only one figure, it applies to all sizes.

KNITTED MEASUREMENTS
• Bust 39½ (42, 45½, 48, 51½)"/98 (106, 113, 121, 128) cm
• Length 24½ (25, 25½, 26, 26½)"/62 (63.5, 64.5, 65.5, 67) cm
• Upper arm 18 (19, 19, 20, 20)"/45 (48, 48, 50, 50) cm

MATERIALS 4
• 23 (23, 24, 24, 25) 1¾oz/50g balls (each approx 80yd/73m) of Melrose *Memory Eight* (cotton/stretch fiber) in #821 purple
• To substitute, seek a worsted-weight yarn with similar fiber content
• One pair each sizes 5 and 8 (3¾ and 5mm) needles OR SIZE TO OBTAIN GAUGE
• Five ⅝"/15mm buttons

GAUGE
24 sts and 28 rows to 4"/10 cm over chevron pat using size 8 (5mm) needles. TAKE TIME TO CHECK GAUGE.

BACK
With smaller needles, cast on 102 (110, 118, 126, 134) sts. Work in k2, p2 rib for 3"/7.5 cm. K next row on RS, then p 2 rows, k 2 rows. P next row, inc 16 (17, 18, 19, 20) sts evenly across—118 (127, 136, 145, 154) sts. Change to larger needles. **Beg chevron pat: Row 1 (RS)** Work first st of chart, work 18-st rep 6 (7, 7, 8, 8) times, then work last 9 sts of chart 1 (0, 1, 0, 1) time more. Cont in pat until piece measures 14½ (14½, 15, 15, 15½)"/37 (37, 38, 38, 39.5) cm from beg.

Armhole shaping
Bind off 9 sts at beg of next 2 rows—100 (109, 118, 127, 136) sts. Work even until armhole measures 9 (9½, 9½, 10, 10)"/22.5 (24, 24, 25, 25) cm.

Neck and shoulder shaping
Bind off 7 (8, 9, 10, 11) sts at beg of next 8 rows, AT SAME TIME, bind off center 12 (13, 14, 15, 16) sts for neck and working both sides at once, bind off from each neck edge 4 sts once, 6 sts twice.

FRONT
Work as for back until armhole measures 6½ (7, 7, 7½, 7½)"/16 (17.5, 17.5, 18.5, 18.5) cm.

Neck shaping
Next row (RS) Work 43 (47, 51, 55, 59) sts, join 2nd ball of yarn and bind off 14 (15, 16, 17, 18) sts, work to end. Working both sides at once, bind off from each neck edge 4 sts once, 3 sts once, 2 sts twice, dec 1 st every other row 4 times, AT SAME TIME, when armhole measures 8 (8½, 8½, 9, 9)"/20 (21.5, 21.5, 22.5, 22.5) cm, work shoulder shaping at left front only (beg of RS rows) as for back, working right front even. When right front is same length as back to shoulder, work shoulder shaping as for back.

SLEEVES
With smaller needles, cast on 46 (46, 46, 50, 50) sts. Work in k2, p2 rib for 2"/5 cm. K next row on RS, then p 2 rows, k 2 rows. P next row, inc 22 (26, 26, 26, 26) sts evenly across—68 (72, 72, 76, 76) sts. Change to larger needles. Beg with first st of chart, work in chevron pat, inc 1 st each end (working inc sts into pat) every 4th row 15 (16, 16, 17, 17) times, every 6th row 5 times—108 (114, 114, 120, 120) sts. Work even in pat until piece measures 15½ (16, 16, 16½, 16½)"/39.5 (40.5, 40.5, 42, 42) cm from beg, end with a WS row. K next row, dec 12 sts evenly across—96 (102, 102, 108, 108) sts. K 1 row, p 2 rows, k 2 rows, p 2 rows. Bind off knitwise.

FINISHING
Block pieces. Sew right shoulder seam.

Neckband
With RS facing and smaller needles, beg at left front neck edge, pick up and k 62 (62, 64, 64, 66) sts to right shoulder, 48 (48, 50, 50, 52) sts along back neck—110 (110, 114, 114, 118) sts. P 2 rows, k 2 rows, p 1 row. Work in k2, p2 rib for 3"/7.5 cm. Bind off in rib.

Back shoulder band
With RS facing and smaller needles, beg at left back neckband edge, pick up and k37 (41, 45, 49, 53) sts along back shoulder edge. P 1 row. Work in k1, p1 rib for 1¼"/3 cm. Bind off knitwise. Place markers on band for 5 buttons, first ½"/1.5 cm from neckband edge, last ½"/1.5 cm from shoulder edge, others evenly between.

Front shoulder band
Beg at left front shoulder edge, work as for back shoulder band for 3 rows. Work buttonholes opposite markers on next row by binding off 2 sts for each buttonhole. On next row, cast on 2 sts over bound-off sts. Complete as for back shoulder band. Place front band over back band and sew sides at shoulder edge. Sew top of sleeves to straight edge of armholes, sewing last 1½"/4 cm of sleeve to bound-off armhole sts. Sew side and sleeve seams. Sew on buttons.

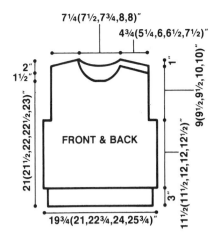

7¼(7½,7¾,8,8)"

4¾(5¼,6,6½,7½)"

2"
1½"

1"

FRONT & BACK

21(21½,22,22½,23)"

9(9½,9½,10,10)"

11½(11½,12,12,12½)"

3"

19¾(21,22¾,24,25¾)"

18(19,19,20,20)"

SLEEVE

14½(15,15,15½,15½)"

2"

11½(12,12,12¾,12¾)"

CHEVRON PATTERN

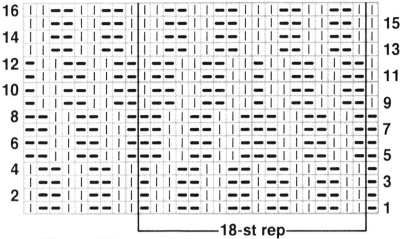

├─ 18-st rep ─┤

☐ k on RS, p on WS
⊟ p on RS, k on WS

Spring/Summer 1988 · No. 29

𝓑ow Beauty

INTERMEDIATE

Loose-fitting, cropped pullover with drop shoulders, rolled, corded edges and placed openings for velvet bows by Louis Dell'Olio for Anne Klein II.

Sized for X-Small, Small, Medium, Large. Directions are for smallest size with larger sizes in parentheses. If there is only one figure, it applies to all sizes.

KNITTED MEASUREMENTS
• Bust 36 (38, 39½, 41½)"/90 (94, 99, 103) cm
• Length 18¼ (18¾, 19¼, 20¼)"/46 (47, 48, 51) cm
• Upper arm 19¾ (20¼, 20¼, 20¾)"/49.5 (50.5, 50.5, 51.5) cm

MATERIALS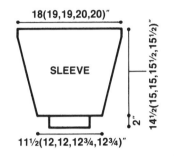
• 10 (11, 11, 12)oz/250g balls (275, 275, 300)g (each approx 150yd/137m per 1oz/25g) of Melrose Yarn Company *70/30 Angora* (angora/wool/cotton) in fuchsia (A)
• 14 (15, 16, 17) 1½oz/40g spools (each approx 100yd/90m) of Melrose Yarn Company *Rayonette* (rayon) in cranberry (B), one ball in black (D)
• 1 ⅜oz/10g ball (each approx

35yd/32m) of 100% French Angora (angora) in black (C)
• To substitute, seek a fingering-weight yarn with similar fiber content
• One pair size 8 (5mm) needles OR SIZE TO OBTAIN GAUGE
• 9½yd/8.5m of black velvet ribbon 1¾"/4.5 cm wide
• 2½yd/2.3m of 1"/2.5 cm cotton/poly cording

GAUGE
18 sts and 24 rows to 4"/10 cm over St st using size 8 (5mm) needles.
TAKE TIME TO CHECK GAUGE.

Notes for working bow openings
1) MC refers to 1 strand A and B held tog. CC refers to 1 strand C and D held tog.
2) Do not twist CC around MC when changing colors.
3) Once opening has been worked, work next row with MC only.

Center bow: (over 3 sts) Work to opening; join CC and k3; add new strands of MC. **Next row** Purl, matching colors. Rep last 2 rows once.
Left bow: Row 1 With MC, k into front, back and front of next st (3 sts), k1; join CC and k3; add new strands of MC, and k1, k2tog. **Row 2** With MC, work to 3 sts before CC sts, p2tog, p1; p3 CC; with MC, p1, p into front and back of next st (2 sts). **Row 3** K3 MC; k3 CC; with MC, k1, k2tog. **Row 4** P2 MC; p3 CC; p3 MC.
Right bow: Row 1 With MC, k2tog, k1; k3 CC; with MC, k1, k3 into 1 st. **Row 2** With MC, work to 2 sts before CC sts, p into front and back of st (2 sts), p1; p3 CC; with MC, p1, p2tog. **Row 3** With MC, work to 3 sts before CC sts, k2tog, k1; k3 CC; k2 MC. **Row 4** P2 MC; p3 CC; p2 MC.
Back bow placement:
Note All bows beg on RS rows. When piece measures 6½"/16.5 cm: **Next row** Cont inc, work 10 (12, 12, 11) sts, work right bow, k51, work left bow, work to end. At 8½"/21.5 cm: **Next row** K49 (51, 53, 55), work center bow, k49 (51, 53, 55). At 12½"/32 cm: **Next row** K17 (19, 21, 23), work left bow, k51, work right bow, k17 (19, 21, 23). At 14½"/37 cm: **Next row** K49 (51, 53, 55), work center bow, k49 (51, 53, 55). At 17½"/44.5 cm: **Next row** K17 (19, 21, 23), work right bow, k51, work left bow, k17 (19, 21, 23).

BACK

With 1 strand A and B, cast on 71 (75, 79, 83) sts. Work in St st for 5 (5, 5½, 6)"/13 (13, 14, 15.5) cm.

Armhole

Inc 1 st each side very row 7 times, then every other row twice. Cast on 3 sts at beg of next 4 rows—101 (105, 109, 113) sts. Work even until armhole measures 10½ (11, 11, 11½)"/26.5 (27.5, 27.5, 29) cm from last cast-on row.

Shoulder and neck shaping

Bind off 5 sts at beg of next 2 (0, 0, 0) rows, 6 sts at beg of next 8 (10, 6, 4) rows, 7 sts at beg of next 0 (0, 4, 6) rows, AT SAME TIME, when piece measures 18¾ (19¼, 19¾, 20¾)"/48 (49, 50, 53) cm from beg, work neck shaping as foll: bind off center 37 (39, 39, 41) sts, and working both sides at once, bind off from each neck edge 2 sts once, 1 st once.

Front bow placement:

When piece measures 5½"/14 cm: **Next row** Cont inc, if necessary, work 37 (39, 38, 40), work center bow, work to end. At 9½"/24 cm: **Next row** K17 (19, 21, 23), work left bow, k51, work right bow, k17 (19, 21, 23). At 10½"/26.5 cm: **Next row** K49 (51, 53, 55), work center bow, k49 (51, 53, 55). At 15½"/39.5 cm: **Next row** K49 (51, 53, 55), work center bow, k49 (51, 53, 55). At 17½"/44.5 cm: **Next row** K17 (19, 21, 23), work right bow, work to last 27 sts, work left bow, k17 (19, 21, 23).

FRONT

Work as for back until piece measures 16¾ (17¼, 17¾, 18¾)"/42.5 (43.5, 44.5, 47.5) cm, from beg, end with a WS row.

Neck shaping

Next row (RS) Work across 43 (45, 46, 48) sts, join 2nd ball of yarn and bind off 15 (15, 17, 17) sts, work to end. Working both sides at once, bind off from each neck edge 5 sts once, bind off from each neck edge 5 sts once, 4 sts once, 2 sts once, dec 1 st every other row 3 (4, 3, 4) times, AT SAME TIME, when same length as back to shoulder, work shoulder shaping as for back.

Sleeve bow placement:

When piece measures 7"/18 cm: **Next row** Work center bow over center 3 sts.
At 10½"/26.5 cm: **Next row** Cont inc, work 13, work left bow, k37, work right bow, work to end. At 15½"/39.5 cm: **Next row** Work center bow over center 3 sts.

SLEEVES

With 1 strand A and B, cast on 43 (45, 45, 47) sts. Work in St st for 2½"/6.5 cm, inc 1 st each side of last row—45 (47, 47, 49) sts. Cont in St st, work 1½"/4 cm even, then inc 1 st each side of next row, then every other row 13 (11, 11, 10) times—every 4th row 8 (10, 10, 11) times—89 (91, 91, 93) sts. Work even until piece measures 15 (15½, 15½, 16)"/37.5 (39, 39, 40.5) cm from beg.

Cap shaping

Bind off 4 (5, 5, 6) sts at beg of next 2 rows, 4 sts at beg of next 14 rows, 3 sts at beg of next 4 rows, 2 sts at beg of next 2 rows. Bind off 9 rem sts.

FINISHING

Block pieces. Sew shoulder seams. Sew top of sleeves to armholes. Sew side and sleeve seams. Cut piece of cord to fit waist. Fold 1½"/4 cm of lower edge of front and back to WS, wrapping around cord. Sew cast-on edge in place. Cut cord for each sleeve edge and work in same way.

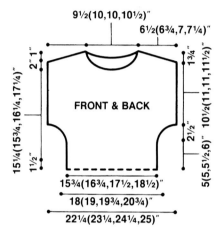

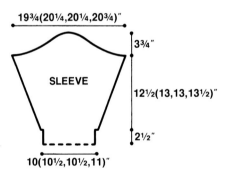

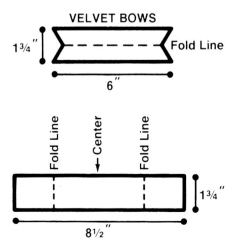

Neckband

With RS facing and 1 strand of A and B, pick up and k 90 (92, 92, 94) sts around neck edge. Work in St st for 2½"/6.5 cm. Bind off loosely. Cut another piece of roll to fit and sew.

Velvet bows

Cut 23 pieces of velvet 6"/15 cm long. Fold each piece lengthwise and cut each end at an angle. Cut 23 pieces 8½"/21.5 cm long. Fold edges to center and fold under small selvage on either side. Stitch down through both thicknesses in center. Place 1 folded piece on top of 1 bow piece and insert into each opening.

Polo Club Sweater

INTERMEDIATE

Standard-fitting cabled pullover with set-in sleeves, updated polo collar and placket. Sized for Small, Medium, Large, and X-Large. Directions are for smallest size with larger sizes in parentheses. If there is only one figure, it applies to all sizes.

SIZES

To fit 32 (34, 36, 38)"/81 (86, 91, 96) cm bust. Directions are for smallest size with larger sizes in parentheses. If there is only one figure it applies to all sizes.

KNITTED MEASUREMENTS
• Bust 34 (36, 38, 40)"/85 (90, 95, 100) cm

• Length 21½ (22, 22½, 23)"/54.5 (56, 57, 58) cm
• Upper arm 14½ (14½, 15, 15)"/36 (36, 37.5, 37.5) cm

MATERIALS [2]
• 13 (14, 14, 15) 1¾oz/50g balls (each approx 176yd/160m) of Froehlich-Wolle/*Renaissance Die tolle Wolle* (wool) in #6252 gold variegated
• To substitute, seek a fingering-weight yarn with similar fiber content
• One pair each sizes 2 and 5 (2.75 and 3.75mm) needles OR SIZE TO OBTAIN GAUGE
• Size 2 (2.75mm) circular needle 16"/40 cm
• Cable needle (cn)
• Stitch holder
• Four ¾"/20mm buttons

GAUGE

40 sts and 37 rows to 4"/10 cm over cable pat using size 5 (3.75mm) needles. TAKE TIME TO CHECK GAUGE.

NOTE

To make gauge swatch, cast on 36 sts. Work cable and rev St st pats as foll: P4, [Work cable pat foll chart over 12 sts, p4] twice. Cont in pats for a total of 32 rows. Piece measures approx 3½"/9 cm square.

STITCH GLOSSARY
12-st Left Cable: Sl 6 sts to cn and hold to front of work, k6, k6 from cn.

BACK

With smaller needles, cast on 136 (144, 152, 160) sts. Work in k1, p1 rib for 3"/7.5 cm, inc 34 (36, 38, 40) sts evenly across last row—170 (180, 190, 200) sts. Change to larger needles. **Beg cable pat: Row 1 (RS)** P4, [work 12-st rep of cable chart, p3 (4, 5, 6)] 10 times, work 12-st rep of cable chart, p4. Cont in pat until piece measures 12½ (13, 13, 13½)"/31.5 (33, 33, 34) cm from beg.

Armhole shaping

Bind off 9 sts at beg of next 2 rows. Dec 1 st each side every other row 8 (9, 10, 11) times—136 (144, 152, 160) sts. Work even until armhole measures 8 (8, 8½, 8½)"/20.5 (20.5, 21.5, 21.5) cm. **Shoulder shaping** Bind off 7 sts at beg of next 4 (0, 0, 0) rows, 8 sts at beg of next 6 (6, 2, 0) rows, 9 sts at beg of next 0 (4, 8, 4) rows, 10 sts at beg of next 0 (0, 0, 6) rows. Bind off rem 60 (60, 64, 64) sts for back neck.

FRONT

Work as for back until piece measures 11½ (12, 12, 12½)"/29 (30.5, 30.5, 31.5) cm from beg, end with a WS row.

Placket shaping

Work 78 (83, 88, 93) sts, place center 14 sts on a holder, join 2nd ball of yarn and work to end. Work both sides at once and working armhole shaping as for back, cont until placket measures 7½ (7½, 8, 8)"/19 (19, 20, 20) cm, end with a WS row.

Neck shaping

Bind off from each neck edge 9 (9, 10, 10) sts once, 5 (5, 6, 6) sts once. Dec 1 st every other row 9 times, AT SAME TIME, when same length as back to shoulder, work shoulder shaping as for back.

SLEEVES

With smaller needles, cast on 66 (72, 78, 82) sts. Work in k1, p1 rib for 3"/7.5 cm, inc 12 (12, 12, 14) sts evenly across last row—78 (84, 90, 96) sts. Change to larger needles. **Beg cable pat: Row 1 (RS)** P3 (4, 5, 6), [work 12-st rep of cable chart, p3 (4, 5, 6)] 5 times. Cont in pat, inc 1 st each side (working inc sts into pat) every 4th row 33 (22, 22, 11) times, every 6th row 0 (8, 8, 16) times— 144 (144, 150, 150) sts. Work even until piece measures 18 (18½, 18½, 19)"/45.5 (47, 47, 48) cm from beg, end with a WS row.

Cap shaping

Bind off 9 sts at beg of next 2 rows. Dec 1 st each side every other row 13 (13, 15, 15) times, every row 8 times. Bind off 7 sts at beg of next 8 rows. Bind off rem 28 (28, 30, 30) sts.

FINISHING

Block pieces. Sew shoulder seams.

Left front placket band

With RS facing and smaller needles, pick up and k16 sts behind sts on holder. Work in k1, p1 rib for 7½ (7½, 8, 8)"/19 (19, 20, 20) cm. Bind off. Sew band to left front. Place markers on band for 4 buttons, the first ¾"/2

cm from lower edge, the last ½"/1.5 cm from top edge and others evenly between.

Right front placket band

Working 14 sts from holder, inc 1 st on either side and work to correspond to left band, working buttonholes opposite markers as foll: **Buttonhole row (RS)** Rib 4 sts, bind off 7 sts, rib to end. On next row, cast on 7 sts over bound-off sts.

Polo collar

With RS facing and circular needle, beg with last 4 sts of right placket band, pick up and k141 (141, 149, 149) sts evenly around neck edge, end with 4 sts of left placket band. Work in k1, p1 rib, inc 1 st each side every 4th row 8 times—157 (157, 165, 165) sts. Cont inc, AT SAME TIME, work short rows as foll: *Next row (RS) Work 8 sts, turn, rib to end. Work 1 row on all sts. **Next row (WS)** Work 8 sts, turn, rib to end. Work 1 row on all sts*. **Next row (RS)** Work 10 sts, turn, rib to end. Work 1 row on all sts. **Next row (WS)** Work 10 sts, turn, rib to end. Work 1 row on all sts. Rep between *'s once more. Bind off all sts. Set in sleeves. Sew side and sleeve seams. Sew on buttons.

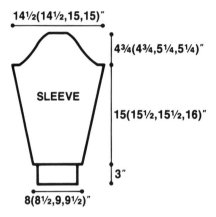

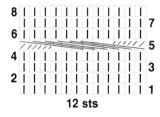

12 sts

☐ k on RS, p on WS
▱ 12-st Cable

Fall 1989 · No. 4

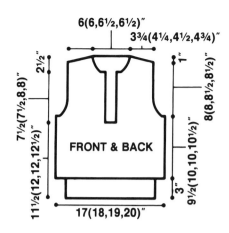

wing Coat

EXPERIENCED

Paneled trapeze coat with set-in sleeves, asymmetrical hem, shawl collar and contrasting trim. One size.

KNITTED MEASUREMENTS

• Total length from center back neck (including ½"/1.5 cm trim) 32½"/81.5 cm
• Upper arm 18"/45 cm

MATERIALS 4

• 26 2oz/60g balls (each approx 100yd/92m) of Melrose *Cablenella* (wool/rayon) in copper (MC)
• To substitute, seek an aran-weight yarn with similar fiber content

23

- 3 balls in black (CC)
- One pair size 7 (4.5mm) needles
OR SIZE TO OBTAIN GAUGE
- Sizes 2 and 6 (2.75 and 4mm)
circular needles 36"/90 cm
- Three 1¼"/3mm large fabric buttons
plus two (optional) for back
- ½yd/.5m seam binding
- Stitch markers

GAUGE
20 sts and 28 rows to 4"/10 cm over
St st using size 7 (4.5mm) needles.
TAKE TIME TO CHECK GAUGE.

NOTES
1) Coat consists of seven panels knit
separately: 3 panels for the back, and 2
panels for each front.
2) For ease in assembling, tag each
piece as it is completed.
3) Since pieces have extensive shaping,
keep careful count of rows.

RIGHT BACK PANEL
With straight needles and MC, cast
on 28 sts. P 1 row on WS, placing
marker at center of row. All length
measurements should be taken from
marker. Cont in St st, cast on 6 sts at
beg of next 8 rows—76 sts. Work in St
st for 6 rows. **Dec row (RS)** K1, ssk,
k to last 3 sts, k2tog, k1. Cont to work
dec row every 8th row 16 times more.
Then dec 1 st at end of RS rows only,
every 8th row twice more, AT SAME
TIME, when piece measures 21¼"/53
cm above marker, end with a WS row
and shape armhole as foll:

Armhole shaping
Bind off 5 sts at beg of next row
(armhole edge), work to end. Cont to
dec 1 st at armhole edge every other
row 9 times, then every 4th row 7
times, then every 6th row 3 times—16
sts. Work even until armhole measures
10¼"/26 cm, end with a WS row.

Shoulder shaping
Bind off from armhole edge 9 sts
once, 7 sts once.

LEFT FRONT SIDE PANEL
Work same as right back panel.

LEFT BACK AND RIGHT FRONT SIDE PANELS
Work as for right back panel, reversing
shaping.

CENTER BACK PANEL
With straight needles and MC, cast
on 28 sts. P 1 row on WS, placing
marker at center of row. All length
measurements should be taken from
marker. Cont in St st, cast on 6 sts at
beg of next 8 rows—76 sts. Work in
St st for 6 rows. Dec 1 st each side of
next row and rep dec every 8th row
18 times more—38 sts. Work even
until piece measures 31½"/79 cm
from marker.

Neck shaping
Next row Work 10 sts, join 2nd ball
of yarn and bind off 18 sts, work to
end. Working both sides at once, bind
off from each neck edge 6 sts once.
Bind off rem 4 sts each side.

LEFT FRONT PANEL
With straight needles and MC, cast
on 33 sts. P 1 row on WS, placing
marker at center of row. All length
measurements should be taken from
marker. Cast on 6 sts at beg of next
row and cont to cast on at same edge
6 sts 3 times more, end with a WS
row—57 sts. Work in St st for 6 rows.
Dec row (RS) K1, ssk, k to end. Cont
to work dec row every 8th row 18
times more—38 sts, end with a RS
row. Work in St st for 3 rows more.

Neck shaping
Row 1 (RS) K to last 3 sts, k2tog
(neck edge), k1. **Row 2 (WS)** P1,
p2tog, p to end. **Row 3** Rep row 1.
Row 4 Purl. Rep last 4 rows 7 times

more—14 sts. Rep rows 3 and 4
until 4 sts rem. Work even until piece
measures 32"/80 cm from marker.
Bind off.

RIGHT FRONT PANEL
With straight needles and MC, cast on
3 sts. P 1 row on WS. Cont in St st,
casting on at beg of WS rows, 3 sts 18
times—57 sts. Place marker at center
of last row. All length measurements
should be taken from marker. Work in
St st for 6 rows. **Dec row (RS)** K to
last 3 sts, k2tog, k1. Cont to work dec
row every 8th row 18 times more—38
sts, end with a RS row. Work even for
1 row. **Next (buttonhole) row (RS)**
K5, bind off 8 sts, k to end. P next row,
casting on 8 sts over bound-off sts.

Neck shaping
Row 1 (RS) K1, ssk, k to end. **Row
2 (WS)** P to last 3 sts, p2tog tbl, p1.
Row 3 Rep row 1. **Row 4** Purl. Rep
last 4 rows 7 times more—14 sts. Rep
rows 3 and 4 until 4 sts rem. Work
even until piece measures 30¾"/77.5
cm from marker. Bind off.

SLEEVES
With straight needles and MC, cast on
54 sts. Work in St st, inc 1 st each side
every 8th row 6 times, every 6th row
6 times, every 4th row 6 times—90
sts. Work even until piece measures
16"/40.5 cm from beg, end with a
WS row.

Cap shaping
Bind off 5 sts at beg of next 2 rows.
Next row (RS) K1, ssk, k to last 3 sts,
k2tog, k1. Cont to work dec row every
other row 4 times more, every 4th
row 8 times, every other row 4 times.
Bind off 2 sts at beg of next 4 rows, AT
SAME TIME, when 60 sts rem, end
with a WS row and work as foll:

Dart shaping
Next row (RS) K28, k2tog, ssk,
k28—58 sts. Cont to work dart dec
row in center every 4th row 5 times
more. Bind off rem 26 sts.

LEFT COLLAR
With straight needles and MC, cast on
40 sts. P 1 row on WS. Work shaping
at front edge (beg of RS rows) and at
center back edge (beg of WS rows)
simultaneously as foll: For front edge,

cast on 5 sts at beg of next row and cont to cast on at same edge 5 sts 5 times more, work 5 rows even. **Next row (RS)** Bind off 2 sts, work to end. P 1 row. **Next row** Bind off 1 st, work to end. P 1 row. Rep last 4 rows twice more. Cont to bind off at same edge 2 sts 3 times, 3 sts 3 times, 4 sts 3 times, 6 sts twice, AT SAME TIME, at center back edge, after 9 rows have been worked from beg, work as foll: **Next row (RS)** Work to last 2 sts, m1 (center back edge), k2. Cont to inc 1 st at this edge every 8th row 4 times more. Bind off rem 27 sts.

RIGHT COLLAR
Work as for left collar, reversing all shaping.

FINISHING
Block pieces. Sew left and right back panels to center back panel. Sew right front side panel to right front panel. Sew two left front panels in same way. Sew side seams.

Right front trim
With WS facing, smaller circular needle and CC, beg at first neck dec, pick up and k2 sts in every 3 rows along front edge to lower edge. Change to larger circular needle. (K 1 row, p 1 row) twice. Bind off. Let trim roll naturally to RS and sew in place. Work trim along left front edge in same way.

Lower edge trim
With WS facing, smaller circular needle and CC, pick up and k68 sts along lower edge of first right front panel, 80 sts along each of next 5 panels, 58 sts along left front panel—526 sts. Change to larger circular needle. Work trim as for right front. Join edges at corners.

Sleeve trim
With WS facing, smaller circular needle and CC, pick up and k 1 st in each cast-on st at lower edge of sleeve. Change to larger circular needle and work trim as for right front.

Collar trim
Sew left and right collars tog along center back inc edge. With WS facing, smaller circular needle and CC, beg at cast-on edge, pick up and k3 sts along short side to bound-off edge, 153 sts along bound-off edge, 3 sts along short side. Change to larger circular needle and work trim as for right front. With WS of collar and RS of coat tog, pin cast-on edge of collar evenly around neck edge and sew in place. Sew seam binding to WS along neck and shoulders. Join edges of trim. Set in sleeves. Sew sleeve seams. Sew button on left front. Sew one button on each sleeve cuff. If desired, sew two buttons on back panel, 3"/7.5 cm and 5½"/14 cm from center back neck.

Fall 1989 · No. 23

ⅅubble Sweater

EXPERIENCED

Very oversized, balloon pullover with angled pockets, ribbed yoke and high neck by Marc Jacobs for Perry Ellis. One size.

KNITTED MEASUREMENTS
• Length 30"/76.5 cm
• Width of lower edge rib 36"/44.5 cm
• Width from sleeve cuff to sleeve cuff 73"/185.5 cm

MATERIALS ④
• 26 1½oz/40g balls (each approx 90yd/82m) of Classic Elite *La Gran* (mohair/wool/nylon) in #3594 purple variegated
• To substitute, seek an aran-weight yarn with similar fiber content
• Sizes 10 and 11 (6 and 8mm) circular needles 29"/80 cm OR SIZE TO OBTAIN GAUGE
• Size 10 (6mm) circular needle 16"/40 cm
• Size 11 (8mm) double pointed needles (dpns)
• Stitch holders and stitch markers

GAUGE
• 12 sts and 16 rows to 4"/10 cm over St stand 2 strands held tog, using size 11 (8mm) needle.
• 13 sts to 4"/10 cm over twisted rib and 2 strands held tog using size 11 (8mm) needle. TAKE TIME TO CHECK GAUGES. **Note** As gauge may differ between working flat in back and forth rows and working circularly in rounds, check work after a few inches and adjust needle size if necessary.

NOTES
1) Body of sweater is knit in one

circular piece to underarm. Sleeves are knit separately to underarm, then joined to body at yoke.
2) Work with 2 strands of yarn held tog throughout.
3) To enlarge rib at lower edge, cast on 128 sts and omit inc on rnd 1.

BODY

With larger 29"/80 cm needle and 2 strands, cast on 116 sts. Join, taking care not to twist sts on needle. Place marker for end of rnd, and sl marker every rnd. **Twisted rib: Rnd 1 (RS)** *k1 tbl, p1; rep from * around. Rep rnd 1 for twisted rib for 2½"/6.5 cm. Work in St st as foll: **Rnd 1** *K10, inc 1 st as foll: k in 1 strand of st, then k in 2nd strand of same st, [k8, inc 1] twice; rep from * 3 times more—128 sts. K 4 rnds. **Note** Use a different color marker for inc rnds to distinguish them from end of rnd marker. **Rnd 6** *K7, inc 1 (placing marker between 2 new sts), k16, inc1 (placing marker), k14, inc 1 (placing marker), k16, inc 1 (placing marker), k7; rep from * once more—136 sts. **Rnd 7** *K to 3 sts before next marker, inc 1; rep from * around—144 sts. K 5 rnds, sl markers every rnd. **Rnd 13** *K to next marker, remove marker, inc 1 (placing marker between 2 new sts); rep from * around—152 sts. Rep rnds 7-13 for 5 times more, then work rnd 7 once more, AT SAME TIME, after 18 rnds have been worked above rib and there are 160 sts on needle, work as foll:

Pocket linings (make 2)

With larger needle and 2 strands, cast on 18 sts. Work in St for 4¾"/12 cm. Place sts on a holder.

Pocket joining

Rnd 19 K12, sl next 18 sts to a holder for left pocket, removing marker, k across sts on one lining, placing marker on lining in correct position, k20, sl next 18 sts to holder for right pocket, k across sts of 2nd lining, k to end of rnd. After all incs have been worked, work even on rem 240 sts until piece measures 17"/43 cm from beg.

Divide for front and back

Bind off 6 sts (underarm) or place sts on a holder to graft tog, work until there are 108 sts from bind-off, sl sts to holder for front, bind off next 12 sts (underarm), work until there are 108 sts from bind-off, sl sts to holder for back, bind off rem 6 sts.

SLEEVES

With smaller 16"/40 cm needle and 2 strands, cast on 52 sts. Join, taking care not to twist sts. Work in twisted rib for 1¼"/3 cm. Change to size 11 (8mm) dpn and k 5 rnds. **Note** Change to circular needle once there are enough sts to fit around needle. **Rnd 6** (Inc 1 st, k12) 4 times—56 sts. K 5 rnds. **Rnd 12** (Inc 1 st, k13) 4 times—60 sts. K 5 rnds. Cont in this way to inc 4 sts (adding 1 more st between incs each inc rnd) every 6th rnd 6 times more—84 sts. K 7 rnds. **Next rnd** (Inc 1 st, k13) 6 times—90 sts. Work even until piece measures 16½"/42 cm from beg. Bind off 6 sts, work until there are 78 sts from bind-off, sl sts to holder, bind off rem 6 sts.

YOKE

Next (joining) row With larger 29"/80 cm needle, k sts from holders as foll: 108 sts of front, 78 sts of right sleeve, 108 sts of back, 78 sts of left sleeve—372 sts. Join and work in rnds as foll: K 4 rnds. **Rnd 5** *K6, k2tog, (k6, k2tog, k7, k2tog) 5 times; rep from * 3 times more—328 sts. K 4 rnds. **Rnd 10** *K2 (k2tog, k6, k2tog, k5) 5 times, k2tog, k3; rep from * 3 times more—284 sts. K 4 rnds. **Rnd 15** *K4, k2tog, (k4, k2tog, k5, k2tog) 5 times; rep from * 3 times more—240 sts. K 4 rnds. **Rnd 20** *K1, (k2tog, k4, k2tog, k3) 5 times, k2tog, k2; rep from * 3 times more—196 sts K 4 rnds. **Rnd 25** *K2, k2tog, (k3, k2tog, k2, k2tog) 5times; rep from * 3 times more—152 sts. K 4 rnds. Work in k2, p2, rib for 2½"6.5 cm. Change to smaller circular needle. **Next rnd** *K2, p2tog; rep from * around—114 sts. Work in k2, p1 rib for 2½"/6.5 cm **Next rnd** *K2tog, p1; rep from * around—76 sts. Work in twisted rib as for body for 5"/12.5 cm. Bind off in rib.

FINISHING

Sew bound-off armhole sts tog at underarm or graft tog.

Right pocket edging

With RS facing and larger needle, work sts from holder as foll: **Next row** K6, turn, p to end. **Next row** K12, turn, purl to end. **Next row** K18. Change to smaller needle and work in twisted rib for 1"/2.5 cm. Bind off. With WS of pocket facing, work left pocket edging to correspond to right pocket. Sew pocket linings to WS of front. Sew sides of pockets to front.

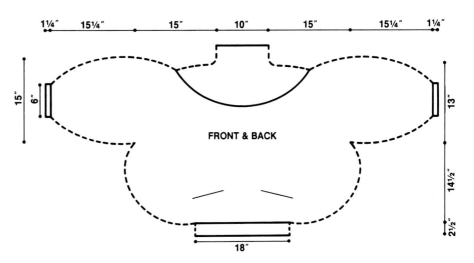

FRONT & BACK

Zigzag Stitch Sweater

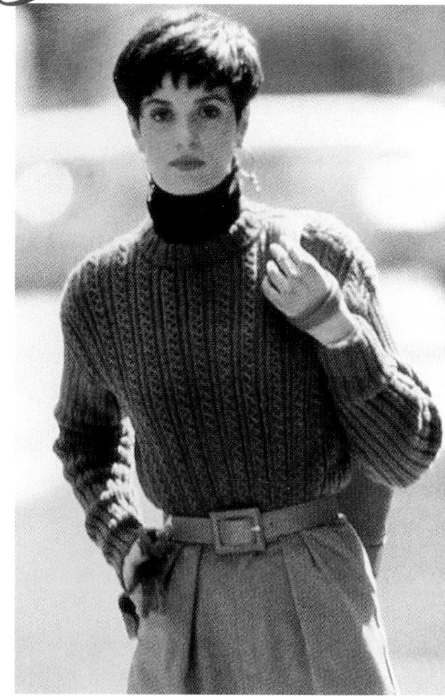

VERY EASY VERY VOGUE

Standard-fitting, zigzag stitch pullover with angled armholes, ribbed sleeves and foldover crewneck. Sized for X-Small, Small, Medium, Large, and X-Large. Directions are for smallest size with larger sizes in parentheses. If there is only one figure, it applies to all sizes.

KNITTED MEASUREMENTS

• Bust at underarm 37½ (40, 42½, 45, 48)"/94 (100, 106, 113, 119) cm
• Length 24½ (25, 25½, 26, 26½)"/62.5 (64, 65, 66, 67.5) cm
• Upper arm 13 (13, 13¾, 13¾, 14½)"/33 (33, 34.5, 34.5, 36.5) cm

MATERIALS 3

• 12 (13, 13, 14, 14) 1¾oz/50g balls (each approx 132yd/120m) of Christian de Falbe *Chandos* (wool) in #27 olive
• To substitute, seek a DK-weight yarn with similar fiber content
• One pair each sizes 4, 5, 6, and 7 (3½, 3¾, 4, and 4.5mm) needles OR SIZE TO OBTAIN GAUGE
• Size 5 (3.75mm) circular needle 16"/40 cm
• Cable needle (cn)

GAUGES

• 31 sts and 30 rows to 4"/10 cm over zigzag
pat using size 7 (4.5mm) needles.
• 28 sts and 30 rows to 4"/10 cm over k2, p2 rib (slightly stretched) using size 6 (4mm) needles. TAKE TIME TO CHECK GAUGES.

NOTES

1) Foll either written or chart instructions for zigzag pat.
2) When binding off in zigzag pat, k3 or p3 tog over 3-st RC or LC.

STITCH GLOSSARY

3-st Right Cross (RC): Sl 2 sts to cn and hold to back of work, k1, k2 from cn.
3-st Left Cross (LC): Sl 1 st to cn and hold to front of work, k2, k1 from cn.

Zigzag pattern

(multiple of 10 sts + 5 extra)
Row 1 (RS) *P2, k1, p2, k1tbl, RC, k1 tbl; rep from *, end p2, k1, p2.
Rows 2 and 4 (WS) *K2, p1, k2, sl 1 wyif, p3, sl 1 wyif; rep from *, end k2, p1, k2. **Row 3** *P2, k1, p2, k1 tbl, LC, k1 tbl; rep from *, end p2, k1, p2.
Rep rows 1-4 for zigzag pat.

Rib pattern

(multiple of 8 sts + 5 extra)
Row 1 (RS) P2, *k1, p2, k3, p2; rep from *, end k1, p2.
Row 2 K the knit sts and p the purl sts.
Rep last row for rib pat.

BACK

With size 5 (3.75mm) needles, cast on 117 (125, 133, 141, 149) sts. Work in rib pat for 2½"/6.5 cm from beg, end with a RS row. Change to size 7 (4.5mm) needles. **Next row (WS)** *K5, ml, k3, ml; rep from *, end k3—145 (155, 165, 175, 185) sts. Work in zigzag pat until piece measures 14 (14½, 14½, 15, 15)"/35.5 (37, 37, 38, 38) cm from beg.

Armhole shaping

Bind off 3 (3, 3, 4, 4) sts at beg of next 2 rows, 2 sts at beg of next 0 (0, 2, 2, 4) rows. Dec 1 st each side every other row 6 (7, 6, 6, 5) times—127 (135, 143, 151, 159) sts. Work even until armhole measures 9 (9, 9½, 9½, 10)", 23 (23, 24, 24, 25.5) cm.

Shoulder and neck shaping

Bind off 6 (7, 7, 8, 8) sts at beg of next 8 (12, 6, 10, 4) rows, 7 (0, 8, 9, 9) sts at beg of next 4 (0, 6, 2, 8) rows, AT SAME TIME, after 6 rows of shoulder shaping have been worked, bind off center 35 (35, 37, 37, 39) sts for back neck and working both sides at once with separate balls of yarn, bind off from each neck edge 8 sts once.

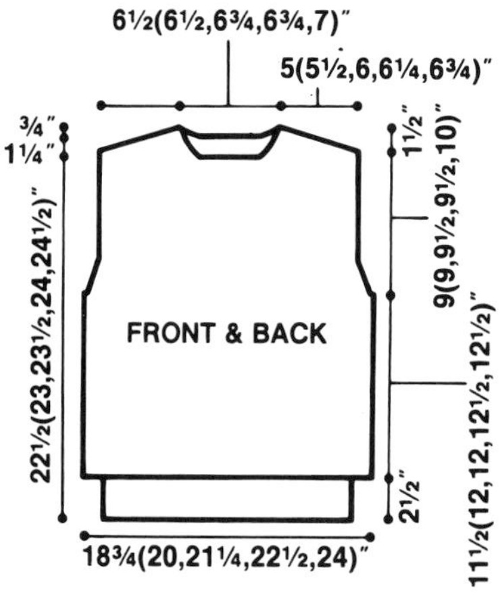
6½(6½,6¾,6¾,7)"
5(5½,6,6¼,6¾)"
¾"
1¼"
1½"
9(9,9½,9½,10)"
22½(23,23½,24,24½)"
FRONT & BACK
11½(12,12,12½,12½)"
2½"
18¾(20,21¼,22½,24)"

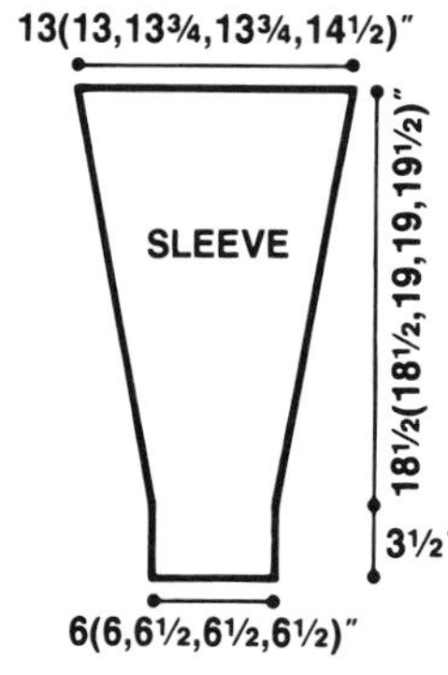
13(13,13¾,13¾,14½)"
SLEEVE
18½(18½,19,19,19½)"
3½"
6(6,6½,6½,6½)"

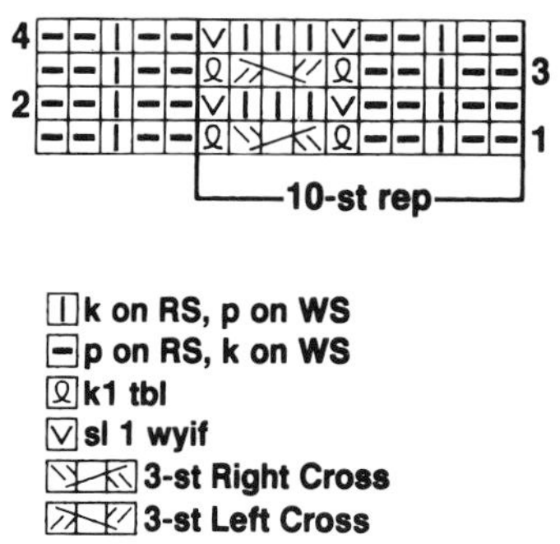
4
3
2
1
10-st rep
k on RS, p on WS
p on RS, k on WS
k1 tbl
sl 1 wyif
3-st Right Cross
3-st Left Cross

FRONT

Work as for back until armhole measures 8½ (8½, 9, 9, 9½)"/22 (22, 23, 23, 24.5) cm, end with a WS row.

Neck and shoulder shaping

Next row (RS) Work 49 (53, 56, 60, 63) sts; join 2nd ball of yarn and bind off 29 (29, 31, 31, 33) sts, work to end. Working both sides at once, bind off from each neck edge 3 sts once, 2 sts 4 times, AT SAME TIME, when same length as back to shoulder, shape shoulder as for back.

SLEEVES

With size 4 (3.5mm) needles, cast on 58 (58, 62, 62, 62) sts. Work in k2, p2 rib for 3½"/9 cm. Change to size 6 (4mm) needles. Cont in rib, inc 1 st each side (working inc sts into rib) every 6th row 3 (3, 1, 1, 11) times, every 8th row 14 (14, 16, 16, 9) times—92 (92, 96, 96, 102) sts. Work even in rib until piece measures 22 (22, 22½, 22½, 23)"/55 (55, 56.5, 56.5, 57.5) cm from beg, end with a WS row. Bind off purlwise on RS.

FINISHING

Block pieces. Sew shoulder seams.

Neckband

With RS facing and circular needle, pick up and k88 (88, 88, 88, 96) sts evenly around neck edge. Join. P 1 rnd. Beg rib pat: **Row 1** ★K1, p2, k3, p2; rep from ★ to end. Cont in rib pat for 2½"/6.5 cm. Bind off in rib. Fold neckband in half to WS and sew in place. Center sleeve at shoulder, stretching sleeve to fit, pin in place. Sew sleeve to armhole. Sew side and sleeve seams.

Fall 1990 • No. 12

$\mathcal{M}$issoni Jacket

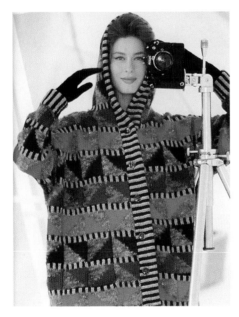

EXPERIENCED

Oversized, diagonal blocked-pattern cardigan with modified set-in sleeves, hood and striped bands. By Missoni. One size.

KNITTED MEASUREMENTS
• Bust at underarm (buttoned) 58½"/148.5 cm
• Length 31¼"/79.5 cm
• Upper arm 16¼"/41 cm

MATERIALS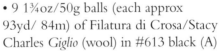
• 9 1¾oz/50g balls (each approx 93yd/ 84m) of Filatura di Crosa/Stacy Charles *Giglio* (wool) in #613 black (A)
• To substitute, seek an aran-weight yarn with similar fiber content
• 5 balls #617 gray (B)
• 3 balls each #618 purple (C), #628 orange (D), and #626 green (E)
• 3 1¾oz/50g balls (each approx 117 yd/105m) of Filatura di Crosa/Stacy Charles *Andros* (mohair/cotton/polyester/nylon) #202 yellow/green variegated (F)
• To substitute, seek a worsted-weight tape or ribbon yarn with similar fiber content
• 2 balls each #203 pink/orange variegated (G) and #204 purple/pink variegated (H)
• One pair each sizes 6 and 8 (4 and 5mm) needles OR SIZE TO OBTAIN GAUGE
• Size 6 (4mm) circular needle 36"/ 90 cm
• Bobbins and stitch holders
• Seven 1"/25mm buttons

GAUGE
36 sts to 7"/18 cm and 40 rows to 6½"/16.5 cm in St st over chart 2 using size 8 (5mm) needles. TAKE TIME TO CHECK GAUGE.

NOTE
Use bobbins for large blocks of color. When changing colors, twist yarns on WS to prevent holes.

BACK
With smaller needles and A, cast on 144 sts. Work in St st for 16 rows (hem facing). Work rows 1-4 of chart 1 for 4 times. Change to larger needles. Beg chart 2 as foll: Work 36-st rep of chart 4 times. Cont in pat as established through row 60. Rep rows 1-50 once more—piece measures approx 18"/45.5 cm from first row of chart 2.

Armhole shaping
Cont in pat, bind off 2 sts at beg of next 4 rows. Dec 1 st each side every other row twice—132 sts. Cont in chart pat until armhole measures 8¾"/22 cm.

Shoulder and neck shaping
Bind off 7 sts at beg of next 10 rows, 8 sts at beg of next 2 rows, AT SAME TIME, after 4 rows of shoulder

shaping have been worked, bind off center 30 sts for neck, and working both sides at once with separate balls of yarn, bind off from each neck edge 6 sts once, 2 sts once.

POCKET LININGS (make 2)
With larger needles and A, cast on 34 sts. Work in St st for 40 rows. Place sts on holder.

LEFT FRONT
With smaller needles and A, cast on 72 sts. Work hem facing and chart 1 as for back. Change to larger needles. Beg chart 2 as foll: Work 36-st rep of chart twice. Cont in pat until 40 rows of chart have been worked.

Pocket joining
Next row (RS) Work 20 sts, place next 34 sts on holder, with RS of lining facing WS of piece, work in pat across sts of one pocket lining, work to end. Cont in pat until same length as back to armhole. Work armhole shaping at side edge only (beg of RS rows) as for back—66 sts. Work even in pat until armhole measures 8"/20.5 cm, end with a RS row.

Neck and shoulder shaping
Next row (WS) Bind off 10 sts (neck edge), work to end. Cont to bind off 3 sts 3 times, then dec 1 st at neck edge every other row 4 times, AT SAME TIME, when same length as back to shoulder, work shoulder shaping at beg of RS rows as for back.

RIGHT FRONT
Work as for left front, reversing all shaping and pocket placement.

SLEEVES
With smaller needles and A, cast on 48 sts. Work hem facing and chart 1 as for back. Change to larger needles.

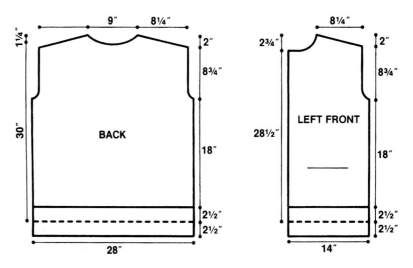

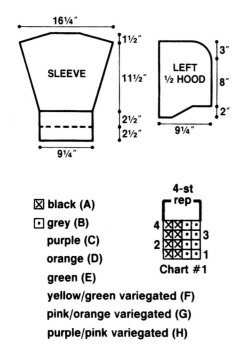

⊠ black (A)
⊡ grey (B)
purple (C)
orange (D)
green (E)
yellow/green variegated (F)
pink/orange variegated (G)
purple/pink variegated (H)

4-st rep
Chart #1

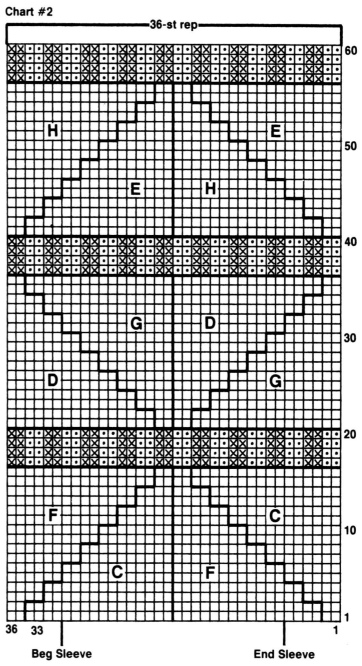

Chart #2

INSTRUCTIONS 218

Next row (RS) Beg with row 41 of chart 2 as indicated, work 36-st rep once, end as indicated. Cont in pat inc 1 st each side (working inc sts into pat) every other row 4 times, every 4th row 14 times—84sts. Work even in pat until piece measures 11½"/29 cm from beg of chart 2, ending with row 50.

Cap shaping
Cont in chart pat, bind off 6 sts at beg of next 10 rows. Bind off rem 24 sts.

HOOD
Left half
Cast on 10 sts with E. Work chart pat and inc simultaneously as foll: Beg with row 43 of chart 2, inc 3 sts at end of next row and every WS row (back edge of hood) 5 times more. Cast on 20 sts at end of next WS row—48 sts. Work even in chart pat

as established until piece measures approx 8"/20.5 cm from last inc row, end with row 48 of chart. Dec 1 st at beg of next RS row (back edge of hood), then at same edge 5 times mores, 3 sts once, 5 sts once, 6 sts once. Bind off rem 28 sts.

Right half
Work as for left half reversing all shaping.

FINISHING
Block pieces. Sew shoulder seams. Sew back edge of hood, then sew hood along neck edge, easing to fit.

Left front band
With circular needle and A, cast on 228 sts. Work 16 rows in St st (facing). Work rows 1-4 of chart 1 4 times. Bind off. Sew bound-off edge of band along left front edge to center of hood. Place markers for 7 buttons,

the first 1"/2.5 cm lower edge and last at neck edge with 5 others evenly between.

Right front band
Work as for left front band, working buttonholes opposite markers on row 7 of facing and row 11 of stripe pat by binding off 2 sts and then casting on 2 sts on next row. Sew right band as for left, seaming band tog at center of hood. Fold band to WS and sew in place. Sew through both thicknesses around buttonholes. Sew on buttons. Set in sleeves. Sew side and sleeve seams, fold hem facings to WS and sew in place.

Fall 1991 • No. 14

𝒮inuous Sweater

EXPERIENCED

Oversized, cropped, blister stitch pullover with drop shoulders and foldover neckband. Sized for Small, Medium and Large. Directions are for smallest size with larger sizes in parentheses. If there is only one figure, it applies to all sizes.

KNITTED MEASUREMENTS
• Bust at underarm 41 (47, 51)"/104 (119.5, 129.5) cm
• Length 21 (22, 23)"/53.5 (56, 58.5) cm
• Upper arm 17 (18, 19)"/43 (45.5, 48) cm

MATERIALS 🔵4
• 10 (11, 12) 1¾oz/50g balls (each approx 146yd/136m) of Filatura di Crosa/Stacy Charles *Sympathie* (wool/mohair/acrylic) in #754 gray heather
• To substitute, seek aran-weight yarn with fiber content similar to the original yarns.
• One pair each sizes 5 and 7 (3.75 and 4.5mm) needles OR SIZE TO OBTAIN GAUGE
• Size 5 (3.75mm) circular needle

16"/40 cm

GAUGE
• 19 sts and 27 rows to 4"/10 cm over St st using size 7 (4.5mm) needles.
• 24 sts to 4¾"/12 cm and 40 rows to 4½"/11.5 cm over chart pat, relaxed using size 7 (4.5mm) needles. TAKE TIME TO CHECK GAUGES.

BACK
With smaller needles, cast on 93 (107, 115) sts. Work in k1, p1 rib for 2"/5 cm, end with a RS row. Change to larger needles. P 1 row, inc 10 (12, 12) sts evenly across—103 (119, 127) sts. Beg and end as indicated, work chart pat until piece measures approx 21 (22, 23)"/53.5 (56, 58.5) cm from beg, end with a WS row. Bind off.

FRONT
Work as for back until piece measures 18½ (19½, 20½)"/47 (49.5, 52) cm

from beg, end with a WS row.

Neck shaping

Next row (RS) Work 44 (51, 55) sts, join 2nd ball of yarn and bind off 15 (17, 17) sts, work to end. Working both sides at once, bind off at each neck edge 4 sts once, 3 sts once, 2 sts twice, 1 st 4 times. Work even until same length as back. Bind off rem 29 (36, 40) sts each side for shoulders.

SLEEVES

With smaller needles, cast on 45 (51, 55) sts. Work in k1, p1 rib for 1"/2.5 cm, end with a WS row. Change to larger needles. Work in St st, inc 1 st each side (working inc sts into St st) every 6th row 18 times—81 (87, 91) sts. Work even until piece measures 18"/45.5 cm from beg. Bind off.

FINISHING

Block pieces. Sew shoulder seams.

Neckband

With RS facing and circular needle, pick up and k 106 (106, 110) sts evenly around neck edge. Work in k1, p1 rib for 3¾"/9.5 cm. Bind of loosely. Fold band in half to WS and sew in place. Place markers 8½ (9, 9½)"/21.5 (23, 24) cm down from shoulders on front and back for arm holes. Sew top of sleeves between markers. Sew side and sleeve seams.

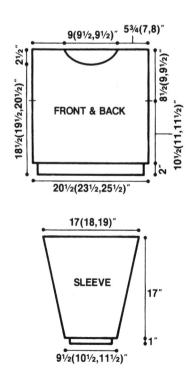

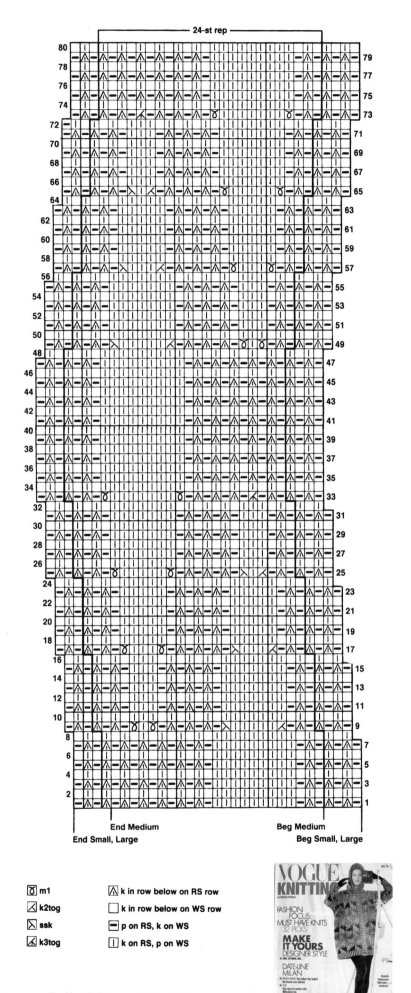

m1	k in row below on RS row
k2tog	k in row below on WS row
ssk	p on RS, k on WS
k3tog	k on RS, p on WS

Fall 1991 · No. 19

$\mathcal{T}$rapeze Dress

relaxed

INTERMEDIATE

Loose-fitting, trapeze-shaped dress with raglan armholes, V-neck, hemmed lower edge and cuffs, contrasting cuff and ribbed tie collar. Sized for Small, Medium, and Large. Directions are for smallest size with larger sizes in parentheses. If there is only one figure, it applies to all sizes.

KNITTED MEASUREMENTS
• Bust at underarm 40 (42, 44)"/102 (107, 112) cm
• Length 33 (34, 35)"/83.5 (86, 89) cm
• Upper arm 15 (15½, 16)"/38 (39.5, 40.5) cm

MATERIALS 4
• 9 (9, 10) 1¾oz/50g balls (each approx 152yd/140m) of Tiber/Classic Elite *Mohair Doux* (kid mohair/acrylic) in #156 toffee (MC)
• 3 balls in #69 brown (CC)
• One pair each sizes 5 and 6 (3.75 and 4mm) needles OR SIZE TO OBTAIN GAUGE
• Size G (4.5mm) crochet hook
• Stitch marker

GAUGE
• 20 sts and 25 rows to 4"/10 cm over St st using size 6 (4mm) needles.
• 30 sts and 28 rows to 4"/10 cm over k1, p1 rib using size 5 (3.75mm) needles. TAKE TIME TO CHECK GAUGE.

STITCH GLOSSARY
sssk: Sl next 3 sts knitwise, one at a time, to RH needle, insert tip of LH needle into fronts of these sts and k them tog.
Double Dec
Row 1 (RS) K1, sssk, work to last 4 sts, k3 tog, k1.
Row 2 (WS) P.
Single Dec
Row 1 (RS) K1, ssk, work to last 3 sts, k2 tog, k1.
Row 2 (WS) P.

BACK
With smaller needles and MC, cast on 150 (156, 160) sts. Work in St st (k on RS, p on WS) for 1½"/4 cm, end with a RS row. K next row on WS for turning ridge. Change to larger needles and work in St st for 1½"/4 cm more. **Beg side shaping: Next row (RS)** Dec 1st at each side on next row, then every 6th row 15 (18, 19) times more, every 4th row 9 (6, 5) times—100 (106, 110) sts. Work even until piece measures 23¼ (24¼, 24¾)"/59 (61.5, 63) cm from turning ridge, end with a WS row.
Raglan armhole shaping
Next row (RS) Work [double dec once, single dec once] 5 (7, 6) times, then work single dec 17 (14, 18) times—36 (36, 38) sts. Work 2 (0, 0) more rows in St st. Bind off rem sts for neck.

FRONT
Work as for back until piece measures 22¼ (23¼, 24¼)"/56.5 (59, 61.5) cm from turning ridge, mark center st on last WS row.
Neck shaping
Next row (RS) Work to last 3 sts before marker, k2 tog, k1, join 2nd ball of yarn, k1, ssk, k to end. Cont to dec as established from each neck edge every 4th row 13 (13, 12) times, then every other row 4 (4, 6) times, AT SAME TIME, when piece measures same length as back to armhole, work raglan armhole shaping as for back.

SLEEVES
With smaller needles and CC, cast on 67 (69, 73) sts. Work in k1, p1 rib for 2"/5 cm. K all sts on next WS row for turning ridge. Cont to work in rib pat as established for 2"/5 cm above turning ridge, end with a WS row. Change to larger needles and MC.
Dec row (RS) K2 (2, 0), *k2 tog, k2; rep from * across row 16 (16, 18) times, k1 (3, 1)—51 (53, 55) sts. P next row. Cont in St st, inc 1 st each side on next row, then every 6th row 6 (5, 7) times more, every 8th row 5 (6, 5) times—75 (77, 81) sts. Work even until piece measures 16 (16½, 17)/40 (41, 42.5) cm from turning ridge.
Raglan cap shaping
Next row (RS) Work (double dec once, single dec once) 5 (6, 6) times, then single dec 18 (16, 18) times. Bind off rem 9 sts.
Tie collar
With smaller needles and CC, cast on 21 sts. Work in k1, p1 rib for 2"/5 cm.
Inc shaping (RS) Cont in rib across row, inc 1 st at end, mark for neck edge. Cont to inc at neck edge 1 st every other row 39 more times—61 sts. **Short row shaping (RS)** *K7, wrap next st, turn. **Next row** Work in rib to end. **Next row (RS)** Work 15 sts, wrap next st, turn. **Next row** Work in rib to end. Cont to work 8 more sts at end of RS row 5 more times. Work 16 rows even in rib on all sts. * Rep between *'s twice, then rep short row shaping once. **Dec shaping (RS)** Dec 1 st at neck edge every other row 40 times—21 sts. Work even in rib for 20"/51 cm. Bind off in rib.

FINISHING
Sew raglan sleeve caps to front and back raglan armholes. Sew side and sleeve seams. Fold hem and cuffs to wrong side and sew in place.

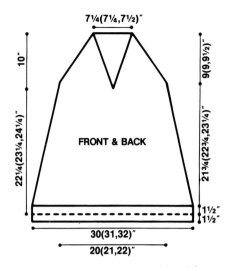

7¼(7¼,7½)"

10"

9(9,9½)"

FRONT & BACK

22¼(23¼,24¼)"

21¾(22¾,23¼)"

1½"
1½"

30(31,32)"

20(21,22)"

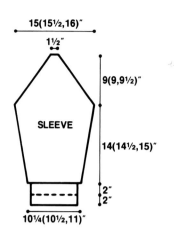

15(15½,16)"

1½"

9(9,9½)"

SLEEVE

14(14½,15)"

2"
2"

10¼(10½,11)"

Collar

Mark 2"/5 cm above beg of front neck shaping on each side. Sew neck edge of tie collar to neck edge of dress between markers. With crochet hook and MC, work 1 row sc evenly along rem front neck between markers.

Fall 1991 · No. 31

VERY EASY VERY VOGUE

Standard-fitting pullover with knit-in sequin yarn, raglan armholes, scoop neck and applied feather trim. Sized for Small, Medium, Large, and X-Large. Directions are for smallest size with larger sizes in parentheses. If there is only one figure, it applies to all sizes.

KNITTED MEASUREMENTS

• Bust at underarm 36 (39, 41, 43½, 45½)"/91.5 (99, 104, 110.5, 115.5) cm
• Length 18 (18¼, 19¾, 20, 21½)"/45.5 (46.5, 50, 50.5, 54.5) cm
• Upper arm 12½ (13½, 14½, 15¼, 16¼)"/32 (34.5, 37, 38.5, 41.5) cm

MATERIALS ④

• 7 (7, 8, 9, 9) 1¾oz/50g balls (each approx 90yd/82m) of Classic Elite *Paisley* (wool/rayon) in #1713 black (MC)
• 14 (15, 17, 19, 22).4oz/10g balls (each approx 32 yd/27m) of Tiber/Classic Elite *Ecailles* (wool/polyester/cotton) in #1802 black (CC)
• To substitute, seek aran-weight yarns with fiber content similar to the original yarns
• One pair each sizes 7 and 8 (4.5 and 5mm) needles OR SIZE TO OBTAIN GAUGE
• One feather boa, approx 40"/101 cm long

GAUGE

17 sts and 24 rows to 4"/10 cm over rev St st with 1 strand of MC and CC held tog using size 8 (5mm) needles. TAKE TIME TO CHECK GAUGE

NOTE

Body of sweater is worked with 1 strand MC and CC held tog, pushing sequins to RS of work.

BACK

With smaller needles and MC, cast on 85 (91, 97, 103, 109) sts. Work in k1,

p1 rib for 1"/2.5 cm, end with a WS row. Change to larger needles, adding 1 strand CC. **Next row (RS)** Work rev St st (p on RS, k on WS), dec 24 (26, 26, 28, 30) sts evenly across—61 (65, 71, 75, 79) sts. Cont in rev St st, inc 1 st each side every 4th row 8 (9, 8, 9, 9) times—77 (83, 87, 93, 97) sts. Work even until piece measures 9 (9, 10, 10, 11)"/23 (23, 25.5, 25.5, 28) cm from beg. end with a WS row.

Raglan armhole shaping

Bind off 4 (4, 4, 5, 5) sts at beg of next 2 rows. Dec 1 st each side every other row, then work 1 row even 1 (0, 1, 0, 1) time. [Dec 1 st each side every row 3 times, then work 1 row even] 4 (5, 5, 6, 6) times—43 (45, 47, 47, 49) sts. Change to smaller needles and MC only. Work in k1, p1 rib for 1¼"/3 cm. Bind off loosely.

FRONT

Work same as for back.

SLEEVES

With smaller needles and MC, cast on 35 (35, 37, 39, 41) sts. Work in k1, p1 rib for 2½"/6.5 cm, end with a WS row. Change to larger needles, adding 1 strand CC. Work in rev St st, inc 1 st each side every 6th row 0 (0, 1, 5,

8) times, every 8th row 0 (9, 11, 8, 6) times, every 10th row 9 (2, 0, 0, 0) times—53 (57, 61, 65, 69) sts. Work even until piece measures 18 (18½, 18½, 19, 19)"/45.5 (47, 47, 48, 48) cm from beg. End with a WS row.

Raglan cap shaping
Bind off 4 (4, 4, 5, 5) sts at beg of next 2 rows. Dec 1 st each side every other row 0 (1, 1, 1, 3) times, every 6th row every 4 (4, 1, 0, 0) times, every 4th row 0 (0, 5, 7, 7) times. Work even on 37 (39, 39, 39, 39) sts until raglan shaping measures 4¾ (5½, 5¾, 6, 6½)"/12 (14, 14.5, 15, 16.5) cm. Change to smaller needles and MC only. Work in k1, p1, rib for 1¼"/ 3 cm. Bind off loosely.

FINISHING
Block pieces. Sew raglan sleeve caps to raglan armholes. Sew side and sleeve seams. Cut feather boa to fit along neck edge and sew in place, joining ends.

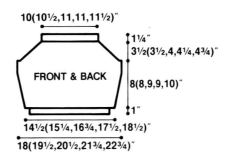

Winter 1991-1992 · No. 19

$\mathcal{D}$esert Garden Pullover

EXPERIENCED

Very oversized, textured stitch pullover with square armholes, front mosaic block pattern, modified highneck and bicolor ribs. By DKNY. One size.

KNITTED MEASUREMENTS
• Bust at underarm 56"/142 cm
• Length 28"/71 cm
• Upper arm 20"/51 cm

MATERIALS 4
• 11 1 1/3oz/50g balls (approx 136yd/124m) of Classic Elite *Willough* (cotton/silk) in #3686 rose-beige (MC)
• To substitute, seek a worsted-weight yarn with similar fiber content
• 3 balls in #3616 natural (A)
• 2 balls in #3676 brown (B)
• 1 ball in #3643 rust (C)
• One pair each size 4 and 6 (3.5 and 4mm) needles OR SIZE TO OBTAIN GAUGE
• Bobbins

GAUGE
21 sts and 30 rows to 4"/10 cm over pat st with MC using size 6 (4mm) needles. TAKE TIME TO CHECK GAUGE.

NOTES
1) Front is worked with four 9"/23 cm squares that are sewn tog to form center square, then all 4 edges are worked outward in border pat to complete front. Back is worked with MC only in pat st.

2) Ribbing is worked after pieces are completed.

BACK
With larger needles and MC, cast on 146 sts. **Beg pat st: Row 1 (RS)** Beg with st 1, work 4-st rep of pat st across, end with st 1. Cont in pat st until piece measures 16"/40.5 cm from beg, end with a WS row.

Armhole shaping
Bind off 8 sts at beg of next 2 rows—130 sts. Work even until armhole measures 9¾"/25 cm.

Neck and shoulder shaping
Bind off 10 sts at beg of next 8 rows, AT SAME TIME, bind off center 38 sts for neck and working both sides at once, bind off 2 sts from each neck edge 3 times.

FRONT
Square (make 4)
With larger needles and A, cast on 3 sts for center of square. Work in pat foll chart for front square. Block to 9"/23 cm square, with a 12"/30.5 cm diagonal. Foll photo, sew 4 squares tog

to form 18"/46 cm center square.

Right side edge
With RS facing, larger needles and B, pick up and k 94 sts along one side of center square. K 1 row. **Beg border pat chart: Next row (RS)** Beg with st 1, work to rep line, work 13-st rep 7 times, end with st 1. Work through 14 rows of chart. With A, k 2 rows. Change to MC, and k 1 row. Change to pat st and work 5 rows more.

Armhole shaping
Bind off 35 sts at beg of next row, then cont in pat on rem 59 sts for 12 rows more. Bind off.

Left side edge
Work to correspond to right side edge, reversing shaping.

Lower edge
With larger needles, pick up and k 12 sts with MC, 2 sts with A, 118 sts with B, 2 sts with A and 12 sts with MC—146 sts. **Next row** With MC, work 4-st rep of pat st over 12 sts, with A work in rev St st over 2 sts, with B k118, with A work in rev St st over 2 sts, with MC work 4-st rep of pat st over 12 sts beg with st 4. Cont in pats on first and last 14 sts as established, work border pat chart over center 118 sts, beg with st 2, working 13-st rep 9 times, and ending with st 15. Work through 14 rows of chart. When chart is completed, cont in pat on first and last 12 sts, and with A k 2 rows on center 122 sts. Change to MC and k 1 row across 146 sts. Work all sts in pat st for 9 rows more.

Ribbed edge
With B, k 2 rows. Change to smaller needles. **Row 1 (RS)** *K1 MC, k1 A; rep from * to end. **Row 2** *K1 A, p1 MC; rep from * to end. Rep last 2 rows twice. With MC, bind off knitwise.

Upper edge
With larger needles, pick up and k 4 sts with MC, 2 sts with A, 118 sts with B, 2 sts with A, and 4 sts with MC—130 sts. Work as for lower edge through row 14 of border pat chart. Keeping in pat on first and last 4 sts, k 2 rows with A on center 122 sts. Cont with MC only and pat st, work 4 rows.

Neck shaping
Next row Work 58 sts, join 2nd ball of yarn and bind off center 14 sts, work to end. Working both sides at once, bind off from each neck edge 5 sts twice, 4 sts once, 2 sts twice, AT SAME TIME, when same length as back to shoulder, shape shoulders as for back.

SLEEVES
With larger needles and MC, cast on 52 sts. Work 4-st rep of pat st, AT SAME TIME, inc 1 st each side (working inc sts into pat st) every 4th row 27 times—106 sts. Work even until piece measures 17"/43 cm from beg. Bind off.

Front Chart

Note: In mosaic pat, 2 rows on chart equal 1 row of knitting.

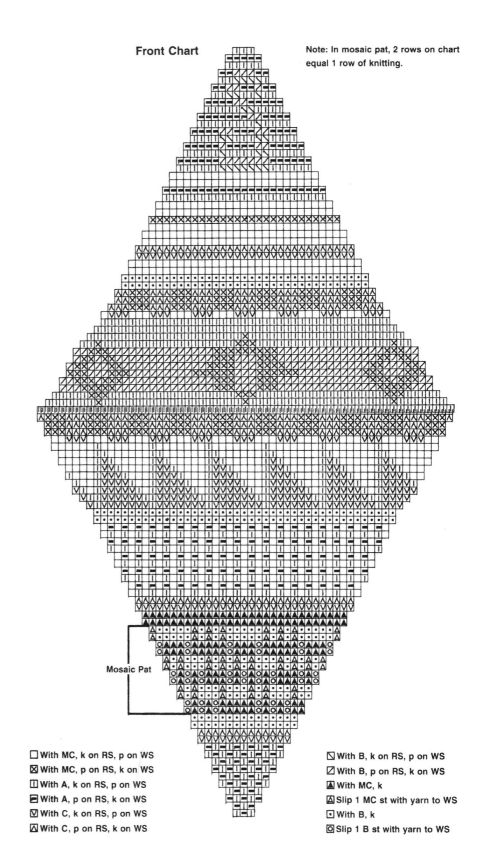

Mosaic Pat

☐ With MC, k on RS, p on WS
☒ With MC, p on RS, k on WS
⊞ With A, k on RS, p on WS
⊟ With A, p on RS, k on WS
☑ With C, k on RS, p on WS
◺ With C, p on RS, k on WS

◧ With B, k on RS, p on WS
◪ With B, p on RS, k on WS
▲ With MC, k
◸ Slip 1 MC st with yarn to WS
⊡ With B, k
◲ Slip 1 B st with yarn to WS

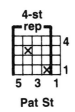

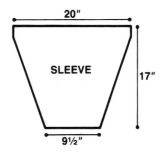

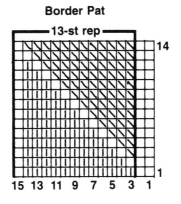

FINISHING

Carefully block pieces. Sew right shoulder seam. With larger needles and B, pick up and k 107 evenly sts around neck edge. Work ribbed edge around neck edge. With larger needles and B, pick up sts and work ribbed edge as for front on lower back and sleeve edges. Sew shoulder including neckband. Sew bound-off sts of sleeve to armhole. Sew bound-off sts of armhole to top side edge of sleeve. Sew side and sleeve seams.

☐ With MC, k on RS, p on WS
☒ With MC, p on RS, k on WS
⊞ With A, k on RS, p on WS
⊟ With A, p on RS, k on WS
☑ With C, k on RS, p on WS
◩ With C, p on RS, k on WS
◿ With B, k on RS, p on WS
◺ With B, p on RS, k on WS
▲ With MC, k
◭ Slip 1 MC st with yarn to WS
⊡ With B, k
⊙ Slip 1 B st with yarn to WS

Border Pat

Spring/Summer 1993 · No. 3

*B*lue Waves Sweater

INTERMEDIATE

Oversized, horizontal wave motif pullover knit in one piece from side-to-side, with drop shoulders, short sleeves and wide, round neck. Sized for Small, Medium, Large, and X-Large. Directions are for smallest

size with larger sizes in parentheses. If there is only one figure, it applies to all sizes.

KNITTED MEASUREMENTS

• Bust at underarm 40 (44, 48, 52)"/101.5 cm (112, 122, 132) cm
• Length 24¾ (24¾, 25½, 26¼)"/63 (63, 65, 66.5) cm
• Upper arm 11½ (11½, 12¼, 13¼)"/29 (29, 31, 33.5) cm

MATERIALS 🧶3

• 11 (12, 13, 14) 1¾oz/50g balls (each approx 123yd/112m) of Reynolds *Saucy Sport* (cotton) in #631 blue
• To substitute, seek a DK-weight yarn with similar fiber content
• One pair each sizes 3 and 5 (3.25

and 3.75mm) needles OR SIZE TO OBTAIN GAUGE
• Size 3 (3.25mm) circular needle 29"/80 cm

GAUGE

• 14 sts to 2¼"/6 cm and 36 rows to 4½"/11.5 cm over chart pat using size 5 (3.75mm) needles. TAKE TIME TO CHECK GAUGE.

NOTES

1) Body is worked in one piece.
2) As body and sleeves are worked sideways, foll chart, it is essential to obtain correct row gauge. Keep careful count of rows.
3) Schematic does not include ribbing at lower edge of body and sleeve.

BODY

With larger needles, cast on 140 (140, 145, 150) sts. **Note** Beg desired size on row indicated by chart. **Beg chart: Next row (RS)** P14 (14, 15, 16), beg as indicated, work 14 sts of chart, p19 (19, 20, 21), 14 sts of chart, p15 (15, 16, 17), 14 sts of chart, p11 (11, 12, 13), 14 sts of chart, p7 (7, 8, 9), 14 sts of chart, p4.

Right back shoulder shaping

Cont in pat as established, keeping sts between chart pats in rev St st, AT SAME TIME, inc 1 st at end of WS rows every 6th row 5 (5, 4, 0) times, every 8th row 0 (0, 1, 5) times—145 (145, 150, 155) sts. Work even for 2 (6, 8, 8) rows.

Back neck shaping

Dec 1 st at end of next WS row, then every 6th row twice, every 8th row twice. Work even on 140 (140, 145, 150) sts for 36 (44, 52, 52) rows. Inc 1 st at end of next WS row, then every 8th row twice, every 6th row twice.

Left back shoulder shaping

Dec 1 st at end of WS rows every other row 1 (0, 0, 0) time, every 6th row 4 (5, 4, 0) times, every 8th row 0 (0, 1, 5) times—140 (140, 145, 150) sts. Work even for 6 (6, 8, 8) rows. At beg of next RS row, bind off 36 (36, 38, 40) sts for left armhole. Cast on 36 (36, 38, 40) sts at end of next row. Shape left front shoulder same as right back shoulder.

Front neck shaping

Dec 1 st at end of next WS row, then every other row 2 (0, 0, 0) times, every 4th row 7 (9, 10, 10) times—135 (135, 139, 144) sts. Work even for 28 rows. Inc 1 st at end of next WS row, then every 4th row 7 (9, 10, 10) times,

every other row 2 (0, 0, 0) times—145 (145, 150, 155) sts. Shape right front shoulder as for left back shoulder. Bind off all sts as indicated on chart.

SLEEVES

With larger needles, cast on 24 sts. Beg chart: **Next row (RS)** P6, beg as indicated, work 14 sts of chart, p4. Work even in pat as established, keeping sts outside of chart pat in rev St st, until 93 (93, 97, 105) rows have been completed. Bind off.

Sleeve ribbing

With smaller needles, pick up and k 80 (80, 84, 90) sts along 4 rev St st edge. Work in k1, p1, rib for ¾"/2 cm. Bind off.

FINISHING

Lower edge rib

With RS facing and circular needle, pick up and k 278 (302, 328, 356) sts along lower edge of body. Work in k1, p1 rib for ¾"/2 cm. Bind off in rib.

Sew side seam including rib, leaving 5¾ (5¾, 6, 6½)"/14.5 (14.5, 15, 16.5) cm at upper edge open for armhole.

Neckband

Sew left shoulder seam. With RS facing and smaller needles, pick up and k 162 (176, 190, 190) sts around neck edge. Work in k1, p1 rib for ¾"/2 cm. Bind off in rib. Sew right shoulder seam and neckband. Sew sleeve seams. Set in sleeves.

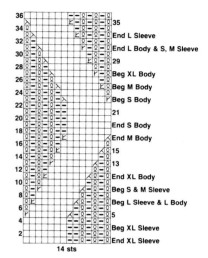

Small = S
Medium = M
Large = L
X-Large = XL

□ k on RS, p on WS
Ľ m1 purl
ᒋ m1 knit
⧄ k2tog
⧅ ssk
− p on RS, k on WS
 Q ktbl on RS, ptbl on WS

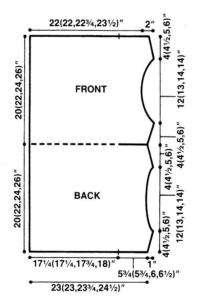

Spring/Summer 1993 · No. 11

Cabled Sweater

VERY EASY VERY VOGUE

Close-fitting, allover cabled pullover with modified set-in sleeves and round

neck. Sized for Small, Medium, and Large. Directions are for smallest size with larger sizes in parentheses. If there is only one figure, it applies to all sizes.

KNITTED MEASUREMENTS

- Bust at underarm 36 (39, 42)"/91.5 (99, 106.5) cm
- Waist 31 (33, 36)"/78.5 (83.5, 91.5) cm
- Length 18 (19, 20)"/46 (48, 51) cm
- Upper arm 15½ (16¼, 17)"/39.5 (41.5, 43) cm

MATERIALS [4]

- 10 (11, 12) 1¾oz/50g balls (each approx 105yd/96m) of Lang/Berroco *Yukon* (wool) in #8023 cream ragg
- To substitute, seek an aran-weight yarn with similar fiber content
- One pair each sizes 5 and 7 (3.75 and 4.5mm) needles OR SIZE TO OBTAIN GAUGE
- Cable needle (cn)
- Stitch markers

GAUGE

- 20 sts and 28 rows to 4"/10 cm over St st using size 7 (4.5mm) needles.
- 25 sts and 28 rows to 4"/10 cm over cable pat using size 7 (4.5mm) needles. TAKE TIME TO CHECK GAUGES.

STITCH GLOSSARY

10-st Back Cable (BC): Sl 5 sts to cn and hold to back of work, k5; k5 from cn.

10-st Front Cable (FC): Sl 5 sts to cn and hold to front of work, k5; k5 from cn.

Floating cable pat

(sizes small and medium: multiple of 18 sts plus 10 extra; size large: multiple of 18 sts plus 1 extra)

Rows 1, 3, 5 (RS) Knit.
Row 2 and all WS rows Purl.
Rows 7, 15, 23 K9, ★10-st FC, k8; rep from ★, end last rep k9 (k9, 10-st FC).
Rows 9, 11, 13, 17, 19, 21, 25, 27, 29, 31 Knit.
Rows 33, 41, 49 10-st BC, k8; rep from ★, end last rep 10-st BC (10-st BC, k9).
Rows 35, 37, 39, 43, 45, 47, 51 Knit.
Row 52 Purl.
Rep rows 1–52 for floating cable pat.

BACK

With smaller needles and 2 strands of yarn held tog, cast on 90 (96, 104) sts. Cut one strand and cont with single strand in k1, p1 rib for 1"/2.5 cm, inc 4 (4, 5) sts evenly across last WS row—94 (100, 109) sts. Change to larger needles. **Beg cable pat: Next row (RS)** K6 (9, 9), place marker (pm), work floating cable pat over next 82 (82, 91) sts, pm, k6 (9, 9). Cont in pats as established, working sts before and after markers in St st and rem sts in floating cable pat, AT SAME TIME, inc 1 st each side (working inc sts into St st) every 6th row 3 (1, 0) times, every 8th row 4 (6, 7) times—108 (114, 123) sts. Work even until piece measures 9 (9½, 10)"/23 (24, 25.5) cm from beg, end with a WS row.

Armhole shaping

Cont in pat, bind off 5 sts at beg of next 2 rows, 2 sts at beg of next 2 rows, dec 1 st each side every other row 1 (2, 2) times—92 (96, 105) sts. Work even in pat until armhole measures 8 (8½, 9)"/20.5 (21.5, 23) cm, end with a WS row.

Shoulder and neck shaping
Bind off 6 (7, 8) sts at beg of next 4 rows, 7 (7, 9) sts at beg of next 2 rows, AT SAME TIME, bind off center 36 (36, 37) sts and working both sides at once, bind off from each neck edge 5 sts once, 4 sts once.

FRONT

Work as for back until armhole measures 7 (7½, 8)"/18 (19, 20.5) cm, end with a WS row.

Neck and shoulder shaping

Next row (RS) Work 30 (32, 36) sts, join 2nd ball of yarn and bind off 32 (32, 33) sts, work to end. Working both sides at once, bind off from each neck edge 3 sts twice, 2 sts twice, dec 1 st every other row once, AT SAME TIME, when same length as back to shoulder, shape shoulders as for back.

SLEEVES

With smaller needles and 2 strands of yarn, cast on 48 sts. Cut one strand and cont with single strand in k1, p1 rib for 2"/5 cm, inc 2 sts across last WS row—50 sts. Change to larger needles. **Beg pat: Row 1 (RS)** K2, pm, work 46 sts in floating cable pat ending as for small, pm, k2. Cont in pats as established, working first and last 2 sts in St st and rem sts in cable pat, AT SAME TIME, inc 1 st each side after first and before last marker (working inc sts into floating cable pat) every 4th row 13 (19, 25) times, every 6th row 11 (7, 3) times—98 (102, 106) sts. Work even until piece measures 20"/50.5 cm from beg, end with a WS row.

Cap shaping

Bind off 5 sts at beg of next 2 rows, 3 sts at beg of next 4 rows, 1 st at beg of next 0 (4, 8) rows, 8 sts at beg of next 8 rows. Bind off rem 12 sts.

FINISHING

Block pieces. Sew left shoulder seam.
Neckband

With RS facing, pick up and k 110 (110, 112) sts evenly around neck edge. Work in k1, p1 rib for 1"/2.5 cm. Bind off loosely in rib. Sew right shoulder seam, including neckband. Set in sleeves. Sew side and sleeve seams.

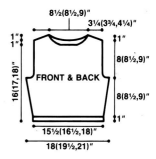

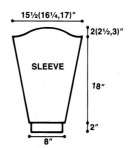

ℛed Hot Sweater

VERY EASY VERY VOGUE

Oversized, seed stitch pullover with dropped shoulders and cowlneck. Sized for X-Small, Small, Medium, Large, and X-Large. Directions are for smallest size with larger sizes in parentheses. If there is only one figure, it applies to all sizes.

KNITTED MEASUREMENTS
• Bust at underarm 43½ (46½, 50, 54, 58)"/110.5 (118, 127, 137, 147) cm
• Length 27½ (27½, 28, 28, 28½)"/70 (70, 71, 71, 72.5) cm
• Sleeve width at upper arm 16 (16, 17, 17, 18)"/40.5 (40.5, 43, 43, 45.5) cm

MATERIALS 3 4
• 7 (8, 8, 9, 9) 3½oz/100g balls (each approx 137yd/125m) of Cascade *Iceland* (wool) in #253 red (A)
• 6 (7, 7, 8, 8) 1¾oz/50g balls (each approx 164yd/150m) of Cascade *Color Kid* (mohair/acrylic) in #148 red (B)
• To substitute, seek a worsted–weight yarn and a DK-weight yarn with fiber content similar to the original yarns.
• One pair size 15 (10mm) needles OR SIZE TO OBTAIN GAUGE

GAUGE
10 sts and 16 rows to 4"/10 cm over seed st using size 15 (10mm) needles and 1 strand each A and B held tog. TO SAVE TIME, TAKE TIME TO CHECK GAUGE.

SEED STITCH
(any number of sts)
Row 1 (RS) ★K1, p1; rep from ★ to end.
Row 2 (WS) K the purl sts and p the knit sts.
Rep rows 1 and 2 for seed st.

BACK
With size 15 needles and 1 strand each A and B held tog, cast on 54 (58, 62, 68, 72) sts. Work in seed st for 27½ (27½, 28, 28, 28½)"/70 (70, 71, 71, 72.5) cm, end with a WS row. **Next row (RS)** Bind off 13 (15, 16, 19, 21) sts, work 28 (28, 30, 30, 30) sts and place on a holder, bind off rem 13 (15, 16, 19, 21) sts.

FRONT
Work as for back until piece measures 26 (26, 26½, 26½, 27)"/66 (66, 67, 67, 68.5) cm from beg, end with a WS row.
Neck shaping
Next row (RS) Work 18 (20, 21, 24, 26) sts, sl center 18 (18, 20, 20, 20) sts to a holder, join 2nd balls of yarn and work to end. Working both sides at once, bind off from each neck edge 3 sts once, 2 sts once. When same length as back, bind off rem 13 (15, 16, 19, 21) sts each side for shoulders.

SLEEVES
With size 15 needles and 1 strand each A and B held tog, cast on 26 (26, 26, 26, 27) sts. Work in seed st, inc 1 st each side (working inc sts into pat) every 8th (8th, 8th, 8th, 6th) row 7 (7, 8, 8, 9) times— 40 (40, 42, 42, 45) sts. Work even until piece measures 16½"/42 cm from beg. Bind off all sts.

FINISHING
Block pieces to measurements. Sew one shoulder seam.
Collar
With RS facing, size 15 (10mm) needles and 1 strand each A and B held tog, work 28 (28, 30, 30, 30) sts from back neck holder in seed st as established, pick up and k 6 sts along left front neck, work 18 (18, 20, 20, 20) sts from front neck holder in seed st as established, pick up and k 6 sts along right front neck—58 (58, 62, 62, 62) sts. Cont in seed st for 8"/20.5 cm. Bind off in pat. Sew 2nd shoulder and collar seam. Place markers 8 (8, 8½, 8½, 9)"/20.5 (20.5, 21.5, 21.5, 23) cm down from shoulder seams on front and back for armholes. Sew top of sleeves between markers. Sew side and sleeve seams.

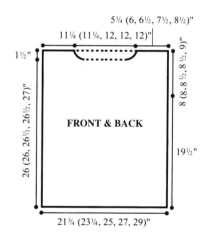

5¼ (6, 6½, 7½, 8½)"
11¼ (11¼, 12, 12, 12)"
1½"
8 (8, 8½, 8½, 9)"
26 (26, 26½, 26½, 27)"
FRONT & BACK
19½"
21¾ (23¼, 25, 27, 29)"

16 (16, 17, 17, 18)"
SLEEVE
16½"
10½ (10½, 10½, 10½, 11)"

*G*arter Ridge Cardigan

VERY EASY VERY VOGUE

Oversized cardigan with drop shoulders, patch pockets and crew neck. Sized for Small, Medium, and Large. Directions are for smallest size with larger sizes in parentheses. If there is only one figure, it applies to all sizes.

KNITTED MEASUREMENTS
• Bust at underarm (buttoned) 46 (52, 58)"/117 (132, 147) cm
• Length 26 (27, 28)"/66 (68.5, 71) cm
• Upper arm 16 (16, 18)"/41 (41, 46) cm

MATERIALS (4)
• 17 (18, 20) 1¾oz/50g balls (each approx 93yd/84m) of Creative Yarns International *Pima Natural* (cotton) in #614N honey
• To substitute, seek a worsted-weight yarn with similar fiber content
• One pair size 6 (4mm) needles OR SIZE TO OBTAIN GAUGE
• Nine ¾"/20mm buttons

GAUGE
20 sts and 32 rows to 4"/10 cm over garter ridge pat using size 6 (4mm) needles. TO SAVE TIME, TAKE TIME TO CHECK GAUGE.

GARTER RIDGE PAT
(any number of sts)
Row 1 (RS) Knit.
Row 2 Purl.
Rows 3 and 4 Knit.
Rep rows 1-4 for garter ridge pat.

BACK
With size 6 (4mm) needles, cast on 116 (130, 144) sts. Work in garter ridge pat for 26 (27, 28)"/66 (68.5, 71) cm. Bind off all sts.

LEFT FRONT
With size 6 (4mm) needles, cast on 65 (72, 80) sts. Work in garter ridge pat for 23 (24, 25)"/58.5 (61, 63.5) cm, end with a RS row.
Neck shaping
Next row (WS) Bind off 8 sts (neck edge), work to end. Cont to bind off from neck edge 3 sts twice, 2 sts 4 times, dec 1 st every row 5 (5, 6) times. Work even until same length as back. Bind off rem 38 (45, 52) sts for shoulder. Place markers at front edge for 6 buttons, the first at 2"/5 cm from lower edge, the last 3"/7.5 cm below neck, and 4 others spaced evenly between.

RIGHT FRONT
Work as for left front, reversing neck shaping and working buttonholes opposite markers as foll: **Buttonhole row (RS)** Work 4 sts, bind off 3 sts, work to end. On next row, cast on 3 sts over bound-off sts.

SLEEVES
With size 6 (4mm) needles, cast on 46 (46, 50) sts. Work in garter ridge pat, inc 1 st each side every 6th row 9 (9, 20) times, every 8th row 8 (8, 0) times—80 (80, 90) sts. Work even until piece measures 16"/41 cm from beg. Bind off all sts.

POCKETS (make 2)
With size 6 (4mm) needles, cast on 35 sts. Work in St st for 6"/15.5 cm.
Next row (RS) K16, bind off 3 sts (buttonhole), k to end. P 1 row, casting on 3 sts over bound-off sts. Work in k1, p1 rib for 1"/2.5 cm. Bind off in rib.

FINISHING
Block pieces to measurements. Sew pockets to fronts, 2"/5 cm from lower edge and 3"/ 7.5 cm from side edge. Sew shoulder seams.

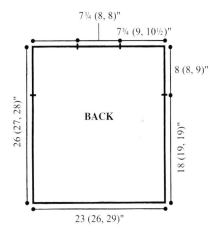

7¾ (8, 8)"
7¾ (9, 10½)"
8 (8, 9)"
26 (27, 28)"
BACK
18 (19, 19)"
23 (26, 29)"

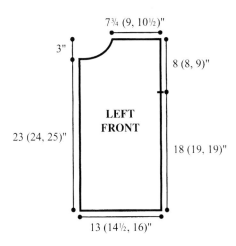

7¾ (9, 10½)"
3"
8 (8, 9)"
23 (24, 25)"
LEFT FRONT
18 (19, 19)"
13 (14½, 16)"

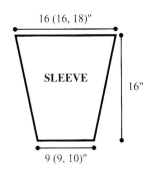

16 (16, 18)"
SLEEVE
16"
9 (9, 10)"

Neckband

With RS facing and size 6 (4mm) needles, beg at right front neck, pick up and k 91 (95, 95) sts evenly around neck edge. Beg and end with p1, work in k1, p1 rib for ¼"/.5 cm. Work a buttonhole on right front as before.

Rib until band measures 1"/2.5 cm. Bind off in rib. Place markers 8 (8, 9)"/20.5 (20.5, 23) cm down from shoulder seams on front and back for armholes. Sew top of sleeves between markers. Sew side and sleeve seams. Sew buttons on left front and pockets.

Spring/Summer 1996 • No. 15

Turtleneck Tunic

EXPERIENCED

Loose-fitting long, turtleneck tunic with circular yoke and cable design body. One size.

KNITTED MEASUREMENTS
• Bust at underarm 46"/117 cm
• Length 33½"/85 cm
• Upper arm 14"/35.5 cm

MATERIALS 4
• 12 3½oz/100g skeins (each approx 220yd/198m) of Cascade *220* (wool) in #8021 wheat (MC)
• 2 skeins each in #8834 rose pink (A) and #8229 soft green (B).
• Small amount of #8622 fawn (C)
• To substitute, seek a worsted-weight yarn with similar fiber content
• One each sizes 5 and 7 (3.75 and 4.5mm) circular needles 16"/40 cm and 24"/60 cm long, OR SIZE TO OBTAIN GAUGE

• One size 7 (4.5mm) circular needle 36"/90 cm long
• One size 4 (3.5mm) circular needle 16"/40 cm long
• Cable needle (cn)
• Stitch holders

GAUGE
• 30 sts and 28 rows to 4"/10 cm over Chart A using size 7 (4.5mm) needles.
• 23 sts and 24 rows to 4"/10 cm over St st and colorwork charts using size 7 (4.5mm) needles. TAKE TIME TO CHECK GAUGES.

STITCH GLOSSARY
12-st Left Cable (LC): Sl 6 sts to cn, hold to front, k6, k6 from cn.

BACK
With size 5 (3.75mm) circular needle (24"/60cm) and MC, cast on 170 sts. Work in k2, p2 rib for 6 rows. Change to size 7 (4.5mm) circular needle (24"/60 cm). **Next (inc) row (RS)** K into front and back of first st (inc l), p1, [k1, (inc 1, k2) twice, inc 1, k1, p4] 6 times, k2, inc 1, k4, inc 1, k2, [p4, k1, (inc 1, k2) twice, inc 1, k1] 5 times, p4, k1, [inc 1, k2] twice, inc 1, k1, p1, inc 1 in last st—210 sts. Beg with row 2 and last st of chart, and reading chart from left to right, work Chart A across row, end with first st of chart. Cont in pat as established until piece measures 18"/46 cm from beg, end with chart row 6. **Next (dec) row (RS)** P3, [k1, ssk, k6, k2tog, k1, p4] 13 times, end last rep p3—184 sts. Next

row K3, [p10, k1, k2tog, k1] 12 times, p10, k3—172 sts. Work 6 rows even. **Next (dec) row (RS)** P3, [k1, ssk, k4, k2tog, k1, p3] 13 times—146 sts. **Next row** ★K3, p8; rep from ★, end k3. Place sts on a holder.

FRONT
Work as for back.

SLEEVES
With size 5 (3.75mm) circular needle (16"/40 cm) and MC, cast on 48 sts. Work in k2, p2 rib for 6 rows, inc 30 sts evenly across last (WS) row—78 sts. Change to size 7 (4.5mm) circular needle (16"/40 cm). Establish Chart A **Next row (RS)** Beg with 3rd st of chart, work Chart A across row, end with first st after rep. Cont in pat as established, AT SAME TIME, inc 1 st each side (working inc sts into pat) on 5th row, then every 4th row 5 times, every 6th row 12 times—114 sts. Work even until piece measures 15"/39 cm from beg, end with chart row 6. **Next (dec) row (RS)** P2tog, p1, [k1, ssk, k6, k2tog, k1, p4] 6 times, k1, ssk, k6, k2tog, k1, p1, p2tog—98 sts. **Next row** K2, p10, [k1, k2tog, k1, p10] 6 times, k2—92 sts. Work 6 rows even. **Next (dec) row (RS)** P2, [k1, ssk, k4, k2tog, k1, p3] 6 times, k1, ssk, k4, k2tog, k1, p2—78 sts. Next row K2, ★p8, k3; rep from ★, end last rep k2. Place sts on a holder.

YOKE
With size 7 (4.5 mm) circular needle

(36"/90 cm) and MC, join all pieces as foll: **Row 1 (RS)** work across 78 sts of left sleeve as foll: K1 (selvage st), k75, k2tog; work across 146 sts of front: ssk, k142, k2tog; work across 78 sts of right sleeve: ssk, k74, k2tog; work across 146 sts of back: ssk, k143, k1 (selvage st)—442 sts. **Row 2** With MC, purl. **Row 3** Establish Chart B K1 (selvage st), work 4-st rep of Chart B across row, end k1 (selvage st). **Rows 4–6** Work 3 rows more Chart B. **Row 7** With MC, knit. **Row 8 (WS)** With MC, k1 (selvage st), p6, p2tog, *p9, p2tog; rep from *, end p3, k1 (selvage st)—402 sts. **Row 9 (RS)** Establish Charts C and D K1 (selvage st), k8 MC, *row 1 of Chart C over 3 sts, k17 MC, row 1 of Chart D over 13 sts, k17 MC; rep from *, end last rep k9 MC, k1 (selvage st). Cont in chart pats as established to end of charts, AT SAME TIME, work dec rows as foll: **Row 10** Work even. **Row 11 (RS)** K1 (selvage st), *k2, ssk, k4, 3 sts Chart C, k4, k2tog, k5, ssk, k4, 13 sts Chart D, k4, k2tog, k3; rep from *, end k1 (selvage st)—370 sts. **Rows 12–14** Work even. **Row 15** K1 (selvage st), *k2, ssk, k3, 3 sts Chart C, k3, k2tog, k5, ssk, k3, 13 sts Chart D, k3, k2tog, k3; rep from *, end k1 (selvage st)—338 sts. **Rows 16–18** Work even. **Row 19** K1 (selvage st), *k2, ssk, k2, 3 sts Chart C, k2, k2tog, k5, ssk, k2, 13 sts Chart D, k2, k2tog, k3; rep from *, end k1 (selvage st)—306 sts. **Rows 20 and 21** Work even. **Row 22** With MC, purl. **Row 23** With MC, k1 (selvage st), k13, k2tog, k20, k2tog, k1; rep from *, end k1 (selvage st)—290 sts. **Row 24 (WS)** Establish Chart E K1 (selvage st), beg with last st of chart and reading chart from left to right, work 4-st rep across row, end k1 (selvage st). **Rows 25–27** Work 3 rows more Chart E. **Row 28** With MC, purl. **Row 29** With MC, k1 (selvage st), k12, k2tog, k19, k2tog, k1; rep from *, end k1 (selvage st)—274 sts. **Row 30** Establish Charts C and D K1 (selvage st), *p9 MC, row 1 of Chart C over 3 sts, p9 MC, row 1 of Chart D over 13 sts; rep from *, end k1 (selvage st). Cont in chart pats as established to end of charts, AT SAME TIME, work dec rows as foll: **Row 31** Work even. **Row 32 (WS)**

K1 (selvage st), *p4, p2tog, p3, 3 sts Chart C, p4, p2tog, p3, 13 sts Chart D; rep from *, end k1 (selvage st)—258 sts. **Rows 33–35** Work even. **Row 36** K1 (selvage st), *p3, p2tog, p3, 3 sts Chart C, p3, p2tog, p3, 13 sts Chart D; rep from *, end k1 (selvage st)—242 sts. **Rows 37–39** Work even. **Row 40** K1 (selvage st), *p2, p2tog, p3, 3 sts Chart C, p2, p2tog, p3, 13 sts Chart D; rep from *, end k1 (selvage st)—226 sts. **Rows 41 and 42** Work even. **Row 43** With MC, knit. **Row 44** K1 (selvage st), *pl, p2tog, p7, p2tog, CHECKp16; rep from *, end k1 (selvage st)—210 sts. **Row 45** Establish Chart B K1 (selvage st), work 4-st rep of Chart B across row, end k1 (selvage st). **Rows 46–48** Work 3 rows more Chart B. **Row 49** With MC, knit. **Row 50** K1 (selvage st), *pl6, p2tog, p3, p2tog tbl, p3; rep from *, end k1 (selvage st)—194 sts. **Row 51** Establish Charts C and D K1 (selvage st), *k4 MC, row 1 of Chart C over 3 sts, k4 MC, row 1 of Chart D over 13 sts; rep from *, end k1 (selvage st). Cont in chart pats as established to end of charts, AT SAME TIME, work dec rows as foll: **Row 52** Work even. **Row 53 (RS)** K1 (selvage st), *k2, ssk, 3 sts

Chart C, k2tog, k2, 13 sts Chart D; rep from *, end k1 (selvage st)—178 sts. **Rows 54–56** Work even. **Row 57** K1 (selvage st), *k1, ssk, 3 sts Chart C, k2tog, k1, 13 sts Chart D; rep from *, end k1 (selvage st)—162 sts. **Rows 58–60** Work even. **Row 61** K1 (selvage st), *ssk, 3 sts Chart C, k2tog, 13 sts Chart D; rep from *, end k1 (selvage st)—146 sts. **Rows 62 and 63** Work even. **Row 64** With MC, purl. **Row 65** K with MC, dec 16 sts evenly across—130 sts. **Rows 66–69** Work 4 rows Chart E. **Row 70** With MC, purl. **Row 71** K With MC, dec 8 sts evenly across—122 sts. Change to size 5 (3.75mm) needle (16"/40 cm).

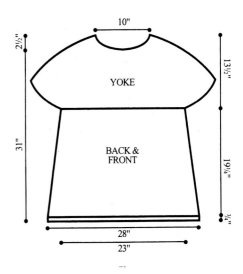

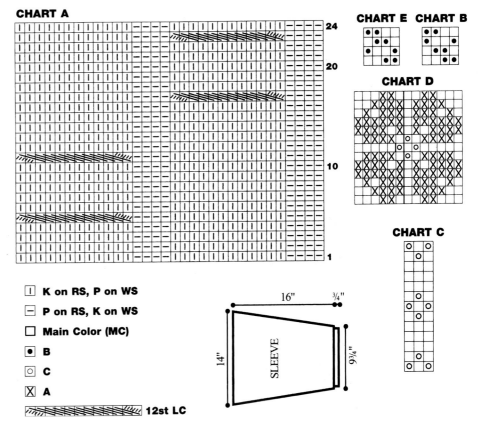

CHART A

CHART E   CHART B

CHART D

CHART C

☐ **K on RS, P on WS**

☐ **P on RS, K on WS**

☐ **Main Color (MC)**

⊡ **B**

⊙ **C**

☒ **A**

〰 **12st LC**

Next row (WS) P2tog, p1, *k2, p2; rep from * across, end k1, p2tog—120 sts. Cont in k2, p2 rib until collar measures 2½"/6.5 cm, end with a RS row. Change to size 4 (3.5mm) circular needle. P1 row, k1 row, p1 row.

Picot edging
Next row (RS) K1, *yo, k2tog; rep from *, end yo, k1. Work 3 more rows in St st. Do not bind off. Fold collar to WS at picot row and weave sts from needle loosely into top of ribbing sts. Sew side and sleeve seams. Sew back yoke seam. Sew collar seam.

Winter 1996-1997 · No. 32

Trellis Cardigan

INTERMEDIATE

Standard fitting lattice cardigan with cabled collar. Sized for Small/Medium and Large/X-Large. Directions are for smallest size with larger size in parentheses. If there is only one figure, it applies to all sizes.

KNITTED MEASUREMENTS
• Bust at underarm 38 (50)"/96.5 (127) cm
• Length 24¼(27¼)"/61.5 (69) cm
• Upper arm 13½ (15¾)"/34.5 (40) cm

MATERIALS
• 17 (23) 1¾oz/50g balls (each approx 139yd/125m) of Ilse Wolle *Setana* (wool/silk/microfiber) in #217 plum
• To substitute, seek a DK-weight yarn with similar fiber content
• One pair each sizes 3 and 5 (3.25 and 3.75mm) needles OR SIZE

TO OBTAIN GAUGE
• Cable needle (cn)
• Seven ½"/13mm buttons

GAUGE
32 sts and 32 rows to 4"/10 cm over cable pat foll chart or one 24-st rep to 3"/7.5 cm using larger needles. TAKE TIME TO CHECK GAUGE.

STITCH GLOSSARY
4-st Right Cable (4-st RC) Sl 2 sts to cn and hold to back, k2, k2 from cn.
4-st Left Cable (4-st LC) Sl 2 sts to cn and hold to front, k2, k2 from cn.
2/2 Right Purl Cable (2/2 RPC) Sl 2 sts to cn and hold to back, k2, p2 from cn.
2/2 Left Purl Cable (2/2 LPC) Sl 2 sts to cn and hold to front, p2, k2 from cn.

BACK
With smaller needles, cast on 138 (178) sts. Work in k2, p2 rib for 1"/2.5 cm, end with a RS row. Purl next (WS) row inc 16 (24) sts evenly spaced—154 (202) sts. Change to larger needles and beg with row 13 (1) of chart as indicated, work to rep line work 24-st rep 5 (7) times, end as indicated. Work rows 1-12 of chart 0 (1) time, then rep rows 13-36 a total of 4 times. Piece measures approx 13 (14½)"/33 (37) cm from beg. Work rows 37-66 once, AT SAME TIME, when piece measures 15½ (17)"/39.5

(43) cm from beg and row 58 of chart is completed, beg armhole shaping.
Armhole shaping
Note Cont foll chart through row 66 during armhole shaping, then rep rows 67-90 to end of piece. Bind off 4 sts at beg of next 2 rows, 3 sts at beg of next 4 (8) rows, 2 sts at beg next 4 (8) rows, dec 1 st each side every other row 2 (4) times-122 (146) sts. Working first and last st in reverse St st, cont in pat rep rows 67-90 until armhole measures 8 (9½)"/20.5 (24) cm.
Shoulder and neck shaping
Bind off 13 sts at beg of next 2 (0) rows, 12 (16) sts at beg of next 4 (6) rows and AT SAME TIME, bind off center 28 (30) sts and working both sides at once, bind off 5 sts from each neck edge twice.

LEFT FRONT
With smaller needles, cast on 71 (87) sts. **Row 1 (RS)** *K2, p2; rep from * end k3, (1 k selvage st at center). Cont in rib for 1"/2.5 cm, end with a RS row. Purl next row, inc 7 (15) sts evenly spaced—78 (102) sts. Change to larger needles and beg with row 13 (1) of chart as indicated, work to rep line, work 24-st rep 2 (3) times then end as indicated. Work rows 1-12 of chart 0 (1) time, then rep rows 13-36 a total of 4 times. Work rows 37-66 once and AT SAME TIME, when piece measures 15½ (17)"/39.5 (43) cm from beg and row 58 of chart is completed, beg armhole shaping.

Armhole shaping

Note As on back, cont foll chart through row 66 during armhole shaping, then rep rows 67-90 to end of piece. Bind off at beg of next RS row (armhole edge) 4 sts once, 3 sts 2 (4) times, 2 sts 2 (4) times, dec 1 st every other row 2 (4) times—62 (74) sts. Work even until armhole measures 7 (8½)"/17.5 (21.5) cm, end with a RS row.

Neck shaping

Bind off 6 (7) sts at beg of next row (neck edge), then bind off 4 sts twice from neck edge, 3 sts twice, 2 sts twice and 1 st once and AT SAME TIME, when same length as back, shape shoulders by binding off 13 sts 1 (0) time and 12 (16) sts 2 (3) times.

RIGHT FRONT

Work to correspond to left front reversing shaping and beg and end chart where indicated.

SLEEVES

With smaller needles, cast on 70 (86) sts. Work in k2, p2 rib for 1"/2.5 cm, end with a RS row. Purl next row, inc 6 (14) sts evenly—76 (100) sts. Change to larger needles. **Next row (RS)** K2, work 24-st rep of chart 2, 3 (4) times, k2. Cont to foll chart, working incs into pat foll chart by working 2 sts into 2nd st (beg inc) and 2 sts into 3rd st from end (end inc) as foll: inc 1 st each side every 6th row 5 times, [every 4th row once, every 8th row once] twice, every 6th row 3 times, every 10th row 4 (1) time and AT SAME TIME, after row 84 of chart, rep rows 61-84 with added inc sts worked in reverse St st. There are 108 (126) sts after all incs. Work even until piece measures 17"/43 cm from beg.

Cap shaping

Bind off 4 sts at beg of next 2 rows, 3 sts at beg of next 2 (4) rows, 2 sts at beg of next 2 (4) rows, dec 1 st each side every other row 4 (15) times, every 4th row 4 (0) times, every other row 3 (0) times, bind off 2 sts at beg of next 4 rows, 3 sts at beg of next 2 rows, 4 sts at beg of next 2 rows, 5 sts at beg of next 2 rows. Bind off rem 36 sts.

FINISHING

Block pieces to measurements. With smaller needles, pick up and k 138 (154) sts from center left front edge. **Row 1 (WS)** K1 (selvage st), ★p2, k2; rep from ★, end k1 (selvage st). Work in rib for 6 more rows. Bind off. Work right front band in same way, working 7 buttonholes in 2nd row, by yo, work 2 sts tog. Work first and last buttonholes at ½"/1.25 cm from edges and space others evenly between. Sew shoulder, side and sleeve seams. Set sleeves in armholes.

#8 CHART 2

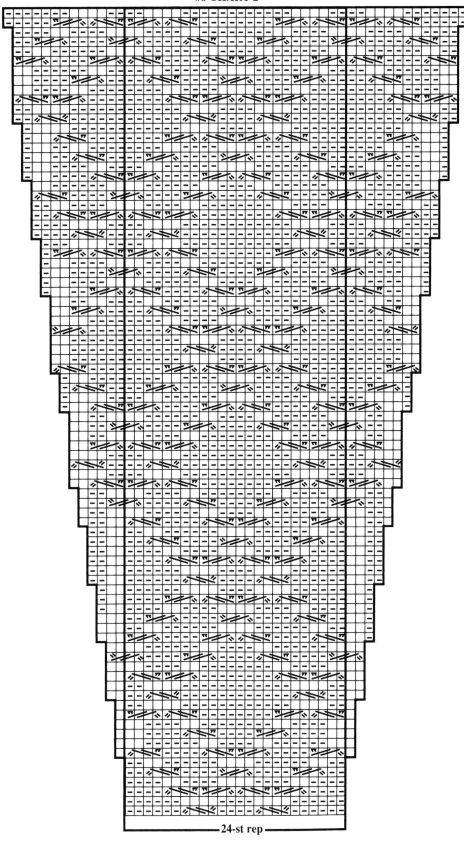

24-st rep

Collar

With smaller needles and RS facing, beg after right front band and end before left front band, pick up and k 112 (118) sts evenly around neck. **Row 1 (RS)** K4, [p2, k4] 17 (18) times, p2, k4. **Row 2** K2, m1, p1, [k1, m1, k1, p4] 17 (18) times, k1, m1, k1, p2, m1, k2. **Row 3** K2, p1, k2, ★p2, sl 2 sts to cn and hold to back, k2, k2 from cn; rep from ★, end p2, k2, p1, k2. Work 3 rows even. Rep last 4 rows until collar measures 5"/12.5 cm. Bind off in pat. Sew on buttons.

Stitch key

☐ k on RS; p on WS

– p on RS; k on RS

4-st RC

4-st LC

2/2 RPC

2/2 LPC

#8 CHART 1

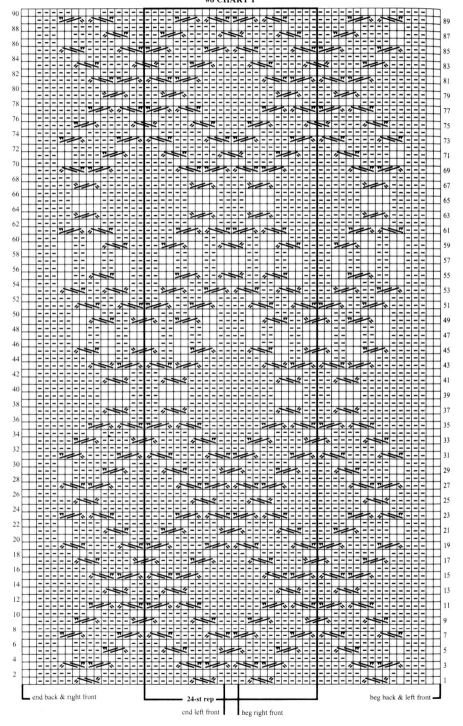

end back & right front · · · 24-st rep · · · beg back & left front
end left front · · · beg right front

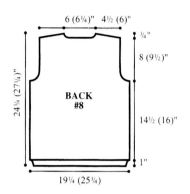

6 (6¼)" · 4½ (6)"
¾"
8 (9½)"
24¼ (27¼)"
BACK #8
14½ (16)"
1"
19¼ (25¼)

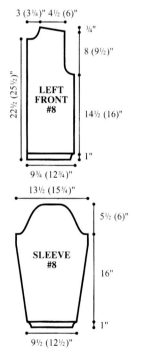

3 (3¼)" 4½ (6)"
¾"
8 (9½)"
22½ (25½)"
LEFT FRONT #8
14½ (16)"
1"
9¾ (12¾)"

13½ (15¾)"
5½ (6)"
SLEEVE #8
16"
1"
9½ (12½)"

Fall 1997 · No. 8

Striped Sweater

Oversized multi-colored ribbed turtleneck pullover. By Isaac Mizrahi. Sized for Small, Medium, Large and X-Large. Directions are for smallest size with larger sizes in parentheses. If there is only one figure, it applies to all sizes.

KNITTED MEASUREMENTS
• Bust at underarm 40 (43, 46½, 50)"/100 (109, 117, 125) cm
• Length 26½ (27, 28, 28½)"/67 (68.5, 71, 72.5) cm
• Upper arm 17 (18, 19, 20)"/43 (46, 48, 51) cm

MATERIALS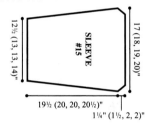
• 1 1½oz/40g balls (each approx 135yd/124m) of Classic Elite *Mini Mohair* (mohair/wool/nylon) each in #8596 clementine, #8502 key lime, #8520 Iznik blue, #8523 garance, #8524 blue moon, #8537 capuchine, #8578 henna, #8553 crushed berries, #8558 scarlet, #8590 pansy, #8563 harvest apple, #8592 lupine, #8546 teal, #8512 mountain green, #8509 winged teal, #8521 herb, #8508 soft shirt blue, #8519 cameo pink, #8544 brass, and #8529 daffodil
• To substitute, seek an aran-weight yarn with similar fiber content
• One pair size 7 (4.5mm) needles OR SIZE TO OBTAIN GAUGE
• Size 7 (4.5mm) circular needle, 16"/40 cm long

GAUGE
19 sts and 26 rows to 4"/10 cm using size 7 (4.5mm) needles in rib pat, slightly stretched. TAKE TIME TO CHECK GAUGE.

STITCH GLOSSARY
Rib Pat (multiple of 4 sts plus 3)
Row 1 ★K2, p2; rep from ★, end k2, p1. Rep row 1 for rib pat.
Stripe Pat
Join colors at varied intervals across rows to create your own variegated effect. When changing colors, twist yarns on WS to prevent holes in work.

BACK
With size 7 (4.5mm) needles and desired color, cast on 95 (103, 111, 119) sts. Work in rib and stripe pat for 17 (17, 17½, 17½)"/43 (43, 44.5, 44.5) cm, end with a WS row.
Armhole shaping
Dec 1 st each side on next row, then every row 3 (3, 3, 5) times more, every other row (3, 4, 3) times—83 (89, 95, 101) sts. Work even in rib until armhole measures 8½ (9, 9½, 10)"/21.5 (23, 24, 25.5) cm.
Shoulder shaping
Bind off 8 (8, 9, 11) sts at beg of next 2 rows, 8 (9, 10, 10) sts at beg of next 4 rows. Bind off rem 35 (37, 37, 39) sts for back neck.

FRONT
Work as for back until armhole measures 6½ (7, 7½, 8)"/16.5 (18, 19, 20.5) cm, end with a WS row.
Neck and shoulder shaping
Next row (RS) Work 32 (34, 37, 39) sts, join 2nd ball of yarn and bind off center 19 (21, 21, 23) sts for neck, work to end. Working both sides at once with separate balls, bind off from each neck edge 2 sts twice, dec 1 st every other row 4 times. When same length as back to shoulders, shape shoulders as on back.

SLEEVES
With size 7 (4.5mm) needles and desired color, cast on 59 (63, 63, 67) sts. Work in rib and stripe pat for 4"/10 cm. Cont in pat, inc 1 st each side (working inc sts into rib pat) every 8th (8th, 6th, 6th) row 9 (7, 8, 6) times, every 10th (10th, 8th, 8th) row 2 (4, 6, 8) times—81 (85, 91, 95) sts. Work even until piece measures 19½ (20, 20, 20½)"/49.5 (51, 51, 52) cm from beg.

Cap shaping
Work as for back armhole shaping. Bind off rem 69 (71, 75, 77) sts.

FINISHING
Block pieces to measurements. Sew shoulder seams.
Collar
With RS facing and circular needle, pick up and k 72 (76, 76, 80) sts evenly around neck. Join and work in rib pat as foll: **Rnd 1** ★K2, p2; rep from ★ around. **Rnd 2** ★K1, p2, k1; rep from ★ around. Rep last 2 rnds and work desired stripes for 6½"/16.5 cm. Bind off in rib. Set in sleeves. Sew side and sleeve seams.

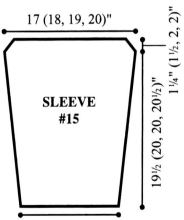

Tape Tee

INTERMEDIATE

Short sleeve pullover by Joan Vass. Sized to fit X-Small, Medium, and Large. Directions are for smallest size with larger sizes in parentheses. If there is only one figure, it applies to all sizes.

KNITTED MEASUREMENTS
• Bust 31 (33, 36, 39)"/78.5 (83.5, 91.5, 99) cm
• Length 18 (18, 18½, 19)"/45.5 (45.5, 47, 48) cm
• Upper arm 12 (13, 13, 14½)"/30.5 (33, 33, 37) cm

MATERIALS 4
• 9 (11, 12, 14) 1¾oz/50g balls (each approx 102yd/95m) of Sesia *Melbourne* (cotton) in #51 offwhite
• To substitute, seek a worsted-weight yarn with similar fiber content
• One pair size 8 (5mm) needles OR SIZE TO OBTAIN GAUGE
• Size 7 (4.5mm) circular needle, 16"/40 cm long

• Cable needle (cn)
• Stitch holders and stitch markers

GAUGE
23 sts and 26 rows = 4"/10 cm over cable pat using size 8 (5mm) needles. TAKE TIME TO CHECK GAUGE.

PATTERN STITCHES
CABLE PATTERN
(multiple of 8 sts plus 1)
Row 1 (RS) *P1, k7; rep from * end p1.
Row 2 (WS) and all even rows *K1, p7; rep from * end k1.
Rows 3 and 5 Rep row 1
Row 7 *P1, sl 4 sts to cn and hold to back, k3, k4 from cn; rep from * end p1.
Rows 9, 11, 13, 15 and 17 Rep row 1.
Row 18 Rep row 2.
Rep rows 7–18 for cable pat.

BACK
Cast on 89 (97, 105, 113) sts and work in k1, p1 rib for 1¾"/4.5 cm, end with a WS row. Then work in cable pat on 11 (12, 13, 14) cables until piece measures 18 (18, 18½, 19)"/45.5 cm (45.5, 47, 48) cm from beg.
Neck and shoulder shaping
Next row (RS) Bind off 25 (25, 33, 33) sts for shoulder, work center 39 (47, 39, 47) sts and place on a holder for neck, bind off last 25 (25, 33, 33) sts for shoulder.

FRONT
Pocket linings (Make 2)
Cast on 17 sts and work in St st for 2"/5 cm. Place sts on holders. Beg at lower edge, cast on and work as for back for 3¾"/9.5 cm.
Join pocket linings
Next row (RS) Work 12 (12, 16, 16) sts, *sl next 17 sts to a holder and replace with 17 pocket lining sts*, work to last 29 (29, 33, 33) sts, rep

between *'s once, work rem 12 (12, 16, 16) sts. Then cont to work front same as for back.

FINISHING
Block pieces to measurements. Sew shoulder seams.
Rolled neck
With circular needle, work across 39 (47, 39, 47) sts from holder, pick up 1 st in corner, work across 39 (47, 39, 47) sts from holder, pick up 1 st in corner—80 (96, 80, 96) sts. Join and work around in St st (k every rnd) for 2"/5 cm. Bind off.
Pocket bands
Work across 17 sts from pocket holder and work in k1, p1 rib for 1"/2.5 cm. Bind off in rib.

SLEEVES
Place markers at 7 (7½, 7½, 8)"/18 (19, 19, 20.5) cm down from shoulders on back and front for armholes. Working into edge p st, pick up and k 65 (73, 73, 81) sts evenly along one armhole edge. Work in cable pat for 3"/7.5 cm, end with 2nd cable row 7. Then work in k1, p1 rib for 2"/5 cm more. Bind off in rib. Work along 2nd armhole in same way.

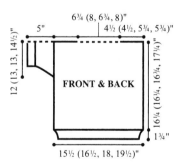

$\mathcal{D}$iagonal-Ridge Turtleneck

EXPERIENCED

Pullover by Oscar de la Renta.
Sized for X-Small, Small, Medium, Large, and X-Large. Directions are for smallest size with larger sizes in parentheses. If there is only one figure, it applies to all sizes.

KNITTED MEASUREMENTS
• Bust 39 (42, 44, 47, 50)"/99 (106.5, 111.5, 119.5, 127) cm
• Length 23 (23½, 24½, 24¾, 25½)"/58 (59.5, 61, 62.5, 64.5) cm
• Upper arm 14 (15, 16, 17, 18)"/35.5 (38, 40.5, 43, 45.5) cm

MATERIALS ④
• 14 (15, 16, 18, 19) 1¾oz/50g balls (each approx 105yd/96m) of Tahki Yarns *Chelsea Silk* (silk/wool) in #166 oatmeal
• To substitute, seek an aran-weight yarn with similar fiber content
• One pair size 7 (4.5mm) needles OR SIZE TO OBTAIN GAUGE
• Size 7 (4.5mm) circular needle, 16"/40 cm long.
• Two cable needles (cn)

GAUGES
• 24 sts and 24 rows= 4"/10 cm over chart pat using size 7 (4.5mm) needles.
• 20 sts and 28 rows = 4"/10 cm over k3, p2 rib (slightly stretched) using size 7 (4.5mm) needles. TAKE TIME TO CHECK GAUGES.

NOTE
Chart pat will bias as you are knitting. Side edges will not be straight. You must pin finished pieces so that side edges are straight and steam block to measurements.

STITCH GLOSSARY
K3, P2 Rib
(multiple of 5 sts plus 1)
Row 1 (RS) K2, ★p2, k3; rep from ★, end last rep k2 instead of k3.
Row 2 K the knit sts and p the purl sts. Rep row 2 for k3, p2 rib.

BACK
With size 7 (4.5mm) needles, cast on 117 (125, 133, 141, 149) sts. Work in k1, p1 rib for 3 rows. P next row on WS. Work in chart pat (rep rows 1–16) until piece measures 14"/35.5 cm from beg, end with a WS row.
Raglan armhole shaping
Note Discontinue the decs at beg of row and incs at end of row on chart.
Next row (RS) K2, SKP, work to last 4 sts, k2tog, k2. **Next row (WS)** P2, p2tog, work to last 4 sts, p2tog tbl, p2. Cont in this way to dec 1 st each side every row until there are 33 (33, 33, 35, 35) sts. Bind off for back neck.

FRONT
Work as for back.

SLEEVES
With size 7 (4.5mm) needles, cast on 51 (56, 56, 56, 56,) sts. Work in k1, p1 rib for 3 rows. P next row on WS. Work in k3, p2 rib for 2"/5 cm. Cont in rib, inc 1 st each side on next row (working inc sts into rib), then every 8th (8th, 6th, 4th, 4th) row 6 (6, 5, 3, 9) times more, every 10th (10th, 8th, 6th, 6th) row 3 (3, 6, 11, 7) times—

71 (76, 80, 86, 90) sts. Work even until piece measures 15"/38 cm from beg, end with a WS row.
Raglan cap shaping
Dec row (RS) K2, SKP, work to last 4 sts, k2tog, k2. **Next row (WS)** P2, rib to last 2 sts, p2. Rep last 2 rows 21 (24, 26, 29 31) times more. Work dec row. Work 3 rows even. Rep last 4 rows 3 (2, 2, 2, 2) times more. Bind off rem 19 (20, 20, 20, 20) sts.

FINISHING
Pin pieces to measurements and steam block making sure that side edges of front and back are straight. Sew raglan sleeve caps to raglan armholes. Sew side and sleeve seams.
Collar
With RS facing and circular needle, pick up and k 104 (104, 104, 108, 108) sts evenly around neck edge. Join and work in k2, p2 rib for 4"/10 cm.

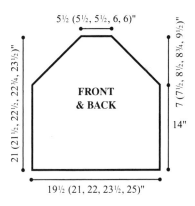

5½ (5½, 5½, 6, 6)"

7 (7½, 8½, 8¾, 9½)"

21 (21½, 22½, 22¾, 23½)"

FRONT & BACK

14"

19½ (21, 22, 23½, 25)"

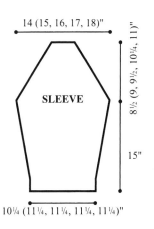

14 (15, 16, 17, 18)"

8½ (9, 9½, 10¼, 11)"

SLEEVE

15"

10¼ (11¼, 11¼, 11¼, 11¼)"

Stitch Key

☐ K on RS, p on WS

Ⅴ K in front and back of st

◩ K2 tog

◪◩ On RS rows: Sl 2 sts to cn and hold to front, k1, k2 from cn
On WS rows: Sl 1 st to cn and hold to front, p2, p1 from cn

*Row 7: Sl 1 st to cn and hold to back, Sl 2 sts to 2nd cn and hold to front, k next st tog with st on first cn, k2 from 2nd cn

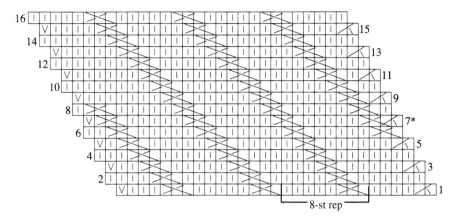

8-st rep

On next rnd, inc 1 st in every p st. Cont in p3, k2 rib for 4"/10 cm more. Bind off in rib. Sew side and sleeve seams. Sew pocket linings and trims in place.

Fall 1998 · No. 16

Seed Stitch Poncho

INTERMEDIATE

Poncho. Sized for Small, Medium, and Large. Directions are for smallest size with larger sizes in parentheses. If there is only one figure, it applies to all sizes.

KNITTED MEASUREMENTS
Width 40 (48, 54)"/101.5 (122, 137) cm
Length 28 (30, 32)"/71 (76, 81.5) cm

MATERIALS (4)
• 28 (36, 42) 1¾oz/50g balls (each approx 107yd/98m) of Lion Brand AL PA KA (acrylic/alpaca/wool) (21–24 sts per 4"/10 cm/medium weight) in #149 silver gray
• To substitute, seek an aran-weight yarn with similar fiber content
• Size 10½ (6.5mm) needles OR SIZE TO OBTAIN GAUGE
• Stitch holders
• Tapestry needle
• Small amount of polyester fiberfill

GAUGE
12 sts and 21 rows = 4"/10 cm over Seed st, using size 10 (6.5mm) needles and 2 strands of yarn held tog. TAKE TIME TO CHECK GAUGE.

NOTE
Use 2 strands of yarn held tog throughout.

STITCH GLOSSARY
Seed Stitch
Row 1 (RS) *K1, p1; rep from *.
Row 2 (WS) K the purl sts and p the knit sts.
Rep row 2 for seed st.

BACK
Cast on 120 (144, 162) sts. Work in seed st for 6 rows. **Twist row (RS)** Cont in seed st, work 6 sts, *rotate LH needle counterclockwise 360°, work next 6 sts; rep from * to end. Cont in seed st until piece measures 28 (30, 32)"/71 (76, 81.5) cm from beg, end with a WS row. **Next row (RS)** Work across 48 (60, 67) sts and place on holder for right shoulder, bind off center 24 (24, 28) sts, work rem 48 (60, 67) sts and place on holder for left shoulder.

FRONT

Work as for back until piece measures 26 (28, 30)"/66 (71, 76) cm from beg, end with a WS row.

Neck shaping

Next row (RS) Work 50 (62, 70) sts, join a 2nd ball of yarn and bind off center 20 (20, 22) sts, work to end. Working both sides at once, dec 1 st at each neck edge every other row 2 (2, 3) times—48 (60, 67) sts each side. Work even until piece measures same length as back to shoulders. Place sts each side on holders.

FINISHING

Join shoulders, using 3-needle bind-off.

Collar

Cast on 74 (74, 80) sts. Work in seed st for 6 rows. **Twist row (RS)** Cont in seed st, work 4 sts, *rotate LH needle counterclockwise 360°, work next 6 sts; rep from *, end last rep work 4 sts. Cont in seed st until collar measures 10"/25.5 cm from beg. Bind off. Sew seam. Sew bound-off edge of collar evenly around neck edge.

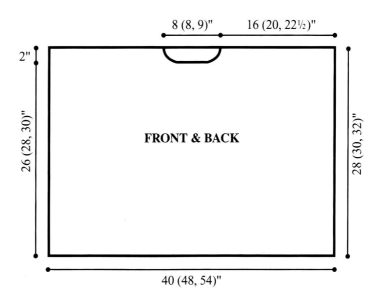

8 (8, 9)"   16 (20, 22½)"

2"

26 (28, 30)"

FRONT & BACK

28 (30, 32)"

40 (48, 54)"

Tassels (make 4)
Cast on 10 sts. Work in seed st for 2½"/6.5 cm, end with a WS row.
Next row (RS) Bind off 5 sts and fasten off st rem on RH needle. Remove 4 sts from LH needle and unravel them down to cast-on edge. Fasten off last st on cast-on row. Sew bound-off and cast-on edges tog. With tapestry needle, run single strand through sts along top of tassel and gather tog tightly. Stuff top of tassel with fiberfill, forming a ball.

Tie
Cast on 8 sts. Work 1 row in Seed st. Bind off in pat. Sew tie around tassel under fiberfill and secure. Trim ends of fringe. Sew tassels to lower corners of poncho.

Fall 1998 · No. 30

Cabled Twinset

Twinset by Isaac Mizrahi with top. Sized for Small, Medium, and Large. Directions are for smallest size with larger sizes in parentheses. If there is only one figure, it applies to all sizes.

KNITTED MEASUREMENTS
Top
• Bust 33 (35, 37)"/84 (89, 94) cm
• Waist 30 (32, 34) "/76 (81, 86) cm
• Length 21¼ (21¾, 22¼)"/54 (55.5, 56.5) cm
Cardigan
• Bust (buttoned) 36 (39, 44)"/91.5 (99, 111.5) cm

• Length 21½ (22, 22½)"/54.5 (56, 57) cm
• Upper arm 12¾ (13½, 14½)"/32.5 (34, 37) cm

MATERIALS [2]
Top
• 4 (5, 5) 1¾oz/50g balls (each approx 187yd/170m) of Lane Borgosesia *Super Lambswool* (wool) in #800 camel
• To substitute, seek a fingering-weight yarn with similar fiber content
Cardigan
• 9 (10, 11) 1¾oz/50g balls (each approx 187yd/170m) of Lane Borgosesia *Super Lambswool* (wool) in #800 camel

• One pair each sizes 2 and 4 (3 and 3.5mm) needles OR SIZE TO OBTAIN GAUGE
• Cable needle (cn)
• Five ⅝"/15mm buttons

GAUGES
• 26 sts and 38 rows= 4"/10 cm in St st using larger needles.
• 26 sts and 44 rows= 4"/10 cm in seed stitch using larger needles.
• 33 sts and 38 rows= 4"/10 cm in chart pats using larger needles. TAKE TIME TO CHECK GAUGES.

STITCH GLOSSARY
Seed Stitch
Row 1 (RS) *K1, p1; rep from * to end.
Row 2 K the purl sts and p the knit sts. Rep row 2 for seed st.

NOTE
Front is wider than back.

TOP
BACK
With smaller needles, cast on 105 (111, 117) sts. **Row 1 (RS)** *K1tbl, p1tbl; rep from * end k1tbl. **Row 2 (WS)** *P1tbl, k1tbl; rep from *, end p1tbl. Rep these 2 rows for twisted rib until piece measures 1¼"/3 cm from beg. Change to larger needles and cont in seed st until piece measures 3¼"/8 cm from beg. Dec 1 st each side of next row and rep dec every 10th row 3 times, every 8th row once—95 (101, 107) sts. Work even until piece measures 7¾"/19.5 cm from beg. Inc 1 st each side of next row and rep inc every 10th row 3 times, every 8th row once—105 (111, 117) sts. Work even until piece measures 13 (13, 13¼)"/33 (33, 33.5) cm from beg.

Armhole shaping
Bind off 6 (7, 7) sts at beg of next 2 rows, 2 sts at beg of next 6 (6, 8) rows, dec 1 st each side every other row 3 times—75 (79, 81) sts. Work even armhole measures 7¼ (7¾, 8)"/18.5 (19.5, 20.5) cm.

Neck and shoulder shaping
On next row, bind off center 19 (19, 21) sts for neck and working both sides at once, cont to bind off 4 sts from each neck edge 3 times, AT SAME TIME, when armhole measures 7½ (8, 8¼"/19 (20.5, 21) cm,

bind off 4 sts from each shoulder edge 4 (2, 2) times, 5 sts 0 (2, 2) times.

FRONT
With smaller needles, cast on 111 (117, 123) sts. Work in twisted rib as on back for 1¼"/3 cm. Change to larger needles and cont in St st, (with k1 selvage sts each side), with Chart I worked on center 9 sts. To foll chart, work rows 1-45, then rep rows 10-45 twice, rows 10-27 (27, 45), once, then discontinue pat at center, and AT SAME TIME, when piece measures 3¼"/8 cm from beg, beg decs. **Dec row (RS)** K1, ssk, work to last 3 sts, k2tog, k1. Rep dec row every 10th row once, every 8th row 3 times—101 (107, 113) sts. Work even until piece measures 7¾"/19.5 cm from beg. Inc 1 st each side of next row (by M1 inside of selvage sts) and rep inc every 10th row once, every 8th row 3 times—111 (117, 123) sts. Work even until piece measures 13 (13, 13¼)"/33 (33, 33.5) cm from beg, end with a WS row.

Armhole shaping
Bind off 9 (10, 10) sts at beg of next 2 rows. Next row K2, SKP, work to last 4 sts, k2tog, k2. Work 1 row even. **Next row (RS)** K2, SK2P, work to last 5 sts, k3tog, k2. Work 1 row even. Rep last 2 rows 3 (3, 4) times more—

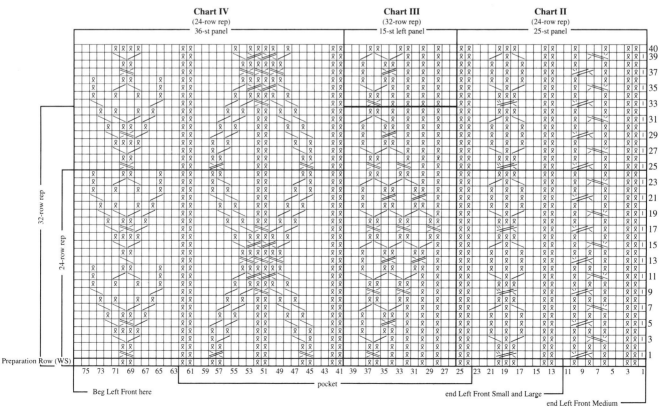

75 (79, 81) sts. Work even armhole measures 4¾ (5¼, 5½)"/12 (13.5, 14) cm.

Neck shaping
Next row (RS) K31 (33, 33) sts, join 2nd ball of yarn and bind off center 13 (13, 15) sts, work to end. Working both sides at once, bind off 3 sts from

each neck edge twice, 2 sts 3 times, dec 1 st every other row 3 times. Shape shoulders when same length as back.

FINISHING
Block pieces to measurements. Sew one shoulder seam.
Neckband
With RS facing and smaller needles, pick up and k 133 (133, 137) sts around neck. Work in twisted rib for ½"/1.25 cm. Bind off. Sew shoulder and neckband seam.
Armhole bands
With RS facing and smaller needles, pick up and k 121 (129, 133) sts evenly around each armhole edge. Work rib same as neckband. Sew side seams.

CARDIGAN
BACK
With smaller needles, cast on 117 (127, 143) sts. Work in twisted rib (see tank top) for 1½"/4 cm end with a RS row. Change to larger needles and cont in seed st until piece measures 13"/33 cm from beg.
Armhole shaping
Bind off 6 (6, 7) sts at beg of next 2 rows, 2 sts at beg of next 2 (4, 6) rows, dec 1 st each side every other row 3 times—95 (101, 111) sts. Work even until armhole measures 7½ (8, 8½)"/19 (20.5, 21.5) cm.
Shape shoulders and neck
Bind off 5 (5, 6) sts at beg of next

4 rows, 5 (6, 7) sts at beg of next 6 rows and AT SAME TIME as 3rd shoulder bind off, bind off center 33 sts then bind off 3 sts from each neck edge twice.

LEFT FRONT
Note All P sts on WS are p1tbl. With smaller needles, cast on 75 (86, 97) sts. Work in twisted rib (end with k1 selvage st at center front) as for back for 1½"/4 cm end with a RS row. Change to larger needles.
Preparation row (WS) [K1tbl, p1tbl] 5 times, (for front band), work preparation row of large chart over the next 64 (75, 86) sts as foll: beg as indicated, and end with st 13 (2, 2), rep sts 23–13 for size Large only, then for all sizes end with a k1 selvage st.
Row 1 (RS) Beg with st 12 (1, 12), k this st (for selvage st), then for size Large only work sts 13–23, then for all sizes work sts 13 (2, 2) through 76 (end of chart), then work 10-st band as established. Cont in pats foll Chart II (24-row rep), Chart III (32-row rep) and Chart IV (24-row rep) until piece measures 13"/33 cm from beg.
Beg armhole, neck, and shawl collar shaping
Next row (RS) From armhole edge, bind off 8 (9, 10) sts, then k2tbl, work across to 1 st before 10-st band, k1tbl, M1 p st, work 10-st band. **Next row (WS)** [K1tbl, p1tbl] 6 times, work pat to end. **Next (dec) row (RS)** K1, k2tbl, SK2P, work in pat to end. **Next row (WS)** [K1tbl, p1tbl] 6 times, M1 k st, p1tbl, work pat to last 3 sts, p2tbl, k1. Cont to work armhole dec row every RS row 2 (3, 4) times more and AT SAME TIME for collar, add 1 st every 3rd row by M1 just before band 21 (22, 22) times more AND add 1 more twisted rib from pat at center every 3rd row 21 (22, 22) times more (displace chart pat sts with twisted rib sts, but do not inc sts). There will be 28 (35, 43) sts rem in chart pat sts for shoulder after sts are displaced with twisted rib sts, 56 (58 58) sts in twisted rib after all incs at center. Work even until armhole measures 7½ (8, 8½)" 19 (20.5, 21.5) cm
Shoulder shaping
Bind off 6 (7, 9) sts from shoulder edge 3 times, 5 (7, 8) sts twice. Work

Chart I

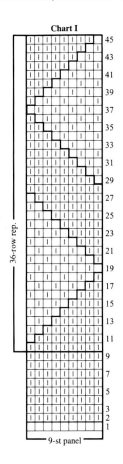

36-row rep.

9-st panel

Chart V

15-st Right Panel

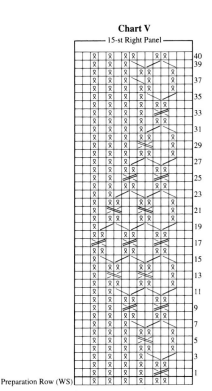

Preparation Row (WS)

Stitch Key
☐ p on RS, k on WS

▯ k on RS, p on WS

⧖ k1 tbl on RS, p1 tbl on WS

1/2 LPC sl 1 st to cn and hold to *front*, k1 tbl, p1, then k1 tbl from cn

1/2 RPC sl 2 sts to cn and hold to *back* k1 tbl, then p1, k1 tbl from cn

2-st RC sl 1 st to cn and hold to *back*, k1 tbl, k1 tbl from cn

2-st RPC sl 1 st to cn and hold to *back*, k1 tbl, p1 from cn

2-st LC sl 1 st to cn and hold to *front*, k1 tbl, k1 tbl from cn

2-st LPC sl 1 st to cn and hold to *front*, p1, k1 tbl from cn

2/1 RC sl 2 sts to cn and hold to *back*, k1 tbl, k2 tbl from cn

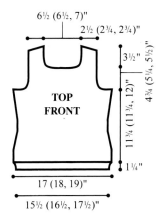

6½ (6½, 7)"

2½ (2¾, 2¾)"

3½"

4¾ (5¼, 5½)"

11¾ (11¾, 12)"

TOP FRONT

1¼"

17 (18, 19)"

15½ (16½, 17½)"

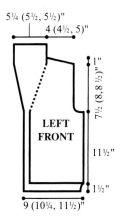

5¼ (5½, 5½)"

4 (4½, 5)"

1"

7½ (8, 8½)"

LEFT FRONT

11½"

1½"

9 (10¼, 11½)"

7"   4 (4½, 5)"

1"

7½ (8, 8½)"

21½ (22, 22½)"

CARDIGAN BACK

11½"

1½"

18 (19½, 22)"

6½ (6½, 7)"

2½ (2¾, 2¾)"

¾"

7½ (8, 8¼)"

11¾ (11¾, 12)"

21¼ (21¾, 22¼)"

TOP BACK

1¼"

16 (17, 18)"

14¼ (15¼, 16¼)"

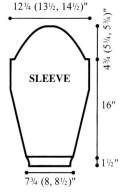

12¾ (13½, 14½)"

4¾ (5¼, 5¾)"

SLEEVE

16"

1½"

7¾ (8, 8½)"

SLEEVES

With smaller needles cast on 51 (53, 55) sts. Work in twisted rib as for back for 1½"/4 cm. Change to larger needles and beg with row 9, center 9-st panel of Chart I on sleeve and work rem sts in St st (with k1 selvage sts), inc 1 st each side every 6th row 16 (17, 19) times—83 (87, 93) sts. Work even until piece measures 17½"/44.5 cm from beg. **Note** Chart I pat will cont to top of sleeve cap. Do not work a partial pat.

Cap shaping

Bind off 6 sts at beg of next 2 rows. Dec 1 st each side every other row 14 (16, 19) times. Bind off 2 sts at beg of next 18 rows. Bind off rem 7 sts.

FINISHING

Block pieces to measurements. Sew on pockets matching pats. Sew on buttons. Weave sts tog at center back neck. Sew collar to back neck. Sew sleeves into armholes. Sew side and sleeve seams.

even on rem 56 (58, 58) sts for collar for 3½"/9cm or to fit to center back neck. Leave sts on a holder.

RIGHT FRONT

Work as for left front, reversing chart at center (and working Chart V instead of Chart III) and working five yo, k2tog buttonholes in center rib of 10-st band, the first one at ½"/1.25 cm from lower edge, the last one ½"/1.25 cm down from beg of neck

shaping and 3 others spaced evenly between.

Left pocket

With larger needles, cast on 41 sts. Working k1 selvage sts at beg and end, work 39 sts foll Chart III and first half of Chart IV (sts 24–62 on chart) for 3¼"/8.5 cm. Work ½"/1.25 cm in twisted rob with smaller needles. Work right pocket in reverse and foll Chart V instead of Chart III.

Winter 1998-1999 · No. 15

15
Very Easy
Very Vogue

VERY EASY VERY VOGUE

Coat. Sized for Small, Medium, and Large. Directions are for smallest size with larger sizes in parentheses. If there is only one figure, it applies to all sizes.

KNITTED MEASUREMENTS

• Bust (wrapped) 37 (40, 42)"/94 (101.5, 106.5) cm
• Length 38 (39, 40)"/96.5 (99, 101.5) cm
• Upper arm 16 (17½, 19½)"/40.5 (44.5, 49.5) cm

MATERIALS

• 23 (24, 26) 1¾oz/50g balls (each approx 39yd/35m) of Filatura di Crosa/Stacy Charles Collection

Muschio (alpaca/wool/acrylic)(13–16 sts per 4"/10 cm, bulky weight) in #356 gray (A)

• 7 (7, 8) 1¾oz/50g balls (each approx 154yd/140m) of *Ultralight* (alpaca/wool/nylon) (13–16 sts per 4"/10 cm, bulky weight) in #1 gray (B)

• 4 (4, 5) 1¾oz/50g balls (each approx 146yd/136m) of *Sympathie* (wool/mohair/nylon) (17–20 sts per 4"/10 cm, medium-heavy weight) in #710 gray (C)

• To substitute, seek a super bulky–weight yarn with similar fiber content

• One pair size 35 (19mm) needles

• Three large coat hook and eye sets

• ½yd/5m of textured weft fusible fabric

• 1 large novelty button

• Size Q (16mm) crochet hook

GAUGE

9 sts and 14 rows = 8"/20 cm over St st using 5 strands of yarn and size 35 (19mm) needles. TAKE TIME TO CHECK GAUGE.

NOTE

Make a test swatch using 2 strands A, 2 strands B and 1 strand C (5 strands of yarn) held tog. Since needle substitution is not a possibility, simply work more tightly or loosely to achieve gauge.

BACK

With 2 strands A, 2 strands B and 1 strand C (5 strands of yarn) held tog, cast on 20 (22, 24) sts. Work in reverse St st (p 1 row, k 1 row) for 8 rows. Then work in St st until piece measures 28"/71 cm from beg, end with a WS row.

Raglan armhole shaping

Bind off 2 sts at beg of next 2 rows. Work even for 2 rows. Dec 1 st each side of next row. Work 1 row even. Rep last 2 rows 4 (5, 6) times more. Bind off rem 6 sts.

LEFT FRONT

With 5 strands of yarn, cast on 10 (12, 14) sts. Work as for back to armholes.

Raglan armhole shaping

Next row (RS)

Bind off 2 sts, work to end. Work even for 3 rows. Dec 1 st at armhole edge on next row then every other row 4 (5, 6) times more—3 (4, 5) sts. Bind off on next WS row.

RIGHT FRONT

With 5 strands of yarn, cast on 16 (18, 20) sts. Work in reverse St st for 8 rows. **Next row (RS)** P7 (front border), k9 (11, 13). Keeping the first 7 sts in reverse St st for front border and rem sts in St st, work as for left front, reversing raglan shaping. Bind off rem 9 (10, 11) sts when armhole shaping is completed.

SLEEVES

With 5 strands of yarn, cast on 14 (16, 18) sts. Work in reverse St st for 8 rows. Then work in St st for 2 rows. Inc 1 st each side of next row, then every 8th row once more—18 (20, 22) sts. Work even until piece measures 18"/45.5 cm from beg.

Raglan cap shaping

Work as for back. Bind off rem 4 sts.

COLLAR

With 5 strands of yarn, cast on 30 (32, 34) sts. (K1 row, p1 row) twice. Bind off loosely.

FINISHING

Block pieces lightly to measurements. Cut fusible fabric to line collar. Foll manufacturer's directions, fuse to WS of collar. With single strand of yarn, sew raglan sleeves into raglan armholes. Sew side and sleeve seams. Sew collar around neck edge. With crochet hook and 5 strands of yarn, work an edge of sc along fronts and all around collar. Sew button to left collar and pull through sc edge. Sew on hook and eye closures to collar and along fronts.

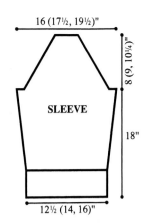

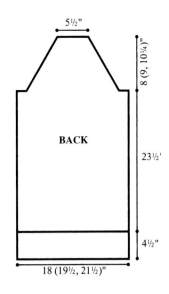

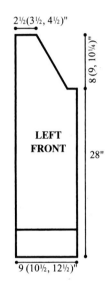

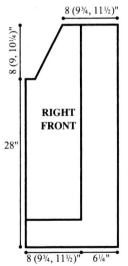

$\mathcal{R}$eversible Rib Shawl

INTERMEDIATE

Shawl. One size.

KNITTED MEASUREMENTS
• Approx 22½"/57 cm wide by 72"/183 cm long

MATERIALS 〔4〕
• 12 1¾oz/50g balls (each approx 192yd/177m) of Filatura di Crosa/Tahki•Stacy Charles, Inc. *Butterfly* (mohair/ acrylic) in #400 white
• To substitute, seek a worsted-weight yarn with similar fiber content
• One pair each sizes 7 and 9 (4.5 and 5.5mm) needles OR SIZE TO OBTAIN GAUGE
• Cable needle (cn)
• Stitch markers

GAUGE
32 sts and 20 rows = 4"/10 cm (blocked) over chart pat using larger needles. TAKE TIME TO CHECK GAUGE.

STITCH GLOSSARY
24-st LC Sl 12 sts to cn and hold to front, [k2, p2] 3 times, work sts from cn as foll: [k2, p2] 3 times.
24-st RC Sl 12 sts to cn and hold to back, [k2, p2] 3 times, work sts from cn as foll: [k2, p2] 3 times.

BACK
With smaller needles, cast on 176 sts.
Beg chart pat
Row 1 (RS) K4, pm, work sts 1 to 48 of chart 3 times, then sts 1 to 24 once more, pm, k4. **Row 2 (WS)** Sl 1 wyif, k3, sl marker, work chart pat to last 4 sts, k3, sl 1 wyif. Cont in this way, working first and last 4 sts in garter and sl st pat as established, until piece measures 72"/183 cm from beg. Switch to larger needles after Row 7. Switch back to the smaller needle for the final 7 rows. Bind off tightly in rib.

FINISHING
Block lightly.

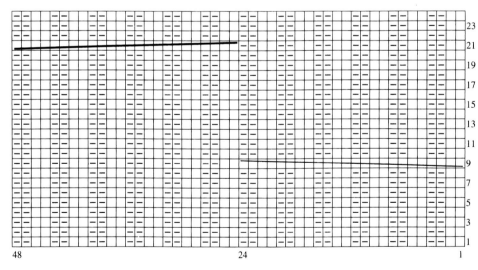

Stitch Key
☐ K on RS, p on WS

⊟ P on RS, k on WS

24-st LC (row 9)
24-st RC (row 21)

Waffle-Knit Coat

EXPERIENCED

Pebble-stitch coat. Sized for Small/Medium and Large. Directions are for smallest size with larger size in parentheses. If there is only one figure, it applies to all sizes.

KNITTED MEASUREMENTS
- Lower edge 54 (58)"/137 (147) cm
- Bust 40 (43)"/101.5 (109) cm
- Length 34 (34½)"/86 (87.5) cm
- Upper arm 15 (16)"/38 (40.5) cm

MATERIALS 〔4〕
- 26 (28) 1¾oz/50g balls (each approx 81yd/75m) of Garnstudio/Aurora Yarns *Alaska* (wool) in #11 red
- To substitute, seek an aran-weight yarn with similar fiber content
- One pair size 7 (4.5mm) needles OR SIZE TO OBTAIN GAUGE
- Size G/6 (4.5mm) crochet hook
- Stitch markers
- Five 1"/25mm button

GAUGE
18 sts and 36 rows = 4"/10 cm over pebble st pat using size 7 (4.5mm) needles. TAKE TIME TO CHECK GAUGE.

NOTE
While knitting, it is important to keep the end of RS rows from being worked too tightly. The tendency of this pat st to bias can be corrected in blocking.

STITCH GLOSSARY
Pebble Stitch
(over an even number of sts)
Row 1 (WS) Sl 2 sts wyib, p to last 2 sts, sl2 sts wyib.
Row 2 (RS) K2tog across row.
Row 3 ★K1, insert RH needle into horizontal thread between st just knit and next st and k1 into this thread; rep from ★, end k last st, pick up and k 1 st in loop at edge.
Row 4 Knit.
Rep rows 1-4 for pebble st pat.

BACK
Cast on 122 (130) sts. Work in pebble st pat for 4"/10 cm, end with pat row 3. **Dec row-pat row 4 (RS)** K44 (48), k3tog, pm, k28, pm, k3tog, k44 (48). Work even for 11 rows. **Next row (RS)** K to 3 sts before marker, k3tog, k to next marker, k3tog after marker, k to end. Rep this row (pat row 4) every 12th row 3 times more, every 28th row 3 times—90 (98) sts. Work even until piece measures 24"/61 cm from beg, end with pat row 1.
Raglan armhole shaping
Bind off 2 sts at beg of next 2 rows. **Dec row-pat row 4 (RS)** K2, k3tog, k to last 5 sts, k3tog, k2. Rep dec row every 6th row 7 (6) times more, every 4th row 7 (10) times—26 sts. Work even, if necessary, until armhole measures 8 (8½)"/20.5 (21.5) cm. Bind off.

LEFT FRONT
Cast on 70 (74) sts. Work in pat st for 4"/10 cm, end with pat row 3. **Dec row-pat row** 4 (RS) K49 (53), k3tog, pm, k18. Cont to dec in this way, working k3tog before marker every 12th row (always on row 4) 4 times more, every 28th row 2 times—54

(58) sts. Work even until piece measures 24"/61 cm from beg, end pat row 1.
Raglan armhole shaping
Next row (RS) Bind off 2 sts, work to end. Work 1 row even. **Dec row-pat row 4 (RS)** K2, k3tog, k to end. Rep dec row every 4th row 13 (14) times more, AT SAME TIME, when armhole measures 4 (4½)"/10 (11.5) cm, work neck shaping.
Neck shaping
Next row (WS) Bind off 6 sts, work to end. Cont to bind off 4 sts from neck edge every other row once, 2 sts 7 times.

RIGHT FRONT
Work to correspond to left front reversing shaping.

LEFT SLEEVE
Cast on 40 (44) sts. Work in pat st for 11 rows. **Inc row (pat row 4)** Work 19 (21) sts, pm, k1 into front, back and front of next st (inc 2 sts inc'd), work to end. Cont to inc 2 sts in this way (before marker) every 8th row 13 times more—68 (72) sts. Work even in pat until piece measures 17"/43 cm from beg, end with pat row 1. **Raglan cap shaping** Bind off 2 sts at beg of next 2 rows. **Dec row (pat row 4)** K2, k3tog, k to last 5 sts, k3tog, k2. For beg of RS rows (back edge), rep dec every 8th row 9 (6) times, every 4th row 2 (6) times and for end of RS rows (front edge), rep dec every 8th row 6 times, every 4th (6th) row 5 (6) times, then bind off 3 sts from LH edge 4 times, 2 sts twice.

RIGHT SLEEVE
Work to correspond to left sleeve until row 11 is completed. **Inc row (RS)** Work 20 (22) sts, pm, inc 2 sts in next st, work to end. Cont to inc in this way (after marker) every 8th row 13 times more—61 (72) sts. When same length as left sleeve, work sleeve cap shaping reversing front and back shaping.

FINISHING

Block pieces to measurements. Sew raglan sleeve seams.

Collar

Pick up and k 29 sts from right neck, 20 sts from sleeve, 26 sts from back neck, other side to correspond—124 sts. Work in pat st for 15 rows.
Next row Dec 2 sts 4 times evenly spaced around. Work 3 rows even.
Next row K20, k3tog, k to last 23 sts, k3tog, k20. Cont in pat until collar measures 3"/7.5 cm. **Next row** K12, k2tog, k to last 15 sts k3tog, k12. Work even until collar measures 3½"/9 cm.

Beg lining

Work 4 rows St st. Inc sts evenly on next row. Work in St st until lining measures 2½"/6.5 cm. Inc 6 sts—120 sts. Work even until lining measures 3¼"/8 cm. Bind off. Fold collar to inside and sew. With crochet hook, work an edge of sc up left front. Do not turn, work 1 backwards sc in each sc. Work an edge in same way up right front working 5 ch 10 button loops on 2nd row, the first one at 15"/38 cm from lower edge and the other spaced evenly to top. Sew side and sleeve seams. Sew on buttons.

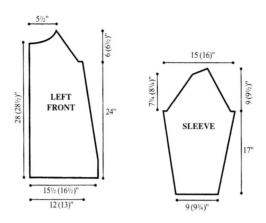

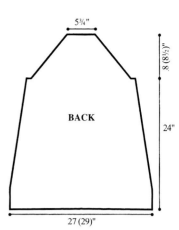

Fall 2000 · No. 34

*R*ibbed Yoke Sweater

INTERMEDIATE

Pullover with rolled neckband. Sized for Small/Medium and Large. Directions are for smallest size with larger size in parentheses. If there is only one figure, it applies to all sizes.

KNITTED MEASUREMENTS
• Bust 36 (40½)"/91.5 (103) cm
• Length 23½"/59.5 cm
• Upper arm 13½"/34 cm

MATERIALS
• 5 (6) 3½oz/100g hanks (each approx 165yd/152m) of Trendsetter Yarns *Dali* (cashmere) in #3 bone
• To substitute, seek a bulky-weight yarn with similar fiber content
• One pair each sizes 7 and 9 (4.5 and 5.5mm) needles OR SIZE TO OBTAIN GAUGE
• Size 9 (5.5mm) circular needle, 36"/92 cm long and 24"/60 cm long
• Large stitch holders

GAUGES
• 15 sts and 21 rows = 4"/10 cm over St st using larger needles.
• 17 sts and 21 rnds = 4"/10 cm over k5, p4 rib for yoke using larger needles. TAKE TIME TO CHECK GAUGES.

BACK

With smaller needles, cast on 74 (82) sts. Work in k1, p1 rib for 2 rows. Change to larger needles and cont in St st, dec 1 st each side every 18th row 3 times—68 (76) sts. Work even until piece measures 14½"/37 cm from beg.
Beg rib: Next row (RS) *P4, k2, m1, k2; rep from * 7 (8) times more, p4—76 (85) sts. Work in k5, p4 rib for 1 row.

Armhole shaping

Bind off 2 sts at beg of next 2 rows—72 (81) sts. Sl sts to a holder to be worked for yoke later.

FRONT

Work as for back.

SLEEVES

With smaller needles, cast on 58 sts. Work in k1, p1 rib for 2 rows. Change to larger needles. **Next row (RS)** P4, *k5, p4; rep from * to end. Cont in k5, p4 rib until piece measures

2½"/6.5 cm from beg.

Armhole shaping
Bind off 2 sts at beg of next 2 rows—54 sts. Sl sts to a holder. Work 2nd sleeve in same way.

Beg yoke
With longer circular needle, work 54 sts of one sleeve, 72 (81) sts of front, 54 sts of other sleeve, 72 (81) sts of back—252 (270) sts. Join and work in rnds of k5, p4 rib for 2½"/6.5 cm. **Dec rnd** Dec 1 p-st in each of the 28 (30) p4 sections around—224 (240) sts. Work even in k5, p3 rib for 2"/5 cm more. **Dec rnd** Dec 1 p-st in each of the 28 (30) p3 sections around—196 (210) sts. Work even in k5, p2 rib for 1½"/4 cm more. **Dec**

rnd Dec 1 p-st in each of the 28 (30) p2 sections around—168 (180) sts. Work 1 rnd in k5, p1 rib. **Next rnd** ★ [K2tog, k1] 16 (10) times, [k2tog] 18 (30) times; rep from ★ once—100 sts. Change to shorter circular needle. P 1 rnd (for ridge). K 8 rnds. **Next rnd** Turn work to WS and working into corresponding st 8 rnds below, p1 st tog from needle with 1 st from 8 rnds below (for edge to roll to inside). Return to work in rnds from RS and k 10 rnds more. Bind off loosely.

FINISHING
Block to measurements. Sew underarm seams at bind offs. Sew side and sleeve seams.

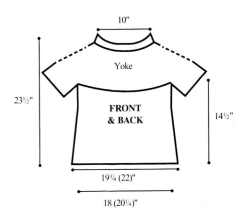

Winter 2000-2001 · No. 16

Diamond-Lace Top

EXPERIENCED

Cardigan Sized for Small, Medium/Large, and X-Large. Directions are for smallest size with larger sizes in parentheses. If there is only one figure, it applies to all sizes.

KNITTED MEASUREMENTS
• Bust (buttoned) 38 (45, 52½)"/96.5 (114, 133) cm
• Length 18½ (19½, 20½)"/47 (49.5, 52) cm
• Upper arm 15¼ (16, 17)"/38.5 (40.5, 43) cm

MATERIALS 2
• 3 (4, 5) .87oz/25g balls (each approx 268yd/245m) of Filatura Di Crosa/Tahki•Stacy Charles, Inc. *Baby Kid Extra* (kid mohair/nylon) in #326 black
• To substitute, seek a fingering-weight yarn with similar fiber content
• One pair each sizes 6 and 8 (4 and 5mm) needles OR SIZE TO OBTAIN GAUGE
• Size 2 (2.5mm) crochet hook
• 1 ball of #20 black crochet cotton
• Thirteen ¾"/10mm buttons

GAUGE
15 sts and 23 rows= 4"/10 cm over chart pat (after blocking) using larger needles. TAKE TIME TO CHECK GAUGE.

NOTES
1) Be sure that there is always a yo to compensate for each dec in every row to keep st count the same. If there is not, then omit the yo or dec and work st in St st.
2) K first and last st of every row for selvage sts.

STITCH GLOSSARY
Scallop Edging
Cast on 7 sts.
Row 1 (RS) Sl 1, k1, yo, k2tog, yo, k1, yo, k2—9 sts.
Row 2 (WS) Yo, k2tog, p4, k1, yo, k2tog.
Row 3 Sl 1, k1, yo, k2tog, yo, k3, yo, k2—11 sts.
Row 4 Yo, k2tog, p6, k1, yo, k2tog.
Row 5 Yo, k1, yo, k2tog, yo, k1, yo, SK2P, yo, k1, yo, k1, k2tog—13 sts.
Row 6 Yo, k2tog, p8, k1, yo, k2tog.
Row 7 Sl 1, k1, yo, k2tog, yo, k3, yo, k1, yo, k3, yo, k2—17sts.
Row 8 Yo, k2tog, p12, k1, yo, k2tog.
Row 9 Sl 1, k1, [yo, SK2P] twice, yo, k3, yo, SK2P, yo, k2tog, k1—15 sts.
Row 10 Yo, k2tog, p10, k1, yo, k2tog.
Row 11 Sl 1, k1, yo, SK2P, k2tog, [yo, SK2P] twice, k2tog—10 sts.

Row 12 Yo, k2tog, p5, k1, yo, k2tog.
Row 13 Sl 1, k1, [yo, SK2P] twice, k2tog—7 sts.
Row 14 Yo, k2tog, p2, yo, k2tog, k1—7 sts.
Rep rows 1-14 for scallop edging.

BACK
With larger needles, cast on 73 (87, 101) sts.
Beg chart pat
Row 1 (RS) K1 (selvage st), work sts 1 to 16, work 14-st rep (sts 3 to 16) 3 (4, 5) times, work sts 17 to 29, k1 (selvage st). Cont in pat as established until piece measures 11"/28 cm from beg, end with a WS row.
Armhole shaping
Bind off 3 (4, 5) sts at beg of the next 2 rows, 3 sts at beg of next 0 (0, 2) rows, 2 sts at beg of next 2 (6, 6) rows, dec 1 st at each side every other row twice—59 (63, 69) sts. Work even until armhole measures 7½ (8½, 9½)"/19 (21.5, 24) cm. Bind off all sts.

LEFT FRONT
With larger needles, cast on 37 (44, 51) sts.
Beg chart pat
Row 1 (RS) K1 (selvage st), work sts 3 (10, 3) to 16, work 14-st rep

(sts 3 to 16) 1 (2, 2) times, work sts 17 to 23, k1 (selvage st). Cont in pat as established until same length as back to armhole.
Armhole shaping
Work armhole shaping as for back at beg of RS rows—30 (32, 35) sts. Work even until armhole measures 2½ (3½, 4)"/6.5 cm (9, 10) cm, end with a RS row.
Neck shaping
Next row (WS) Bind off 4 sts (neck edge), work to end. Cont to bind off from neck edge 2 (2, 3) sts once, dec 1 st every other row 6 (7, 7) times. When piece measures same as back, bind off rem 18 (19, 21) sts for shoulder.

RIGHT FRONT
Work to correspond to left front, reversing shaping and beg chart pat with st 9.

SLEEVES
With smaller needles, work 14 rows of scallop edging 4 (5, 5) times. Bind off. With RS facing and smaller needles, pick up and k 35 (39, 39) sts evenly across top of edging. **Next row (WS)** Purl. Change to larger needles.

Beg chart pat
Row 1 (RS) K1 (selvage st), work at 7 (5, 5) to 16, work 14-st rep once, work st 17 to 25 (27, 27), k1 (selvage st). Cont in pat as established, inc 1 st each side (working incs into chart pat inside of selvage sts) every 4th (6th, 4th) row 2 (8, 2) times, every 6th (8th, 6th) row 10 (3, 11) times—59 (61, 65) sts. Work even until piece measures 15 (15½, 16)"/38 cm (39.5, 40.5) cm from beg.
Cap shaping
Bind off 3 (4, 4) sts at beg of next 2 rows, 2 sts at beg of next 2 rows, dec 1 st each side every other row 2 (4, 5) times. Bind of rem 45 (41, 43) sts.

FINISHING
Block pieces to measurements. Sew shoulder seams. Set in sleeves. Sew side and sleeve seams. With smaller needles work 14 rows of scallop edging 7 (7, 8) times. Sew edging around neck. With crochet hook and cotton, work 2 rows sc along fronts including side edge of collar, and around lower edge.
Row 3 Work buttonhole picot on right front as foll: 10 (12, 14) sc, ★ch 3, skip 2 sc, 5 sc in next 5 sts; rep from ★10 times, then at neck: ★ch 3, skip 2 sc, sc in last 2 sc. Sew on buttons opposite button loops.

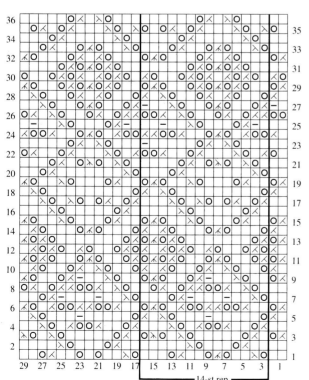

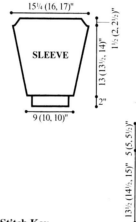

15¼ (16, 17)"

SLEEVE

1½ (2, 2½)"

13 (13½, 14)"

2"

9 (10, 10)"

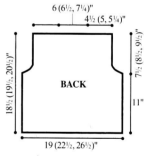

6 (6½, 7¼)"

4½ (5, 5¼)"

BACK

7½ (8½, 9½)"

18½ (19½, 20½)"

11"

19 (22½, 26½)"

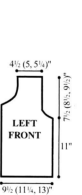

4½ (5, 5¼)"

13½ (14½, 15)"

5 (5, 5½)"

7½ (8½, 9½)"

LEFT FRONT

11"

9½ (11¼, 13)"

Stitch Key
☐ K on RS, p on WS
⊟ P on RS, k on WS
◿ K3tog on RS, p3 tog on WS
◺ Sk2p on RS, p3 tog tbl on WS
◹ K2tog on RS, p2 tog on WS
◸ Ssk on RS, p2tog tbl on WS
⊡ Yo

$\mathcal{C}$otton Tunic

INTERMEDIATE

Loose-fitting, cabled pullover knit in one piece. Sized for Small, Medium, and Large. Directions are for smallest size with larger sizes in parentheses. If there is only one figure, it applies to all sizes.

KNITTED MEASUREMENTS
• Bust 39 (41, 43)"/99 (104, 109) cm
• Length 20½ (21, 21½)"/52 (53, 54.5) cm
• Upper arm 15 (16, 17)"/38 (40.5, 43) cm

MATERIALS 🔵4
• 15 (16, 17) 1¾oz/50g balls (each approx 87yd/80m) of Adrienne Vittadini/JCA *Miranda* (cotton) in #1250 white
• To substitute, seek an aran-weight yarn with similar fiber content
• Size 6 and 8 (4 and 5mm) circular needle, 16"/40 cm and 36"/92 cm long OR SIZE TO OBTAIN GAUGE
• Cable needle (cn)
• Stitch holders

GAUGE
20 sts and 31 rows = 4"/10 cm over St st using size 8 (5mm) needles. TAKE TIME TO CHECK GAUGE.

NOTE
Pullover is made all in one piece beg at front lower edge and ending at back lower edge.

STITCH GLOSSARY
12-st RC sl next 6 sts to cn and hold to back, k6, k6 from cn.

FRONT
Beg at lower edge with size 8 (5mm) circular needle, cast on 101 (105, 111) sts. **Row 1 (WS)** P34 (36, 39), k4, p4, k4, p9, k4, p4, k4, p34 (36, 39). **Row 2 (RS)** Work 46 (48, 51) sts as established, [k2, M1] 3 times, k3 (for central cable pat), work as established to end—104 (108, 114) sts. Work even in pat as established for 3 rows. **Next row (RS)** Work 46 (48, 51) sts, 12-st RC, work to end. Cont to work in this way, working 12-st RC every 16th row, until piece measures 13"/33 cm from beg, end with a WS row.

SLEEVES
Next row (RS) Cast on 90 sts, p18, k4, p4, k12, p4, k4, p4, k40, work from established to end. **Next row (WS)** Cast on 90 sts, k18, p4, k4, p12, k4, p4, k4, p40, work as established to end—284 (288, 294) sts. Work as established, working 12-st RC over the 12 sts on each sleeve as on front, until sleeve measures 5 (5½, 6)"/12.5 (14, 15) cm.
Neck shaping
Next row (RS) Work 124 (126, 129) sts, join another ball of yarn and work across center 36 sts, dec 3 sts across 12 center cable sts and sl these 33 sts to a holder, work with separate ball to end. Working both sides at once, bind off 4 sts from each neck edge once, 3 sts once, 2sts once, 1 st once. Work even on 114 (116, 119) sts each side until sleeve cuff measures 7½ (8, 8½)"/19 (20.5, 21.5) cm.
Back neck shaping
To rejoin piece and form neck, cast on

5 sts at each neck edge every other row once, then cast on 33 sts and join to complete row. **Next row (WS)** Work to center 33 sts, k4, p4, k4, p9, k4, p4, k4, work to end. **Next row (RS)** Work to center 9 sts, [k2, M1] 3 times, k3 (for central cable pat), work to end. Cont on all 284 (288, 294) sts for back until sleeve cuff measures 15 (16, 17)"/38 (41, 43) cm. Bind off 90 sts at beg of next 2 rows to complete sleeves. Cont on 104 (108, 114) sts for back until there are same number of rows as on front. Bind off in pat, dec 3 sts across cable section while binding off.

FINISHING
Block pieces to measurements. Sew side and sleeve seams.
Neckband
With smaller circular needle, pick up and k 125 sts evenly around neck edge. Join and k 7 rnds. Bind off.

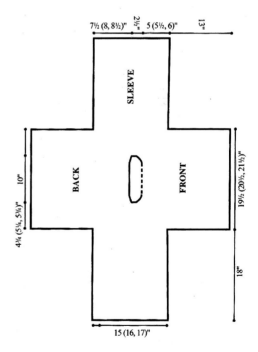

Coral Cables

EXPERIENCED

Close-fitting cabled pullover with ribbed yoke. Sized for X-Small, Small, Medium, and Large. Directions are for smallest size with larger sizes in parentheses. If there is only one figure, it applies to all sizes.

KNITTED MEASUREMENTS
• Bust 31 (34, 37, 40)"/78.5 (86.5, 94, 101.5) cm
• Length 19½ (20½, 21, 22)"/49.5 (52, 53, 56) cm
• Upper arm 10 (11, 13, 13½)"/25.5 (28, 33, 34) cm

MATERIALS 6
• 10 (11, 12, 13) 3½100g balls (each approx 88yd/80m) of Karabella Yarns *Softig* (cotton) in #102 coral
• To substitute, seek a super bulky–weight yarn with similar fiber content
• One pair size 10½ (7mm) needles OR SIZE TO OBTAIN GAUGE
• Size 10½ (7mm) circular needle, 32"/80 cm long
• Cable needle (cn)

GAUGES
• 16 sts and 18 rows = 4"/10 cm over cable pat using size 10½ (7mm) needles.
• 18 sts and 18 rows = 4"/10 cm over k1, p1 rib (unstretched) using size 10½ (7mm) needles. TAKE TIME TO CHECK GAUGES.

STITCH GLOSSARY
Cable pattern
(multiple of 12 sts)
Rows 1 and 3 (RS) ★K8, p4; rep from ★ to end.
Row 2 and all WS rows K the knit sts and p the purl sts.
Row 5 ★Sl 4 sts to cn and hold to front, k4, k4 from cn, p4; rep from ★ to end.
Rows 7, 9, 11 and 13 Rep row 1.
Rows 14 Rep row 2.
Rep rows 1–14 for cable pat.

Left-slanting double dec
Sl next st knitwise to RH needle, sl next st to cn and hold to back, sl next st knitwise to RH needle, sl 2 sts from RH needle back to LH needle, sl st from cn to LH needle and k3tog tbl.

Right-slanting double dec
Sl 2 sts to cn and hold to back, sl next st knitwise to RH needle, sl p st from cn knitwise to LH needle then sl k st from cn purlwise to LH needle, place slipped st on RH needle back to LH needle and k3tog tbl.

BACK
Cast on 62 (68, 74, 80) sts. Work in k1, p1 rib for 3"/7.5 cm.
Beg cable pat
Row 1 (RS) P3 (6, 3, 6); rep from ★ of cable pat to last 3 (6, 3, 6) sts, p to end. Cont in pat as established, working sts outside of cable pat in rev St st, until piece measures 11½ (12, 12, 12½)"/29 (30.5, 30.5, 31.5) cm from beg, end with a WS row. Place sts on a holder.

FRONT
Work as for back.

SLEEVES
Cast on 29 (29, 31, 33) sts. Work in k1, p1 rib, inc 1 st each side (working inc sts into rib) every 6th (4th, 4th, 4th) row 8 (6, 11, 12) times, every 0 (6th, 2nd, 2nd) row 0 (4, 3, 2) times— 45 (49, 59, 61) sts. Work even until piece measures 11 (11½, 12, 12½)"/28 (29, 30.5, 31, 5) cm from beg, end with a WS row. Place sts on a holder.

YOKE
With circular needle, work sts from holder as foll: Work 62 (68, 74, 80) sts from back holder, pm, 45 (49, 59, 61) sts from one sleeve holder, pm, 62 (68, 74, 80) sts from front holder, pm, 45 (49, 59, 61) sts from 2nd sleeve holder, pm—214 (234, 266, 282) sts. Join and cont in rnds, slipping markers every rnd, as foll: **Next rnd** K1, cont back sts in pat as established to 1 st before next marker, k1, ★sl marker, k1, p1 work right-slanting double dec, rib to last 5 sts of sleeve, work left-slanting double dec, p1 k1, sl marker★, k1, cont front sts in pat as established to 1 st before next marker, k1; rep between ★'s once. Cont in this way to dec 2 sts each side of each sleeve every 4th rnd 4 times more, every 2nd rnd 0 (1, 2, 3) times, AT SAME TIME, **for sizes Small and Large only**, dec 1 st each side on front and back (in p-4 section) every 4th rnd (3, 2) times, AT SAME TIME, after 8 rnds have been worked in the yoke, dec 6 (6, 12, 10) sts on front and 6 (6, 12, 10) sts on back on next rnd as foll: **For sizes X-Small and Small only** K1, p2tog, [work to next p-section, p1 p2tog, p1] 4 times, work to last 3 sts before next marker, p2tog, k1, sl marker, cont sleeve sts as established, work back sts same as front sts, cont sleeve sts as established. **For size Medium only** K1, p2tog, [work to next p-section, (p2tog) twice] 5 times, work to last 3 sts before next marker, p2tog, k1, sl marker, cont sleeve sts as established, work back sts same as front sts, cont sleeve sts as established. **For size Large only** K1, p2tog, work to next

p-section, p1 p2tog, p1 [work to next p-section, (p2tog) twice] 3 times, work to next p-section, p1 p2tog, p1 work to last 3 sts before next marker, p2tog, k1, sl marker, cont sleeve sts as established, work back sts same as front sts, cont sleeve sts as established. **For all sizes** Mark center 20 (20, 22, 22) sts on front and back. On next rnd, work center marked sts in k1, p2 rib, beg and end with p2 (p2, k1, k1) and rem sts as established. Cont to work 2 more rib sts each side of center sts every rnd 9 (9, 10, 10) times. After all decs have been worked, there are 162 (162, 186, 186) sts. Cont in p2, k1 rib over all sts for 2"/5 cm.

Next rnd Work p2tog in each p-2 section—108 (108, 124, 124) sts. Cont in k1, p1 rib for 2"/5 cm. Bind off knitwise.

FINISHING
Block lightly. Sew side and sleeve seams.

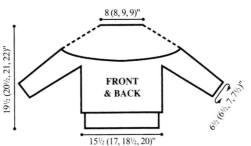

8 (8, 9, 9)"

19½ (20½, 21, 22)"

FRONT & BACK

6½ (6½, 7, 7½)"

15½ (17, 18½, 20)"

Spring/Summer 2001 · No. 15

Wrap Star Cardigan

EXPERIENCED

Loose-fitting, wrapped cardigan with diagonal ribs and cabled front panels. Designed by Oscar for Oscar de la Renta. Sized for Small, Medium, and Large. Directions are for smallest size with larger sizes in parentheses. If there is only one figure, it applies to all sizes.

KNITTED MEASUREMENTS
• Bust 38 (42, 46)"/96.5 (106.5, 117) cm
• Length 23 (23½, 24)"/58.5 (59.5, 61) cm
• Upper arm 14 (15, 16)"/35.5 (38, 40.5) cm

MATERIALS 4
• 23 (25, 27) 1¾oz/50g balls (each approx 70yd/65m) of Needful Yarns and Things *Modigliani* (wool) in #03 taupe
• To substitute, seek a worsted-weight yarn with similar fiber content
• One pair each sizes 9 and 10½ (5.5 and 6.5mm) needles OR SIZE TO OBTAIN GAUGE
• Cable needle (cn)

GAUGES
• 19 sts and 22 rows = 4"/10 cm over k3, p6 diagonal rib using larger needles.
• 17 sts and 23 rows = 4"/10 cm over k3, p6 rib using larger needles. TAKE TIME TO CHECK GAUGES.

STITCH GLOSSARY
Left-Slating Diagonal Rib
(multiple of 9 sts)

Row 1 (RS) ★P6, k3; rep from ★to end.
Row 2 P2, k, k2tog, ★p3, M1, k4, k2tog; rep from ★ to last 6 sts, M1, k5, p1.
Row 3 and all foll RS rows K the knit sts and p the purl sts.
Row 4 P1, k5, k2tog; rep from ★in row 2 to last 7 sts, M1, k, p2.
Row 6 K5, k2tog; rep from ★ in row 2 to last 8 sts, Ml, k5, p3.
Row 8 K4, k2tog; rep from ★ in row 2 to last 3 sts, p2, M1-p, k1.
Row 10 K3, k2tog; rep from ★ in row 2 to last st, Ml, k1.
Row 12 K2, k2tog; rep from ★ in row 2 to last 2 sts, M1, k2.
Cont in this way to shift p6, k3 rib to the left every WS row for left-slanting diagonal rib.

Right-Slanting Diagonal Rib
(multiple of 9 sts)
Row 1 (RS)★K3, p6; rep from ★ to end.
Row 2 P1, k5, M1, ★p3, k2tog, k4, M1; rep from ★ to last 9 sts, k2tog, k5, p2.
Row 3 and all foll RS rows
K the knit sts and p the purl sts.
Row 4 P2, k5, M1; rep from ★ in row 2 to last 8 sts, k2tog, k5, p1.
Row 6 P3, k5, M1; rep from ★ in row 2 to last 7 sts, k2tog, k5.

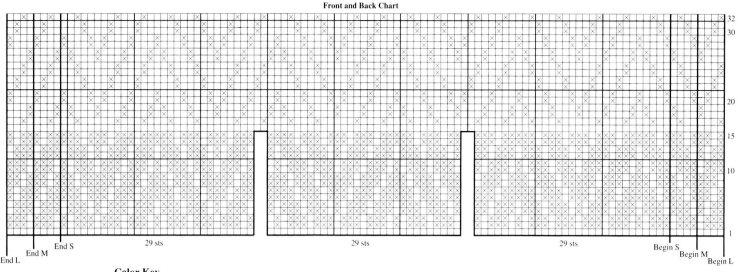

End L | End M | End S | 29 sts | 29 sts | 29 sts | Begin S | Begin M | Begin L

32
30
20
15
10
1

Color Key

☒ Tan (A)

☐ Off-white ombre (B)

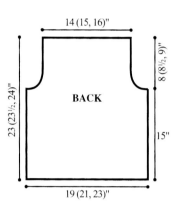

14 (15, 16)"

BACK

23 (23½, 24)"

8 (8½, 9)"

15"

19 (21, 23)"

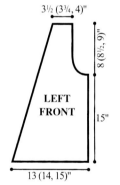

3½ (3¾, 4)"

8 (8½, 9)"

LEFT
FRONT

15"

13 (14, 15)"

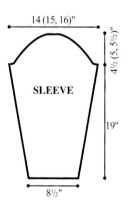

14 (15, 16)"

4½ (5, 5½)"

SLEEVE

19"

8½"

Row 8 K1, P3, k5, M1; rep from ★in row 2 to last 6 sts, k2tog, k4.

Row 10 K1, M1; rep from ★ in row 2 to last 5 sts, k2tog, k3.

Row 12 K2, M1; rep from ★ in row 2 to last 4 sts, k2tog, k2.

Row 14 K3, M1; rep from ★ in row 2 to last 3 sts, k2tog, k1.

Cont in this way to shift p6, k3 rib to the right every WS row for right-slanting diagonal rib.

Left Twist (LT)

(over 2 sts)

Row 1 (RS) Skip first st on LH needle and k 2nd st behind first st, then k first st and drop both sts from LH needle.

Row 2 (WS) P2.

Rep rows 1 and 2 for left twist.

6-ST LC

(over 6 sts)

Rows 1 and 3 (RS) K6.

Rows 2, 4 and 6 P6.

Row 5 Sl 3 sts to cn and hold to front, k3, k3 from cn. Rep rows 1–6 for 6-st LC.

8-ST RC

(over 8 sts)

Rows 1, 3, 5 and 7 (RS) K8.

Rows 2, 4, 6, 8 and 10 (WS) P8.

Row 9 Sl 4 sts to cn and hold to back, k4, k4 from cn.

Rep rows 1–10 for 8-st RC.

BACK

With larger needles, cast on 90 (100, 108) sts. Beg with p6 (p2, p6), work left-slanting diagonal rib over first 45 (50, 54) sts, pm, beg with k3, work right-slanting diagonal rib over last 45 sts, end with p6 (p2, p6). Cont in pats as established until piece measures 15"/38 cm from beg, end with a WS row.

Armhole shaping

Bind off 4 sts at beg of next 2 rows, 3 sts at beg of next 2 rows, 2 sts at beg of next 2 (4, 4) rows. Dec 1 st each side every other row 3 (3, 5) times—66 (72, 76) sts. Work even until armhole measures 8 (8½, 9)"/20.5 (21.5, 23) cm. Bind off all sts.

LEFT FRONT

With larger needles, cast on 63 (67, 71) sts. Beg with p6 (p1, p5), work left-slanting diagonal rib, AT SAME TIME, dec 1 st at front edge every 4th row 25 times, every other row 10 times, AT SAME TIME, when same length as back to armhole, shape armhole at side edge as for back. When same length as back, bind off rem 16 (18, 20) sts for shoulder.

RIGHT FRONT

With larger needles, cast on 63 (67, 71) sts. Beg with k3, work right-slanting diagonal rib, and reverse shaping as for left front.

CABLE BAND

With larger needles, cast on 30 sts. Beg cable pats **Row 1 (RS)** P2, LT, p2, 8-st RC, p2, k3, p2, 6-st LC, p3. Cont in past as established, working sts outside cable pats as k the knit sts and p the purl sts, until piece fits along left front, back neck and right front edges. **Note** Sew shoulder seams and pin band in place while knitting, beg at right front edge, if desired for ease in measuring. Bind off. Sew band to fronts and back neck.

SLEEVES

With larger needles, cast on 39 sts.

Beg cable and rib pats

Row 1 (RS) K1, p4, work 30 sts cable pats as for cable band, p3, k. Cont in pats as established, working sts outside cable pats in p6, k3 rib, AND inc 1 st each side (working inc sts into p6, k3 rib) every 8th (6th, 4th) row 12 (16, 9) times, every 0 (0, 6th) row 0 (0, 10) times—63 (71, 77) sts. Work even until piece measures 19"/48 cm from beg, end with a WS row.

Cap shaping

Bind off 4 sts at beg of next 2 rows, 3 sts at beg of next 2 rows, 2 sts at beg of next 2 (4, 4) rows. Dec 1 st each side every other row 8 (8, 9) times. Bind off 4 (5, 6) sts at beg of next 4 rows. Bind off rem 13 sts.

BELT

With smaller needles, cast on 7 sts.

Preparation row (RS) ★K1, p1; rep from ★, end p1. **Row 1** ★P1, k1; rep from ★, end p1. **Row 2** Sl 1 wyib, ★p1, k1; rep from ★ to last st, sl 1 wyib. Rep rows 1 and 2 until piece measures 31"/78.5 cm. Bind off. Make a 2nd belt 45"/114 cm long.

FINISHING

Block pieces to measurements. Sew shoulder seams. Set in sleeves. Sew side seams, leaving a 1"/2.5 cm opening at 8"/20.5 cm above lower edge on right seam for belt. Sew sleeve seams. Sew one end of longer belt to left front edge at 8"/20.5 cm above lower edge (to make opening on right seam). Sew shorter belt to right front edge.

Fall 2001 · No. 2

$\mathcal{F}$ine Lines Cowlneck

INTERMEDIATE

Close fitting striped pullover with deep U-neck and cowl collar. Sized for X-Small, Small, Medium, and Large. Directions are for smallest size with larger sizes in parentheses. If there is only one figure, it applies to all sizes.

KNITTED MEASUREMENTS

• Bust 30½ (31½, 34, 36)"/77.5 (80, 86, 91.5) cm
• Waist 28 (30, 31½, 33½)"/71 (76, 80, 85) cm
• Length 21 (21½, 21½, 22)"/53 (54.5, 54.5, 56) cm
• Upper arm 11½ (12½, 12½, 13½)"/29 (32, 32, 34) cm

MATERIALS 🔵4

• 7 (7, 8, 9) 1¾oz/50g balls (each approx 109yd/100m) of Dive/Lane Borgosesia *Christine* (mohair/wool/acrylic) in #1807 ecru (A)
• To substitute, seek an aran-weight yarn with similar fiber content
• 2 (2, 3, 3) balls in #1810 green (B)
• One pair each sizes 8 and 10 (5 and 6mm) OR SIZE TO OBTAIN GAUGE
• Size 10 (6mm) circular needle, 36"/92 cm long
• Size I/9 (5.5mm) crochet hook

GAUGE

17 sts and 26 rows = 4"/10 cm over St st and stripe pat using larger needles.
TAKE TIME TO CHECK GAUGE.

NOTE

Green stripe in stripe pat is formed over 2 rows using slipped sts to show as a 1-row color stripe.

STRIPE PATTERN

(over an odd number of sts)
Row 1 (WS) With A, purl.
Row 2 With A, knit.
Row 3 Rep row 1.
Row 4 With B, k1, ★sl 1 purl-wise wyib, k1; rep from ★ to end.
Row 5 With B, sl 1 purlwise wyif, ★pl, sl 1 purlwise wyif; rep from ★ to end.
Row 6 With A, knit.
Rep rows 1-6 for stripe pat.

BACK

With smaller needles and A, cast on 67 (71, 75, 79) sts. K1 row, p1 row. Change to larger needles. Beg with row 1 (WS row) of stripe pat, work in stripe pat until piece measures 2"/5 cm from beg. Dec 1 st each side of next row, then every 10th row 3 times more—59 (63, 67, 71) sts. Work even until piece measures 7½"/19 cm from beg. Inc 1 st each side of next row, then rep inc every 12th row twice more—65 (69, 73, 77) sts. Work even until piece measures 13½"/34 cm from beg.

Armhole shaping
Bind off 3 sts at beg of next 2 rows, 2 sts at beg of next 2 rows. Dec 1 st each side every other row 2 (3, 4, 5) times—51 (53, 55, 57) sts. Work even until armhole measures 6½ (7, 7, 7½)"/16.5 (18, 18, 19) cm.

Neck and shoulder shaping Bind off 5 sts at beg of next 4 (6, 6, 4) rows, 4 (0, 0, 6) sts at beg of next 2 rows. Bind off rem 23 (23, 25, 25) sts for back neck.

FRONT
Work as for back until piece measures 11 (11½, 11½, 12)"/28 (29, 29, 30.5) cm.

Neck shaping
On next row, bind off center 5 (5, 7, 7) sts. Working both sides at once, bind off 2 sts from each neck edge twice, dec 1 st each side every other row 3 times, every 4th row twice, AT SAME TIME, work armhole shaping and shoulder shaping when same length as back.

SLEEVES
With smaller needles and A, cast on 43 (45, 45, 47) sts. K1 row, p1 row. Change to larger needles and work in Stripe pat as on back, inc 1 st each side every 20th row 3 (4, 4, 5) times—49 (53, 53, 57) sts. Work even until piece measures 17½"/44.5 cm

from beg (end with same stripe row as on back).

Cap shaping
Bind off 3 sts at beg of next 2 rows, 2 sts at beg of next 2 rows. Dec 1 st each side every other row 13 (15, 15, 17) times. Bind off rem 13 sts.

FINISHING
Block pieces to measurements. Sew shoulder seams.

Cowlneck
With circular needle and A, pick up and k 136 (136, 140, 140) sts evenly around neck edge from WS of piece working in rnds, work in stripe pat for 7½"/19 cm. P 1 rnd for turning ridge. K 1 rnd. Bind off. Block cowlneck and fold to WS. With crochet hook and A, work long sl sts to join edge at turning ridge by ★sl st through one st and corresponding st on WS, skip 1 st; rep from ★ until edge is joined to WS. Sew sleeves into armholes. Sew side and sleeve seams.

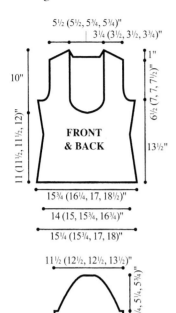

5½ (5½, 5¾, 5¾)"
3¼ (3½, 3½, 3¾)"
1"
10"
6½ (7, 7, 7½)"
FRONT & BACK
11 (11½, 11½, 12)"
13½"
15¾ (16¼, 17, 18½)"
14 (15, 15¾, 16¾)"
15¼ (15¾, 17, 18)"

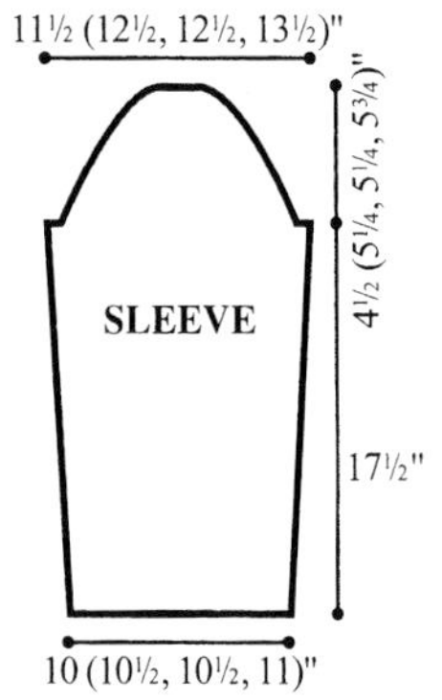

11½ (12½, 12½, 13½)"
4½ (5¼, 5¼, 5¾)"
SLEEVE
17½"
10 (10½, 10½, 11)"

*A*ran Attitude Pullover

EXPERIENCED

Close-fitting, aran pullover with deep ribs, raglan armholes and turtleneck. Sized for Small, Medium, and Large. Directions are for smallest size with larger sizes in parentheses. If there is only one figure, it applies to all sizes.

KNITTED MEASUREMENTS
• Bust 34 (38½, 44½)"/86.5 (97.5, 113) cm
• Length 18¾ (20, 20¾)"/47.5 (51, 52.5) cm
• Upper arm 12 (13½, 14½)"/30.5 (34.5, 37) cm

MATERIALS 🄌
• 16 (17, 18) 1¾oz/50g balls (each approx 86yd/78m) of Debbie Bliss/ Knitting Fever *Merino Aran* (wool) in #101 cream
• To substitute, seek an aran–weight yarn with similar fiber content
• One pair each sizes 7 and 8 (4.5mm and 5mm) needles OR SIZE TO OBTAIN GAUGE
• Sizes 7 and 8 (4.5mm and 5mm) circular needles 16"/40 cm long
• Cable needle (cn)
• Stitch holders

GAUGES
• 18 sts and 24 rows= 4"/10 cm over St st using larger needles.
• 27 sts and 27 rows= 4"/10 cm (slightly stretched) over all chart pats using larger needles. TAKE TIME TO CHECK GAUGE.

STITCH GLOSSARY
RT Skip first st and k into front on 2nd st, then k into front of first st; sl both sts tog from LH needle.
3-st RPT Sl 1 st to cn and hold to back, k2, then p1 from cn.
3-st LPT Sl 2 sts to cn and hold to front, p1 then k2 from cn.
4-st RC Sl 2 sts to cn and hold to back, k2, then k2 from cn.
4-st LC Sl 2 sts to cn and hold to front, k2, then k2 from cn.

BACK
With smaller needles, cast on 102 (114, 130) sts.
Size Small Only
Beg rib pat
Row 1 (**RS**) K2, [p2, k2] 3 times, p4, k2, p4, k2, [p2, k2] 13 times, p4, k2, p4, k2, [p2, k2] 3 times. **Row 2 (WS)** K the knit sts and p the purl sts. Cont in rib as established until piece measures 4¾"/12 cm from beg, end with a RS row. **Next (inc) row (WS)** Rib 4, m1 p-st, p2, m1 p-st, rib 12, m1 p-st, p2, m1, p-st, rib 12, m1-p-st, p2, m1 p-st, rib 34, m1 p-st, p2, m1 p-st, rib 12, m1 p-st, p2, m1 p-st, rib 12, m1 p-st, p2, m1 p-st, rib 4—114 sts. Change to larger needles.
Beg chart pats
Row 1 (RS) K2; work 8 sts chart 1, 24 sts chart 2, 8 sts chart 1, 30 sts chart 3, 8 sts chart 1, 24 sts chart 2, 8 sts chart 1; k2, Cont in pats as established, working first and last 2 sts in St st, until piece measures 9½"/24 cm from beg, end with a WS row.
Size Medium Only
Beg rib pat
Row 1 (RS) [P2, k2] 5 times, p4, k2, p4, k2, [p2, k2] 13 times, p4, k2, p4, [k2, p2] 5 times. **Row 2** K the knit sts and p the purl sts. Cont in rib as established until piece measures 4¾"/12 cm from beg, end with a RS row.

Next (inc) row (WS) Rib 2, ml p-st, p2, ml p-st, rib 6, [ml p-st, p2, ml p-st, rib 12] twice, ml p-st, p2, ml, p-st, rib 34, [ml p-st, p2, ml p-st, rib 12] twice, ml p-st, p2, ml p-st, rib 6, ml p- st, p2, ml p-st, rib 2—130 sts. Change to larger needles.
Beg chart pats
Row 1 (RS) Work 8 sts chart 1, k2, work 8 sts chart 1, 24 sts chart 2, 8 sts chart 1, 30 sts chart 3, 8 sts chart 1, 24 sts chart 2, 8 sts chart 1, k2, work 8 sts chart 1. Cont in pats as established, working sts outside of charts in St st, until piece measures 10"/25.5 cm from beg, end with a WS row.
Size Large Only
Beg rib pat
Row 1 (RS) [P2, k2] 7 times, p4, k2, p4, k2, [p2, k2] 13 times, p4, k2, p4, [k2, p2] 7 times. **Row 2** K the knit sts and p the purl sts. Cont in rib as established until piece measures

4¾"/12 cm from beg, end with a RS row. **Next (inc) row (WS)** Rib 2, [ml p-st, p2, ml p-st, rib 6] twice, [ml p-st, p2, ml p-st, rib 12] twice, ml p-st, p2, ml p-st, rib 34 [ml p-st, p2, ml p-st, rib 12] twice, ml p-st, p2, ml p-st, [rib 6, ml p-st, p2, ml p-st] twice, rib 2—150 sts. Change to larger needles.
Beg chart pats
Row 1 (RS) [Work 8 sts chart 1, k2] twice, work 8 sts chart 1, 24 sts chart 2, 8 sts chart 1, 30 sts chart 3, 8 sts chart 1, 24 sts chart 2, 8 sts chart 1, [k2, work 8 sts chart 1] twice. Cont in pats as established, working sts outside of charts in St st, until piece measures 10"/25.5 cm from beg, end with a WS row.

FOR ALL SIZES
Raglan armhole shaping Bind off 10 sts at beg of next 2 rows.
For sizes Medium and Large Only
Next row (RS) K2, SK2P, work to

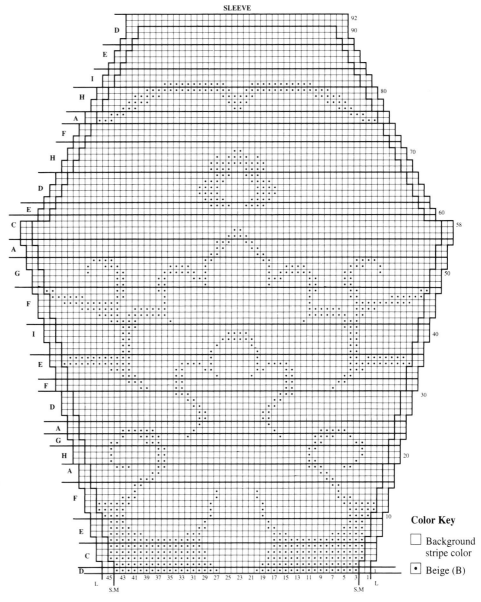

SLEEVE

Color Key
☐ Background stripe color
⊡ Beige (B)

last 5 sts, k3tog, k2. **Next row (WS)** P3, work to last 3 sts, p3. Rep last 2 rows (4, 12) times more. **For all sizes—Next row (RS)** K2, SKP, work to last 4 sts, k2tog, k2. **Next row** P3, work to last 3 sts, p3. Rep last 2 rows 26 (24, 18) times more. Place rem 40 sts on a holder for back neck.

FRONT
Work as for back.

SLEEVES
With smaller needles, cast on 42 sts. Beg and end with p2, work in k2, p2 rib for 2½"/6 cm. Change to larger needles and cont rib until piece measures 5"/12 cm from beg, end with a RS row. **Next (inc) row (WS)** K2, m1 p-st, p2, m1 p-st, rib to last 4 sts, m1 p-st, p2, m1 p-st, k2—46 sts. Change to larger needles.

Beg chart pats
Row 1 (RS) Work 8 sts chart 1, 30 sts chart 3, 8 sts chart 1. Cont in pats as established, inc 1 st each side (working inc sts as foll: work first 2 incs in k2 rib, next 8 incs in chart 1, next 2 incs in k2 rib and rem incs in rev St st) every 4th row—80 (92, 98) sts. Work even until piece measures 20½ (21, 21½)/52 (53.5, 54.5) cm from beg,

end with a WS row.

Raglan cap shaping
Bind off 10 sts at beg of next 2 rows. **Next row (RS)** K2, SKP, work to last 4 sts, k2tog, k2. Next 3 rows. Work even in pat, working first and last 3 sts in St st. Rep last 4 rows 4 (2, 0) times more. Then work dec row every other row 17 (26, 30) times. Place rem 16 sts on a holder.

FINISHING
Block pieces to measurements. Sew raglan sleeve caps to raglan armholes.

Collar
With RS facing, sl sts from holders to larger circular needle—112 sts. Join and work in k2, p2 rib (matching k2 ribs) for 2¾"/7 cm. Change to smaller circular needle and cont in rib for 3½"/9 cm more. Bind off in rib. Sew side and sleeve seams, reversing seam on one half of cuff for turnback.

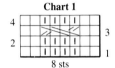

Chart 1

8 sts

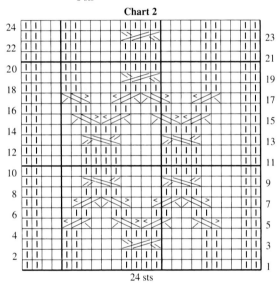

Chart 2

24 sts

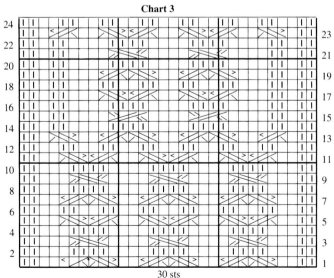

Chart 3

30 sts

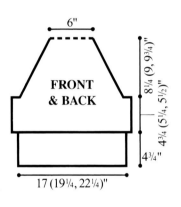

6"
FRONT & BACK
8¼ (9, 9¾)"
5¼, 5½)"
4¾ (5¼, 5½)"
4¾"
17 (19¼, 22¼)"

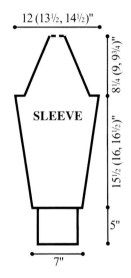

12 (13½, 14½)"
SLEEVE
8¼ (9, 9¾)"
15½ (16, 16½)"
5"
7"

Stitch Key

| | K on RS, p on WS
| | P on RS, k on WS
3-st RPT
3-st LPT
4-st RC
4-st LC

Shawl Collar Sweater

INTERMEDIATE

Standard-fitting pullover with crossover cowlneck. Sized for Small, Medium, Large, and X-Large. Directions are for smallest size with larger sizes in parentheses. If there is only one figure, it applies to all sizes.

KNITTED MEASUREMENTS
• Bust 39 (41, 44, 47)"/99 (104, 112, 119) cm
• Length 23¾ (25, 25¾, 26½)"/60 (63.5, 65.5, 67) cm
• Upper arm 14½ (16, 17, 18)"/37 (40.5, 43, 45.5) cm

MATERIALS ⒋
• 7 (7, 8, 9) 3½oz/100g skeins (each approx 183yd/168m) of Tahki Yarns/Tahki•Stacy Charles, Inc. *Donegal Tweed* (wool) in #863 cranberry
• To substitute, seek an aran-weight yarn with similar fiber content
• One pair size 8 (5mm) needles OR SIZE TO OBTAIN GAUGE
• Size 8 (5mm) circular needle, 24"/60 cm long
• Stitch marker and holder

GAUGES
• 21 sts and 23 rows = 4"/10 cm over k1, p1 rib using size 8 (5mm) needles.
• 22 sts and 23 rows = 4"/10 cm over k2, p2 slanting rib using size 8 (5mm) needles. TAKE TIME TO CHECK GAUGES.

BACK
With size 8 (5mm) needles, cast on 105 (113, 121, 129) sts. **Row 1 (WS)** K1, [p2, k2] 8 (9, 10, 11) times, pm, k1 [p1 k1] 19 times, pm, [k2, p2] 8 (9, 10, 11) times, k1. **Row 2 (RS)** K1, M1 rib st, work k2, p2 rib until 2 sts before first marker, dec 1 st in rib (by k2tog or p2tog as necessary), work k1, p1 rib over center 39 sts, sl marker and dec 1 st in rib (by ssk or p2tog as necessary), work k2, p2 rib to last st, M1, k1. Work in ribs as established, with center 39 sts in k1, p1 rib and rem sts in slanting k2, p2 rib until piece measures 22 (23, 23½, 24)"/56 (58, 60, 61) cm from beg, measuring piece at center.

Shoulder and neck shaping
Bind off 3 sts at beg of next 22 (22, 26, 30) rows, 0 (4, 2, 0) sts at beg of next 0 (2, 2, 0) rows. Sl rem 39 sts to a holder for back neck.

FRONT
Work as for back until piece measures 18 (19, 19½, 20)"/46 (48, 50, 51) cm from beg.

Neck shaping
Next row (RS) Work 33 (37, 41, 45) sts slanting rib, join a 2nd ball of yarn and bind off center 39 sts, work slanting rib to end. Work both sides at once until same length as back to shoulders.

Shoulder shaping
Bind off 3 sts from each shoulder edge 11 (11, 13, 15) times, 0 (4, 2, 0) sts 0 (1, 1, 0) time.

SLEEVES
With size 8 (5mm) needles, cast on 45 (49, 53, 57) sts. Work in k1, p1 rib, inc 1 st each side every 6th row 14 (13, 13, 10) times, every 4th row 2 (4, 5, 9) times—77 (83, 89, 95) sts. Work even until piece measures 16½ (17, 17½, 17½)"/42 (43, 44.5, 44.5) cm from beg.

Cap shaping
Bind off 6 sts at beg of next 12 (13, 14, 15) rows. Bind off rem 5 sts.

FINISHING
Block pieces to measurements, pinning lower edge to straighten hem. Sew shoulder seams.

Collar
With circular needle, pick up and k 39 sts from side of right front neck edge, 39 sts from back neck holder, 39 sts from side of left front neck edge—117 sts. Work in k1, p1 rib for 7½"/19 cm OR until side edge of piece fits along center front 39 sts. Bind off in rib. Sew collar to front neck, overlapping right edge over left edge. Place markers at 8½ (9, 9½, 10)"/21.5 (23, 24, 25.5) cm down from shoulders at armholes. Sew shaped sleeve caps to straight armhole between markers. Sew side and sleeve seams.

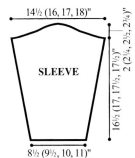

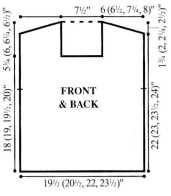

FRONT & BACK

7½"   6 (6½, 7¼, 8)"

5¾ (6, 6¼, 6½)"   1¾ (2, 2¼, 2½)"

18 (19, 19½, 20)"   22 (23, 23½, 24)"

19½ (20½, 22, 23½)"

14½ (16, 17, 18)"

SLEEVE

2 (2¼, 2½, 2¾)"

16½ (17, 17½, 17½)"

8½ (9½, 10, 11)"

Fall 2002 • No. 7

$\mathcal{T}$ake Two Twinset

EXPERIENCED

Standard-fitting cabled cardigan and close fitting shell. Sized for Small, Medium, and Large. Directions are for smallest size with larger sizes in parentheses. If there is only one figure, it applies to all sizes.

KNITTED MEASUREMENTS
Cardigan
• Bust 39½ (42½, 45½)"/100 (108, 115.5) cm
• Length 27 (29, 31)"/68.5 (73.5, 78.5) cm
• Upper arm 13¾ (14¼, 15)"/35 (36, 38) cm
Shell
• Bust 35 (38, 41)"/89 (96.5, 104) cm
• Length 19½ (21, 21¾)"/49.5 (53, 55) cm

MATERIALS 🔲4
Cardigan
• 24 (25, 26) 1¾oz/50g balls (each approx 88yd/78m) of Debbie Bliss/ KFI *Merino Aran* (wool) in #102 cream
• To substitute, seek an aran-weight yarn with similar fiber content
• One pair each sizes 7 and 8 (4.5 and 5mm) needles OR SIZE TO

OBTAIN GAUGE
• Size 7 (4.5mm) circular needle, 24"/60 cm long
Shell
• 8 (9, 10) 1¾oz/50g balls (each approx 88yd/78m) of Debbie Bliss *Merino Aran* (wool) in #102 cream
• To substitute, seek an aran-weight yarn with similar fiber content
• One pair each sizes 3 and 4 (3 and 3.5mm) needles OR SIZE TO OBTAIN GAUGE
Both
• Cable needle (cn)

GAUGES
Cardigan
• 18 sts and 24 rows = 4"/10 cm over St st using size 8 (5mm) needles.
• 28 sts and 24 rows = 4"/10 cm over all pats using size 8 (5mm) needles.
Shell
• 22 sts and 30 rows = 4"/10 cm over St st using size 4 (3.5mm) needles.
• 29 sts and 30 rows = 4"/10 cm over all pats using size 4 (3.5mm) needles.
TAKE TIME TO CHECK GAUGES.

STITCH GLOSSARY
C4B (C4F) Sl 2 sts to cn, hold to back (front), k2, k2 from cn.
T4B (T4F) Sl 2 sts to cn and hold to back (front), k2 (p2), p2 (k2) from cn.

Short Row Wrap and Turn (w&t)
On RS row (on WS row)
1) Wyib (wyif), Sl next st purlwise.
2) Move yarn between the needles to the front (back).
3) Sl the same st back to LH needle. Turn work. One st is wrapped.
4) When working the wrapped st, insert RH needle under the wrap and work it tog with the corresponding st on needle.

Panel A
(over 8 sts)
Row 1 (RS) K8.
Row 2 and all WS rows P8.
Row 3 C4F, C4B.
Row 5 Rep row 1.
Row 7 C4B, C4F.
Row 9 Rep row 1.

Row 11 Rep row 7.
Row 13 Rep row 1.
Row 15 Rep row 3.
Row 16 P8.
Rep rows 1-16 for panel A.

Panel B (over 26 sts)
Row 1 (RS) P3, C4B, [p4, C4B] twice, p3.
Row 2 (WS) K3, p4, [k4, p4] twice, k3. Row 3 P1, [T4B, T4F] 3 times, p1.
Row 4 K1, p2, k4, [p4, k4] twice, p2, k1.
Row 5 P1, k2, p4, [C4F, p4] twice, k2, p1.
Row 6 K1, p2, k4, [p4, k4] twice, p2, k1.
Row 7 P1, [T4F, T4B] 3 times, p1.
Row 8 K3, p4, [k4, p4] twice, k3.
Rep rows 1-8 for panel B.

CARDIGAN
BACK
With smaller needles, cast on 140 (150, 160) sts. Work in k1, p1 rib for 5"/12.5 cm. Change to larger needles.
Next row (RS) P3, [k2, p3] 1 (2, 3) times, work panel A over next 8 sts, p3, k2, p3, work panel B over next 26 sts, p3, k2, p3, ★work panel A over next 8 sts, p3, k2, p3; rep from ★ 1 more time, work panel B over next 26 sts, p3, k2, p3, work panel A over next 8 sts, [p3, k2] 1 (2, 3) times, p3. Cont in pats as established until piece measures 18 (19¼, 20½)"/45.5 (49, 52) cm from beg.
Armhole shaping
Bind off 10 sts at beg of next 2 rows, dec 1 st each side every other row 11 (13, 15) times—98 (104, 110) sts. Work even in pats until armhole measures 7½ (8¼, 9)"/19 (21, 23) cm.
Neck shaping
Next row (RS) Work 33 (35, 37) sts, join 2nd ball of yarn and bind off center 32 (34, 36) sts, work to end. Working both sides at once, dec 1 st at each neck edge every row 4 times. Work even until armhole measures 8½ (9¼, 10)"/21.5 (23.5, 25.5) cm.
Shoulder shaping
Bind off 15 (16, 17) sts at beg of next 2 rows, 14 (15, 16) sts at beg of next 2 rows.

LEFT FRONT

With smaller needles, cast on 72 (77, 82) sts. Work in k1, p1 rib for 5"/12.5 cm. Change to larger needles. **Next row (RS)** P3, [k2, p3] 1 (2, 3) times, work panel A over next 8 sts, p3, k2, p3, work panel B over next 26 sts, p3, k2, p3, work panel A over next 8 sts, p3, k2, p1. Cont in pats as established until piece measures 18 (19¼, 20½)"/45.5 (49, 52) cm from beg.

Armhole and neck shaping

Next row (RS) Bind off 10 sts, work to end. Dec 1 st at armhole edge every other row 11 (13, 15) times, AT SAME TIME, dec 1 st at neck edge every other row 22 (23, 24) times—29 (31, 33) sts. Work even until piece measures same length as back to shoulder, shape shoulder as on back.

RIGHT FRONT

With smaller needles, cast on 72 (77, 82) sts. Work in k1, p1 rib for 5"/12.5 cm. Change to larger needles. Beg cable pats.

Next row (RS) P1, k2, p3, work panel A over next 8 sts, p3, k2, p3, work panel B over next 26 sts, p3, k2, p3, work panel A over next 8 sts, [p3, k2] 1 (2, 3) times. Cont in pats as established, work to correspond to left front, reversing all shaping.

SLEEVES

With smaller needles, cast on 60 (62, 64) sts. Work in k1, p1 rib for 5"/12.5 cm. Change to larger needles. **Next row (RS)** P1 (2, 3), work panel A over next 8 sts, p3, k2, p3, work panel B over next 26 sts, p3, k2, p3, work panel A over next 8 sts, k1 (2, 3). Cont in pats as established, AT SAME TIME, inc 1 st each side on next RS row, then every 4th row 17 (18, 19) times, working first 7 (6, 5) inc sts each side in k2, p3, rib, the next 8 inc sts each side in panel A, and rem inc sts in rev St st—96 (100, 104) sts. Work even until piece measures 17½ (18, 18½)"/44.5 (45.5, 47) cm from beg.

Cap shaping

Bind off 10 sts at beg of next 2 rows, dec 1 st each side every other row 12 (14, 16) times, every row 10 times, bind off 3 sts at beg of next 4 rows. Bind off rem 20 sts.

FINISHING

Block pieces to measurements. Sew shoulder seams.

Right front band

With RS facing and circular needle, beg at lower edge and pick up and k 86 (90, 94) sts to neck shaping, 63 (66, 69) sts to shoulder, cast on 23 (24, 25) sts—172 (180, 188) sts. **Next row (WS)** Rib 26 sts, w&t. **Next row** Rib to end. **Next row (WS)** Rib 30 sts, w&t. **Next row** Rib to end. Cont in this way to rib 4 more sts at the end of every WS row 13 times more, end with a RS row—86 sts worked in rib. Work 19 row in rib across all sts. Bind off in rib.

Left front band

With RS facing, cast on 23 (24, 25) sts, pick up and k 63 (66, 69) sts to beg of neck shaping, 86 (90, 94) sts to lower edge. Work 1 row in rib. **Next row (RS)** Rib 26 sts, w&t. **Next row** Rib to end. **Next row (RS)** Rib 30 sts, w&t. **Next row** Rib to end. Cont in this way to rib 4 more sts at the end of every RS row 13 times more, end with a WS row—86 sts worked in rib. Work 18 rows in rib across all sts. Bind off in rib.

FINISHING

Sew sleeves into armholes. Sew side and sleeve seams. Sew cast on sts of collar to back neck edge.

SHELL

BACK

With smaller needles, cast on 128 (138, 148) sts. Work in k1, p1 rib for 4"/10 cm. Change to larger needles. **Next row (RS)** P3, [k2, p3] 3 (4, 5) times, work panel A over next 8 sts, p3, k2, p3, work panel B over next 26 sts, p3, k2, p3, work panel B over next 26 sts, p3, k2, p3, work panel A over next 8 sts, [p3, k2] 3 (4, 5) times, p3. Cont in pats as established until piece measures 11½ (12, 12½)"/29 (30.5, 31.5) cm from beg.

Armhole shaping

Bind off 8 (10, 12) sts at beg of next 2 rows, dec 1 st each side every other row 8 (9, 10) times—96 (100, 104) sts. Work even in pats until armhole measures 7 (7¾, 8¼)"/18 (19.5, 21) cm.

Neck shaping

Next row (RS) Work 33 (35, 37)

sts, join 2nd ball of yarn and bind off center 30 sts, work to end. Working both sides at once, dec 1 st at each neck edge every row 4 times. Work even until armhole measures 7¾ (8½, 8¾)"/19.5 (21.5, 22) cm.

Shoulder shaping

Bind off 15 (16, 17) sts at beg of next 2 rows, 14 (15, 16) sts at beg of next 2 rows.

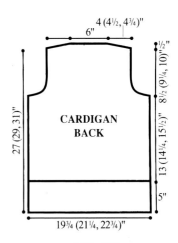

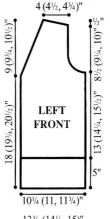

FRONT

Work as for back until piece measures 16½ (17¼, 18½)"/42 (44, 47) cm.

Neck shaping

Work 36 (38, 40) sts, join 2nd ball of yarn and bind off center 24 sts, work to end. Working both sides at once, bind off from each neck edge every other row 7 times—29 (31, 33) sts. Work even until piece measures same length as back to shoulders, shape shoulders as on back.

FINISHING

Block pieces to measurements. Sew right shoulder seam.

Turtleneck

With RS facing and smaller needles, pick up and k 106 sts evenly around neck edge. Work in k1, p1 rib for 4"/10 cm. Change to larger needles and work 6"/15 cm more. Bind off in rib. Sew left shoulder and turtleneck, reversing seam on last 6"/15 cm for turnback of turtleneck.

Armhole bands

With RS facing and smaller needles, pick up and k 114 (120, 124) sts evenly around armhole edge. Work 4 rows in k1, p1 rib. Bind off in rib. Sew side and armhole seams.

Fall 2002 · No. 44

Shaped Camisole

EXPERIENCED

Close-fitting side-shaped camisole with lower back and eyelet pattern shaping. Sized for one size, Small.

KNITTED MEASUREMENTS
• Bust 32"/81 cm
• Waist 27"/68.5 cm
• Length 21"/53 cm

MATERIALS ③
• 4 1¾oz/50g balls (each approx

114yd/104m of Dale of Norway *Svale* (cotton/viscose/silk) in #0010 white
• To substitute, seek a DK-weight yarn with similar fiber content
• Size 3 (3.25mm) needles OR SIZE TO OBTAIN GAUGE
• Liquid starch
• Stitch holders

GAUGE

One 26-st pat rep foll chart = 5¼"/13.5 cm at widest point of diamond and 5¼"/13.5 cm long over a 40-row rep. TAKE TIME TO CHECK GAUGE.

NOTES

1) Chart is worked showing the odd-numbered RS rows only. On WS (even) rows, k the knit sts and p the purl sts and always k the yos of previous row.
2) Chart is drawn for front only. Back neck shaping is worked in a similar way. Make front first.

FRONT

With size 3 (3.25mm) needles, cast on 87 sts. K3 rows. **Beg chart pat: Row 1 (RS)** Work foll row 1 of chart across. **Row 2 and all even rows** K the knit sts, p the purl sts and k all the yos. Cont to foll chart in this way, with

natural side seam shaping formed by the pat (see chart) through row 78.

Neck shaping

Row 79 (RS) Work to center 8 sts on chart, sl next 4 sts to cn and hold to front, with separate ball of yarn, k4, k4 from cn, (8-st LC) work chart to end.
Row 80 Working both sides at once, k the knit sts and p the purl sts.

Armhole shaping

Row 81 Bind off 5 sts, work to end.
Row 82 Bind off 5 sts, work to end. Cont to foll chart in this way, cont neck shaping and working p3tog at 2 sts in from each armhole edge for armhole shaping until there are 4 sts for the strap. Cont on these strap sts, working a sl 1 at beg of each row for edge st, until strap measures 14"/35.5 cm. Sl sts to holders.

BACK

Work as for front to row 38.

Neck shaping

Next row (RS) Work as for row 79 of frontneck. Working both sides at once, work neck shaping foll pat as on front and cont to work side seams as on front to row 80.

Armhole shaping

Bind off 13 sts at beg of next 2 rows. When 4 sts rem for straps, sl these sts to a holder for finishing later.

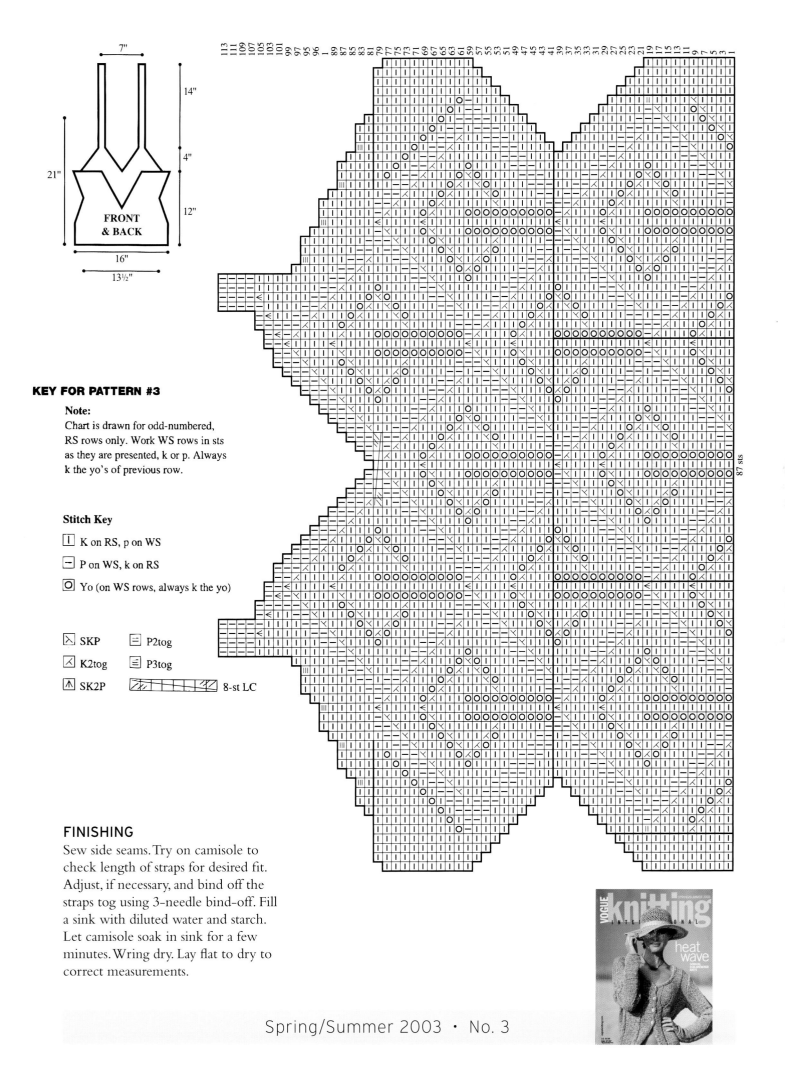

7"

14"

4"

21"

12"

FRONT & BACK

16"

13½"

KEY FOR PATTERN #3

Note:
Chart is drawn for odd-numbered, RS rows only. Work WS rows in sts as they are presented, k or p. Always k the yo's of previous row.

Stitch Key

☐ K on RS, p on WS

⊟ P on WS, k on RS

⊡ Yo (on WS rows, always k the yo)

⊠ SKP   ⊟ P2tog

⊡ K2tog   ⊟ P3tog

⊼ SK2P   ⬚⬚⬚⬚ 8-st LC

FINISHING

Sew side seams. Try on camisole to check length of straps for desired fit. Adjust, if necessary, and bind off the straps tog using 3-needle bind-off. Fill a sink with diluted water and starch. Let camisole soak in sink for a few minutes. Wring dry. Lay flat to dry to correct measurements.

87 sts

VOGUE knitting INTERNATIONAL
heat wave

Spring/Summer 2003 · No. 3

Woven Cable Twinset

EXPERIENCED

Standard-fitting turtleneck pullover with set-in sleeves and loose-fitting cape with fold-back collar designed by Oscar de la Renta. Pullover sized for Small, Medium, and Large. Cape sized for Small/Medium and Large/X-large. Directions are for smallest size with larger sizes in parentheses. If there is only one figure, it applies to all sizes.

KNITTED MEASUREMENTS
Pullover
- Bust 36 (40, 44)"/91.5 (101.5, 111.5) cm
- Length 21 (21½, 22½)"/53.5 (55, 57) cm
- Upper arm 10½ (12, 13½)"/26.5 (30.5, 34.4) cm
Cape
- Width at lower edge 62"/157.5 cm
- Length 26 (27½)"/66 (70) cm

MATERIALS ⓸
Pullover
- 16 (17, 18) 1¾oz/50g balls (each approx 88yd/80m) of Filatura di Crosa/Tahki•Stacy Charles, Inc., *Luna* (wool) in #231 burgundy
Cape
- 17 (18) 1¾oz/50g balls (each approx 88yd/80m) of Filatura di Crosa/Tahki•Stacy Charles, Inc., *Luna* (wool) in #231 burgundy

FOR ALL PIECES
- To substitute, seek an aran-weight yarn with similar fiber content
- One pair each sizes 7 and 11 (4.5 and 8mm) needles OR SIZE TO OBTAIN GAUGE
- Size 7 (4.5mm) circular needle, 16"/40 cm long for turtleneck
- Cable needle (cn)

GAUGE
24 sts and 18 rows = 4"/10 cm over pat st using larger needles. TAKE TIME TO CHECK GAUGE.

NOTES
1) K first and last stitch of every row for selvage sts. Work all increases and decreases inside of the selvage sts.
2) If there are not enough sts to work a full cable, then work these sts in St st.
3) When binding off sts, work k2tog while binding off to keep edge even.

PATTERN GLOSSARY
Pattern Stitch
(multiple of 4 sts)
Row 1 (RS) K2, ★4-st RC (sl 2 sts to cn and hold to back, k2, k2 from cn); rep from ★ to last 2 sts, end k2.
Rows 2 and 4 Purl.
Row 3 ★4-st LC (sl 2 sts to cn and hold to front, k2, k2 from cn); rep from ★ to end. Rep rows 1-4 for pat st.

PULLOVER
BACK
With smaller needles, cast on 114 (126, 138) sts. Work in k2, p2 rib for 3"/7.5 cm. Change to larger needles. P next row on WS, then work in pat st, with 1 selvage st each side, and dec 1 st each side inside of selvage sts every 4th row 6 times—102 (114, 126) sts. Work even until piece measures 9"/23 cm from beg. Inc 1 st each side (inside of selvage sts) on next row, then every 4th row 3 times more—110 (122, 134) sts. Work even until piece measures 13½ (13½, 14)"/34.5 (34.5, 35.5) cm from beg.

Armhole shaping
Bind off 0 (4, 4) sts at beg of next 2 rows, 3 sts at beg of next 2 (2, 4) rows, 2 sts at beg of next 4 rows, dec 1 st each side every other row 4 times—88 (92, 98) sts. Work even until armhole measures 7½ (8, 8½)"/19 (20.5, 21.5) cm. Bind off, working k2tog while binding off to keep edge even.

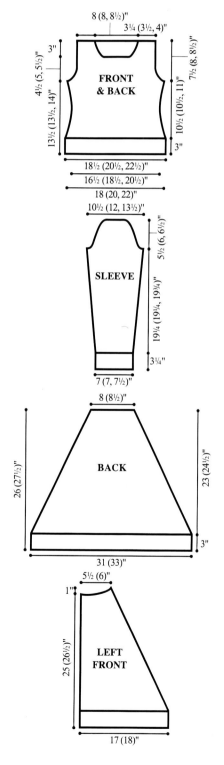

FRONT
Work as for back.
Neck shaping
Next row (RS) Work 32 (34, 36) sts, join 2nd ball of yarn and bind off center 24 (24, 26) sts, work to end. Working both sides at once, bind off 4 sts from each neck edge once, 2 sts 3 times, dec 1 st every other row twice. When same length as back, bind off rem 20 (22, 24) sts each side for shoulders.

SLEEVES
With smaller needles, cast on 42 (42, 46) sts. Work in k2, p2 rib for 3¼"/8.5 cm. Change to larger needles. P next row on WS, then work in pat st, with selvage sts each side, and inc 1 st each side (working inc sts into pat inside of selvage sts) every 4th row 0 (7, 12) times, every 6th row 7 (6, 9) times, every 8th row 5 (0, 0) times—66 (74, 82) sts. Work even until piece measures 22½ (22½, 23)"/57 (57, 58.5) cm from beg.
Cap shaping
Bind off 0 (4, 4) sts at beg of next 2 rows, 3 sts at beg of next 2 (2, 4) rows, 2 sts at beg of next 4 rows, dec 1 st each side every row 16 times, bind off 4 sts at beg of next 2 rows. Bind off rem 12 (12, 14) sts.

FINISHING
Block pieces to measurements. Sew shoulder seams. Set in sleeves. Sew side and sleeve seams.
Turtleneck
With RS facing and circular needle, pick up and k 68 (68, 72) sts evenly around neck edge. Join and work in k2, p2 rib for 6"/15.5 cm. Bind off in rib.

CAPE
BACK
With smaller needles, cast on 186 (198) sts. Work in k2, p2 rib for 3"/7.5 cm. Change to larger needles. P next row on WS, then cont in pat st, dec 1 st each side (inside of selvage sts) every other row once. [Dec 2 sts each side (working k3tog) every other row once. Dec 1 st each side every other row twice] 17 (18) times. Bind off rem 48 (52) sts for back neck.

LEFT FRONT
With smaller needles, cast on 102 (108) sts. Work in k2, p2 rib for 3"/7.5 cm. Change to larger needles and p next row on WS. Cont in St st, working decs at side edge (beg of RS rows) as for back, AT SAME TIME, when piece

measures 25 (26½)"/63.5 (67.5) cm from beg, work neck shaping as foll: bind off from neck edge (beg of WS rows) 11 sts once, 11 (12) sts twice.

RIGHT FRONT
Work to correspond to left front, reversing shaping.

FINISHING
Block pieces to measurements. Sew side seams.
Left front band
With RS facing and smaller needles, pick up and k 138 (146) sts evenly along left front edge. Work in k2, p2 rib for 1½"/4 cm. Bind off in rib. Work right front band in same way.

COLLAR
With smaller needles, pick up and k 118 (126) sts evenly around neck edge. Work in k2, p2 rib for 6½"/16.5 cm. Bind off in rib.

Winter 2003-2004 · No. 12

Lace Cape

EXPERIENCED

Lace cape with beaded rib collar designed by Pierrot. One size.

KNITTED MEASUREMENTS
• Lower edge (around) 72"/183 cm
• Length 31"/78.5 cm

MATERIALS
• 18 1¾oz/50g balls (each approx 55yd/50m) of Knit One Crochet Too *Temptation* (alpaca/wool) in #212 pink

• To substitute, seek a worsted-weight yarn with similar fiber content
• One pair size 11 (8mm) needles OR SIZE TO OBTAIN GAUGE
• Stitch markers

GAUGES
• 34 sts = 9"/23 cm in lace pat using size 11 (8mm) needles.
• 12 sts and 20 rows = 4"/10 cm over beaded rib pat using size 11 (8mm) needles. TAKE TIME TO CHECK GAUGES.

STITCH GLOSSARY
Lace Pattern
(multiple of 34 sts plus 2)
Row 1 (RS) K1, *yo, ssk, k2, yo, ssk, p2, yo, k4, ssk, k6, k2tog, k4, yo, p2, k2, yo, ssk, k2; rep from *, end k1.
Row 2 K1, *yo, p2tog, p2, yo, p2tog, k2, p1, yo, p4, p2tog, p4, p2tog tbl, p4, yo, p1, k2, p2, yo, p2tog, p2; rep from *, end k1.
Row 3 K1, *yo, ssk, k2, yo, ssk, p2, k2, yo, k4, ssk, k2, k2tog, k4, yo, k2, p2, k2, yo, ssk, k2; rep from *, end k1.

k3; rep from ★, end k1.

Row 14 K1, ★p2, p2tog tbl, p4, yo, p1, k2, [p2, yo, p2tog] 3 times, k2, p1, yo, p4, p2tog, p2; rep from ★, end k1.

Row 15 K1, ★k1, k2tog, k4, yo, k2, p2, [k2, yo, ssk] 3 times, p2, k2, yo, k4, ssk, k1; rep from ★, end k1.

Row 16 K1, ★p2tog tbl, p4, yo, p3, k2, [p2, yo, p2tog] 3 times, k2, p3, yo, p4, p2tog; rep from ★, end k1.

Rows 17-24 Rep rows 13-16 twice more.

Rep rows 1-24 for lace pat.

Beaded Rib
Row 1 (RS) Sl 1, p to end.
Row 2 Sl 1, ★k1, p1; rep from ★ to end.

Rep rows 1 and 2 for beaded rib.

CAPE
Cast on 274 sts. Work in lace pat for 48 rows.

Beg shaping
Next row (RS) Work 73 sts, (do not work last yo), k3tog, place marker,

Row 4 K1, ★yo, p2tog, p2, yo, p2tog, k2, p3, yo, p4, p2tog, p2tog tbl, p4, yo, p3, k2, p2, yo, p2tog, p2; rep from ★, end k1.

Rows 5-12 Rep rows 1-4 twice more.

Row 13 (RS) K1, ★k3, k2tog, k4, yo, p2, [k2, yo, ssk] 3 times, p2, yo, k4, ssk,

SK2P (sl 1, k2tog, psso), work 116 sts, k3tog, place marker, SK2P, (do not work next yo), work to end. Cont in this way to dec 2 sts each side of both markers (working dec sts into lace pat) every 4th row 4 times more, every other row 20 times—74 sts. Work even until 108 rows have been worked from beg. Piece measures approx 31"/78.5 from beg. Bind off all sts.

COLLAR
Cast on 119 sts. Work in beaded rib, dec 1 st each side (1 st in from edge) every 4th row 6 times—107 sts. Work even until collar measures 7½"/19 cm. Bind off. Beg at 2"/5 cm in from each front neck edge, sew bound-off edge of collar around neck.

Fall 2004 · No. 3

Striped Kimono

INTERMEDIATE

Oversized, striped, cropped kimono. One size.

KNITTED MEASUREMENTS
• Width 42"/106.5 cm
• Length 22½"/57 cm

MATERIALS (3)
• 4 4oz/125g balls (each approx 175yd/161m) of Fiesta Yarns *Kokopelli DK* (mohair/wool) in #01 black (A)
• 2 8oz/250g balls (each approx 290yd/267m) of Fiesta Yarns *La Boheme* (mohair/rayon) in #1248 rust (B)
• To substitute, seek DK-weight yarns with similar fiber content
• One pair size 8 (5mm) needles OR

SIZE TO OBTAIN GAUGE
• Size G/6 (4mm) crochet hook

GAUGE
15 sts and 22 rows = 4"/10 cm over St st using size 8 (5mm) needles. TAKE TIME TO CHECK GAUGE.

STITCH GLOSSARY
Stripe Pattern
(Over 4 rows)
Working in St st, work 2 rows A, 2 rows B.
Rep these 4 rows for stripe pat.

NOTE
Kimono is knit side to side.

BACK
With A, cast on 84 sts. Work in stripe

pat until piece measures 16"/40.5 cm from beg, end with a RS row.

Neck shaping
Next row (WS) Cont in stripe pat, bind of 2 sts, work to end. Work 1 row even. Rep last 2 rows 4 times more—74 sts. Work even for 6"/18 cm. **Next row (RS)** K to end, cast on 2 sts.

Work 1 row even. Rep last 2 rows 4 times more—84 sts. Work even until piece measures 42"/106.5 cm from beg. Bind off.
FRONT (make 2)
With A, cast on 84 sts. Work in stripe pat until piece measures 16"/40.5 cm. Bind off.

SLEEVES
With A, cast on 98 sts. Work in stripe pat until piece measures 8"/20.5 cm. Bind off.
FINISHING
Block pieces to measurements. Sew fronts to back at shoulder. Place markers 13"/33 cm down from each shoulder edge. Sew in sleeves between markers. Sew side and sleeve seams. With crochet hook and A, work sc evenly around outside edges.

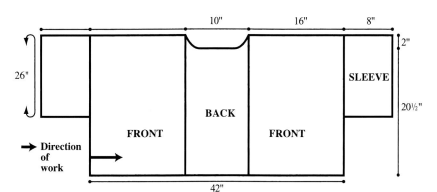

Fall 2004 · No. 12

ℬelted Lace Pullover

17

EXPERIENCED

Standard-fitting V-neck pullover with crossover neckline and matching belt. Sized for Small/Medium, Large/X-Large, and XX-Large. Directions are for smallest size with larger sizes in parentheses. If there is only one figure, it applies to all sizes.

KNITTED MEASUREMENTS
• Bust 42 (49, 56)"/107 (124, 142) cm
• Length 26 (26½, 27)"/66 (67, 68.5) cm
• Upper arm 15 (16, 17)"/38 (40.5, 43) cm

MATERIALS
• 16 (18, 20) 1¾oz/50g balls (each approx 175yd/ 160m) of Lana Grossa/ Unicorn Books & Crafts *Cool Wool 2000* (wool) in #475 tan
• To substitute, seek a DK-weight yarn with similar fiber content
• One pair size 6 (4mm) needles OR SIZE TO OBTAIN GAUGE

GAUGES
• 25 sts and 30 rows = 4"/10 cm over diamond pat st using size 6 (4mm) needles.

• 42 sts and 48 rows = 6"/15 cm over twisted rib pat using size 6 (4mm) needles. TAKE TIME TO CHECK GAUGES.

STITCH GLOSSARY
Twisted Rib Pattern Stitch
(over a multiple of 3 sts plus 2 selvage sts)
Row 1 (RS) K1 (selvage st), ★ p2, k1tbl; rep from ★ end k1 (selvage st).
Row 2 (WS) K1, ★ k2, pl tbl; rep from ★, end k1.
Rep these 2 rows for twisted rib pat st.

Sloped bind-off
To eliminate the "stair-step" resulting from regular bind-offs, use sloped bind-off method on all bind-offs. To work sloped bind-off, sl the last st worked (or the first st of the bind-off on the next row). On the bind-off, wyib, sl this st over the next st to make the first st bind-off, then bind off as usual.

Diamond Pattern Stitch

(over a panel of 22 sts)

Row 1 K1 (selvage st), *yo, k2tog tbl, [p2, k1 tbl] 5 times, p2, k2tog, yo, k1; rep from *, end k1 (selvage st).

Row 2 K1, *p2, yo, p2tog, k1 [p1 tbl, k2] 4 times, p1 tbl, k1, p2tog tbl, yo, p1; rep from *, end k1.

Row 3 K1, *k2, yo, k2tog tbl, k1 tbl, [p2, k1tbl] 4 times, k2tog, yo, k3; rep from *, end k1.

Row 4 K1, *[p1, yo, p2tog] twice, [k2, p1 tbl] 3 times, k2, p2tog tbl, yo, p1, p2tog tbl, yo; rep from *, end k1.

Row 5 K1, *[k1, yo, k2tog tbl] twice, p1, [k1 tbl, p2] twice, k1 tbl, p1, k2tog, yo, k2tog, yo, k2; rep from *, end k1.

Row 6 K1, *p3, yo, p2tog, p1, yo, p2tog [p1 tbl, k2] twice, p1 tbl, p2tog tbl, yo, p1, p2tog tbl, yo, p2; rep from *, end k1.

Row 7 K1, *[yo, k2tog tbl, k1] twice, yo, k2tog tbl, p2, k1 tbl, p2, [k2tog, yo, k1] 3 times; rep from *, end k1.

Row 8 K1, *p2, [yo, p2tog, p1] twice, yo, p2tog, k1, p1 tbl, k1, p2tog tbl, [yo, p1, p2tog tbl] twice, yo, p1; rep from *, end k1.

Row 9 K1, *k2, [yo, k2tog tbl, k1] twice, yo, k2tog tbl, k1 tbl, k2tog, [yo, k1, k2tog] twice, yo, k3; rep from *, end k1.

Row 10 K1, *p4, [yo, p2tog, p1] twice, yo, p3tog tbl, [yo, p1, k2tog tbl] twice, yo, p3; rep from *, end k1.

Row 11 K1, *[p2, k1tbl] twice, p2, k2tog, yo, k1, yo, k2tog tbl, [p2, k1 tbl] 3 times; rep from *, end k1.

Row 12 K1, *[p1 tbl, k2] twice, p1 tbl, k1, p2tog tbl, yo, p3, yo, p2tog, k1, [p1 tbl, k2] twice; rep from *, end k1.

Row 13 K1, *[p2, k1 tbl] twice, k2tog, yo, k5, yo, k2tog tbl, [k1 tbl, p2] twice, k1 tbl; rep from *, end k1.

Row 14 K1, *[p1 tbl, k2] twice, p2tog tbl, yo, p1, p2tog tbl, yo, p1, yo, p2tog, p1, yo, p2tog, k2, p1 tbl, k2; rep from *, end k1.

Row 15 K1, *p2, k1 tbl, p1, [k2tog, yo, k1] twice, k2, yo, k2tog tbl, k1, yo, k2tog tbl, p1, k1 tbl, p2, k1 tbl; rep from *, end k1.

Row 16 K1, *p1 tbl, k2, p1 tbl, p2tog tbl, yo, p1, p2tog tbl, yo, p5, yo, p2tog, p1, yo, p2tog, p1 tbl, k2; rep from *, end k1.

Row 17 K1, *p2, [k2tog, yo, k1] 3 times, yo, [k2tog tbl, k1, yo] twice, k2tog tbl, p2, k1 tbl; rep from *, end k1.

Row 18 K1, *p1 tbl, k1, [p2tog tbl, yo, p1] 3 times, p2, [yo, p2tog, p1] twice, yo, p2tog, k1; rep from * end k1.

Row 19 K1, *[k2tog, yo, k1] 3 times, k4, [yo, k2tog tbl, k1] twice, yo, k2tog tbl, k1 tbl; rep from *, end k1.

Note On the first rep of row 20 only, beg as p2tog tbl instead of p3tog tbl, and on the last rep only, end last rep p1 (instead of yo).

Row 20 K1, *p3tog tbl (or p2tog tbl on first rep),[yo, p1, p2tog tbl] twice, yo, p7, [yo, p2tog, p1] twice, yo (or p1 on last rep); rep from *, end k1.

BACK

Cast on 134 (156, 178) sts. Work in diamond pat st until piece measures 18½ (18, 17½)"/47 (45.5, 44.5) cm from beg.

Armhole shaping

Bind off 5 (5, 6) sts at beg of next 2 rows, 3 (4, 4) sts at beg of next 2 rows, 2 (3, 3) sts at beg of next 6 (4, 6) rows, 1 (2, 2) sts at beg of next 6 (8, 10) rows, 0 (1, 1) st at beg of next 0 (4, 6) rows—100 (106, 114) sts. Work even until armhole measures 6¾ (7¾, 8¾)"/17 (19.5, 22) cm.

Neck shaping

Next row (RS) Work 37 (40, 42) sts, join a 2nd ball of yarn and bind off center 26 (26, 30) sts, work to end. Working both sides at once, bind off 7 sts from each neck edge twice. When armhole measures 7½ (8½, 9½)"/19 (21.5, 24), bind off rem 23 (26, 28) sts each side for shoulders.

FRONT

Work as for back until piece measures 15 (15½, 16)"/38 (39.5, 40.5) cm from beg.

V-neck shaping

Next row (RS) Work 66 (77, 88) sts, join a 2nd ball of yarn and bind off center 2 sts, work to end. Working both sides at once, bind off (using sloped bind-off method), binding off 1 st 26 (26, 28) times, AT SAME TIME, work armhole shaping when same length as back. When all neck shaping is completed and 23 (26, 28) sts rem each side, work even until same length as back to shoulder. Bind off sts each side for shoulders.

SLEEVES

Cast on 68 (68, 80) sts. Set up diamond pat st as foll: **For sizes Small/Medium and Large/X-Large:** Work k1 (selvage st), work 3 reps of 22-st pat, k1 (selvage st) **For size XX-Large**: k1 (selvage st), work the last 6 pat sts of the rep, work 3 reps of 22-st pat, work the first 6 pat sts of the rep, k1 (selvage st). Work even in diamond pat st until piece measures 4"/10 cm from beg. Inc 1 st each side of next row then every 6th row 6 (5, 6) times, every 7th (5th, 7th) row 7 (11, 7) times—96 (102, 108) sts. Work even until piece measures 17"/43 cm from beg.

Cap shaping

Bind off 6 sts at beg of next 2 rows, 4 sts at beg of next 2 rows, 3 sts at beg of next 4 rows, [2 sts at beg of next 2 rows, 1 st at beg of next 2 rows] 5 (6, 6) times, 3 (3, 1) sts at beg of next 4 (4, 2) rows, 3 sts at beg of next 0 (0, 4) rows. Bind off rem 22 (22, 26) sts.

Neckband

Cast on 23 sts. **Row 1 (RS)** K1 (selvage st), p1, k1 tbl, * p2, k1 tbl; rep from *, end p1, k1 (selvage st). **Row 2 (WS)** K2, * p1 tbl, k2; rep from *, end p1 tbl, k2. Rep these 2 rows for twisted rib pat st for 30¼ (30¾, 31¾)"/77 (78, 80.5) cm. Bind off loosely in pat.

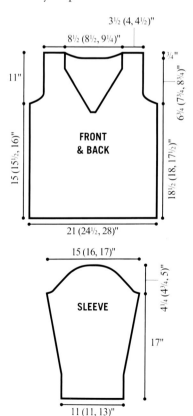

BELT

Cast on 3 sts. K1 row. Purl next row inc 1 p st at each end of row—5 sts.

Next row (RS) K1 into front and back of first st, p1, k1 tbl, p1, k1 into front and back of last st—7 sts. Cont to inc 1 st each side every row (and add sts at center into pat) until there are 23 sts (there are 19 sts in pat with 4 edges sts) and this is pat row 9. On next row (pat row 10), inc 1 st only at beg of row for 24 sts. Then, beg with pat row 11, cont in pat on the 22 sts (with 2 selvage sts) until 19 (20 rows) pat reps are completed, end with row 17 of last pat rep.

Prepare trim for back point

On row 18, inc 1 st inside the selvage sts—26 sts. On row 20, inc again at end of row—27 sts. To dec for the back point, work dec'ing over 13 rows as foll: Dec 1 st at each edge on every row inside the selvage sts. On RS rows, ssk after the selvage and k2tog before the end of selvage. On WS rows, p2tog after the selvage and ssp before the end selvage. After working row 10 of pat, there are 7 sts.

Next row (RS) K1, ssk, k1, k2tog, k1—5 sts. **Next row** P3tog.

Next row Sl 2 knitwise, k next st, pass the sl sts over the k st. Fasten off. Belt measures approx 56"/142 cm long.

FINISHING

Block pieces to measurements. Sew shoulder, side and sleeve seams. Set in sleeves. Sew collar around neck overlapping the right side over the left.

Winter 2004-2005 • No. 17

Wrap Front Pullover

INTERMEDIATE

Very loose-fitting hooded pullover with wide sleeves and foldover reversible lace trim at the hem. Sized for Small, Medium, Large, and X-Large. Directions are for smallest size with larger sizes in parentheses. If there is only one figure, it applies to all sizes.

KNITTED MEASUREMENTS

• Bust 36 (40½, 45, 49)"/91.5 (103, 114, 124.5) cm
• Length 17½ (18, 18½, 19)"/44.5 (45.5, 47, 48) cm
• Upper arm 15 (16, 17, 18)"/38 (41, 43, 46) cm

MATERIALS

• 13 (14, 16, 18) 1¾oz/50g balls (each approx 110yd/90m) of Trendsetter Yarns *Spiral* (acrylic/nylon) in #96 aqua
• To substitute, seek a worsted-weight yarn with similar fiber content
• One pair each sizes 6 and 7 (4 and 4.5mm) needles OR SIZE TO OBTAIN GAUGE

GAUGE

19 sts and 24 rows = 4"/10 cm over St st using larger needles. TAKE TIME TO CHECK GAUGE.

STITCH GLOSSARY
Two-Sided Frost Flowers
(over 34 sts)

Row 1 Sl 2 (Purlwise wyib on all odd rows), p3, p2tog tbl, k4, yo, k2, yo, ssk, p2, yo, p2tog, k2, yo, ssk, yo, k4, p2tog, p3, k2.

Row 2 Sl 2 (Purlwise wyif on all even rows), k2, k2tog, p4, yo, k1, p2, yo, p2tog, k2, yo, ssk, p2, yo, p2tog, k1, yo, p4, ssk, k2, p2.

Row 3 Sl 2, p1, p2tog tbl, k4, yo, p2, k2, yo, ssk, p2, yo, p2tog, k2, yo, ssk, p2, yo, k4, p2tog, p1, k2.

Row 4 Sl 2, k2tog, p4, yo, k3, p2, yo,

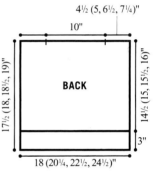

4½ (5, 6½, 7¼)"
10"
17½ (18, 18½, 19)"
BACK
14½ (15, 15½, 16)"
3"
18 (20¼, 22½, 24½)"

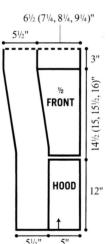

6½ (7¼, 8¼, 9¼)"
5½"
3"
½ **FRONT**
14½ (15, 15½, 16)"
HOOD
12"
5½" 5"

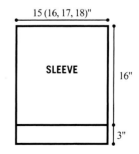

15 (16, 17, 18)"
SLEEVE
16"
3"

p2tog, k2, yo, ssk, p2, yo, p2tog, k3, yo, p4, ssk, p2.

Row 5 Sl 2, k3, k2tog, p4, yo, k2, yo, ssk, p2, yo, p2tog, k2, yo, ssk, yo, p4, ssk, k5.

Row 6 Sl 2, p2, k2tog tbl, k4, yo, p3, yo, p2tog, k2, yo, ssk, p2, yo, p2tog, p1, yo, k4, p2tog, p4.

Row 7 Sl 2, k1, k2tog, p4, yo, k4, yo, ssk, p2, yo, p2tog, k2, yo, ssk, k2, yo, p4, ssk, k3.

Row 8 Sl 2, k2tog tbl, k4, yo, p5, yo, p2tog, k2, yo, ssk, p2, yo, p2tog, p3, yo, k4, p2tog, p2.

Rows 9-16 Rep rows 1-8.

Row 17 Sl 2, yo, ssk, p2, yo, p2tog, yo, k4, p2tog, p6, p2tog tbl, k4, yo, p2, yo, p2tog, yo, ssk, k2.

Row 18 Sl 2, p2, k2, yo, ssk, k1, yo, p4, ssk, k4, k2tog, p4, yo, k1, k2, yo, ssk, p4.

Row 19 Sl 2, yo, ssk, p2, yo, p2tog, p2, yo, k4, p2tog, p2, p2tog tbl, k4, yo, p4, yo, p2tog, yo, ssk, k2.

Row 20 Sl 2, p2, k2, yo, ssk, k3, yo, p4, ssk, k2tog, p4, yo, k3, k2, yo, ssk, p4.

Row 21 Sl 2, yo, ssk, p2, yo, p2tog, yo, p4, ssk, k6, k2tog, p4, yo, p2, yo, p2tog, yo, ssk, k2.

Row 22 Sl 2, p2, k2, yo, ssk, p1, yo, k4, p2tog, p4, p2tog tbl, k4, yo, p1, k2, yo, ssk, p4.

Row 23 Sl 2, yo, ssk, p2, yo, p2tog, k2, yo, p4, ssk, k2, k2tog, p4, yo, k2, p2, yo, p2tog, yo, ssk, k2.

Row 24 Sl 2, p2, k2, yo, ssk, p3, yo, k4, p2tog, p2tog tbl, k4, yo, p3, k2, yo, ssk, p4.

Rows 25-32 Rep rows 17-24.

Rep rows 1-32 for two-sided frost flowers.

BACK

With smaller needles, cast on 102 (114, 126, 138) sts. Row 1 (RS) K2, ★p2, k2; rep from ★ to end. Cont in k2, p2 rib for 3"/7.5 cm, dec 16 (18, 20, 22) sts evenly spaced across last WS row—86 (96, 106, 116) sts. Change to larger needles and cont in St st until piece measures 17½ (18, 18½, 19)"/44.5 (45.5, 47, 48) cm from beg. Bind off.

Note The front begins at the top of the right side of the hood, then is worked down the right front to the

lower ribbed edge. The right front ribbed edge is bound off and the two-sided frost flowers panel continues for 1½"/38 cm. The left front ribbed edge is cast on at the end of an odd-numbered row of the frost flowers pattern. At this point, the RS of the left front is worked with even-numbered rows of the two-sided frost flowers pattern, becoming the WS of the right front. When knitting is finished, the two-sided frost flowers panel is folded with the Left front on top. With larger needles, cast on 58 sts for top of hood. **Next row (RS)** K 24, work 34 sts in Row 1 of frost flower pat. Work even in St st and Frost flower pat until piece measures 12"/30.5 cm from cast on row, end with a WS row. **Next row (RS)** Bind off 23 sts, work to end in pat. **Next row** Work 34 sts in frost flowers pat, p1, cast on 19 (23, 28, 33) sts for right shoulder.

Beg Right Front

Next row (RS) Knit 19 (23, 28, 33) sts, cont in frost flowers to end—54 (58, 63, 68) sts. Work even in frost flowers pat and rem st in St st for 11 (13, 15, 17) more rows. **Next (inc) row (RS)** Work to 2 sts before the 34-st band, M1, k2, complete the 34-st band. Rep inc row every 8th row 9 times more—64 (68, 73, 78) sts. Place marker on both sides of last inc row. Work even until piece measures 14½ (15, 15½, 16)"/37 (38, 39.5, 40.4) cm from shoulder cast-on, end with RS row. **Next (inc) row (WS)** Work 34 sts in frost flowers, inc 6 (6, 9, 8) sts evenly across rem St sts—70 (74, 82, 86) sts. Change to smaller needles.

Begin rib

Next row (RS) [K2, p2] 9 (10, 12, 13) times, work 34 sts in frost flowers. Work even in frost flowers pat and k2, p2 rib for 3"/7.5 cm, end with WS row. **Next row (RS)** Bind off 36 (40, 48, 52) rib sts, work to end. Work even on rem 34 sts in frost flowers for 1½"/38 cm, end with a odd numbered row, cast on 36 (40, 48, 52) sts at end of row for left front.

Beg left front

After this point, even-numbered frost

flowers pat rows will be worked on the RS of left front.

Next row (RS) [K2, p2] 9 (10, 12, 13) times, work rem 34 sts in frost flowers—70 (74, 82, 86) sts. **Next row (WS)** Work 34 sts in frost flowers, [k2, p2] 9 (10, 12, 13) times to end of row. Continue in k2, p2 rib and frost flowers until 3"/7.5 cm from cast-on row, end with a WS row. Change to larger needles. **Next row (RS)** Knit and dec 6 (6, 9, 8) sts evenly across rib sts, work rem 34 sts in frost flowers—64 (68, 73, 78) sts. Work even until same length as right front to marker, end with WS row. **Next (dec) row (RS)** Work to last 4 sts in St st, k2, ssk, work pat to end. Rep dec row every 8th row 9 times more—54 (58, 63, 68) sts. Work even for 10 (12, 14, 16) rows. **Next row (RS)** Bind off 19 (23, 28, 33) sts (for shoulder), work to end. Work 1 row even. **Next row (RS)** Cast on 19 (23, 28, 33) sts, work to end. Work even on all 54 (58, 63, 68) sts for 2nd half of hood for 12"/30.5 cm. Bind off.

SLEEVES

With smaller needles, cast on 86 (90, 98, 102) sts. Work in k2, p2 rib as for back for 4"/10 cm, dec 15 (14, 17, 16) sts evenly spaced across last WS row—71 (76, 81, 86) sts. Change to larger needles and cont in St st until piece measures 19"/48 cm from beg. Bind off.

FINISHING

Block pieces lightly to measurements. Fold up the front at the lower hem so that both sides are in St st. Sew top of hood seam along the cast-on and bind-off edges of front. Sew shoulder seams. Place markers at 7½ (8, 8½, 9)"/19 (20.5, 21.5, 23) cm from shoulders. Sew sleeves to armholes between markers. Sew side and sleeve seams.

Seed Stitch Suit

INTERMEDIATE

Close-fitting, seed stitch jacket with shaped patch pockets and crocheted trim and ties. Matching skirt with side seam zipper. Designed by Anna Sui. Sized for Small, Medium, Large, and X-Large. Directions are for smallest size with larger sizes in parentheses. If there is only one figure, it applies to all sizes.

KNITTED MEASUREMENTS
Jacket
• Bust (buttoned) 33 (37, 41, 45)"/84 (94, 104, 114.5) cm
• Length 23½ (24½, 25½, 26½)"/60 (62, 65, 67.5) cm
• Upper arm 12 (13, 14, 15)"/30.5 (33, 35.5, 38) cm
Skirt (Note Skirt is worn below waist.)
• Width at top edge 30 (34, 38, 42)"/76 (86.5, 96.5, 106.5) cm
• Width at lower edge 41 (46, 51, 57)"/104 (117, 130, 145) cm
• Length 24"/61 cm

MATERIALS (4)
Jacket
• 7 (8, 9, 10) 1¾oz/50g balls (each approx 131yd/120m) of Naturally *Sensation* (merino/angora) in #306 black (A)
• To substitute, seek an aran-weight yarn with similar fiber content
• 6 (7, 8, 9) balls in #300 white (B)
• 1 ball in #237 yellow (C)
Skirt
• 6 (8, 10, 12) 1¾oz/50g balls (each approx 131yd/120m) of Naturally *Sensation* (merino/angora) in #306 black
• To substitute, seek an aran-weight yarn with similar fiber content
• 5 (7, 9, 11) balls in #300 white (B)
• 1 ball in #237 yellow (C)
• One pair size 11 (8mm) needles OR SIZE TO OBTAIN GAUGE
• Size F/5 (3.75mm) crochet hook
• Five ¾"/19mm buttons (for jacket)
• One 8"/20 cm skirt zipper

GAUGE
12 sts and 20 rows = 4"/10 cm over seed st and 2 strands of yarn held tog using size 11 (8mm) needles. TAKE TIME TO CHECK GAUGE.

STITCH GLOSSARY
Seed Stitch
Row 1 (RS) ★K1, p1; rep from ★ to end.
Row 2 (WS) K the purl sts and p the knit sts.
Rep row 2 for seed st.

JACKET
BACK
With 1 strand each A and B held tog, cast on 50 (56, 62, 68) sts. Work in seed st for 15 (15½, 16, 16½)"/38 (39.5, 40.5, 42) cm.
Armhole shaping
Bind off 2 (2, 3, 4) sts at beg of next 2 rows. Dec 1 st each side every other row 3 (4, 5, 5) times—40 (44, 46, 50) sts. Work even until armhole measures 7½ (8, 8½, 9)"/19 (20.5, 21.5, 23) cm.
Shoulder and neck shaping
Bind off 3 (4, 4, 4) sts at beg of next 6 (2, 4, 6) rows, then 0 (3, 3, 0) sts at beg of next 0 (4, 2, 0) rows, AT SAME TIME, bind off center 18 (20, 20, 22) sts and working both sides at once, bind off 2 sts from each neck edge once.

LEFT FRONT
With 1 strand each A and B held tog, cast on 27 (30, 33, 36) sts. Work in seed st until piece measures same as back to armhole. Shape armhole at side edge (beg of RS rows) as for back—22 (24, 25, 27) sts. Work even until armhole measures 6 (6½, 7, 7½)"/15 (16.5, 18, 19) cm, end with a RS row.
Shape neck and shoulder
Next row (WS) Bind off 6 sts (neck edge), work to end. Cont to bind off from neck edge 2 (3, 3, 3) sts twice (once, once, twice), then 0 (2, 2, 0) sts 0 (once, once, 0), dec 1 st every other row 3 times, AT SAME TIME, when same length as back to shoulder, shape shoulder at side edge as for back. Place markers on front edge for 5 buttons, the first one at 1"/2.5 cm from lower edge, the last one at ½"/1.5 cm just below neck shaping, and the others spaced evenly between.

RIGHT FRONT
Work to correspond to left front, reversing all shaping and working buttonholes opposite markers as foll:
Buttonhole row (RS) Work 2 sts, bind off 2 sts, work to end. On foll row, cast on 2 sts over bound-off sts.

SLEEVES
With 1 strand each A and B held tog,

cast on 28 (29, 30, 31) sts. Work in seed st for 3"/7.5 cm. Cont in seed st, inc 1 st each side every 14th (12th, 10th, 10th) row 4 (5, 6, 7) times—36 (39, 42, 45) sts. Work even until piece measures 16½ (17, 17½, 18)"/42 (43, 44.5, 45.5) cm from beg.

Cap shaping

Bind off 3 sts at beg of next 2 rows, dec 1 st each side every other row 5 (6, 7, 7) times, every 4th row 2 (2, 2, 3) times. Bind off 3 sts at beg of next 2 rows, 2 sts at beg of next 2 rows. Bind off rem 6 (7, 8, 9) sts.

POCKETS (make 4)

With 1 strand each A and B held tog, cast on 6 sts. Work in seed st for 2 rows. Cont in seed st, inc 1 st each side on next row, then every row 3 times more—14 sts. Work even until pocket measures 4"/10 cm. Bind off.

FINISHING

Block pieces to measurements. Sew shoulder seams. Set in sleeves. Sew side and sleeve seams.

Crochet edging

With RS facing, crochet hook and 1 strand A, work 1 row sc evenly around all outside edges of body, lower edge of each sleeve and bound-off edge of each pocket. Sew pockets to left front as foll: the first one at 2"/5 cm from front edge and 2½"/6.5 cm from lower edge, the 2nd one 2"/5 cm from front edge and 5½"/14 cm above top of first pocket. Sew pockets to right front in same way.

Crochet pocket bands

With crochet hook and 1 strand C, ch 21. Sc in 2nd ch from hook, [ch 1, skip next ch, sc in next ch] 9 times, ch 1, work 3 sc in last ch; work along opposite edge of foundation ch as foll: [ch 1, skip next ch, sc in next ch] 9 times, sc in end of ch. Join with sl st to first sc. Fasten off. Join strand A with sl st in joining sl st. Next rnd With A, ch 1, sc in each sc and each ch-1 space around, join. Fasten off. Sew band to top of pocket, approx ¾"/.75cm below crocheted edge.

Crochet sleeve ties

With crochet hook and 1 strand C, ch for approx 35"/89 cm. Complete ties to match pocket trim. Sew center portion of tie to sleeve, approx 2"/5 cm from lower edge so that piece can be tied at outside edge of sleeve.

Neck tie

With crochet hook and 1 strand C, ch approx 56"/142 cm. Work as for sleeve ties. Sew center portion of tie around neck edge at approx 2"/5 cm from neck edge, and tie at center front. Sew on buttons to correspond to buttonholes.

SKIRT
BACK

With 1 strand each A and B held tog, cast on 61 (69, 77, 85) sts. Work in seed st, dec 1 st each side every 12th (10th, 8th, 8th) row 8 (6, 2, 7) times, then every 0 (12th, 10th, 10th) row 0 (3, 8, 4) times—45 (51, 57, 63) sts. Work even until piece measures 24"/61 cm from beg. Bind off.

FRONT

Work as for back.

Pockets (make 2)

Work as for pockets on jacket.

FINISHING

Block pieces to measurements. Sew side seams, leaving 8"/20.5 cm of top left seam open for zipper placement.

Crochet edging

With RS facing, crochet hook and 1 strand A, work 1 row sc evenly around top and lower edges of skirt. Sew pockets to fronts 2"/5 cm in from each side edge and 2½"/6.5 cm down from top edge.

Crochet pocket bands (make 2)

Work same as jacket. Sew to pockets.

Waist ties

With crochet hook and 1 strand C, ch approx 19"/48 cm. Work as for sleeve ties on jacket. Make a 2nd tie approx 35"/89 cm long in same way. Mark each side of center 2"/5 cm at top edge of front with a pin. Sew shorter tie along top front edge of skirt, just below crocheted edging, from zipper

to first pin. Sew longer tie from 2nd pin around back of skirt to zipper. Tie at center front.

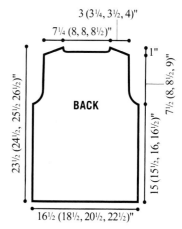

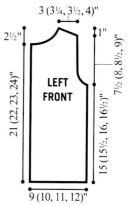

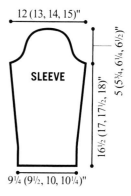

$\mathcal{S}$triped Tunic

EXPERIENCED

Very close-fitting sleeveless tunic with deep cowlneck is worked all in one piece in a reverse stockinette pattern. Designed by Twinkle. Sized for X-Small, Small, Medium, and Large. Directions are for smallest size with larger sizes in parentheses. If there is only one figure, it applies to all sizes.

KNITTED MEASUREMENTS
• Bust 32 (34½, 40, 42½)"/81.5 (87.5, 101.5, 108) cm
• Length approx 29 (29, 30, 31)"/73.5 (73.5, 76, 78.5) cm

MATERIALS 5
• 3 (3, 3, 4) 3½oz/100g balls (each approx 110yd/100m) of Naturwolle/ Muench Yarns *Black Forest* (wool) in #52 white (B)
• To substitute, seek a bulky-weight yarn with similar fiber content
• 2 (2, 2, 3) each in #02 black (A), and #47 yellow (C)
• 2 (2, 2, 2) each in #46 peach (D), #26 purple (E), #05 orange (F) and #48 pink (G)
• Size 19 (15mm) circular needle or size to obtain gauge, in various lengths to accommodate the number of stitches for your size
• Stitch holders and stitch markers

GAUGE
6 sts and 10 rnds = 4"/10 cm over rev St st using size 19 (15mm) needle and 3 strands of yarn held tog. TAKE TIME TO CHECK GAUGE.

STRIPE PATTERN
6 rnds each A, B, C, D, E, F, G; rep from ★ (42 rows) for stripe pat.

NOTE
Work with 3 strands of yarn held tog throughout.

POCKET LININGS (make 2)
With 3 strands B, cast on 7 (7, 8, 8) sts. Work in rev St st for 6 rows. Place sts on a holder.

BODY
With 3 strands A, cast on 48 (52, 60, 64) sts. Join, taking care not to twists sts on needle. Place a marker for beg of rnd (this will be center back) and slip marker every rnd. Work in garter st (k 1 rnd, p 1 rnd) for 4 rnds. Cont in rev St st (p every rnd), working 2 more rnds with A (for first 6 rnds of stripe pat), then beg with color B, cont in stripe pat to end of piece, AT SAME TIME, work as foll: Work until there are 12 rnds from beg, ending with B stripe.

Pocket joining
Next rnd With C, p15 (17, 19, 21), sl next 7 (7, 8, 8) sts to a holder, p across 7 (7, 8, 8) sts from one pocket lining holder, p4 (4, 6, 6), sl next 7 (7, 8, 8) sts to a holder, p across 7 (7, 8, 8) sts from 2nd pocket lining holder, p to end. **Next rnd** P12, (13, 15, 16), pm, p24 (26, 30, 32), pm, p to end of rnd. **Dec rnd** P to 2 sts before first marker, p2tog, sl marker, p2tog, p to 2 sts before 2nd marker, p2tog, sl marker, p2tog, p to end. Work 12 rnds even. Rep dec rnd—40 (44, 52, 56) sts. Work 10 rnds even. Inc rnd P to first marker, M1 p-st, sl marker, M1 p-st, p to next marker, M1 p-st, sl marker, M1 p-st, p to end. Work 6 rnds even. Rep inc rnd—48 (52, 60, 64) sts. Work even until piece measures 20"/50.5 cm from beg.

SLEEVES
Cont in stripe pat as foll: **Next rnd** P11 (12, 14, 15), bind off 2 sts, p22 (24, 28, 30), bind off 2 sts, p to end of rnd.
Next rnd P to bound off sts, cast on 14 (14, 15, 16) sts, p to bound off sts, cast on 14 (14, 15, 16) sts, p to end of rnd—72 (76, 86, 92) sts.
Dec rnd 1 P8 (8, 10, 11), *p2tog, p2, p2tog*, p8 (9, 10, 11); rep between *'s once, p16 (18, 22, 24); rep between *'s once, p8 (9, 10, 11); rep between *'s once, p to end of rnd—64 (68, 78, 84) sts. P 2 rnds. **Dec rnd 2** P7 (7, 9, 10), *p2tog, p2, p2tog*, p6 (7, 8, 9); rep between *'s once, p14 (16, 20, 22); rep between *'s once, p6 (7, 8, 9), rep between *'s once, p to end of rnd—56 (60, 70, 76) sts. P 2 rnds. **Dec rnd 3** P6 (6, 8, 9), *p2tog, p2, p2tog*, p4 (5, 6, 7); rep between *'s once, p12 (14, 18, 20); rep between *'s once, p4 (5, 6, 7), rep between *'s once, p to end of rnd—48 (52, 62, 68) sts. P 2 rnds. **Dec rnd 4** P5 (5, 7, 8), *p2tog, p2, p2tog*, p2 (3, 4, 5); rep between *'s once, p10 (12, 16, 18); rep between *'s once, p2 (3, 4, 5), rep between *'s once, p to end of rnd—40 (44, 54, 60) sts.

For sizes Medium and Large only
P 2 rnds. **Dec rnd 4** P (6, 7), *p2tog, p2, p2tog*, p (2, 3); rep between *'s once, p (14, 16); rep between *'s once, p (2, 3), rep between *'s once, p to end of rnd—(46, 52) sts.

For size Large only
P 2 rnds. **Dec rnd 4** P (6), *p2tog, p2, p2tog*, p (1); rep between *'s once, p (14); rep between *'s once, p to end of rnd—(46) sts.

For all sizes
Work even on 40 (44, 46, 46) sts until piece measures approx 13½"/34.5 cm from last dec row. Bind off loosely purlwise using last color worked.

FINISHING
Block lightly to measurements. Sew pocket linings in place. With C, pick up sts from pocket holders and work in k1, p1 rib for 4 rows. Bind off. Sew in place.

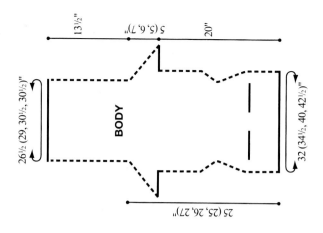

BODY

13½"

5 (5, 6, 7)"

20"

26½ (29, 30½, 30½)"

32 (34½, 40, 42½)"

25 (25, 26, 27)"

*L*oop Stitch Cardigan

EXPERIENCED

Standard-fitting, cropped cardigan with loop stitch and cable pattern fronts, stockinette stitch back and loop stitch down center of sleeves. Sized for X-Small, Small, Medium, Large, X-Large, and XX-Large. Directions are for smallest size with larger sizes in parentheses. If there is only one figure, it applies to all sizes.

KNITTED MEASUREMENTS
• Bust (closed) 32 (36, 40, 44, 48, 52)"/81 (91.5, 101.5, 111.5, 122, 132) cm
• Length (with lower edge rolled) 17 (18, 18½, 19½, 20, 21)"/43 (45.5, 47, 49.5, 51, 53.5) cm
• Upper arm 12 (13, 14, 15, 15½, 16)"/30.5 (33, 35.5, 38, 39.5, 40.5) cm

MATERIALS 🧵2
• 9 (10, 11, 12, 13, 14) 1¾oz/50g

skeins (each approx 175yd/160m) of Koigu Wool Designs *Painter's Palette Premium Merino* (wool) in #0000 cream
• To substitute, seek a fingering-weight yarn with similar fiber content
• One pair each sizes 2 and 3 (2.75 and 3.25mm) needles OR SIZE TO OBTAIN GAUGE
• One set dpn size 3 (3.25mm),
• Cable needle (cn)
• Stitch markers
•1 button

GAUGES
• 28 sts and 38 rows = 4"/10 cm over St st using larger needles.
• 36 sts = 4"/10 cm over cable panel and loop st pat using larger needles.
TAKE TIME TO CHECK GAUGES.

NOTE
All length measurements reflect the lower edge rolled.

STITCH GLOSARY
Cable Panel
(over 12 sts)
Rows 1 and 5 (RS) Knit.
Row 2 and all WS rows Purl. Row 3 Sl 4 sts to cn and hold to front, k4, k4 from cn, k4.
Row 7 K4, sl 4 sts to cn and hold to back, k4, k4 from cn.
Row 8 Rep row 2.

Rep rows 1–8 for cable panel.
Loop Stitch Pattern
(over 9 sts)
Row 1 (RS) K3, [turn, p3, turn, k3] 3 times, turn, p3, turn, k9, [turn, p3, turn, k3] 4 times.
Row 2 and all WS rows Purl.
Rows 3 and 5 Knit.
Row 7 K6, [turn, p3, turn, k3] 3 times, turn, p3, turn, k6.
Rows 9 and 11 Knit. Row 12 Rep row 2.
Rep rows 1–12 for loop st pat.

BACK
With smaller needles, cast on 112 (126, 140, 154, 168, 182) sts. Work in St st for 10 rows. Change to larger needles and cont in St st until piece measures 10 (10½, 10½, 11, 11, 11)"/25.5 (26.5, 26.5, 28, 28, 28) cm from beg (with edge rolled).
Armhole shaping
Bind off 4 (5, 5, 6, 6, 7) sts at beg of next 2 rows, 3 sts at beg of next 0 (0, 0, 2, 4, 4) rows, 2 sts at beg of next 2 (2, 4, 4, 4, 4) rows. Dec 1 st each side every other row 4 (7, 8, 8, 8, 11) times—92 (98, 106, 112, 120, 126) sts. Work even until armhole measures 7 (7½, 8, 8½, 9, 10)"/17.5 (19, 20.5, 21.5, 23, 25.5) cm. Bind off all sts.

LEFT FRONT
With smaller needles, cast on 71 (78,

88, 97, 104, 115) sts. Work in St st for 10 rows. Change to larger needles.

Beg cable and loop st pat

Row 1 (RS) K7 (14, 12, 12, 19, 18), work 0 (0, 12, 0, 0, 12) sts in cable pat, [work 9 sts in loop st pat, 12 sts in cable pat] 3 (3, 3, 4, 4, 4) times, k1.

Row 2 K1, [work 12 sts in cable pat, 9 sts in loop st pat] 3 (3, 3, 4, 4, 4) times, 0 (0, 12, 0, 0, 12) sts in cable pat, p7 (14, 12, p12, 19, 18). Cont in pats as established until same length as back to armhole.

Armhole and neck shaping

Shape armhole at side edge (beg of RS rows) as for back, AT THE SAME TIME, when armhole measures ½ (½, 1, 1, 1½, 2)"/1.5 (1.5, 2.5, 2.5, 4, 5) cm, shape neck at end of RS rows as foll: **Next row (RS)** Work to last 4 sts, k3tog, k1. Cont to dec 2 st at neck edge every other row 7 (6, 9, 11, 11, 14) times more, then dec 1 st (by working to last 3 sts, k2tog, k1) every other row 22 (25, 22, 22, 22, 22) times—23 (25, 29, 30, 34, 35) sts. Work even until same length as back. Bind off sts for shoulder.

RIGHT FRONT

Work to correspond to left front, reversing all shaping and placement of pat as foll:

Beg cable and loop st pat

Row 1 (RS) K1, [work 12 sts in cable pat, 9 sts in loop st pat] 3 (3, 3, 4, 4, 4) times, 0 (0, 12, 0, 0, 12) sts in cable pat, k7 (14, 12, 12, 19, 18).

SLEEVES

With smaller needles, cast on 60 (60,

62, 62, 64, 64) sts. Work in St st for 10 rows. Change to larger needles.

Beg loop st pat

Row 1 (RS) K14 (14, 15, 15, 16, 16), work 9 sts in loop st pat, k14, 9 sts in loop st pat, k14 (14, 15, 15, 16, 16).

Row 2 (WS) P14 (14, 15, 15, 16, 16), work 9 sts in loop st pat, p14, 9 sts in loop st pat, p14 (14, 15, 15, 16, 16). Cont in pat as established, inc 1 st at each side (working inc sts into St st) every 10th (8th, 6th, 6th, 6th, 6th) row 10 (14, 4, 20, 17, 25) times, every 12th (10th, 8th, 8th, 8th, 8th) row 4 (4, 16, 4, 7, 1) times—88 (96, 102, 110, 112, 116) sts. Work even in pat until piece measures 17½ (18, 18, 18, 18½, 18½)"/44.5 (45.5, 45.5, 45.5, 47, 47) cm from beg.

Cap shaping

Bind off 4 (5, 5, 6, 6, 7) sts at beg of next 2 rows, 3 sts at beg of next 0 (0, 0, 2, 4, 4) rows, 2 sts at beg of next 2 (2, 4, 0, 0, 0) rows. Dec 1 st each side every row 8 (8, 8, 8, 0, 0) times, every other row 13 (16, 17, 20, 26, 23) times, every 4th row 0 (0, 0, 0, 0, 4) times. Bind off 4 sts at beg of next 4 rows. Bind off rem 18 (18, 18, 20, 20, 20) sts.

FINISHING

Block pieces to measurements. Sew shoulder seams. With RS facing and smaller needles, pick up and k 140 (144, 144, 150, 150, 156) sts evenly around neck edge. Bind off knitwise. Set in sleeves. Sew side and sleeve seams.

I-cord loop

With dpn, cast on 3 sts. **∗Next row (RS)** Knit. Do not turn. Slide sts

to beg of row to work next row from RS. Rep from ∗ until cord measures 2"/5 cm. Bind off. Attach loop to right front edge below neck shaping. Sew button to left front in corresponding position.

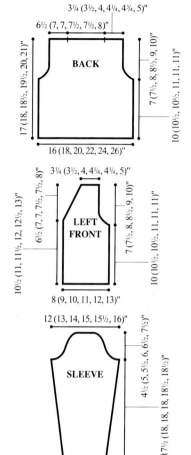

Winter 2005-2006 • No. 1

Whip-Stitch Tunic

Winter 2005-2006 • No. 1

INTERMEDIATE

Loose-fitting tunic with side slits, set-in sleeves and crocheted whip-stitch edges. Designed by Michael Kors.

Sized for X-Small, Small, Medium, Large, and X-Large. Directions are for smallest size with larger sizes in parentheses. If there is only one figure, it applies to all sizes.

KNITTED MEASUREMENTS

• Bust 36 (38, 40, 42, 44)"/91.5 (96.5, 101.5, 106.5, 111.5) cm

• Length 30½ (31, 31½, 32, 32½)"/77.5 (78.5, 80, 81, 82.5) cm

- Upper arm 11 (12, 13, 14, 15)"/28 (30.5, 33, 35.5, 38) cm

MATERIALS 4

- 8 (9, 10, 11, 12) 1¾oz/50g hanks (each approx 125yd/114m) of Classic Elite Yarns *Posh* (cashmere/silk) in #93049 orange (MC)
- To substitute, seek a worsted-weight yarn with similar fiber content
- 1 hank in #93046 snow (CC)
- One pair size 8 (5mm) needles OR SIZE TO OBTAIN GAUGE
- Size H/8 (5mm) crochet hook

GAUGE

19 sts and 26 rows = 4"/10 cm over St st using size 8 (5mm) needles. TAKE TIME TO CHECK GAUGE.

BACK

With MC, cast on 96 (100, 104, 110, 114) sts. Work in k1, p1 rib for ½"/1.5 cm. Cont in St st until piece measures 6"/15 cm from beg. Dec 1 st each side every 18th row 5 times—86 (90, 94, 100, 104) sts. Work even until piece measures 22"/56 cm from beg.

Armhole shaping

Bind off 3 sts at beg of next 2 rows, 2 sts at beg of next 4 rows. **Next (dec) row (RS)** K2, k2tog, k to last 4 sts, ssk,

k2. Rep dec row every other row 3 (4, 5, 6, 7) times—64 (66, 68, 72, 74) sts. Work even until armhole measures 7¼ (7¾, 8¼, 8¾, 9¼)"/18.5 (19.5, 21, 22, 23.5) cm.

Shoulder and neck shaping

Bind off 4 (4, 4, 6, 6) sts at beg of next 6 (4, 2, 2, 4) rows, 5 sts at beg of next 2 (4, 6, 6, 4) rows, AT SAME TIME, after 2 rows of shoulder shaping have been worked, bind off center 22 sts for neck and working both sides at once, bind off 2 sts from each neck edge twice.

FRONT

Work as for back until piece measures 19½ (20, 20½, 21, 21½)"/49.5 (51, 52, 53, 54.5) cm from beg.

Placket shaping

Next row (RS) Work 43 (45, 47, 50, 52) sts, join 2nd ball of yarn and work to end. Working both sides at once, and working armhole shaping as for back, work even on rem 32 (33, 34, 36, 37) sts each side until armhole measures 4½ (5, 5½, 6, 6½)"/11.5 (12.5, 14, 15, 16.5) cm.

Neck shaping

Bind off from each neck edge 5 sts once, 2 sts once. Dec 1 st at each neck edge every other row 8 times as foll: **Next row (RS)** Work to last 4 sts on first side, k2tog, k2; on 2nd side, k2, ssk, work to end. When same length as back to shoulder, shape shoulder as on back.

SLEEVES

With MC, cast on 52 (57, 62, 66, 71) sts. Work in k1, p1 rib for ½"/1.5 cm. Then, cont in St st for 19½"/49.5 cm.

Cap shaping

Bind off 3 sts at beg of next 2 rows, 2 sts at beg of next 4 rows, dec 1 st each side (as for armhole dec row) every other row 12 (13, 15, 16, 17) times. Bind off 2 sts at beg of next 4 rows. Bind off rem 6 (9, 10, 12, 15) sts.

FINISHING

Block pieces lightly to measurements. Sew shoulder seams. Set in sleeves. Sew side seams, leaving first 6"/15 cm

at lower edge unsewn for side slits.

Crochet edging

With RS facing, crochet hook and CC, work evenly around lower edge of body as foll: join with sl st in one side seam at top of slit, ★ work 1 sc into space between 3rd and 4th st from edge, ch 3, skip 3 rows; rep from ★ to hem corner, work (1 sc, ch 3, 1 sc, ch 3, 1 sc) into corner, ★★ch 3, skip 2 sts, work 1 sc into base of rib; rep from ★★ along lower edge, then work opposite corner and side slits and other lower edge in same way. Fasten off. Work crochet edge on cuffs and around neck and placket in same way, using photo as a guide.

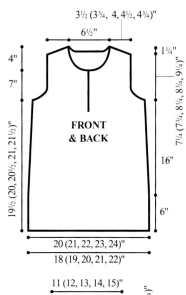

$\mathcal{F}$itted Jacket

EXPERIENCED

Close-fitting shaped jacket in textured bee stitch pattern with set in sleeves and knitted belt. Sized for Small, Medium, Large, and X-Large. Directions are for smallest size with larger sizes in parentheses. If there is only one figure, it applies to all sizes.

KNITTED MEASUREMENTS
• Bust 35¼ (38½, 41¾, 45)"/89.5 (98, 106, 114) cm
• Length 23 (23½, 24, 24½)"/58.5 (59.5, 61, 62) cm
• Upper arm 13½ (14, 14½, 15¼)"/34.5 (35.5, 37, 38.5) cm

MATERIALS 〔3〕
•16 (18, 20, 22) 1¾oz/50g balls (each approx 137yd/125m) of Lane Borgosesia/Trendsetter Yarns *Merinos Sei* (merino wool) in #42000 ash
• To substitute, seek a DK-weight yarn with similar fiber content
• One pair each sizes 4 and 6 (3.5 and 4mm) needles
OR SIZE TO OBTAIN GAUGE
• Size 6 (4mm) 12"/30 cm circular or double pointed needles
• One size E-4 (3.5mm) crochet hook
• Four ⅞"/22mm buttons, eight

⅜"/10mm buttons for sleeve cuffs
• One 2"/5cm wide buckle
• ½yd/.5m heavy sew-in facing, ½yd/.5m lightweight cotton jersey in dark gray
•Dark gray sewing thread and needle

GAUGES
• 23 sts = 5"/12.5 cm and 44 rows = 4"/10 cm over bee st pat using size 6 (4mm) needles.
• 40 sts = 7"/17.5 cm and 53 rows = 6"/15 cm over St st using size 6 (4mm) needles. TAKE TIME TO CHECK GAUGES.

STITCH GLOSSARY
K1-b Insert the needle through the center of the stitch below the next st on the needle and knit this stitch in the usual way, slipping the stitch above off the needle at the same time.
Bee Stitch
(over an even number of sts)
Rows 1 and 3 (WS) Knit.
Row 2 (RS) Sl 1, ★k1, k1-b; rep from ★, end sl 1.
Row 4 (RS) Sl 1, ★k1-b, k1; rep from ★, end sl 1.
Rep row 1-4 for bee st.
Garter selvedge Knit the first and last sts on every row unless otherwise indicated.
Sloped Bind Off Do not work the last st of the row before the bind off. On the bind off row slip the first st from the LH needle purlwise, then bind off the rem stitch from the previous row over the slipped st. This technique is used only on the first bind off stitch.
Sloped Cast On Add sts on at the end of RS rows for purl side increases and at the end of WS rows for knit side increases. Using a simple cast on add on the number of sts for the increase, turn, on the purl rows keep the yarn in front and slip the first st from the LH needle to the RH needle from the front, purl the next st tbl. On knit rows keep the yarn in back and slip the first st from LH needle to RH needle from the back and knit the 2nd

st tbl. **Note** When slipping the first st on both rows hold the yarn tight or the loop cast on will come undone.

BACK
With size 6 (4mm) needles, cast on 84 (92, 100, 108) sts. Work in bee st for 12 rows. Cont in pat, dec 1 st each side (inside of selvage sts) on next RS row, then every 10th row 5 times, every 12th row twice—68 (76, 84, 92) sts. Work even until piece measures 10"/25.5 cm from beg. Inc 1 st at each side on next RS row (inside of selvage sts), then every 6th row twice, then every 8th row 4 times—82 (90, 98, 106) sts. Work even until piece measures 16"/40.5 cm from beg.

ARMHOLE SHAPING
(Use Sloped Bind Off)
Bind off 2 (3, 3, 4) sts at beg of next 4 (2, 2, 2) rows, 1 (2, 2, 3) sts at beg of next 8 (4, 6, 2) rows, 0 (1, 1, 2) sts at beg of next 0 (8, 8, 6) rows, 0 (0, 0, 1) st at beg of next 0 (0, 0, 6) rows—66 (68, 72, 74) sts. Work even until armhole measures 7 (7½, 8, 8½)"/17.5 (19, 20.5, 21.5) cm. Work last RS row as foll: Work in pat across first 19 (20, 21, 22) shoulders sts, bind off center 28 (28, 30, 30) back neck sts, work across rem 19 (20, 21, 22) shoulder sts. Place shoulder sts on holders for the 3-needle bind off.

RIGHT FRONT
(Use Sloped Cast On)
With size 6 (4mm) needles, cast on 29 (33, 37, 41) sts. Working in bee st, casting on at the RH side (end of the first row, then at end of foll WS rows and working inc sts into pat) every other row as foll: 3 sts once, 2 sts twice, 1 st 7 times, then cast on every 4th row 1 st 3 times—17 sts added at RH side, AT SAME TIME, work decs and incs at LH side as for back.
Armhole shaping
For Small Size Only Bind off 3 sts at the beg of the first row = 1 st more than on first row on back. Work rem bind offs at LH side as for

back—35 sts. **For Medium, Large, and X-Large Sizes Work** at LH side as for back. **For All Sizes** AT SAME TIME, make four, 3-st buttonholes beg on the 3rd st after the RH side selvage st. Work the first at 3¼ (3¼, 3½, 3½)"/8 (8, 9, 9) cm after the last RH side cast-on row (WS), the rem 4 spaced 30 (32, 32, 34) rows apart. Work even until piece measures 15 (15½, 16, 16½)"/38 (39.5, 40.5, 42) cm from beg.

Lapel Shaping

(Use Sloped Cast On for RH side incs)

Work the selvage and the first st in reverse (WS rows out, RS rows in). Then to form lapel cont to work additional sts in reverse pat toward the armhole (LH side), AT SAME TIME, inc while working in reverse at the outside (RH side) edge as foll:

For Small Size Only LH side

[Reverse 1 st on the foll 4th row, then on the foll 6th row] 7 times, then reverse 1 st on every foll 4th row twice—17 sts rev pat. **RH side** [Inc 1 st at beg of 4th row, then at beg of 6th row] 5 times, then inc 1 st at beg of every foll 4th row 8 times—18 sts inc'd and worked in reverse pat at RH side—54 total sts, 35 sts reverse for lapel. **Note** Bring inc sts immediately into reversed pat at RHS. Work even on these sts for 3 rows, then bind off 9 sts at beg of next 3 RS rows—27 sts. Work next WS row as foll: slip 19 back shoulder sts from holder to needles. Seam front and back shoulders tog using the 3-needle bind off technique. Cont across row working on rem 8 back collar sts casting on 1 st at each edge to form selvage sts—10 sts. When piece measures 3"/7.5 cm from shoulder bind-offs, place all sts on a holder. **For Medium Size Only**

LH side

Reverse 1 st on every foll 6th row 5 times, then on every foll 4th row 12 times—18 sts in reverse pat. **RH side** Work incs on same rows at RH side as reverse sts on LH side. Bring inc sts at RH side immediately into reversed pat—18 sts inc'd and worked in reversed pat—56 sts, 36 reversed for lapel. Work even on these sts for 3 rows, then bind off 10 sts at beg of next RS row, 9 sts at beg of next 2 RS rows—28 sts. Slip 20 back

shoulder sts to needles. Seam front and back shoulders tog as you work across the next WS row using 3-needle bind off technique. Cont across row working rem 8 back collar sts, casting on 1 selvage st at each edge—10 sts. When piece measures 3"/7.5 cm from shoulder, place sts on a holder. **For Large and X-Large Sizes Only**

LH side

Reverse 1 st on every foll 6th row 3 times, then on every foll 4th row 15 times—19 sts in reversed pat. **RH side** Inc 1 st at the beg of every foll 6th row 5 times, then at the beg of every foll 4th row 12 times—18 sts. Bring inc sts at RH side immediately into reversed pat. There are 58 (59) sts on needles—37 in reversed pat for lapel. Work even on these sts for 3 rows, then bind off 9 sts at beg of next RS row, 10 sts at beg of next 2 RS rows—29 sts rem. Slip the 21 (22) back shoulder sts to needles. Work next WS row as foll: seam front and back shoulders tog using the 3-needle bind off technique. Cont across row working on rem 8 back collar sts, casting on 1 st at each edge for selvage sts—10 sts. When piece measures 3¼"/8 cm from shoulder bind-offs place all sts on a holder.

LEFT FRONT

Work as for right front reversing all shaping. Increase sts are added at the end of RS rows and the Sloped Cast On technique worked on the foll WS rows. Work incs, and decs at RH side as for back.

SLEEVES

With size 6 (4mm) needles, using a provisional cast-on, cast on 46 (48, 48, 52) sts. Work in bee st, inc 1 st each side (working inc sts into pat) every 14th (14th, 12th, 12th) row 9 (9, 7, 7) times, then every 0 (0, 14th, 14th) row 0 (0, 3, 3) times—64 (66, 68, 72) sts. Work even until piece measures 13½"/34.5 cm from beg.

Cap shaping

(Use Sloped Bind Off)

Bind off 2 (3, 3, 4) sts at beg of next 4 (2, 2, 2) rows, dec 1 st each side every other row 19 (19, 16, 16) times, every 4th row 0 (2, 5, 6) times, bind off 2 sts at beg of next 2 rows. Bind off rem 14 (14, 16, 16) sts.

Cuff

Note The Cuff will be reversed to RS of sleeve when turned back. Seam sleeve seam, then turn them to WS. Remove temporary cast on and place 46 (48, 48, 52) sts on either a size 6 (4mm) 12"/30 cm circular needle, or on a set of size 6 (4mm) double pointed needles. Beg working in rnds placing a marker at the seam to indicate end of rnd. Working the bee st in rnds (without selvage sts), work as foll: Purl first rnd, work row 2 of pat, purl 3rd rnd, work row 4 of pat.

Split cuff Row 5 (Circular pat Rnd 1) P23 (24, 24, 26) sts to center of cuff, pm, p to end. Slip sts back around to center marker, cut yarn. Reattach yarn to the 24th (25th, 25th, 27th) st of the previous row that began at sleeve seam marker. Change to regular size 6 (4mm) needles and beg working back-and-forth in pat (beg with row 2). Inc 1 st at each side (inside selvage sts and into pat) on foll row, then every 4th row twice, every 6th row 4 times—60 (62, 62, 66) sts. Work 1 WS row.

Center cuff shaping

(Use Sloped Bind Off)

Next row (RS) Work in pat across 16 sts, bind off the center 28 (30, 30, 34) sts, work across the rem 16 sts.

LH side Knit next 2 WS rows, then bind off 8 sts at beg of next 2 RS rows. **RH side** Reattach yarn at inside edge and slip first 2 sts purlwise from LH needle to RH needle, then bind first st off over second, bind off 7 additional sts. On foll WS row bind of rem 8 sts.

BIAS BANDS
Body

With size 6 (4mm) needles, cast on 3 sts and work as foll: **Row 1** Inc in first and last sts. **Row 2** Purl. Rep rows 1 and 2 until there are 9 sts. Work on these 9 sts as foll: **RS rows** Inc in first st, work to last 2 sts, k2tog. **WS rows** Purl 9. Cont to work in this way until band measures 125 (130, 136, 139)"/317 (330, 345, 353) cm. Place sts on a holder.

Sleeve cuff

Cast on and inc to 9 sts as with body bands. Work bias as for bands until piece measures 25 (26, 26, 28)"/63.5

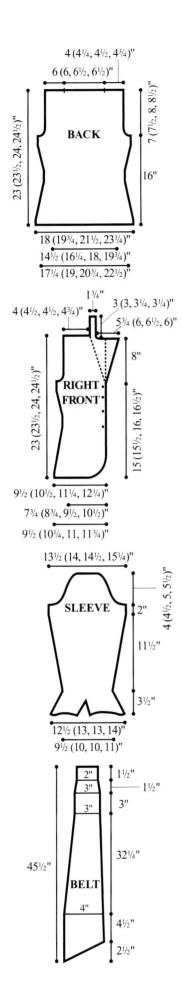

BACK
4 (4¼, 4½, 4¾)"
6 (6, 6½, 6½)"
7 (7½, 8, 8½)"
16"
23 (23½, 24, 24½)"
18 (19¾, 21½, 23¼)"
14½ (16¼, 18, 19¾)"
17¼ (19, 20¾, 22½)"

RIGHT FRONT
1¾"
4 (4½, 4½, 4¾)"
3 (3, 3¼, 3¼)"
5¾ (6, 6½, 6)"
8"
23 (23½, 24, 24½)"
15 (15½, 16, 16½)"
9½ (10½, 11¼, 12¼)"
7¾ (8¾, 9½, 10½)"
9½ (10¼, 11, 11¾)"

SLEEVE
13½ (14, 14½, 15¼)"
4 (4½, 5, 5½)"
2"
11½"
3½"
12½ (13, 13, 14)"
9½ (10, 10, 11)"

BELT
2"
1½"
3"
1½"
3"
3"
32¼"
45½"
4"
4½"
2½"

(66, 66, 71) cm ending on a WS row. Work as foll: **RS rows** K2tog, work to last 2 sts, K2tog. **WS rows** Purl. Rep these 2 rows until 3 sts rem. Bind off all sts.

BELT (Beg at buckle end)

With size 4 (3.5mm) needles cast on 11 sts. Work even for 1½"/4 cm, end with a WS row. Inc 1 st each side of next RS row, then every 6th row once, then every 7th row once—17 sts. Work even until piece measures 6"/15.5 cm from beg, end with a WS row. On next RS row, inc 1 st at each side, then every 142 rows twice—23 sts. Work even for 4½"/11.5 cm more, end with a WS row. Bind off 2 sts at beg of next RS row, then every RS row 10 times more—1 st rem. Pull yarn through st.

FINISHING

Block pieces to measurements. Slip back collar sts back to needles and seam using the 3-needle bind off technique. Whip st collar to back neck. Sew side seams. Steam bias bands to measurements. Pin body bias band around the entire jacket, beg and end at the center back neck, folding the band in half over the edge, add more length or rip back if necessary until band fits. When piece is pinned to within 1"/2.5 cm of completion, bind off as foll: **RS rows** K2tog, work to last 2 sts, k2tog. **WS rows** Purl. Rep these 2 rows 3 times—3 sts. Bind off all sts. Seam edges tog at center back neck, baste entire band to jacket, then seam using mattress st on RS of collar, then whip st bands in place on WS. Pin, baste, then seam bias bands around the sleeve cuffs using the same techniques used on fronts and back above. Beg and end at base of cuff opening. Sew buttons on each front opposite buttonholes and 4 on each cuff = one on back and one on front as shown in photo. Set in sleeves.

BELT FINISHING

Trace belt on tissue paper. Using tissue paper as a pattern, cut facing to belt measurements minus about ⅛"/3mm width. Cut length approx 2"/5 cm below the top. Again, using tissue pattern cut jersey fabric approx ¼"/6mm wider than belt and ¼"/6mm higher than facing at top. Lay facing inside belt, then place jersey on top as belt back. Tuck jersey in around facing, pin, then baste the 3 pieces together. Steam lightly, then seam the facing and jersey to belt along the sides and around the bottom using a whip st. with sewing thread and needle. Sew through 1 side of st on belt, then through edge of both jersey and facing. Using a size E (3.5mm) crochet hook, work 1 row of sc around the entire buckle. Pull the 2"/5 cm unlined top portion of the belt across the buckle and seam it down to the top of the facing and jersey, then seam it just below the crossing bar.

$\mathcal{R}$ainbow Shawl

VERY EASY VERY VOGUE

Large shawl knitted in ten colors with knitted-on facings. One size.

MEASUREMENTS
• Neck 16"/40.5 cm
• Length approx 35"/89 cm

MATERIALS

• 1 1¾oz/50g ball (each approx 126yd/115m) of S. Charles Collezione/Tahki•Stacy Charles, Inc. *Cashmere Breeze* (cashmere) in #303566 pink (B) and #303326 dark pink (C)
• 2 balls each in #303324 dark blue (A), #303331 red (D), #303329 orange (E), #303328 light orange (F), #303327 yellow (G), #303337 lime (H), #303321 light blue (I), #303323 blue (J)

• Shawl can also be made using Filatura Di Crosa/Tahki•Stacy Charles, Inc. *Zara* (1¾oz/50g balls, each approx 138yd/125m, wool) in #1499 (A), #1723 (B), #1716 (C), #1449 (D), #1738 (E), #1743 (F), #429 (G), #1727 (H), #1462 (I) and #1472 (J)
• To substitute, seek a bulky-weight yarn with similar fiber content
• 1 each size 7 (4.5mm) circular needles, 32"/80 cm and 47"/120 cm lengths OR SIZE TO OBTAIN GAUGE
• Stitch markers

GAUGE
18 sts and 29 rows to 4"/10 cm over St st. TAKE TIME TO CHECK GAUGE.

NOTE
To M1, with the needle tip, lift the strand between the last stitch knit and the next stitch on the left-hand needle and knit into back of it. One stitch has been added.

STITCH GLOSSARY
Pattern Stitch
Row 1 (RS) [K1, M1, k to 1 st before marker, M1, k1, sl marker] 3 times, k1, M1, k to last st, M1, k1.
Row 2 (WS) Purl.
Rep rows 1 & 2 for pattern stitch.

Shawl
With A and 32"/80 cm needle, cast on 72 sts.
Next row (RS) [K18, place marker] 3 times, k to end. Work 9 more rows even in St st. **Next row (RS)** Change to B and work row 1 of pattern stitch. Changing to longer circular needle when required to accommodate number of sts, work evenly in pattern stitch for 27 more rows. Change to C and work even in pattern stitch for 26 rows. Change to D and work even in pattern stitch for 24 rows. Change to E and work even in pattern stitch for 22 rows. Change to F and work even in pattern stitch for 20 rows or to end of second ball, ending at end of row. Change to G and work even in pattern stitch to end of second ball, ending at end of row. Change to H and work even in pattern stitch to end of second ball, ending at end of row. Change to I and work even in pattern stitch to end of second ball, ending at end of row. Change to J and work even in pattern stitch to end of second ball, ending with a WS row. Change to A and work even in pattern stitch for 6 rows. Continuing in A, work as foll:
Row 1 (RS) [K1, k2tog, k to 3 sts before marker, ssk, k1, sl marker] 3 times, k1, k2tog, k to last 3 sts, ssk, k1.
Row 2 (WS) Purl. Rep last 2 rows once more. Bind off.

FINISHING
Front edges
With 47"/120 cm needle and A, beg at bound-off edge, work along right front and with RS facing, pick up 3 sts for every 4 rows. Work in St st for 8 rows. Bind off. With 47"/120 cm needle and A, beg at cast-on edge, work along left front and with RS facing, pick up 3 sts for every 4 rows. Work in St st for 8 rows. Bind off. Fold front edges in half to WS. Fold cast-on and bound edges in half to WS, so that half of A becomes a hem. Sew hems to front edges, neatly mitering the corners.

Fair Isle Cardigan

EXPERIENCED

Close-fitting, fair isle V-neck cardigan with shaped sides, set-in sleeves and ribbed borders. Sized for Small, Medium, Large, X-Large, and XX-Large. Directions are for smallest size with larger sizes in parentheses. If there is only one figure, it applies to all sizes.

KNITTED MEASUREMENTS
• Bust (buttoned) 36¾ (41¾, 46, 50¾, 55½)"/93.5 (106, 117, 129, 142) cm
• Length 21½ (22, 23, 23½, 24½)"/55 (56, 58.5, 59.5, 62.5) cm
• Upper arm 14 (14¾, 15½, 16, 17)"/35.5 (37.5, 39.5, 40.5, 43) cm

MATERIALS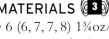
• 6 (6, 7, 7, 8) 1¾oz/50g balls (each approx 137yd/125m) of Debbie Bliss/KFI *Cashmerino Baby* (merino/microfiber/cashmere) in #12 silver (MC)

• To substitute, seek a DK-weight yarn with similar fiber content
• 3 balls in #203 teal (B)
• 2 balls in #101 ecru (C)
• 1 (1, 2, 2, 2) balls each in #16 celadon green (A), #700 red (D), and #15 pale salmon (E)
• 1 ball in #17 citrus (F)
• One pair each sizes 2 and 3 (2.75 and 3.25mm) needles OR SIZE TO OBTAIN GAUGE
• Size 2 (2.75mm) circular needle, 29"/74 cm long
• Seven ½"/13mm buttons

GAUGE
28 sts and 29 rows = 4"/10 cm over St st and Fair Isle chart using larger needles. TAKE TIME TO CHECK GAUGE.

NOTE
When changing colors, twist yarns on WS to prevent holes in work. Carry yarns not in use loosely across WS of work.

BACK
With smaller needles and MC, cast on 130 (146, 162, 178, 194) sts. Beg and end with K2 on RS, work in k2, p2 rib for 6 rows, dec 1 st at center of last row—129 (145, 161, 177, 193) sts. Change to larger needles. Work in St st and stripes as foll: 2 rows each MC, D, MC, A, MC, F, MC and E.
Beg chart pat
Row 1 (RS) Beg with st 9, work sts 9–24 (16-st rep) 8 (9, 10, 11, 12) times, work st 25. Cont in chart pat as established, dec 1 st each side (working dec sts into pat) on next row, then every 6th row 5 times more—117 (133, 149, 165, 181) sts. Work 9 (9, 11, 11, 13) rows even. Inc 1 st each side on next row, then every 8th row 4 times more—127 (143, 159, 175, 191) sts. Work even until piece measures 13½ (13½, 14, 14, 14½)"/34.5 (34.5, 35.5, 35.5, 37) cm from beg.
Armhole shaping
Bind off 8 (9, 10, 11, 11) sts at beg of next 2 rows. Dec 1 st each side every

row 5 (7, 11, 13, 15) times, then every other row 6 (7, 6, 7, 9) times—89 (97, 105, 113, 121) sts. Work even until armhole measures 8 (8½, 9, 9½, 10)"/20.5 (21.5, 23, 24, 25.5) cm. Bind off all sts.

LEFT FRONT
With smaller needles and MC, cast on 67 (75, 83, 91, 99) sts. Beg with K2 and end with p1 on RS, work in k2, p2 rib for 6 rows, dec 2 sts across last row—65 (73, 81, 89, 97) sts. Change to larger needles. Work in St st and stripes as for back.
Beg chart pat
Row 1 (RS) Beg with st 9, work sts 9–24 (16-st rep) 4 (4, 5, 5, 6) times, work st 25 (sts 25–33, st 25, sts 25–33, st 25). Cont in chart pat as established, working side decs at beg RS rows as for back—59 (67, 75, 83, 91) sts, then side inc's—64 (72, 80, 88, 96) sts. Work even until piece measures same length as back to armhole.
Armhole and neck shaping
Shape armhole at side edge as for back, AT SAME TIME, after 2 rows have been worked in armhole, dec 1 st at neck edge (end of RS rows) on next row, then every other row 17 (17, 21, 21, 22) times and every 4th row 3 (4, 2, 3, 3) times. Work even until same length as back. Bind off rem 24 (27, 29, 32, 35) sts for shoulder.

RIGHT FRONT
Work to correspond to left front, reversing all shaping and working chart pat as foll:
For sizes Small, Large and XX-Large
Row 1 (RS) Work sts 9–24 (16-st rep) 4 (0, 5, 0, 6) times, work st 25.
For sizes Medium and Large
Row 1 (RS) Beg with st 0 (1, 0, 1, 0) and work to st 8, work sts 9–24 (16-st rep) 0 (4, 0, 5, 0) times, work st 25.

SLEEVES
With smaller needles and MC, cast on 58 (62, 66, 70, 74) sts. Beg and end with K2 on RS, work in k2, p2 rib

for 10 rows, inc 1 st at center of last row—59 (63, 67, 71, 75) sts. Change to larger needles. Work in St st and stripes as for back AT SAME TIME, inc 1 st each side as foll: work 4 rows even, then inc 1 st each side on next row, then every 4th row twice more— 65 (69, 73, 77, 81) sts. After all stripe rows have been worked cont as foll:

Beg chart pat

Row 1 (RS) Beg with st 0 (7, 5, 3, 1) and work to st 0 (8, 8, 8, 8), work sts 9–24 (16-st rep) 4 times, work st 25 (sts 25–27, sts 25–29, sts 25–31, sts 25–33).

Cont in chart pat as established and work 1 row even. Inc 1 st each side (working inc sts in chart pat) on next row, then every 4th row 0 (1, 4, 2, 5) times, every 6th row 15 (15, 13, 15, 13) times—97 (103, 109, 113, 119) sts. Work even until piece measures 17 (17½, 17½, 18, 18)"/43 (44.5, 44.5, 45.5, 45.5) cm from beg.

Cap shaping

Bind off 8 (9, 10, 11, 11) sts at beg of next 2 rows. Dec 1 st each side every

row 6 (6, 6, 6, 8) times, then every other row 16 (18, 20, 21, 22) times. Bind off 6 sts at beg of next 4 rows. Bind off rem 13 sts.

FINISHING

Block pieces to measurements. Sew shoulder seams. Set in sleeves. Sew side and sleeve seams.

Front band

With RS facing, circular needle and MC, pick up and k 80 (80, 86, 86, 88) sts along right front edge to beg of neck shaping, 50 (53, 53, 56, 59) sts to shoulder, k 42 (44, 48, 50, 52) sts from back neck holder, pick up and k 50 (53, 53, 56, 59) sts along left front edge to beg of neck shaping, then 80 (80, 86, 86, 88) sts to cast-on edge—302 (310, 326, 334, 346) sts. Beg and end with P2 on WS, work in k2, p2 rib for 3 rows. **Buttonhole row (RS)** K2, p2tog, yo, [rib 10 (10, 12, 12, 12), rib 2tog, yo] 6 times, rib to end. Rib 2 more rows. Bind off in rib. Sew buttons to left front, opposite buttonholes.

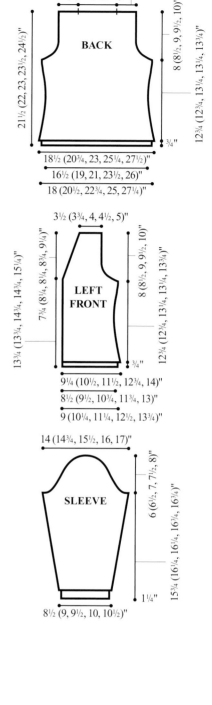

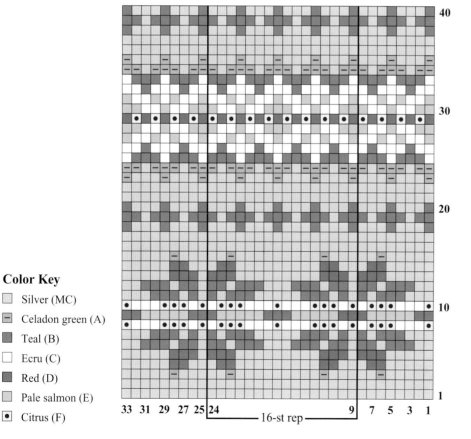

Color Key

- ☐ Silver (MC)
- ⊟ Celadon green (A)
- ▨ Teal (B)
- ☐ Ecru (C)
- ▨ Red (D)
- ☐ Pale salmon (E)
- ⊡ Citrus (F)

$\mathcal{F}$orestry Cardigan

EXPERIENCED

Standard-fitting raglan cardigan with front coin-cable panels. Sized for X-Small, Small, Medium, Large, X-Large, XX-Large, XXX-Large. Directions are for smallest size with larger sizes in parentheses. If there is only one figure, it applies to all sizes.

KNITTED MEASUREMENTS
• Bust (closed) 33½ (36¾, 40, 43¼, 46½, 49½, 52¾)"/85 (93.5, 101.5, 110, 118, 125.5, 134) cm
• Length 21¾ (22¾, 23¾, 24½, 25½, 26¼, 27¼)"/55 (58, 60.5, 62, 65, 66.5, 69) cm
• Upper arm 13¼ (14¾, 16, 17¼, 18½, 19½, 20¾)"/33.5 (37.5, 40.5, 44, 47, 49.5, 52.5) cm

MATERIALS (4)
• 12 (13, 15, 16, 17, 19, 21) 1¾oz/50g balls (each approx 93yd/85m) of Needful Yarns, Inc. *London Tweed* (wool/viscose) in #10 olive
• One pair each sizes 3 and 6 (3.25 and 4mm) needles OR SIZE TO OBTAIN GAUGES
• One size 3 (3.25mm) circular needles 32"/80 cm length
• Five ¾"/19mm snaps
• Cable needle (cn)
• Stitch holders and stitch markers

GAUGES
• 20 sts and 28 rows = 4"/10 cm over St st using size 6 (4mm) needles.
• 22 sts and 32 rows = 4"/10 cm over k2, p2 ribbing using size 3 (3.25mm) needles. TAKE TIME TO CHECK THE GAUGES.

STITCH GLOSSARY
RT
Row 1 Sl 1 to cn and hold in back, k1, k1 from cn.
Row 2 Purl.

LT
Row 1 Sl 1 to cn and hold in front, k1, k1 from cn.
Row 2 Purl.

Right Coin Cable
(over 5 sts)
Row 1 and all WS rows Purl.
Rows 2 and 6 Knit.
Row 4 Sl 4 sts to cn and hold in back, k1, sl last 3 sts on cn back to LH needle, k3, k1 from cn.
Rep rows 1–6 for Right Coin Cable.

Left Coin Cable
(over 5 sts)
Row 1 and all WS rows Purl.
Rows 2 and 6 Knit.
Row 4 Sl 4 sts to cn and hold in front, k1, sl last 3 sts on cn back to LH needle, k3, k1 from cn.
Rep rows 1–6 for Left Coin Cable.

Short Row Wrap and Turn (w&t)
On RS row (on WS row)
1) Wyib (wyif), Sl next st purlwise.
2) Move yarn between the needles to the front (back).
3) Sl the same st back to LH needle. Turn work. One st is wrapped.
4) When working the wrapped st, insert RH needle under the wrap and work it tog with the corresponding st on needle.

BACK
With smaller needles, cast on 90 (98, 106, 114, 122, 130, 138) sts. **Set-up row (WS)** ★P2, k2; rep from ★ to last 2 sts, end p2. Work in rib for 2"/5 cm, end with a WS row. Change to larger needles and St st, decreasing 4 sts evenly across row—86 (94, 102, 110, 118, 126, 134) sts. Work in St st until piece measures 2½"/6.5 cm from beg, end with a WS row. **Next (dec) row (RS)** K2, ssk, k to last 4 sts, k2tog, k2. Rep dec row every 6th row 4 times—76 (84, 92, 100, 108, 116, 124) sts. Work even until piece measures 7¾ (7¾, 7¾, 8, 8, 8¼, 8¼)"/20 (20, 20, 20.5, 20.5, 21, 21) cm, end with a WS row. **Next (inc) row (RS)** K3, M1, k to last 3 sts, M1, k3. Rep inc row every 8th row 4 (4, 3, 2, 1, 0, 0) times and every 10th row 0 (0, 1, 2, 3, 4, 4) times—86 (94, 102, 110, 118, 126, 134) sts. Work even until piece measures 13¾ (14, 14¼, 14¾, 15, 15½, 15¾)"/35 (35.5, 36, 37.5, 38, 39.5, 40) cm, end with a WS row.
Raglan armhole shaping
Bind off 2 (3, 3, 4, 5, 5, 6) sts at beg of next 2 rows, then 2 (2, 3, 3, 4, 5, 5) sts at beg of next 2 rows—78 (84, 90, 96, 100, 106, 112) sts. **Next (dec) row (RS)** K2, ssk, k to last 4 sts, k2tog, k2. Rep dec row every other row 20 (22, 24, 26, 28, 30, 32) times—36 (38, 40, 42, 42, 44, 46) sts. Work 1 WS row. Bind off all sts.

LEFT FRONT
With smaller needles, cast on 43 (47, 51, 55, 59, 63, 67) sts. **Set-up row (WS)** P3, ★k2, p2; rep from ★ to end. Work in rib for 2"/5 cm, end with a WS row. **Next (dec) row (RS)** K14 (18, 22, 26, 30, 34, 38), p2, [k2, k2tog, k2, p2] twice, k2, k2tog, k2, p2, RT, k1—40 (44, 48, 52, 56, 60, 64) sts. Change to larger needles. **Next row (WS)** P3, [work row 1 of Right Coin Cable over next 5 sts, k2] twice, work row 1 of Right Coin Cable over next 5 sts, k2, purl to end. Keep selvage in St st, work in pats as established until piece measures 2½"/6.5 cm from beg,

end with a WS row. **Next (dec) row (RS)** K2, ssk, work to end. Rep dec row on every 6th row 4 times—35 (39, 43, 47, 51, 55, 59) sts. Work even until piece measures 7¾ (7¾, 7¾, 8, 8, 8¼, 8¼)"/20 (20, 20, 20.5, 20.5, 21, 21) cm from beg, end with a WS row. **Next (inc) row (RS)** K3, M1, work to end. Rep inc row on every 8th row 4 (4, 3, 2, 1, 0, 0) times and on every 10th row 0 (0, 1, 2, 3, 4, 4) times—40 (44, 48, 52, 56, 60, 64) sts. Work even until piece measures 13¾ (14, 14¼, 14¾, 15, 15½, 15¾)"/35 (35.5, 36, 37.5, 38, 39.5, 40) cm from beg, end with a WS row.

Raglan armhole shaping
Bind off 2 (3, 3, 4, 5, 5, 6) sts at beg of next RS rows, then 2 (2, 3, 3, 4, 5, 5) sts at beg of next RS row—36 (39, 42, 45, 47, 50, 53) sts. **Next (dec) row (RS)** K2, ssk, work to end. Rep dec row on every RS row 20 (22, 24, 26, 28, 30, 32) times. AT SAME TIME, when armhole measures 4 (4¼, 4½, 5, 5½, 5½, 5¾)"/10 (11, 11.5, 12.5, 14, 14, 14.5), shape neck as foll: Bind off 3 sts at beg of next 2 WS rows and dec 1 st at neck edge every row 5 (6, 7, 8, 8, 9, 10) times—4 sts rem after all decreases have been worked. Bind off all sts.

RIGHT FRONT
Work as for left front, reversing all shaping and substituting Left Coin Cable for Right Coin Cable, and LT for RT.

SLEEVES
With smaller needles, cast on 50 (54, 58, 58, 62, 62, 66) sts. **Set-up row (WS)** ★P2, k2; rep from ★ to last 2 sts, end p2. Work in pat as established for 3½"/9 cm, end with a WS row. Change to larger needles and St st and dec 4 sts evenly on next row—46 (50, 54, 54, 58, 58, 62) sts. Work in St st until sleeve measures 6½"/16.5 cm from beg, end with a WS row. **Next (inc) row (RS)** K3, M1, k to last 3 sts, M1, k3. Rep inc row every 8th row 10 (9, 10, 5, 4, 0, 0) times, every 6th row 0 (2, 0, 8, 10, 13, 13) times

and every 4th row 0 (0, 2, 2, 2, 6, 7) times—68 (74, 80, 86, 92, 98, 104) sts. Work even until piece measures 19½ (20, 20½, 20¾, 21¼, 21½, 22)"/49.5 (51, 52, 52.5, 54, 55.5, 56) cm from beg, end with a WS row.

Raglan armhole shaping
Bind off 2 (3, 3, 4, 5, 5, 6) sts at beg of next 2 rows, then 2 (2, 3, 3, 4, 5, 5) sts at beg of next 2 rows—60 (64, 68, 72, 74, 78, 82) sts. **Next (dec) row (RS)** K2, ssk, k to last 4 sts, k2tog, k2. Rep dec row every other row 20 (22, 24, 26, 28, 30, 31) times—18 (18, 18, 18, 16, 16, 16) sts. Work 1 WS row. Place all sts on holder.

FINISHING
Sew raglan seams.

Collar and neck band
With RS facing and beg at right front edge, pick up and knit 100 (102, 105, 109, 113, 115, 119) right front edge sts, 13 (14, 16, 17, 18, 18, 19) right front neck sts, place marker (pm), 14 (14, 14, 14, 12, 12, 12) right sleeve sts, 32 (34, 36, 38, 38, 40, 42) back neck sts, 14 (14, 14, 14, 12, 12, 12) left sleeve sts, pm, 13 (14, 16, 17, 18, 18, 19) left neck sts and 100 (102, 105, 109, 113, 115, 119) left front edge sts—286 (294, 306, 318, 324, 330, 342) sts. **Set up row** ★K2, p2; rep from ★ to last 2 sts, end k2. **Next (inc) row** K4, [work in est rib to 2 sts before next marker, yo, p2, slip marker, yo] twice, work in est rib to last 4 sts, end k4. Working in pats as established, rep inc row every other row 7 times more—318 (326, 338, 350, 356, 362, 374) sts. Work 1 row even.

Back neck short rows
Row 1 Work to 4 sts before second marker, w & t. **Row 2** Work to 4 sts before opposite marker, w & t. **Row 3** Work to 4 sts before last wrapped stitch, w & t. Repeat row 3 nine times more. **Row 13** Work to 2 sts before last wrapped stitch, w & t. Repeat row 13 eleven times more. **Row 25** Work across, picking up all wraps. Work 3 more rows in rib. Bind off in rib. Sew side seams. Sew on snaps.

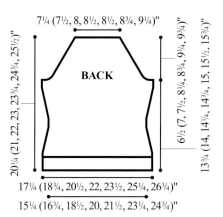

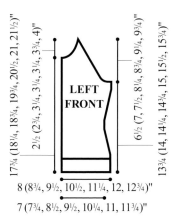

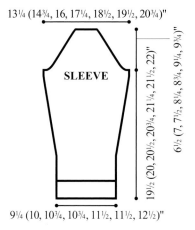

Bulky Coat

EXPERIENCED

Loose-fitting bubble coat with three-quarter sleeves, bubble-shaped back, and deep collar. Designed by Twinkle. Sized for Small, Medium, Large, X-Large. Directions are for smallest size with larger sizes in parentheses. If there is only one figure, it applies to all sizes.

KNITTED MEASUREMENTS
• Bust (closed) 44 (46½, 49, 51½)"/111.5 (118, 124.5, 131) cm
• Length at center back (without lower edge band) 26½ (28, 29, 30¾)"/67 (71, 73.5, 78) cm
• Length at front side seam (without lower edge band) 25 (26½, 28, 29½)"/63.5 (67, 71, 72.5) cm
• Upper arm 18 (19, 20¼, 21½)"/45.5 (48, 51.5, 54.5) cm

MATERIALS 6
• 7 (9, 10, 11) 7oz/200g hanks (each approx 83yd/76m) of Twinkle by Wenlan/Classic Elite Yarns *Soft Chunky* (wool) in #12 riviera
• To substitute, seek a super bulky–weight yarn with similar fiber content

• One pair size 19 (15mm) needles OR SIZE TO OBTAIN GAUGE
• Size 19 (15mm) circular needle, 47"/120 cm long
• Size N/15 (10mm) crochet hook
• Six 1¼"/32mm buttons
• Stitch holders and stitch markers

GAUGE
11 sts = 7"/18 cm and 14 rows = 6"/15 cm over St st using size 19 (15mm) needles. TAKE TIME TO CHECK GAUGE.

STITCH GLOSSARY
Sloped Bind-Off Method
One row before the next bind-off row, work to the last st of row. Do not work this st. Turn work. With yarn in back, sl first st purlwise from LH needle. Pass the unworked st of previous row over the slipped st. The first st is bound-off. Bind off the remaining number of sts in that row in the normal way.

Short Row Wrap and Turn (w&t)
On RS row (on WS row)
1) Wyib (wyif), Sl next st purlwise.
2) Move yarn between the needles to the front (back).
3) Sl the same st back to LH needle. Turn work. One st is wrapped.
4) When working the wrapped st, insert RH needle under the wrap and work it tog with the corresponding st on needle.

NOTES
1) Coat is constructed by first working the bubble-shaped lower body piece. Then each sleeve/yoke piece is worked from cuff to center back and joined by a three-needle bind-off at center back.
2) Collar is picked up and worked around neck edge and front bands are worked separately, then sewn to front.

POCKET LININGS (make 2)
Cast on 10 sts. Work in St st for 12 rows. Leave sts on holder.

LOWER BODY
With circular needle, beg at lower back edge, cast on 40 (42, 44, 46) sts. K 1 row. Cont in St st, cast on 2 sts at beg of next 10 rows—60 (62, 64, 66) sts. Then, cast on 19 (20, 21, 22) sts at beg of next row. **Dec row 13 (RS)** Cast on 19 (20, 21, 22) sts, k43 (45, 47, 49), k2tog, pm, k8, SKP, (for center back dec), k43 (45, 47, 49)—96 (100, 104, 108) sts. **Rows 14-18** Work even. **Dec row 19 (RS)** K10, SKP, k2, SKP (for right pocket dec), k to 2 sts before marker, k2tog, sl marker, k8, SKP, k to the last 16 sts, k2tog, k2, k2tog, k10 (for left pocket dec). **Rows 20-22** Work even. **Dec row 23** K9, SKP, k2, SKP (for right front dec), k to 2 sts before marker, k2tog, sl marker, k8, SKP, k to last 15 sts, k2tog, k2, k2tog, k9 (for left front dec).

Join the pockets
Using sloped bind-off method, shape pocket as foll: **Row 24 (WS)–Left front** P17, turn. **Next row (RS)** Bind off 4 sts, k to end. **Next row (WS)** P13. **Next row (RS)** Bind off 4 sts, k to end. **Next row (WS)** P9. **Next row (RS)** Bind off 2 sts, k to end. **Next row–Join pockets** P7, p10 sts from one pocket lining, p to last 17 sts, bind off 4 sts (for right front pocket), p to end. **Next row (RS)** K13, turn. **Next row (WS)** Bind off 4 sts, p to end. **Next row (RS)** K9, turn. **Next row (WS)** Bind off 2 sts, p to end. **Row 25 (RS)–Join pocket** K7, k10 sts from pocket lining, k to end. **Row 26** Purl 84 (88, 92, 96) sts. **Row 27** Rep dec row 23. **Rows 28-30** Work even. **Dec row 31** K8, SKP, k2, SKP (for right front dec), k to 2 sts before marker, k2tog, sl marker, k8, SKP, k to last 14 sts, k2tog, k2, k2tog, k8—72 (76, 80, 84) sts. **Row 32** Purl.
For Sizes Large and X-Large Only
Rows 33-36 Work even.
For all sizes
Work short row shaping on right front sts as foll: **Short row 1 (RS)** K12, w&t. Purl to end. **Short row 2 (RS)** K7, w&t. Purl to end. **Row 33 (33, 37, 37) (RS)** Knit across all sts hiding

wraps. Work short row shaping on left front sts as foll: **Short row 1 (WS)** P12, w&t. Knit to end. **Short row 2 (WS)** P7, w&t. Knit to end. **Row 34 (34, 38, 38)** Purl across all sts hiding wraps. **Dec row 35 (35, 39, 39) (RS)** K7, SKP, k2, SKP (for right front dec), k to 2 sts before marker, k2tog, sl marker, k8, SKP, k to last 13 sts, k2tog, k2, k2tog, k7 (for left front dec)—66 (70, 74, 78) sts. **Next 1 (3, 1, 3) rows** Work even. Bind off.

LEFT SLEEVE

With straight needles, cast on 28 (30, 32, 34) sts. Work in St st for 8 rows. **Note** Compensating eyelets (either k2tog, yo or yo, ssk) are worked for eyelet decoration. For eyelet inc's, yos are worked without the compensating dec.
Eyelet row 9 (RS) K7, k2tog, yo (for compensating eyelet), k10 (12, 14, 16), yo, ssk (for compensating eyelet), k7. **Rows 10-14** Work even. **Row 15** Rep eyelet row 9. **Rows 16-20** Work even. **Row 21** Rep eyelet row 9. **Rows 22-26** Work even. Place a removable marker at each end of the last row worked for the end of the sleeve seaming. **Row 27** Rep eyelet row 9. **Rows 28-32** Work even. **Inc row 33** K9, yo (for eyelet inc), k to last 9 sts, yo (for eyelet inc), k9—30 (32, 34, 36) sts. **Row 34** Purl.
For Sizes Large and X-Large
Rows 35 and 36 Work even.
For All Sizes—Short Row Shaping
Row 35 (35, 37, 37) (RS) Knit. **Short row 1 (WS)** P10, w&t. Knit to end. **Short row 2 (WS)** P6, w&t. Knit to end. **Row 36 (36, 38, 38)** Purl across all sts, hiding wraps. **Next 2 rows** Work even. **Row 39 (39, 41, 41)** K10, yo (for back eyelet inc), k to end—31 (33, 35, 37) sts. **Next 2 rows** Work even.

Front neck shaping

Row 42 (42, 44, 44) (WS) Bind off 15 (16, 17, 18) sts (for neck edge), purl to end. **Next 2 rows** Work even. **Row 45 (45, 47, 47)** K11, yo (for back eyelet inc), k to end—17 (18, 19, 20) sts. **Next 3 (5, 5, 7) rows** Work even. Sl these 17 (18, 19, 20) sts to a st holder for (center back edge).

RIGHT SLEEVE

Work as for left sleeve through row 34 (34, 36, 36).

Short row shaping

Short row 1 (RS) K10, w&t. Purl to end. **Short row 2 (RS)** K6, w&t. Purl to end. **Row 35 (35, 37, 37)** Knit across all sts hiding wraps. **Next 3 rows** Work even. **Row 39 (39, 41, 41) (RS)** K20 (22, 24, 26), yo (for back eyelet inc), k to end—31 (33, 35, 37) sts. **Next 2 rows** Work even.

Front neck shaping

Row 42 (42, 44, 44) (WS) P16 (17, 18, 19), join 2nd ball of yarn and bind off rem 15 (16, 17, 18) sts (for neck edge). **Next 2 rows** Work even. **Row 45 (45, 47, 47) (RS)** K5 (6, 7, 8), yo, k to end—17 (18, 19, 20) sts. **Next 3 (5, 5, 7) rows** Work even. With these 17 (18, 19, 20) sts on one needle and 17 (18, 19, 20) sts from left sleeve on a parallel needle with RS of pieces tog (in position with the shaped front neck edge matching), join the sts tog at center back using three-needle bind-off method.

FINISHING

Matching the removable markers on row 26 of each sleeve, sew the sleeve seams up to the markers for approx 11"/28 cm.

COLLAR

Place a removable marker at 6 sts in from the center front (neck) edge of each sleeve. Beg and end at these markers, pick up and k 35 (37, 39, 41) sts evenly along yoke edge between these markers. [P 1 row, k 1 row] twice. **Dec row 5 (WS)** P1, p2tog, p to last 3 sts, p2tog tbl, p1. **Rows 6-9** Work even in St st. **Dec row 10 (RS)** K1, SKP, k to last 3 sts, k2tog, k1. **Rows 11-14** Work even. Dec row 15 Rep dec row 5. **Rows 16-19** Work even. **Dec row 20** Rep dec row 10—27 (29, 31, 33) sts. **Row 21** Work even. Bind off loosely.

Lower edge band

Place a marker at lower center back edge. With circular needle, pick up and k sts from lower edge as foll: 7 sts to the pocket, 10 sts from both the right front and pocket lining thickness, 32 (34, 36, 38) sts to the center back, 32 (34, 36, 38) sts to the left front pocket, 10 sts from both the left front and pocket lining thickness, 7 sts to the end—98 (102, 106, 110) sts. **Row 1 (WS)** K2, k2tog, k1, k2tog, [k1, k2tog] 4 times, k10 (12, 14, 16), [k2tog] 20 times, k10 (12, 14, 16), [k2tog, k1] 4 times, k2tog, k1, k2tog, k2—66 (70, 74, 78) sts. P 1 row. Bind off knitwise. Center the sleeve seam at center back and seam the sleeve piece to the lower edge. With crochet hook, work 14 (15, 16, 17) sc firmly around each sleeve cuff edge (skipping every other st) to pull in cuff. With crochet hook, work an edge on each pocket edge by working sl st loosely in the front loop of each bound-off st. Seam sides of pocket linings to WS of fronts.

Left front band

With straight needles, cast on 9 sts. **Row 1 (RS)** K1, [p1, k1] 4 times. Work in k1, p1 rib for 66 (68, 70, 72) rows. Bind off in rib.

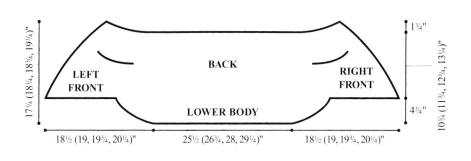

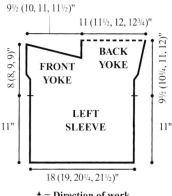

↑ = Direction of work

Right front band

Work as for left front band for 12 (14, 16, 18) rows.

Buttonhole row (RS) Rib 3 sts, k2tog, yo, rib 4 sts. Work even for 9 rows. Rep the last 10 rows 4 times more. Work buttonhole row on next row. Work 3 rows even. Bind off. Sew the bands to center fronts. Sew on buttons.

Winter 2008-2009 · No. 17

Dolman Pullover

INTERMEDIATE

Standard-fitting, cropped dolman sleeve pullover with diagonal stripe shift. Sized for Small, Medium, Large/ X-Large, and XX-Large. Directions are for smallest size with larger sizes in parentheses. If there is only one figure, it applies to all sizes.

KNITTED MEASUREMENTS

• Bust (at end of dolman) 54 (56, 59, 61)"/137 (142, 150, 155) cm
• Length 20 (20½, 21, 22½)"/51 (52, 53.5, 57) cm
• Upper arm 16 (17, 18, 20)"/40.5 (43, 45.5, 51) cm

MATERIALS 5

• 3 (4, 4, 4) 3½oz/100g hanks (each approx 175yd/160m) of Rowan/ Westminster Fibers, Inc. *Colourscape Chunky* (lambswool) in #437 camouflage (A)
• To substitute, seek a bulky-weight yarn with similar fiber content
• 2 (3, 3, 3) hanks in #434 candy pink (B)
• One size 10½ (6.5mm) circular needle, 36"/91 cm long OR SIZE TO OBTAIN GAUGE.

GAUGE

14 sts and 22 rows = 4"/10 cm over St st (after blocking) using size 10½ (6.5mm) needle. TAKE TIME TO CHECK GAUGE.

STITCH GLOSSARY
Diagonal Stripe Shift Pattern
For back
Row 1 (RS) With B, k2; with A, knit to end.
Row 2 With A, purl to last 3 sts; with B, p3.
Row 3 With B, k4; with A, knit to end.
Row 4 With A, purl to last 5 sts; with B, p5.
Cont to work diagonal stripe shift pat for back by working 1 less st in A and 1 more st in B every row as established, for 8 rows more. Then, using same shift technique, change first set of sts to A and last set to B and work for 12 rows more—24 rows make up the diagonal stripe shift pat for back.
For front
Row 1 (RS) With A, k to last 2 sts; with B, k2.

Row 2 With B, p3; with A, purl to end.
Row 3 With A, knit to last 4 sts; with B, k4.
Row 4 With B, p5; with A, purl to end.
Cont to work diagonal stripe shift pat for front by working 1 less st in A and 1 more st in B every row as established, for 8 rows more. Then, using same shift technique, change first set of sts to B and last set to A and work for 12 rows more. 24 rows make up diagonal stripe shift pat for front.

NOTES

1) When changing colors on every row, twist yarn tog at the color point to avoid holes in work.
2) The selvage sts are not counted in the finished measurements.

BACK

With A, cast on 61 (65, 69, 73) sts. Work 12 rows in garter st. Then work in St st and diagonal stripe shift pat for back (24-row rep), AT SAME TIME, after 4 (4, 4, 8) rows of stripe pat as completed, shape the dolman as foll:
Inc row (RS) K1, inc 1 st in next st, k to last 3 sts, inc 1 st in next st, k2. Rep inc row every 8th row once, every 6th row once, every 4th row once—69 (73, 77, 81) sts. Then, rep inc row every 2nd row 14 times—97 (101, 105, 109) sts. This is end of dolman.

EXTENDED SLEEVES

Cast on 5 sts at beg of next 6 rows, 6 sts at beg of next 6 rows—163 (167, 171, 175) sts. Place a marker each end of the last row worked. Work even until sleeve cuffs measure 5 (5½, 6, 7)"/12.5 (14, 15, 18) cm from the markers, end with a WS row.

Neck and top of sleeve shaping
Bind off 11 (11, 12, 12) sts at beg of next 5 rows. **Next row (WS)** Bind off 11 (11, 12, 12) sts, purl until there are 39 (41, 40, 41) sts on RH needle, with a separate ball of yarn, bind off center 19 (19, 19, 21) sts, purl to end. Working on the right shoulder only, bind off 11 sts from shoulder edge (beg of RS rows) 3 (1, 2, 1) times, then 12 sts 0 (2, 1, 2) times, AT SAME TIME, for the neck edge, bind off 2 sts twice. Bind off rem 2 sts at end of shaping. Rejoin yarn to neck edge to work the left shoulder and reverse shaping by binding off 2 sts from the neck edge twice AT SAME TIME, bind off 11 sts from shoulder edge (beg of WS row) 3 (1, 2, 1) times, then 12 sts 0 (2, 1, 2) times. Bind off rem 2 sts at end of shaping.

FRONT
With A, cast on 61 (65, 69, 73) sts. Work 12 rows in garter st. Then work in St st and work diagonal shift pat for front (24-row rep), AT SAME TIME, shape dolman as for back—97 (101, 105, 109) sts.

EXTENDED SLEEVES
Work as for back on 163 (167, 171, 175) sts until sleeve cuffs measure approx 5 (5½, 6, 7)"/12.5 (14, 15, 18) cm from the markers, end with RS row. **Note** This is 1 row before the back top of sleeve shaping.
Neck and top of sleeve shaping
Next row (WS) P72 (74, 76, 77), join a 2nd ball of yarn and bind off center 19 (19, 19, 21) sts, p to end. Cont to shape top of sleeve by binding off 11 sts from each shoulder edge 6 (4, 2, 1) times, then 12 sts 0 (2, 4, 5) times, AT SAME TIME, bind off 2 sts from each side of neck edge 3 times.

FINISHING
Block pieces to measurements. Sew right sleeve and shoulder seam.
Neckband
With A, pick up and k 73 (73, 73, 77)

sts evenly spaced around neck edge. K 7 rows. Bind off. Sew other sleeve and shoulder seam.
Sleeve cuffs
With RS facing and A, pick up and K 35 (39, 42, 49) sts evenly along one sleeve cuff edge. K 7 rows. Bind off. Sew side and underarm sleeve seams.

9 (9, 9, 9½)" 19 (19½, 20, 20¼)"
2"
FRONT & BACK
20 (20½, 21, 22½)"
13 (13, 13 13½)"
5 (5½, 6, 7)"
17 (18, 19, 20¼)"
27 (28, 29½, 30½)"

Holiday 2009 · No. 4

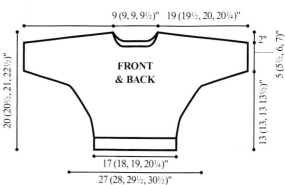

$\mathscr{P}$eplum Cardigan

EXPERIENCED

Loose-fitting peplum cardigan in multiple lace patterns and knit from the neck down. Designed by Nanette Lepore. Sized for Small/Medium, Large/X-Large. Directions are for smallest size with larger sizes in parentheses. If there is only one figure, it applies to all sizes.

KNITTED MEASUREMENTS
• Bust (closed) 35 (41)"/89 (104) cm
• Length (back of neck to bottom of peplum) 27 (28)"/68.5 (71) cm

MATERIALS
• 17 (19) 1¾oz/50g hanks (each approx 87yd/80m) of Tahki Yarns/Tahki•Stacy Charles, Inc., *Rio* (alpaca/fine merino wool/silk) in #3 tan (A)
• 6 (7) .88oz/25g balls (each approx 268yd/245m) of Filatura di Crosa/Tahki•Stacy Charles, Inc., *Baby Kid Extra* (mohair/nylon) in #495 rose (B)
• To substitute, seek a bulky-weight yarn and a fingering-weight yarn with fiber content similar to the original yarns
• One each sizes 8 and 9 (5 and 5.5mm) circular needle, 24"/60 cm long, OR SIZE TO OBTAIN GAUGE

- One size 6 (4mm) needle for sleeve bind off only
- Stitch holders and stitch markers

GAUGES

- 20 sts and 20 rows = 4"/10 cm over k1, p1 rib (unstretched) using smaller circular needle and 1 strand each A & B held tog.
- 14 sts and 18 rows =4"/10 cm over Fisherman's rib, using smaller circular needle and 1 strand each A & B held tog.
- 16 sts and 20 rows = 4"/10 cm over St st using larger circular needle and 1 strand each A & B held tog. TAKE TIME TO CHECK GAUGES

STITCH GLOSSARY

S2KP Sl 2 sts together knitwise, k1, psso.

VI (visible increase) Insert the LH needle from front to back into the strand between last st worked and the next st on the LH needle. Knit into the front loop for an open increase.

Inc 1 Increase 1 st by knitting into the front and back of the next st.

K1B Knit 1 st in the row below the st on needle.

Fisherman's Rib

(over an even number of sts)
Set-up row (WS) Purl.
Row 1 *K1B, p1; rep from * to end. Rep row 1 for Fisherman's rib.

NOTES

1) Work with 1 strand each A and B held tog throughout.
2) Circular needles are used to accommodate large number of sts. Work back and forth as with straight needles.

BODY

Using 1 strand each A & B held tog and smaller circular needle, cast on 93 sts for neck edge.
Set-up row (WS) *P1, k1; rep from *, end p1.
Note Work all inc'd sts into k1, p1 rib.
Row 1 (RS) Inc 1 st in first st, rib 5 sts, yo, place marker (pm), k1, pm, yo, rib 39 sts, yo, pm, k1, pm, yo, rib 39 sts, yo, pm, k1, pm, yo, rib 5 sts, inc 1 st in last st—101 sts. Cont to inc 1 st each side every row 5 (7) times more (for front neck shaping), AT SAME TIME, work a yo each side of the marked "k1" sts every RS row 12 (14) times more—183 (199) sts. Work 1 row even in rib on WS, dropping markers. Change to larger circular needle. K 4 rows. **Eyelet row** K1, *yo, k2tog; rep from * to end. P 1 row. K 4 rows, dec 4 (inc 4) sts evenly across last row—179 (203) sts.

Beg chart 1

Work rows 1-14 of chart 1. When chart is complete 62 (70) sts have been inc'd—241 (273) sts.

Divide for body

Next row (RS) K2tog, k36 (42) (for left front), place next 50 (54) sts on holder (for left sleeve), k2tog, k29 (35), k2tog, k29 (35), k2tog, place next 50 (54) sts on holder (for right sleeve), k36 (42), S2KP—135 (159) sts for body. K 3 rows. **Next row (RS)** Rep eyelet row. P 1 row. Knit 4 rows. **Next row (RS)** Rep eyelet row. P 1 row.

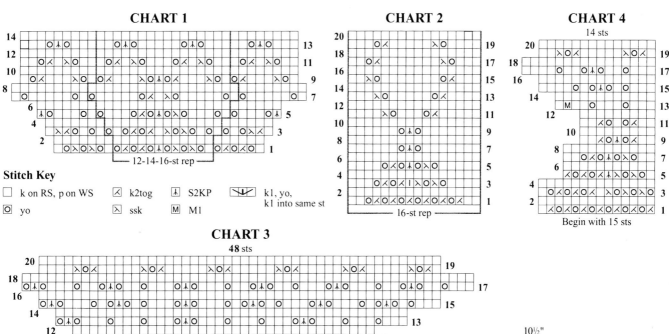

CHART 1

Stitch Key:
- □ k on RS, p on WS
- ☒ k2tog
- S2KP
- ⊠ ssk
- Ⓞ yo
- M M1
- k1, yo, k1 into same st

— 12-14-16-st rep —

CHART 2 — 16-st rep —

CHART 4 — 14 sts — Begin with 15 sts

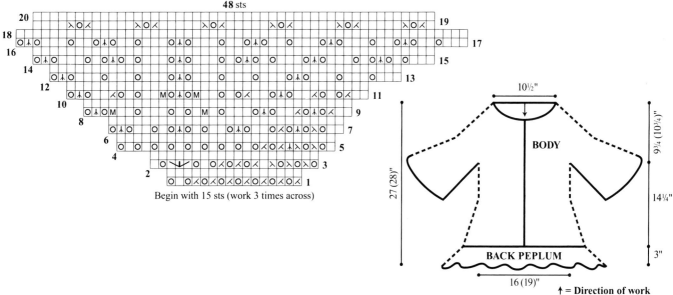

CHART 3 — 48 sts
Begin with 15 sts (work 3 times across)

10½"
BODY
9¾ (10¾)"
14¼"
27 (28)"
BACK PEPLUM
16 (19)"
3"
↑ = Direction of work

Rep last 2 rows 3 times more. K 4 rows. **Next row (RS)** Rep eyelet row. P 1 row. K 2 rows. **Next row (RS)** Rep eyelet row. P 1 row. K 4 rows.

Beg charts
Next row K4 (2), work row 1 of chart 2, working 16-st rep 2 (3) times, k2, work row 1 of chart 3 three times, work row 1 of chart 4, work row 1 of chart 2, working 16-st rep 2 (3) times, k5 (1). Cont to work chart pats as established through row 20, dec 0 (2) sts on last row—233 (257) sts. **Next row (RS)** *K1, yo, ssk, k3, k2tog, yo; rep from * to last st, k1. Purl one row. **Next row** *K2, yo, ssk, k1, k2tog, yo, k1; rep from * to last st, k1. Purl one row. **Next row** *K3, yo, S2KP, yo, k2; rep from * to last st, k1. Purl one row.

Beg bottom rib
Change to smaller circular needle.
Next row (RS) Work in Fisherman's Rib pat over next 86 (92) sts, [k1,VI] 60 (72) times, work in Fisherman's rib to end of row—293 (329) sts. Work in Fisherman's rib over all sts for 3½"/9 cm. Then, maintaining pat, dec one st each side of next 4 rows. Bind off all sts loosely.

SLEEVES
Place sleeve sts on smaller circular needle. Rejoin yarn to work on RS. K 4 rows. **Eyelet row 2** K1, *yo, k2tog; rep from * to last st, k1. Purl 1 row. K 4 rows, inc 29 (33) sts evenly across last row—79 (87) sts.

Beg Fisherman's Rib
Next row (RS) K1, [k1B, p1] to last 2 sts, end k1B, k1. Keeping first and last st as St st, work 3 more rows of Fisherman's Rib.

Beg sleeve pattern
Row 1 (RS) K1, p2tog, *[K1B, p1] 8 (9) times, K1B, pm,VI, p1,VI, pm, [K1B, p1] 8 (9) times, K1B *, S2KP (slip 2 sts tog, k1, pass 2 sl sts over k1), pm on the st formed by S2KP; rep from * to * once more, end p2tog, k1. **Next row and all WS rows** Keeping first and last st as St st, cont in Fisherman's Rib, working inc'd sts into pat. **Row 3** K1, p2tog, *rib to marker, slip marker,VI, K1B, p1, K1B,VI, sm*, rib to 1 st before S2KP marker, S2KP; rep from * to * once more, rib to last 3 sts, p2tog, k1. Cont to in this way to work incs and decs until length directed in magazine, moving up S2KP marker when necessary, until sleeve measures 6½"/16.5 cm from eyelet

row, end with WS row. K 4 rows. Work eyelet row. P 4 rows. With size 6 (4mm) straight needle, bind off all sts knitwise.

LAPEL BANDS
Right band
With size 8 needle, cast on 30 sts and purl one WS row. Work in Fisherman's Rib for 4 rows. **Next row (RS)** P2tog, rib to end. Cont in Fisherman's Rib, dec 1 st at beg of every 6th row 15 times more. Work even until piece measures 26 (27)"/66 (68.5) cm from beg. Bind off.

Left band
Work to correspond to right band by working decs at end of rows.

FINISHING
Sew lapel bands to front edges, beg at center back neck with narrow end and sewing wide end to top of the final lace pat, allowing it to fold over. Sew bands tog at back of neck. Sew sleeve seams.

Fall 2009 · No. 33

Striped Cardigan

EXPERIENCED

Very oversized cardigan knit sideways for vertical stripes on the bodice. One size.

KNITTED MEASUREMENTS
• Bust (buttoned) 67"/170 cm
• Length 24½"/62 cm
• Upper arm 20"/50.5 cm

MATERIALS (4)
• 14 1¾oz/50g balls (each approx 85yd/78m) of Mission Falls *1824 Wool* (superwash wool) in #3 oyster (MC),

8 balls in #4 charcoal (CC)
• To substitute, seek an aran-weight yarn with similar fiber content
• One pair size 8 (5mm) needles OR SIZE TO OBTAIN GAUGE
• Five ¾"/20mm buttons
• Stitch holders and stitch markers

GAUGE
18 sts and 24 rows = 4"/10 cm over St st using size 8 (5mm) needles. TAKE TIME TO CHECK GAUGE.

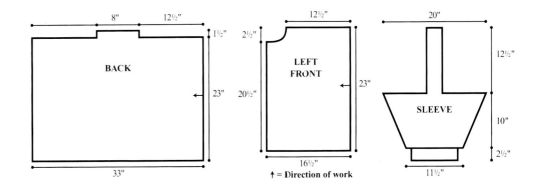

STITCH GLOSSARY
Ridge Pattern
(over 4 sts)
Rows 1 and 3 (RS) P4.
Rows 2 and 5 K4.
Rows 4 and 6 P4.
Rep rows 1–6 for ridge pat.

NOTES
1) Back and fronts are worked sideways.
2) When changing colors, twist yarns on WS to prevent holes in work.

BACK
With MC, cast on 104 sts for side edge. Work in St st for 2 rows. Beg stripe and ridge pat. **Row 1 (RS)** With CC, work 46 sts, with MC, work to last 4 sts, work 4 sts in ridge pat. **Note** Keep 4 sts in ridge pat with MC and work rem sts in St st and stripe pat to end of piece. **Rows 2 and 3** Work matching colors. **Rows 4-6** Work all sts with MC. **Row 7 (RS)** With CC, work 42 sts, with MC, work to end. **Rows 8 and 9** Work matching colors. **Rows 10-12** Work all sts with MC. **Rows 13-15** Rep rows 1-3. **Rows 16-18** Work all sts with MC. **Row 19** With CC, work 50 sts, with MC, work to end. **Rows 20 and 21** Work matching colors. **Rows 22-24** Work all sts with MC. **Row 25** With CC, work 54 sts, with MC, work to end. **Rows 26 and 27** Work matching colors. **Rows 28-30** Work all sts with MC. **Rows 31-33** Rep rows 19-21. **Rows 34-36** Work all sts with MC. Rep rows 1-36 for stripe and ridge pat, until 74 rows have been worked in stripe and ridge pat. **Row 75 (RS)** With CC, cast on 6 sts, work to end—110 sts. Cont in pat, working 6 cast-on sts in stripe pat, for 23 rows more. Mark last row for center of back. Work 22 rows more. **Next row (RS)** Bind off 6 sts, work to end. Cont in pat over 104 sts for 75 rows. With MC, work 2 rows in St st over all sts. Bind off.

LEFT FRONT
With MC, cast on 104 sts for side edge. Work in St st for 2 rows. Work in stripe and ridge pat same as back for 74 rows.

Neck shaping
Next row (RS) Bind off 3 sts, work to end. Cont to dec 1 st at neck edge every row 6 times, then every other row 3 times—92 sts. Work even until 98 rows have been worked in stripe and ridge pat, ending with a stripe row 26. Bind off all sts, matching colors.

RIGHT FRONT
With MC, cast on 50 sts, with CC, cast on 42 sts—92 sts for front edge. Beg with row 25 of stripe pat, work in stripe and ridge pat as on left front for 10 rows.

Neck shaping
Next row (RS) Inc 1 st, work to end. Cont to inc 1 st at neck edge every other row twice more, then every row 6 times, then cast on 3 sts at beg of next RS row—104 sts. Cont in pats until same number of rows as left front, ending with stripe pat row 16. Bind off all sts with MC.

SLEEVES
With MC, cast on 51 sts.
Beg corrugated rib
Row 1 (RS) *K3 MC, p3 CC; rep from *, end k3 MC. Cont in k3, p3 corrugated rib, matching colors, until piece measures 2½"/6.5 cm, cut MC and work all sts with CC in St st, inc 1 st each side every other row 13 times, every 4th row 7 times—91 sts. Work even until piece measures 12½"/31.5 cm from beg.
Cap shaping
Bind off 39 sts at beg of next 2 rows. Work even on rem 13 sts for 12½"/31.5 cm for saddle shoulder. Bind off.

FINISHING
Block pieces to measurements. Sew sides of saddle shoulder at top of sleeve to shoulders on fronts and back, sewing 6 sts at top to 6 cast-on and bound-off sts on back.
Neckband
With RS facing and CC, pick up and k 93 sts evenly around neck edge, including 7 sts at top of each sleeve saddle shoulder. **Next row (WS)** P3, *k3, p3; rep from * to end. Cont in k3, p3 rib for 1"/2.5 cm. Bind off in rib.
Left front button band
With RS facing and CC, pick up and k 111 sts evenly along left front edge, including side of neckband. Work in k3, p3 rib as on neckband for 1"/2.5 cm. Bind off in rib. Place markers on band for 5 buttons, the first and last ¾"/2 cm from each edge and 3 others spaced evenly between.
Right front buttonhole band
With RS facing and MC, pick up and k 111 sts evenly along right front edge, including side of neckband. Work in k3, p3 rib, working buttonholes opposite markers after ¼"/.5 cm by binding off 3 sts for each buttonhole, then casting on 3 sts over bound-off sts on the next row. When band measures 1"/2.5 cm, bind off in rib. Sew side and sleeve seams. Sew on buttons.

$\mathcal{L}$ace Capelet

EXPERIENCED

Shaped capelet with allover lace pattern and lace edging. One size.

KNITTED MEASUREMENTS
• Lower edge 50"/127 cm
• Upper edge 48"/122 cm
• Length (at center back with collar unfolded) 26"/66 cm
• Length (at center back with collar turned back) 22"/56 cm

MATERIALS ③
• 9 1¾oz/50g balls (each approx 110yd/100m) of Debbie Bliss/KFI, *Prima* (bamboo/merino) in #24 light gray
• Contrasting DK-weight yarn (scrap yarn)
• To substitute, seek a DK-weight yarn with similar fiber content
• Size 7 and 8 (4.5 and 5mm) circular needles, 29"/74 cm long OR SIZE TO OBTAIN GAUGE
• One pair size 8 (5mm) needles
• Size H/8 (5mm) crochet hook

GAUGE
18 sts and 19 rows = 4"/10 cm over chart pat 1 using larger circular needle. TAKE TIME TO CHECK GAUGE.

STITCH GLOSSARY
Lace Pattern
(over a multiple of 12 sts plus 1)

Rows 1, 3 and 5 (RS) P1, ★ssk, k3, yo, p1, yo, k3, k2tog, p1; rep from ★ to end.

Rows 2, 4, 6 and 8 (WS) K1, ★p5, k1; rep from ★ to end.

Row 7 P1, ★yo, k3, k2tog, p1, ssk, k3, yo, p1; rep from ★ to end.

Row 9 P2, ★yo, k2, k2tog, p1, ssk, k2, yo, p3; rep from ★, end last rep p2.

Row 10 K2, ★p4, k1, p4, k3; rep from ★, end last rep k2.

Row 11 P3, ★yo, k1, k2tog, p1, ssk, k1, yo, p5; rep from ★, end last rep p3.

Row 12 K3, ★p3, k1, p3, k5; rep from ★, end last rep k3.

Row 13 P4, ★yo, k2tog, p1, ssk, yo, p7; rep from ★, end last rep p4.

Row 14 K4, ★p2, k1, p2, k7; rep from ★, end last rep k4.

Rows 15, 17 and 19 Rep row 7.

Rows 16, 18, 20 and 22 Rep row 2.

Row 21 Rep row 1.

Row 23 P1, ★ssk, k2, yo, p3, yo, k2, k2tog, p1; rep from ★ to end.

Row 24 K1, ★p4, k3, p4, k1; rep from ★ to end.

Row 25 P1, ★ssk, k1, yo, p5, yo, k1, k2tog, p1; rep from ★ to end.

Row 26 K1, ★p3, k5, p3, k1; rep from ★ to end.

Row 27 P1, ★ssk, yo, p7, yo, k2tog, p1; rep from ★ to end.

Row 28 K1, ★p2, k7, p2, k1; rep from ★ to end.

Rep rows 1–28 for lace pat.

LACE PATTERN

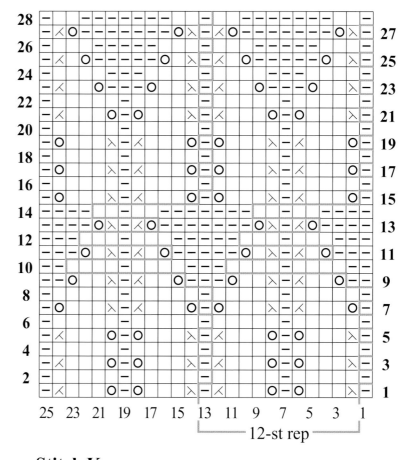

12-st rep

Stitch Key

☐ k on RS, p on WS

⊟ p on RS, k on WS

🞅 yarn over

⧄ k2tog on RS and WS

Border Pattern

Row 1 Yo, k2tog, k1, yo, k10, yo, k2tog, k1.

Row 2 K2, yo, k2tog, k12, p1.

Row 3 Yo, k2tog, k1, yo, k2tog, yo, k9, yo, k2tog, k1.

Row 4 K2, yo, k2tog, k13, p1.

Row 5 Yo, k2tog, k1, [yo, k2tog] twice, yo, k8, yo, k2tog, k1.

Row 6 K2, yo, k2tog, k14, p1.

Row 7 Yo, k2tog, k1, [yo, k2tog] 3 times, yo, k7, yo, k2tog, k1.

Row 8 K2, yo, k2tog, k15, p1.

Row 9 Yo, k2tog, k1, [yo k2tog] 4 times, yo, k6, yo, k2tog, k1.

Row 10 K2, yo, k2tog, k16, p1.

Row 11 Yo, k2tog, k1, [yo, k2tog] 5 times, yo, k5, yo, k2tog, k1.

Row 12 K2, yo, k2tog, k17, p1.

Row 13 Yo, k2tog, k1, [yo, k2tog] 6 times, yo, k4, yo, k2tog, k1.

Row 14 K2, yo, k2tog, k18, p1.

Row 15 Yo, k2tog, k1, [yo k2tog] 7 times, yo, k3, yo, k2tog, k1.

Row 16 K2, yo, k2tog, k19, p1.

Row 17 Yo, [k2tog] twice, [yo, k2tog] 7 times, k3, yo, k2tog, k1.

Rows 18, 20, 22, 24, 26, 28 and 30 Rep rows 14, 12, 10, 8, 6, 4 and 2.

Row 19 Yo, [k2tog] twice, [yo, k2tog] 6 times, k4, yo, k2tog, k1.

Row 21 Yo, [k2tog] twice, [yo, k2tog] 5 times, k5, yo, k2tog, k1.

Row 23 Yo, [k2tog] twice, [yo, k2tog] 4 times, k6, yo, k2tog, k1.

Row 25 Yo, [k2tog] twice, [yo, k2tog] 3 times, k7, yo, k2tog, k1.

Row 27 Yo, [k2tog] twice, [yo, k2tog] twice, k8, yo, k2tog, k1.

Row 29 Yo, [k2tog] twice, yo, k2tog, k9, yo, k2tog, k1.

Row 31 Yo, [k2tog] twice, k10, yo, k2tog, k1.

Row 32 K2, yo, k2tog, k11, p1.

Rep rows 1–32 for border pat.

NOTES

1) Body of caplet is worked in one piece from the bottom up.

2) Lace border is worked separately, then joined to outer edge of body using three-needle bind-off.

3) The lace pattern and lace border are given in chart and written form. If working from the charts, work RS rows from right to left and WS rows from left to right.

BODY

With crochet hook and waste yarn, ch 187 for chain-st provisional cast-on. Cut yarn and draw end though lp on hook. Turn ch so bottom lps are at top and cut end is at left. With larger circular needle beg 2 lps from right end, pick up and k 1 st in each of next 181 lps. If working from written instructions, work in lace pat for 56 rows.

If working from chart, work lace pat chart as foll:

Beg lace pattern chart

Row 1 (RS) Beg at st 1, work 12-st rep (sts 2-13) 14 times, then work sts 14-25.

Row 2 (WS) Beg at st 25 and work to st 14, work 12-st rep (sts 13-2) 14 times, then work st 1. Cont to foll chart in this way, carefully foll the shift of the 12-st rep lines, to row 28, then rep rows 1-28 once more. Change to smaller circular needle, then rep rows 1-28 once more. Cut yarn leaving a 12"/30.5 cm tail; leave sts on needle. Set aside.

Lace border

With straight needles, cast on 16 sts. Knit next row. Work in border pat following either the written instructions or lace border chart, until 32 rows of pat have been worked 28 times. Bind off.

FINISHING

Joining lace border

With RS facing, release cut end from lp of waste yarn ch. Pulling out 1 ch at a time, place live sts from bottom edge of body onto larger circular needle. Join yarn at LH end of needle. Pick up and k 43 sts evenly spaced along right side edge of body, k 181 sts from smaller circular needle, pick up and k 43 sts evenly spaced along left side

BORDER PATTERN

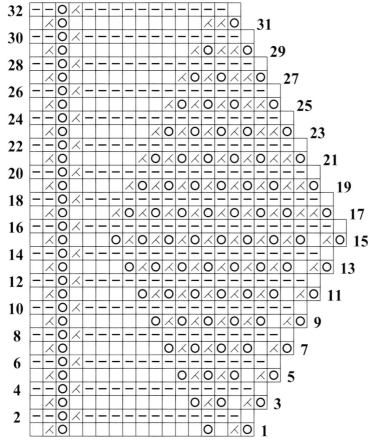

16 sts

Stitch Key

☐ k on RS, p on WS

⊟ p on RS, k on WS

◙ yarn over

⊠ k2tog on RS and WS

edge of body, then k 181 sts on larger circular needle—448 sts. With RS facing and smaller circular needle, pick up and k 448 sts along straight edge of lace border (1 st in side edge of every 2 garter st rows). With RS tog, join lace border to body using three-needle bind-off. Sew cast-on and bound-off ends of lace border. Lightly block piece to measurements.

Cabled Cardigan

EXPERIENCED

Standard fitting long coat in cable patterns. Designed by Lutz and Patmos. Sized for X-Small/Small, Medium, Large/X-Large, and XX-Large.

KNITTED MEASUREMENTS
• Bust (closed) 38 (43, 48, 53)"/96.5 (109, 122, 134.5) cm
• Length 27 (27½, 29½, 31)"/68.5 (70, 75, 78.5) cm
• Upper arm 15 (16, 17, 18)"/38 (40.5, 43, 45.5) cm

MATERIALS 6
• 10 (12, 13, 15) 3½oz/100g hanks (each approx 130yd/120m) of Tahki Yarns/Tahki•Stacy Charles, Inc. *Montana* (wool) in #003 light gray
• To substitute, seek a super bulky–weight yarn with similar fiber content
• One pair size 13 (9mm) needles OR SIZE TO OBTAIN GAUGE
• Cable needle (cn)
• Stitch holders and stitch markers

GAUGE
13 sts and 15 rows = 4"/10 cm over 4-st chart rep (slightly stretched) using size 13 (9mm) needles. TAKE TIME TO CHECK GAUGE.

STITCH GLOSSARY
3-st RPC Sl 2 sts to cn and hold to back, k1, then p1, k1 from cn.
10-st RC (LC) Sl 5 sts to cn and hold to back (front), k5, k5 from cn.

BACK
Cast on 73 (81, 89, 97) sts. **Row 1 (WS)** K1, *p1, k1; rep from * to end. **Row 2 (RS)** P1, *k1, p1; rep from * to end. Rep rows 1 and 2 once more. **Set-up row (WS)** K1, [p1, k1] 8 (10, 12, 14) times, pm, p4, M1 p-st, p5, k1, p10, M1 p-st, p9, k1, p5, M1 p-st, p4, pm, k1, [p1, k1] 8 (10, 12, 14) times—76 (84, 92, 100) sts.
Beg chart pat
Row 1 (RS) Beg with st 1, work first 4-st rep (sts 2-5) 4 (5, 6, 7) times, sl marker, work 42 sts (sts 6-47) once, sl marker, work 2nd 4-st rep (sts 48-51) 4 (5, 6, 7) times, work st 52. Cont to foll chart in this way through row 8, then rep rows 1-8 until piece measures

18 (18, 19, 20)"/45.5 (45.5, 48, 51) cm from beg, end with a WS row.
Armhole shaping
Bind off 5 (6, 6, 7) sts at beg of next 2 rows. Dec 1 st each side on next row, then every other row 6 (7, 8, 9) times more—52 (56, 62, 66) sts. Work even until armhole measures 8 (8½, 9½, 10)"/20.5 (21.5, 24, 25.5) cm, end with a WS row.
Shoulder shaping
Bind off 6 (7, 9, 10) sts at beg of next 2 rows, then 6 (7, 8, 9) sts at beg of next 2 rows. Place rem 28 sts on holder for back neck.

LEFT FRONT
Cast on 48 (52, 56, 60) sts. **Row 1 (WS)** P3, pm, k1, *p1, k1; rep from * to end. **Row 2 (RS)** P1, *k1, p1; rep from * to marker, sl marker, sl 1 knitwise wyib, k2. Slipping marker each row, rep rows 1 and 2 once more, then row 1 once.
Beg chart pat
Row 1 (RS) Beg with st 1, work first 4-st rep (sts 2-5) 11 (12, 13, 14) times, sl marker, sl 1 knitwise wyib, k2. Keeping 3 sts at front edge as established, cont to foll chart in this way to row 4, then rep rows 1-4 for cable rib pat, AT SAME TIME, when piece measures 4½"/11.5 cm from beg, end with row 2 of cable rib pat.
Pocket placement
Next row (RS) Work row 3 of cable rib pat over first 8 (8, 12, 12) sts, place next 25 sts on holder for pocket, cast on 25 sts, work to end. Keeping 3 sts at front edge as established, beg with row 4, cont in cable rib pat, until piece measures same length as back to

underarm, end with a WS row (same cable rib pat row).

Armhole shaping
Bind off 5 (6, 6, 7) sts at beg of next row. Work next row even. Dec 1 st from armhole edge on next row, then every other row 6 (7, 8, 9) times more. Work even on 36 (38, 41, 43) sts until piece measures same length as back to shoulder, end with a WS row (same cable rib pat row).

Shoulder shaping
Bind off from armhole edge 6 (7, 9, 10) sts once, then 6 (7, 8, 9) sts once. Place rem 24 sts on holder for left front neck.

RIGHT FRONT
Cast on 48 (52, 56, 60) sts. **Row 1 (WS)** K1, ★p1, k1; rep from ★ to last 3 sts, pm, p3. **Row 2 (RS)** K2, sl 1 knitwise wyib, sl marker, p1, ★k1, p1; rep from ★ to end. Slipping marker each row, rep rows 1 and 2 once more, then row 1 once.

Beg chart pat
Row 1 (RS) K2, sl 1 knitwise wyib, sl marker, work st 1, work first 4-st rep (sts 2-5) 11 (12, 13, 14) times. Keeping 3 sts at front edge as established, cont to foll chart in this way to row 4, then rep rows 1-4 for cable rib pat. AT SAME TIME, when piece measures 4½"/11.5 cm from beg, end with row 2 of cable rib pat.

Pocket placement
Next row (RS) K2, sl 1 knitwise wyib, sl marker, work row 3 of cable rib pat over next 12 (16, 16, 20) sts, place next 25 sts on holder for pocket, cast on 25 sts, work to end. Keeping

3 sts at front edge as established, beg with row 4, cont in cable rib pat, until piece measures same length as back to underarm, end with a WS row (same cable rib pat row), then work 1 row more, end with a RS row. Shape armhole as for left front. Work even on 36 (38, 41, 43) until piece measures same length as back to shoulder, end with a WS row (same cable rib pat row), then work 1 row more, end with a RS row. Shape shoulder as for left front. Place rem 24 sts on holder for right front neck.

SLEEVES
Cast on 49 (49, 53, 57) sts. **Row 1 (WS)** K1, ★p1, k1; rep from ★ to end. **Row 2** P1, ★k1, p1; rep from ★ to end. Rep rows 1 and 2 once more, then row 1 once.

Beg chart pat
Row 1 (RS) Beg with st 1, work first 4-st rep (sts 2-5) 12 (12, 13, 14) times. Cont to foll chart in this way to row 4, then rep rows 1-4 for cable rib pat. AT SAME TIME, inc 1 p-st each side every 0 (3, 5, 5)"/0 (7.5, 12.5, 12.5) cm 0 (2, 1, 1) times—49 (53, 55, 59) sts. Work even until piece measures approx 10 (10, 11, 12)"/25.5 (25.5, 28, 30.5) cm from beg, end with a WS row (same cable rib pat row as back to underarm).

Cap shaping
Bind off 5 (6, 6, 7) sts at beg of next 2 rows. Dec 1 st each side on next row, then every other row 6 (7, 8, 9) times more. Bind off 4 sts at beg of next 4 rows. Bind off rem 9 sts.

FINISHING
Lightly block pieces to measurements. Sew shoulder seams.

Collar
With RS facing, place 24 sts from left front holder on LH needle, then place 28 sts from back neck holder on LH needle, then 24 sts from right front holder on LH needle—76 sts.

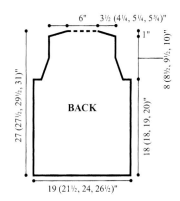

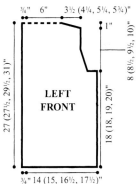

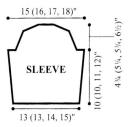

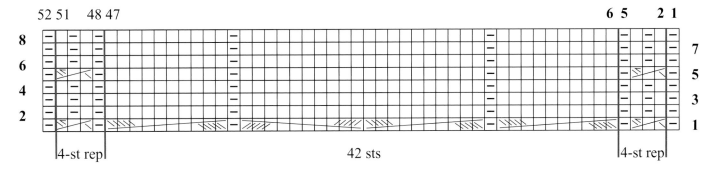

Stitch Key
☐ k on RS, p on WS
☐ p on RS, k on WS
▱ 3-st RPC
▱ 10-st RPC
▱ 10-st LPC

Next row (RS) K2, sl 1 knitwise wyib, p1, work in cable rib over next 20 sts, [k1, p1] twice, pm, k20, pm, p1, [k1, p1] twice, work in cable rib pat over next 20 sts, sl 1 knitwise wyib, k2. Keeping 3 sts each side in pat as established and center 20 sts between markers in St st, work rem sts in cable rib pat. Work even for 3"/7.5 cm, end with a WS row. Bind off in pat sts.

Pockets

With RS facing, place 25 sts from pocket holder back to LH needle ready for a RS row. Beg with row 3, cont in cable rib pat to row 4, then rep rows 1-4 four times more, then rows 1-3 once. Bind off in rib. Sew side edges of pockets in place. On WS, sew cast-on sts from pocket placement in place. Fold each front edge to WS along sl st and sew in place. Set in sleeves. Sew side and sleeve seams.

Early Fall 2010 · No. 1

Cabled Swing Poncho

INTERMEDIATE

Oversized square poncho with hood in cable and texture patterns. Sized for Small/Large and X-Large/XXX-Large. Directions are for smallest size with larger size in parentheses. If there is only one figure, it applies to all sizes.

KNITTED MEASUREMENTS

• Lower edge 84 (92)"/213.5 (233.5) cm
• Length 25½ (28)"/64.5 (71) cm

MATERIALS 🔳5

•14 (17) 3½oz/100g skeins (each approx 121yd/111m) of Zealana *Aspire Tui* (wool/possum/cashmere) in #T03 red pepper
• To substitute, seek a bulky-weight yarn with similar fiber content
• Two size 9 (5.5mm) circular needles, 40"/100 cm long OR SIZE TO OBTAIN GAUGE
• One pair size 9 (5.5mm) needles
• Cable needle (cn)
• Stitch holders and stitch markers

GAUGE

15 sts and 20 rows = 4"/10 cm over broken rib using size 9 (5.5mm) circular needle. TAKE TIME TO CHECK GAUGE.

STITCH GLOSSARY

4-st RC Sl 2 sts to cn and hold to back, k2, k2 from cn.
4-st LC Sl 2 sts to cn and hold to front, k2, k2 from cn.

Broken Rib

(over an even number of sts)
Row 1 (RS) Knit.
Row 2 (WS) Purl.
Row 3 *K1, p1; rep from * to end.
Row 4 *P 1, k 1; rep from * to end.
Rep rows 1-4 for broken rib.

Cartridge Rib

(multiple of 5 sts plus 3)
Row 1 (RS) K1, *p1, k4; rep from *, end p1, k1.
Row 2 (WS) *K3, p2; rep from *, end k3.
Rep rows 1 and 2 for cartridge rib.

Seed Stitch

(over an even number of sts)
Row 1 (WS) *K1, p1; rep from * to end.
Row 2 (RS) K the purl sts and p the knit sts.
Rep row 2 for seed st.

BACK

With circular needle, cast on 158 (172) sts. Do not join. **Row 1 (RS)** K1 (selvage st), pm, work broken rib over next 4 (6) sts, pm, work cartridge rib to last 5 (7) sts, pm, work broken rib over next 4 (6) sts, pm, k1 (selvage st). **Row 2 (WS)** K1, sl marker, work broken rib over next 4 (6) sts, sl marker, work cartridge rib to next marker, sl marker, work broken rib over next 4 (6) sts, sl marker, k1. Keeping 1 selvage st each side in garter st, cont to work rem sts as established for 12 (16) rows more. **Next row (RS)** K1, sl marker, work broken rib over next 4 (6) sts, sl marker, purl to next marker, sl marker, work broken rib over next 4 (6) sts, sl marker, k1. **Next row** K1, sl marker, work broken rib over next 4 (6) sts, sl marker, knit to next marker, sl marker, work broken rib over next 4 (6) sts, sl marker, k1.

Beg chart pat

Working row 1 of chart and each pat st, work as foll: **Row 1 (RS)** K1, sl marker, work broken rib over next 4 (6) sts, sl marker, work cartridge rib over next 28 (33) sts, pm, work chart over next 32 sts, pm, work cartridge rib over next 28 sts, work chart over next 32 sts, pm, work cartridge rib over next 28 (33) sts, sl marker, work broken rib over next 4 (6) sts, sl marker, k1. Cont to work pats as established until piece measures approx 18 (20½)"/45.5 (52) cm from beg, end with a broken rib row 2. Mark beg and end of last row for beg of yoke.

YOKE

Next row (RS) K1, sl marker, work row 3 of broken rib to last st, dropping all markers except last marker, sl last marker, k1. Cont to keep 1 selvage st each side in garter st, cont to work rem sts in broken rib until piece measures 4"/10 cm above marked row, end with a row 4.

Shoulder shaping

Slipping first st (for sloped bind-off), bind off 8 (9) sts at beg of next 14 rows, then 8 sts at beg of next 2 rows. Bind off rem 30 sts.

FRONT

Work as for back until 3 (4) cable chart reps have been completed, end with a WS row.

Left pocket

Next row (RS) With 2nd circular needle, work across first 33 (40) sts, pm, cast on 30 sts (pocket lining)—63 (70) sts. Leave rem sts on first needle.
Next row Work in seed st over first 30 sts, sl marker, work to end. Keeping 30 sts in seed st, work even for 28 rows more, end with a RS row. **Next row (WS)** Bind off first 30 sts in seed st, drop marker, work to end. Do not cut yarn; leave rem 33 (40) sts on needle.

Center section

Change to straight needles. **Next row (RS)** Join yarn and work across center 92 sts. Work even for 29 rows more, end with a WS row. Cut yarn; place sts on 2nd needle along with left front sts.

Right pocket

Next row (RS) Cast on 30 sts (pocket lining) to first needle, pm, work to end—63 (70) sts. **Next row** Work to last marker, sl marker, work seed st over last 30 sts. Keeping 30 sts in seed st, work even for 27 rows more, end with a WS row. **Next row (RS)** Bind off first 30 sts in seed st, drop marker, work to end—33 (40) sts. Work 1 row more. Cut yarn; place sts on 2nd needle along with center section and left front sts. **Next (joining) row (RS)** Work across 33 (40) sts of left front, 92 sts of center section, then 33 (40) sts of right front—158 (172) sts. Cont to work as for back to yoke.

LEFT YOKE

Next row (RS) With 2nd circular needle, k1, sl marker, work row 3 of broken rib across next 75 (82) sts, dropping markers, pm, cast on 6 sts (left front placket)—82 (89) sts. Leave rem sts on first needle.
Next row (WS) Work seed st across first 6 sts, sl marker, work broken rib to last marker, sl marker, k1. Cont to keep 1 selvage st at side edge in garter st, 6 sts for left front placket in seed st and rem sts in broken rib until piece measures 4"/10 cm above marked row, end with a row 4.

Left shoulder shaping

Slipping first st (for sloped bind-off), bind off 8 (9) sts at beg of next 7 RS rows, then 8 sts at beg of next RS row. Cont to work across rem 18 sts as foll: work row 3 of broken rib across first 12 sts, sl marker, work in seed st across last 6 sts. **Next row (WS)** Work seed st across first 6 sts, sl marker, work row 4 of broken rib across last 12 sts. Place these 18 sts on holder for hood. Cut yarn.

RIGHT YOKE

Next row (RS) [P1 k1] 3 times (right front placket), pm, work row 3 of broken rib across next 75 (82) sts, dropping all but last marker, sl last marker, k1—82 (89) sts.
Next row (WS) K1, sl marker, work in broken rib to last marker, sl marker, work seed st across last 6 sts. Cont to keep 1 selvage st at side edge in garter st, 6 sts for right front placket in seed st and rem sts in broken rib until piece measures 4"/10 cm above marked row, end with a RS row 1.

Right shoulder shaping

Slipping first st (for sloped bind-off), bind off 8 (9) sts at beg of next 7 WS rows, 8 sts at beg of next WS row. Cont to work across rem 18 sts as foll: work row 4 of broken rib across first 12 sts, sl marker, work in seed st across last 6 sts. Place these 18 sts on holder for hood. Do not cut yarn.

FINISHING

Sew shoulder seams.

HOOD

With RS facing and circular needle, work in seed st over first 6 sts of right front holder, sl marker, knit next 12 sts, pick up and k 42 sts evenly spaced across back neck edge, knit next 12 sts from left front holder, sl marker, work in seed st over last 6 sts—78 sts. **Next row (WS)** Work seed st over first 6 sts, sl marker, p33, pm (center back), p33,

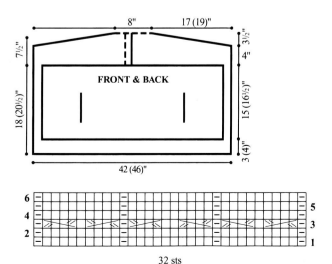

FRONT & BACK

8"   17 (19)"
7½"
3½"
4"
18 (20½)"
15 (16½)"
3 (4)"
42 (46)"

32 sts

Stitch Key

☐ k on RS, p on WS

⊟ p on RS, k on WS

4-st RC

4-st LC

sl marker, work seed st over last 6 sts. Beg with row 3, work center 66 sts in broken rib and cont to work 6 sts each side in seed st. Work even until hood measures 10"/25.5 cm from beg, end with a WS row. **Dec row (RS)** Work to 2 sts before 2nd marker, ssk, sl marker, k2tog, work to end—76 sts.

Work next 3 rows even. Rep last 4 rows 7 times more—62 sts. Divide sts in half, placing 31 sts each on a straight needle so tip of needle extends beyond seed st border. With RS tog, hold halves on two parallel needles. Cont to work 3-needle bind-off. Sew bottom edge of left front placket in place. Sew

pocket linings in place. Sew 9 (11)"/23 (28) cm side seams.

Lace Jacket

EXPERIENCED

Lace jacket knit in the round, with close fitting St st sleeves, lace edge and cuffs. Sized for X-Small, Small/Medium, Large, and X-Large. Directions are for smallest size with larger size in parentheses. If there is only one figure, it applies to all sizes.

KNITTED MEASUREMENTS
• Total diameter when flat 37 (37, 38½, 39)"/94 (94, 98, 99) cm
• Upper arm 12¼ (14½, 17, 18)"/31 (37, 43, 45.5) cm

MATERIALS ①
• 4 (5, 5, 5) .88oz/25g balls (each approx 269yd/245m) of Filatura di

Crosa/Tahki•Stacy Charles, Inc. *Baby Kid Extra* (mohair/polyamide) in #324 Navy
• Four size 5 (3.75mm) circular needles, one each 16"/40 cm, 24"/60 cm, 40"/100 cm, 60"/150 cm long OR SIZE TO OBTAIN GAUGE
• Six size 5 (3.75mm) double-pointed needles
• Two size 4 (3.5mm) dpns for picking up sleeves
• 5 stitch markers in different colors
• Scrap yarn in a similar weight and contrasting color with a smooth texture

GAUGE
20 sts and 32 rows = 4"/10cm over St st using size 5 (3.75mm) needle.
TAKE TIME TO CHECK GAUGE.

NOTES
1) Visit our website for charts 2 and 4.
2) Jacket is worked in the round from the center outward. The lace edge is added to body after chart 2 has been worked.

BODY
With larger dpns and main yarn, cast on 5 sts. Join, being careful not to twist sts, place marker (pm) for beg of rnd. Place 1 st on each of 5 dpn. **Rnd 1** Knit. **Rnd 2** *K1, yo; rep from * around—10 sts. **Rnds 3 and 4** Rep rnds 1 and 2—20 sts. **Rnd 5** Knit.
For Sizes XS, S/M Only
Rnd 6 [K1, yo, k3, yo, pm] 5

times—30 sts. **Rnds 7 and 8** Knit.
Rnd 9 [K1, yo, k to next marker, yo, slip marker (sm)] 5 times—40 sts total, 8 in each of the 5 sections. **Rnds 10 and 11** Knit. **Rnds 12-17** Rep rnds 9-11 twice—12 sts in each section.
For Sizes L, XL Only
Rnd 6 *K1, yo; rep from * around—40 sts. **Rnds 7 and 8** Knit.
Rnd 9 [K2, yo, k5, yo, k1, pm] 5 times around—50 sts, 10 sts in each of the 5 sections. **Rnds 10 and 11** Knit.
Rnd 12 [K2, yo, k to 1 st before next marker, yo, k1, sl marker (sm)] 5 times around—12 sts in each section. **Rnds 13-15** Rep rnds 10-12 once more—14 sts in each section.
Rnds 16 and 17 Knit.
For Size XL Only
Rnd 18 Rep rnd 12—16 sts in each section.
Rnds 19 and 20 Knit.
Beg chart 1
For Sizes X-Small and Small/Medium Only
Rnd 1 Work sts between blue lines five times around—14 (14) sts in each section.
For Size Large Only
Rnd 1 Work sts between green lines five times around—16 sts in each section.
For Size X-Large Only
Rnd 1 *Beg as indicated and work first set of sts between red lines, then work sts between red lines in center of chart, then work last set of sts between red lines, ending as indicated; rep from * a total of five times around—18 sts

in each section.

For All Sizes
Use circular needle when necessary and cont to work chart 1 as established until rnd 37 has been worked—38 (38, 40, 42) in each section.

Separate for armholes
For Size X-Small Only
Rnd 1 Knit. **Rnd 2** Knit to and slip next marker, ★ k4, then with scrap yarn k 30, sl these 30 sts back to LH needle and knit again with main yarn★, [knit to and slip next marker] twice, rep from ★ to ★ once more, knit to end of rnd. **Rnd 3** [K1, yo, k to next marker, yo, sm] 5 times around—40 sts in each section. **Rnds 4 and 5** Knit. **Rnds 6-11** Rep rnds 3–5 twice—44 sts in each section.

For Size Small/Medium
Rnds 1 and 2 Knit. **Rnd 3** [K1, yo, k to next marker, yo, sm] 5 times around—40 sts in each section.
Rnds 4 and 5 Knit. **Rnd 6** [K1, yo, k to next marker, yo, sm] 5 times around—42 sts in each section.
Rnd 7 Knit. **Rnd 8** Knit to and slip next marker, ★k3, then with scrap yarn k36, sl these 36 sts back to LH needle and knit again with main yarn★, [knit to and slip next marker] twice, rep from ★ to ★ once more, knit to end of rnd.
Rnd 9 Rep rnd 6 once—44 sts in each section. **Rnds 10 and 11** Knit.

For Size Large
Rnds 1 and 2 Knit. **Rnd 3** [K2, yo, k to 1 st before next marker, yo, k1, sm] 5 times around—42 sts in each section.
Rnds 4-9 Rep rnds 1–3 twice—46 sts in each section.
Rnd 10 Knit. **Rnd 11** Knit to and slip next marker, ★k2, then with scrap yarn k42, sl these 42 sts back to LH needle and knit again with main yarn★, [knit to and slip next marker] twice, rep from ★ to ★ once more.

For Size X-Large
Rnds 1 and 2 Knit. **Rnd 3** [K2, yo, k to 1 st before next marker, yo, k1, sm] 5 times around—44 sts in each section. **Rnds 4-9** Rep rnds 1–3 twice—48 sts in each section. **Rnd 10** Knit.
Rnd 11 Knit to and slip next marker, ★k2, then with scrap yarn k44, sl these 44 sts back to

LH needle and knit again with main yarn★, [knit to and slip next marker] twice, rep from ★ to ★ once more.

Beg chart 2 (see website)
Working same as for Chart 1, beg and end as indicated for each size on chart 2, work rnd 1 five times around—46 (46, 48, 50) sts in each section. Use longer circular needles when necessary and cont to work chart 2 until rnd 52 has been worked—80 (80, 82, 84) sts in each section. **Rnds 53 and 54** Knit—400 (400, 410, 420) sts rem on needle to be worked with lace edge.

LACE EDGE
NOTE Lace edge is joined to body at the end of every WS row by working k2tog tbl over last st of lace edge tog with next st of body, so for each body st worked, 2 rows of chart 3 are worked. To work lace edge around the 5 points of shawl body, multiple rows will be worked in corner sts as indicated for each size.

4-row corner
Work to end of WS row and join sts and drop the lace edge st but do not drop the body st from LH needle. Turn and work next RS and WS rows, joining sts and allowing body st to drop from needle. Turn and work next RS row—4 rows have been joined to 1 body st.

6-row corner
Work to end of WS row and join sts and drop the lace edge st but do not drop the body st from LH needle. Turn and work next RS row. Turn and work to end of next WS row and join sts and drop the lace edge st but do not drop body st from LH needle. Turn and work next RS and WS rows, joining sts and allowing body st to drop from needle. Turn and work next RS row—6 rows have been joined to 1 body st.

Beg chart 3
With RS of shawl body facing and scrap yarn, cast on 21 sts onto LH needle for lace edge. With main yarn, knit these sts onto RH needle of work. Turn work for WS row. Beg with chart row 1, reading from left to right, work as foll:

For Sizes XS and S/M Only
Joining row (WS) ★Work chart row to last lace edge st, join sts and drop the lace st but do not drop body st, then

Stitch Key
□	k on RS, p on WS	☑	k2tog on RS, k2tog tbl on WS
⊟	p on RS, k on WS		
⊙	yo	⅄	SK2P
�ℚ	k1 tbl	☒	k3tog
⊠	ssk on RS, k2tog on WS	☑	slip 1 wyib

CHART 1

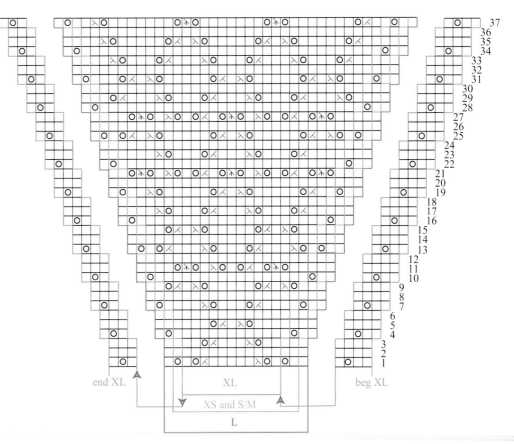

cont working a 6-row corner in first body st. Work a 4-row corner in next body st. Work 2 rows in each body st to 1 st before next marker, work a 4-row corner in that st, sm; rep from ★ to end of body sts, cont chart rows in sequence, working 30-row rep, ending with row 30.

For Size L Only
Joining row (WS) ★Work chart row to last lace edge st, join sts and drop the lace st but do not drop body st, then continue working a 6-row corner in first body st. Work a 6-row corner st in next body st. Work a 4-row corner st in next body st. Work 2 rows in each body st to 2 sts before next marker, work a 4-row corner in next st, work a 6-row corner in last st, sl m; rep from ★ to end of body sts cont chart rows in sequence, ending with row 30.

For Size XL Only
Joining row (WS) ★Work chart row to last lace edge st, join sts and do not drop body st, then cont working a 6-row corner in first body st. Work a 4-row corner in each of next 2

body sts. Work 2 rows in each body st to 2 sts before next marker, work a 4-row corner in each of next 2 sts, sm; rep from ★ to end of body sts continuing chart rows in sequence, ending with row 30.

For All Sizes
Carefully remove scrap yarn and place sts on spare needle, graft ends of lace edge tog.

SLEEVES
Work right sleeve first, carefully remove scrap yarn from sleeve opening and work as foll:
Beg at A on schematic drawing and place 30 (36, 42, 44) sts from inner side of opening on smaller dpn, place 31 (37, 43, 45) sts from outer side of opening on second smaller dpn. Place marker on this rnd for length. With shortest circular needle, join main yarn, pick up and k 1 st at bottom of sleeve opening, then k sts from LH needle, pick up and k 1 st at top of sleeve opening, then k sts from RH needle, pick up and k 1 more st at bottom of sleeve opening—64 (76, 88, 92) sts. Pm for beg of rnd, join and work sleeve sts in St st for 16 rnds. Cont in St st and dec 1 st at beg and end of rnd on next rnd, then every 8th (6th, 6th, 6th) rnd 2 (7, 13, 9) times more, then every 6th (4th, 4th, 4th) rnd 12 (13, 4, 10) times, then dec 0 (0, 1, 1) st on next rnd—34 (34, 51, 51) sts. Work even until sleeve measures 14 (14½, 15, 15)"/35.5 (37, 38, 38) cm. Work left sleeve in same manner.

LACE CUFF
Beg chart 4 (see website)
With RS of sleeve facing and scrap yarn, cast on 23 sts to LH needle for lace cuff.
Work chart 4 as for lace edge over 34-row rep, joining sts but do not work any multiple row corners, end with row 34.

Schematic measurements:
37 (37, 38½, 39)"
27 (27, 28½, 29)"
13(13, 13¾, 14)"
12¼(14½, 17, 18)"
6"
14(14½, 15, 15)"
5"

↑ = Direction of work
Beg of rnd
A

CHART 3

(Chart rows numbered on left: 1 (WS), 3, 5, 7, 9, 11, 13, 15, 17, 19, 21, 23, 25, 27, 29; on right: 2, 4, 6, 8, 10, 12, 14, 16, 18, 20, 22, 24, 26, 28, 30)

$\mathscr{M}$ultitextured Cardigan

INTERMEDIATE

Oversized cardigan worked in one long rectangle with sewn on cabled pockets. Designed by Rebecca Taylor. Sized for Small/Medium, Large/X-Large, and XX-Large. Directions are for smallest size with larger sizes in parentheses. If there is only one figure, it applies to all sizes.

KNITTED MEASUREMENTS
• Bust approx 52 (58, 64)"/132 (147.5, 162.5, 111.5) cm
• Finished rectangle approx 18½ (20½, 22½)"/47 (52, 57) cm wide x 72 (76, 80)"/183 (193, 203) cm long

MATERIALS ②④
• 10 (12, 14) 3½oz/100g balls (each approx 100yd/90m) of Blue Sky Alpacas *Worsted Hand Dyes* (royal alpaca/merino) in #2003 ecru (A)
• 1 3½oz/100g hank (approx 288yd/263m), Blue Sky Alpacas *Royal* (alpaca) in #700 alabaster (B)
• To substitute, seek a worsted-weight and fingering-weight yarn with fiber content similar to the original yarns.
• One pair each sizes 3, 4, 9 and 11 (3.25, 3.5, 5.5 and 8mm) needles OR SIZE TO OBTAIN GAUGE
• 8 locking stitch ring markers (not closed)
• Cable needle (cn)
• Marking pins

GAUGES
• 16 sts and 16 rows = 4"/10 cm over elongated bobbles & trinity stitch using size 11 (8mm) needles and A.
• 39½ sts and 38½ rows = 4"/10 cm over cable pat using size 4 (3.5mm) needles and B. TAKE TIME TO CHECK GAUGES.

STITCH GLOSSARY
Elongated Bobbles & Trinity Stitch
(Multiple of 4 sts plus 2)
Row 1 (RS - inc row) P3, ★(k1, p1, k1) in next st, p3; rep from ★, end p2.
Row 2 Knit.
Row 3 Purl.
Row 4 Knit.
Row 5 (RS - dec row) P3, ★p3tog, p3; rep from ★, end p2.
Row 6 K1, ★p3tog, (k1, p1, k1) in next st; rep from ★, end k1.
Row 7 Purl.
Row 8 K1, ★(k1, p1, k1) in next st, p3tog; rep from ★, end k1.
Row 9 Purl.
Row 10 K1, ★p3tog, (k1, p1, k1) in next st; rep from ★, end k1.
Row 11 Purl.
Row 12 K1, ★(k1, p1, k1) in next st, p3tog; rep from ★, end k1.
Rep rows 1-12 for elongated bobbles & trinity st.

CABLE PATTERN
(over a multiple of 10 sts plus 2)
Rows 1, 3 and 5 (WS) K1, purl to last 2 sts, k1.
Rows 2 and 4 Knit.
Row 6 K1, ★sl 5 sts to cn and hold to front, k5, k5 from cn; rep from ★, end k1.
Rows 7, 9 and 11 K1, p to last 2 sts, k1.
Rows 8 and 10 Knit.
Row 12 K6, ★sl 5 sts to cn and hold to back, k5, k5 from cn; rep from ★, end k6. Rep rows 1-12 for cable pat.

BODY
With size 9 (5.5mm) needles and A, cast on 91 (101, 111) sts. Work in k1, p1 rib for 3"/7.5 cm. **Next (inc) row (RS)** Knit, dec 17 (19, 21) sts evenly spaced across—74 (82, 90) sts. Change to size 11 (8mm) needles. Work rows 6-8 of elongated bobbles & trinity st, ★work rows 1-12 of pat; rep from ★ until piece measures 69"/175 cm from beg, ending with a pat row 8, AT SAME TIME, place marker at end of RS rows when piece measures 6"/15 cm, 14"/35.5 cm, 21 (22, 23)"/53 (56, 58.5) cm, 28 (30, 32)"/71 (76, 81) cm, 44 (46, 68)"/111.5 (117, 172.5) cm, 51 (54, 57)"/129.5 (137, 146) cm, 58 (62, 66)"/147 (157.5, 167.5) cm and 66 (70, 74)"/1675. (177.5, 188) cm from beg. Change to size 9 (5.5mm) needles. **Next (inc) row (RS)** Knit, inc 17 (19, 21) sts evenly spaced across—91 (101, 111) sts. Work in k1, p1 rib for 3"/7.5 cm. Bind off all sts in rib.

POCKETS (make 2)
Note Work first and last st in garter st for selvedge.
With size 3 (3.25mm) needles and B, cast on 53 sts. Work in k1, p1 rib for 1"/2.5 cm, inc 9 sts evenly spaced across last RS row—62 sts. Change to size 4 (3.5mm) needles. Work rows 1-12 of cable pat 4 times. **Next row (WS)** Purl. **Bind off row** K2, bind off next st, ★k2tog, bind off next st, [k1, bind off next st] twice; rep from ★ to end.

FINISHING
Position and sew pockets using photo as guide. Sew cardigan together along marked side as foll: Fold in half widthwise so that ribbing edges meet.

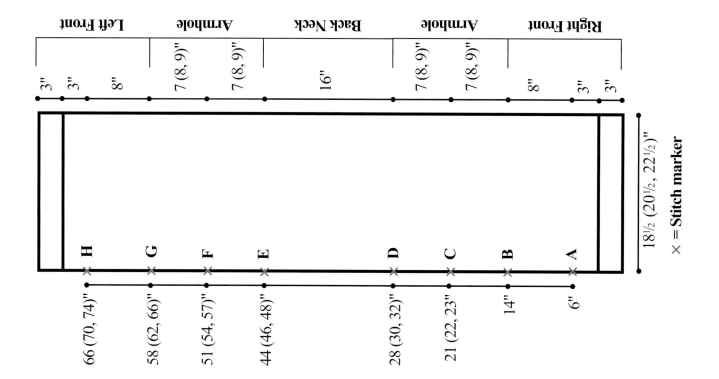

	Left Front			Armhole		Back Neck		Armhole			Right Front	
3"	3"	8"	7 (8, 9)"	7 (8, 9)"		16"		7 (8, 9)"	7 (8, 9)"	8"	3"	3"

18½ (20½, 22½)"

× = Stitch marker

H G F E D C B A

66 (70, 74)" 58 (62, 66)" 51 (54, 57)" 44 (46, 48)" 28 (30, 32)" 21 (22, 23)" 14" 6"

Sew seam beg at ribbing edges to markers A & H. Fold at markers C and F and place tog B & D markers and E & G markers. Beg at B & D markers, sew seam across to E & G markers. Remaining unsewn seams are the armholes.

Fall 2010 · No. 16

$\mathscr{C}$abled Pullover

INTERMEDIATE

Loose-fitting pullover with crossways cables, boat neck, and deep waistband. Sized for Small, Medium, and Large. Directions are for smallest size with larger sizes in parentheses. If there is only one figure, it applies to all sizes.

KNITTED MEASUREMENTS
• Waist circumference 30 (38, 44)"/76 (96.5, 111.5) cm
• Length 18¾"/47.5 cm
• Upper arm 27½"/70 cm

MATERIALS
• 16 (17, 17) 1¾oz/50g hanks (each approx 150yd/135m) of Manos del Uruguay/Fairmount Fibers *Silk Blend* (wool/silk) in #3014 natural

• One pair size 10 (6mm) needles OR SIZE TO OBTAIN GAUGE
• Size 9 (5.5mm) circular needle, 29"/74 cm long
• Cable needle (cn)
• Stitch holders and stitch markers

GAUGES
• 16 sts and 24 rows = 4"/10 cm over St st using
larger needles.
• One 20-st cable panel = 3½"/9 cm width. TAKE TIME TO CHECK GAUGES.

STITCH GLOSSARY
6-st RC (LC) Sl 3 sts to cn and hold to back (front), k3, k3 from cn.
8-st RC (LC) Sl 4 sts to cn and hold to back (front). k4, k4 from cn.

NOTES

1) Garment is worked with yarn held double throughout.

2) The length and width of the main piece is same for all 3 sizes. Only the waist circumference (and the opening at the lower edge) is different.

MAIN PIECE

Beg at the right sleeve opening edge, with size 10 (6mm) needles and yarn held double, cast on 140 sts.

Set up patterns

Row 1 (RS) P4, ★work 20 sts of row 1 of chart 1, p8; rep from ★ 3 times more, work 20 sts of row 1 of chart 1, p4. **Row 2 (WS)** K4, ★work 20 sts of row 2 of cable chart 1, k8; rep from ★ 3 times more, work 20 sts of chart 1, k4. Cont to foll chart pat and work rem sts in rev St st as established until piece measures 16"/40.5 cm from beg, end with pat row 12 of chart 1.

Divide for neck opening

Row 1 (RS) P4, [work 20 sts of row 1 of cable chart 1, p8] twice, k8, k2tog, turn, leaving the rem 70 sts on hold for back.

FRONT

Row 2 (WS) P9, work rem sts as established. **Row 3 (RS)** Work as established to the last 9 sts, work row 3 of chart 2 over the last 9 sts. Cont as established on these 69 sts for approx 10"/25.5 cm, end with a chart 1 row 12. Leave the front sts on hold.

BACK

Return to the 70 sts on hold for the back. **Row 1 (RS)** Ssk, k8, work to end. Complete the back neck as for the front neck, end with the same row as the front.

Join front and back

Next row (RS) Work the 69 sts of front in established pats foll row 1 of chart 1, inc 1 st at end, then inc 1 st in next st of beg of back and cont to end—140 sts. Work in chart 1 and rev St st pats as before on these sts until there are same number of rows as the first half. Bind off loosely.

FINISHING

Block lightly. Fold piece in half lengthwise and place markers to mark the center of the body front and back at the lower edge. Place markers at 7½ (9½, 11)"/19 (24, 28) cm each side of the center markers. Seam the sleeve up to these markers, leaving an opening of 15 (19, 22)"/38 (48, 56) cm on each piece.

Waistband

With circular needle and yarn held double, pick up and k 66 (83, 97) sts from front lower edge and 66 (83, 97) sts from back lower edge—132 (166, 194) sts. Join and pm to mark beg of rnd. Work in rnds of k1, p1 rib for 5"/12.5 cm. Bind off in rib.

CHART 1

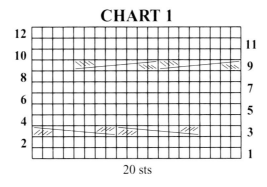

20 sts

CHART 2

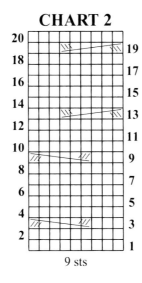

9 sts

Stitch Key

☐ k on RS, p on WS

6-st RC

6-st LC

8-st RC

8-st LC

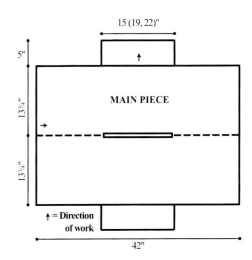

$\mathcal{F}$isherman's Cardigan

INTERMEDIATE

Over-sized, man's-style cardigan worked in a rib pattern with reversed front bands and knit-in pockets. Sized for Small, Medium, Large, and X-Large. Directions are for smallest size with larger sizes in parentheses. If there is only one figure, it applies to all sizes.

KNITTED MEASUREMENTS
• Bust 41 (46, 51, 55)"/104 (116.5, 129.5, 139.5) cm
• Length 25 (25½, 26, 27)"/63.5 (64.5, 66, 68.5) cm
• Upper arm 14 (15½, 16½, 17¾)"/35.5 (39.5, 42, 45) cm

MATERIALS ⑤
• 12 (13, 15, 17) 3½oz/100g hanks (each approx 109yd/98m) of Misti Alpaca *Tonos Chunky* (alpaca/wool) in #07 dark salmon
• One pair each sizes 9 and 10½ (5.5 and 6.5mm) needles, OR SIZE TO OBTAIN GAUGE
• Spare size 10½ (6.5mm) needle
• Four 1⅜"/34mm buttons
• Stitch holders
• Scrap yarn and tapestry needle

GAUGE
13 sts and 25 rows = 4"/10 cm over Half Fisherman's Rib using larger needles. TAKE TIME TO CHECK GAUGE.

STITCH GLOSSARY
k1B (knit 1 below) Insert RH needle into center of stitch below next stitch and k, slipping the stitch above off the needle at the same time.
SSKP [Sl 1 knitwise] twice, insert LH needle into slipped sts and k2tog tbl. Slip this stitch back to LH needle; pass 2nd stitch on LH needle over first stitch and slip stitch back to RH needle.

Short Row Wrap and Turn (w&t)
On RS row (on WS row)
1) Wyib (wyif), Sl next st purlwise.
2) Move yarn between the needles to the front (back).
3) Sl the same st back to LH needle. Turn work. One st is wrapped.
4) When working the wrapped st, insert RH needle under the wrap and work it tog with the corresponding st on needle.

Half Fisherman's Rib
(over an odd number of sts)
Row 1 (RS) Sl 1, k to end.
Row 2 *P1, k1b; rep from * to last st, p1.
Rep rows 1 and 2 for Half Fisherman's Rib.

BACK
With smaller needles, cast on 74 (82, 90, 98) sts. **Row 1 (RS)** *K2, p2; rep from * to last 2 sts, k2. **Row 2 (WS)** P2, *k2, p2; rep from * to end. Rep rows 1 and 2 until back measures 2"/5 cm from beg, ending with a RS row. **Dec row (WS)** [P2, k2] 1 (2, 2, 2) times, *p1, p2tog, k1, [p2, k2] twice, p1, p2tog, k1, p2, k2; rep from * 2 (2, 2, 3) times more, p2, k2, p1, p2tog, k1, p2, [k2, p2] 0 (1, 3, 0) times—67 (75, 83, 89) sts. **Set-up row 1 (RS)** Sl 1, k to last st, p1. **Set-up row 2** Sl 1, *p1, k1b; rep from * to last 2 sts, p1, k1.

Change to larger needle. Work even in Half Fisherman's Rib until back measures 6"/15 cm from beg, ending with a WS row.

Waist shaping
Dec row 1 (RS) Sl 1, SSKP, work to last 4 sts, SK2P, p1—63 (71, 79, 85) sts. Work 15 rows in pat. **Dec row 2 (RS)** Sl 1, SSKP, work to last 4 sts, SK2P, p1—59 (67, 75, 81) sts. Work 13 rows in pat. **Inc row 1 (RS)** Sl 1, (k1, p1, k1) into next st, work to last 2 sts, (k1, p1, k1) into next st, p1—63 (71, 79, 85) sts. Work 15 rows in pat. **Inc row 2 (RS)** P1, (k1, p1, k1) into next st, work to last 2 sts, (k1, p1, k1) into next st, p1—67 (75, 83, 89) sts. Work even in pat until back measures 17½"/44.5 cm from beg, ending with a WS row.

Armhole shaping
Bind off 3 (4, 5, 6) sts at beg of next 2 rows—61 (67, 73, 77) sts. **Dec row (RS)** Sl 1, SK2P, work to last 4 sts, SSKP, p1—57 (63, 69, 73) sts. Cont in pat, rep dec row every RS row twice more, then every 4th row 1 (2, 3, 3) times—45 (47, 49, 53) sts. Work even until armhole measures 7 (7½, 8, 9)"/18 (19, 20.5, 23) cm, ending with a WS row.

Neck and shoulder shaping
Next row (RS) Sl 1, k10 (11, 12, 13), bind off next 23 (23, 25, 25) sts, k10 (11, 12, 13), p1—11 (12, 13, 14) sts each shoulder. Cont in pat, work each side separately.

Left shoulder
Next row (WS) Bind off 4 sts, work to end. Bind off 4 (4, 4, 5) sts at beg of next WS row, then bind off rem 3 (4, 5, 5) sts on next WS row.

Right shoulder
With WS facing, join yarn at neck edge. **Next row (WS)** Work 11 (12, 13, 14) sts in pat. **Next row (RS)** Bind off 4 sts, k to last st, p1. Bind off 4 (4, 4, 5) sts, at beg of next RS row, then bind off rem 3 (4, 5, 5) sts on next RS row.

RIGHT FRONT
Button band
With smaller needles, cast on 16 sts.
Row 1 (RS) Sl 1, *p1, k1; rep from *
to last st, p1. Rep row 1 until button
band measures 17½"/44.5 cm, slightly
stretched. Place sts on holder, and break
yarn, leaving a long tail for sewing.
Body
With smaller needles, cast on 36 (40,
44, 48) sts. **Row 1 (RS)** *P2, k2; rep
from * to end. Rep row 1 until front
measures 2"/5 cm, end with a RS row.
Sizes Small (X-Large) Only
Dec row (WS) [P1, p2tog, k1] once
(twice), [p1, p2tog, k1, p2, k2] 4 (5)
times—31 (41) sts.
Sizes Medium (Large) Only
Dec row (WS) [P1, p2tog, k1, p2, k2]
5 times, [p2, k2] 0 (1) time—35 (39) sts.
For All Sizes
Set-up row 1 (RS) Sl 1, k to end.
Set-up row 2 Sl 1 wyif, *k1b, p1;
rep from * to end. Change to larger
needles.
Pocket front
Next row (RS) Sl 1, k17 (20, 22, 23),
turn. Place rem 13 (14, 16, 17) sts on
holder for side front. Work even in
pat as established on 18 (21, 23, 24) sts
until front measures 9"/23 cm from
beg, end with a WS row. Place sts on
holder.
Side front and pocket lining
Place 13 (14, 16, 17) side front sts
onto needle. With WS facing and scrap
yarn, cast on 17 (20, 22, 23) lining sts;
turn. With RS facing, join yarn and
k to end—30 (34, 38, 40) sts. **Next
row** Work 13 (14, 16, 17) sts in Half
Fisherman's Rib as established, p17
(20, 22, 23) sts. Cont working 17 (20,
22, 23) lining sts in St st and 13 (14,
16, 17) side front sts in pat until piece
measures 7½"/19 cm from beg, end
with a WS row.
Waist shaping and pocket joining
Dec row 1 (RS) Sl 1, k to last 5 sts,
SK2P, k2—28 (32, 36, 38) sts. Work
even in pat until piece matches pocket
front, ending with a WS row. Place
18 (21, 23, 24) pocket front sts onto a
spare needle. With RS tog and pocket
front in front, k1 pocket front st, *k 1
st from front needle tog with 1 st from
back needle; rep from * until pocket
lining and front sts are joined, k11 (12,
14, 15) side front sts—29 (33, 37, 39)

sts. **Next row (WS)** Sl 1 wyif, *k1B,
p1; rep from * to end. Work 4 rows
in Half Fisherman's Rib. **Dec row 2**
Sl 1, k to last 5 sts, SK2P, k2—27 (31,
35, 37) sts. Work 7 rows in pat. **Inc
row 1** Sl 1, k to last 3 sts, (k1, p1, k1)
into next st, k2—29 (33, 37, 39) sts.
Work 13 rows in pat. **Inc row 2** Sl 1,
k to last 3 sts, (k1, p1, k1) into next
st, k2—31 (35, 39, 41) sts. Work even
until front measures 17½"/44.5 cm
from beg, ending with a RS row.
Armhole and lapel shaping
Row 1 (WS) Bind off 3 (4, 5, 6) sts,
work to end. Place 16 button band
sts onto LH needle and work in Half
Fisherman's Rib as established—44
(47, 50, 51) sts. **Row 2** Sl 1, k to last
5 sts, SSKP, k2—42 (45, 48, 49) sts.
Row 3 and all WS rows Work in pat
to end. **Row 4** Sl 1, k to last 5 sts,
SSKP, k2—40 (43, 46, 47) sts. **Row 6**
Sl 1, k15, (k1, p1, k1) into next st, k to
last 5 sts, SSKP, k2. **Row 8** Sl 1, k to
end. **Row 10** Sl 1, k to last 5 sts, SSKP,
k2—38 (41, 44, 45) sts. **Row 12** Sl 1, k
to end. **Row 14** Sl 1, k17, (k1, p1, k1)
into next st, k to last 5 sts, SSKP, k2.
Work even in pat as established until
armhole measures same as back, end
with a RS row.
Shoulder shaping
Row 1 (WS) Bind off 4 sts, work in
pat to end. **Row 2** Work even in pat.
Row 3 Bind off 4 (4, 4, 5) sts, work
in pat to end. **Row 4** Work even in
pat. Bind off 3 (4, 5, 5) sts—27 (29, 31,
31) sts.
Collar
Work even in pat on 27 (29, 31, 31)
sts for 3"/7.5 cm, ending with a WS
row. **Row 1 (RS)** Sl 1, k24, w&t. **Row
2 and all WS rows** Work in pat to
end. **Row 3** Sl 1, k20, w&t. **Row 5**
Sl 1, k16, w&t. **Row 7** Sl 1, k12, w&t.
Row 9 Sl 1, k8, w&t. **Row 11** Sl 1, k4,
w&t. **Row 13** Sl 1, k to end, lifting
wraps and k tog with wrapped st.
Row 14 Work in pat to end. Rep rows
1–14 once more. Work even in Half
Fisherman's Rib until shorter edge of
collar measures 4 (4, 4, 4¼)"/10 (10,
10, 11) cm from shoulder. Place sts
on holder.

LEFT FRONT
Buttonhole band
With smaller needles, cast on 16 sts.

Row 1 (RS) Sl 1 wyif, *k1, p1; rep
from * to last st, k1. Rep row 1 until
band measures 1½"/4 cm from beg,
end with a WS row. **Buttonhole
row 1 (RS)** Sl 1 wyif, k1, [p1, k1]
twice, bind off 6 sts, [p1, k1] twice.
Buttonhole row 2 Sl 1 wyif, k1,
p1, k1, using cable cast-on method,
cast on 6 sts, [p1, k1] 3 times. Work
in rib as established, rep buttonhole
rows when band measures 6½, 11
and 15½"/16.5, 28 and 39.5 cm from
beg. Work even until band measures
17½"/16.5 cm from beg. Place sts on
holder and break yarn, leaving a long
tail for seaming.
Body
With smaller needles, cast on 36 (40,
44, 48) sts.
Row 1 (RS) *K2, p2; rep from * to
end. Rep row 1 until front measures
2"/5 cm, end after a RS row.
Sizes Small (X-large) Only
Dec row (WS) [K2, p1, p2tog, k1, p2]
3 (4) times, k2, [p1, p2tog, k1], 2 (3)
times, p2—31 (41) sts.
Sizes Medium (Large) Only
Dec row (WS) [K2, p2] 0 (1) time,
[k2, p1, p2tog, k1, p2] 5 times—35
(39) sts.
For all sizes
Set-up row 1 (RS) Sl 1, k to end.
Set-up row 2 Sl 1 wyif, *k1b, p1;
rep from * to end. Change to larger
needles.
Pocket front
Next row (RS) Sl 1, k12 (13, 15, 16)
and place these sts on holder for side
front; k to end—18 (21, 23, 24) sts.
Work even in Half Fisherman's Rib
until front measures 9"/23 cm from
beg, ending with a WS row. Place sts
on holder.
Side front and pocket lining
Place 13 (14, 16, 17) side front sts onto
needle. With RS facing and scrap yarn,
cast on 17 (20, 22, 23) sts; turn. With
WS facing, join yarn and p17 (20, 22,
23), work 13 (14, 16, 17) sts in Half
Fisherman's Rib as established—30
(34, 38, 40) sts.
Next row Sl 1, k to end. Cont
working 17 (20, 22, 23) lining sts in St
st and 13 (14, 16, 17) side front sts in
pat until piece measures 7½"/11.5 cm
from beg, ending with a WS row.
Waist shaping and pocket joining
Dec row 1 (RS) Sl 1, k1, SSKP, k to

end—28 (32, 36, 38) sts. Work even in pat until piece matches pocket front, ending with a WS row. K11 (12, 14, 15) side front sts. Place 18 (21, 23, 24) pocket front sts onto a spare needle. With RS tog and pocket front in front, *k 1 st from front needle tog with 1 st from back needle; rep from * until pocket lining and front sts are joined, and 1 front st rem, k1—29 (33, 37, 39) sts. **Next row (WS)** Sl 1 wyif, *k1B, p1; rep from * to end. Work 4 rows in Half Fisherman's Rib. **Dec row 2** Sl 1, k1, SSKP, k to end—27 (31, 35, 37) sts. Work 7 rows in pat. **Inc row 1** Sl 1, k1, (k1, p1, k1) into next st, k to end—29 (33, 37, 39) sts. Work 13 rows in pat. **Inc row 2** Sl 1, k1, (k1, p1, k1) into next st, k to end—31 (35, 39, 41) sts. Work even until front measures 17½"/44.5 cm from beg, ending with a WS row.

Armhole and lapel shaping
Row 1 (RS) Bind off 3 (4, 5, 6) sts, work to end. Place 16 buttonhole band sts onto LH needle and work in Half Fisherman's Rib—44 (47, 50, 51) sts. **Row 2 and all WS rows** Sl 1, *k1B, p1; rep from * to end. **Row 3** Sl 1, k1, SK2P, k to end—42 (45, 48, 49) sts **Row 5** Sl 1, k1, SK2P, k to end—40 (43, 46, 47) sts. **Row 7** Sl 1, k1, SK2P, k to last 17 sts, (k1, p1, k1) into next st, k to end. **Row 9** Sl 1, k to end. **Row 11** Sl 1, k1, SK2P, k to end—38 (41, 44, 45) sts. **Row 13** Sl 1, k to end. **Row 15** Sl 1, k1, SK2P, k to last 19 sts, (k1, p1, k1) into next st, k to end. Work even in Half Fisherman's Rib as established until armhole measures same as back, end with a WS row.

Shape shoulder
Row 1 (RS) Bind off 4 sts, work in pat to end. **Row 2 (WS)** Work even in pat. **Row 3** Bind off 4 (4, 4, 5) sts, work in pat to end. **Row 4** Work even in pat. Bind off 3 (4, 5, 5) sts—27 (29, 31, 31) sts.

Collar
Work even in pat on 27 (29, 31, 31) sts for 3"/7.5 cm, ending with a RS row. **Row 1 (WS)** Work 25 sts in pat, w&t. **Row 2 (RS)** and all RS rows K to end. **Row 3** Work 21 sts in pat, w&t. **Row 5** Work 17 sts in pat, w&t. **Row 7** Work 13 sts in pat, w&t. **Row 9** Work 9 sts in pat, w&t. **Row 11** Work 5 sts in pat, w&t.

Row 13 Work 29 sts in pat, lifting wraps and working tog with wrapped st. **Row 14** K to end. Rep rows 1-14 once more. Work even in Half Fisherman's Rib until shorter edge of collar measures 4 (4, 4, 4¼)"/10 (10, 10, 11) cm from shoulder. Place sts on holder.

RIGHT SLEEVE
With smaller needles, cast on 38 (42, 46, 46) sts on smaller needle. **Row 1 (RS)** *K2, p2; rep from * to last 2 sts, k2. **Row 2 (WS)** P2, *k2, p2; rep from * to end. Rep rows 1 and 2 until cuff measures 2"/5 cm from beg, ending with a RS row. **Dec row (WS)** [P2, k2, p1, p2tog, k1] twice, [p2, k2] 2 (3, 4, 4) times, p1, p2tog, k1, p2, k2, p1, p2tog, k1, p2—34 (38, 42, 42) sts. **Set-up row 1 (RS)** Sl 1, k to end. **Set-up row 2** Sl 1 wyif, *k1b, p1; rep from * to last st, k1. Work 10 rows even in Half Fisherman's Rib. **Inc row 1 (RS)** Sl 1, (k1, p1, k1) into next st, k to end—36 (40, 44, 44) sts. Work 11 rows even in Half Fisherman's Rib. **Inc row 2** Sl 1, k to last 3 sts, (k1, p1, k1) into next st, k2—38 (42, 46, 46) sts. Work 11 rows even in Half Fisherman's Rib. Rep last 24 rows 2 (2, 2, 3) times more—46 (50, 54, 58) sts. Work even until sleeve measures 17 (17, 17½, 18)"/43 (43, 44.5, 45.5) cm from beg, ending with a WS row.

Cap shaping
Bind off 3 (4, 5, 6) sts at beg of next 2 rows—40 (42, 44, 46) sts. Work 2 rows even in pat. **Dec row (RS)** Sl 1, SK2P, k to last 5 sts, SSKP, k2—36 (38, 40, 42) sts. Rep dec row every 8th row twice more, then every 4th row once, then every other row twice—16 (18, 20, 22) sts. Work even until sleeve cap measures 5 (5½, 6, 7)"/12.5 (14, 15, 16) cm. Bind off 3 (4, 5, 6) sts at beg of next 2 rows. Bind off rem 10 sts.

LEFT SLEEVE
Work same as right sleeve through first dec row—34 (38, 42, 42) sts. **Set-up row 1 (RS)** Sl 1, k to last st, p1. **Set-up row 2** Sl 1, *p1, k1b; rep from * to last st, p1. Work 10 rows even in Half Fisherman's Rib. **Inc row 1 (RS)** Sl 1, k1, (k1, p1, k1) into next st, k to last st, p1—36 (40, 44, 44) sts. Work 11 rows even in Half Fisherman's Rib. **Inc row 2** Sl 1, k

to last 2 sts, (k1, p1, k1) into next st, p1—38 (42, 46, 46) sts. Work 11 rows even in Half Fisherman's Rib. Rep last 24 rows 2 (2, 2, 3) times more—46 (50, 54, 58) sts. Work even until sleeve measures 17 (17, 17½, 18)"/43 (43, 44.5, 45.5) cm from beg, end with a WS row.

Cap shaping
Bind off 3 (4, 5, 6) sts at beg of next 2 rows—40 (42, 44, 46) sts. Work 2 rows even in pat.

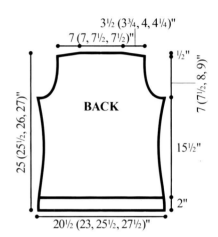

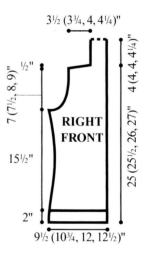

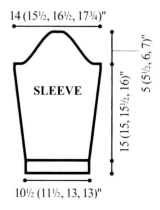

Dec row (RS) Sl 1, k1, SK2P, k to last 4 sts, SSKP, p1—36 (38, 40, 42) sts. Rep dec row every 8th row twice more, then every 4th row once, then every other row twice—16 (18, 20, 22) sts. Work even until sleeve cap measures 5 (5½, 6, 7)"/12.5 (14, 15, 16) cm. Bind off 3 (4, 5, 6) sts at beg of next 2 rows. Bind off rem 10 sts.

FINISHING

Graft left and right sides of collar together. With WS facing, sew short edge of collar to back neck. With RS facing, sew shoulder seams, set in sleeves, sew side and sleeve seams. Remove scrap yarn while grafting lower edges of pocket linings to top of ribbing. With RS facing, sew button bands to fronts, beg at top and sewing through all thickness at pocket linings.

Right pocket edging

With smaller needles and scrap yarn, cast on 12 sts. **Row 1** ★P1, k1; rep from ★ to end. Rep row 1 until piece measures 7"/18 cm from beg. Place sts on holder.

Left pocket edging

With smaller needles and scrap yarn, cast on 12 sts. **Row 1** ★K1, p1; rep from ★ to end. Rep row 1 until piece measures 7"/18 cm from beg. Place sts on holder. Sew pocket edgings to pocket fronts and graft upper and lower edges to fronts. Sew on buttons.

Winter 2010-2011 · No. 11

Hooded Lace Cardigan

EXPERIENCED

Very oversized, double-breasted jacket with lace and texture patterns, garter stitch hood and front bands, and raglan sleeves. Designed by Rebecca Taylor. Sized for Small-Large, and X-Large. Directions are for smallest size with larger sizes in parentheses. If there is only one figure, it applies to all sizes.

KNITTED MEASUREMENTS
• Bust (closed) 48½ (58½)"/123 (148.5) cm
• Length 26½ (28½)"/67 (72) cm
• Upper arm 24¾ (28)"/63 (71) cm

MATERIALS 🔵4
•22 (28) 1¾oz/50g balls (each approx 98yd/90m) of Rowan/Westminster Fibers, Inc. *All Seasons Cotton* (cotton/acrylic microfibre) in #178 organic
• One pair size 11 (8mm) needles OR SIZE TO OBTAIN GAUGE
• One pair size 13 (9mm) needles (for hood and front bands)
• Four 1"/25mm buttons

GAUGES
• 10 sts and 15 rows = 4"/10 cm over chart pats using smaller needles and 2 strands of yarn.
• 11 sts and 18 rows = 4"/10 cm over garter st using larger needles and 2 strands of yarn. TAKE TIME TO CHECK GAUGES.

NOTES
1) Jacket is worked with 2 strands of yarn held tog throughout.
2) The charts are drawn for the Small to Large size only.

BACK
With smaller needles, cast on 67 (79) sts. Work in k1, p1 rib for 6 rows. P next row on RS, dec 5 sts evenly spaced across—62 (74) sts. Beg chart for back (see page 104) Work rows 1-40 of chart, and for size X-Large work two more 6-st reps (shaded area). Raglan shaping Cont in chart pat, dec 1 st each side on next row then every other row 25 (29) times more. Bind off rem 10 (14) sts.

LEFT FRONT
With smaller needles, cast on 27 (33) sts. Work in k1, p1 rib for 6 rows. P next row on RS, dec 3 sts evenly spaced across—24 (30) sts. K next row on WS. Beg chart for left front (see page 105) Work rows 1-40 of chart, and for size X-Large work one more 6-st rep (shaded area). **Raglan shaping** Cont to work in chart pat, dec 1 st at armhole edge (beg of RS row) on next row, then every other

row 13 (21) times more, every 4th row 6 (4) times. Bind off rem 4 sts.

RIGHT FRONT
Work as for left front except foll chart for right front and work armhole decs at end of RS rows.

SLEEVES
With smaller needles, cast on 31 (35) sts. Work in k1, p1 rib for 8 rows. P next row on WS, inc 5 (7) sts evenly spaced across—36 (42) sts. K 1 row. **Beg sleeve chart.** Work row 1 of chart, and for size X-Large only work one more 6-st rep (shaded area). Cont in chart as established, inc 1 st each side on next (WS) row and rep inc every other row 12 (13) times more— 62 (70) sts. Work even through chart row 30. **Raglan cap shaping** Cont in chart pat, dec 1 st each side on next row, then every other row 25 (29) times more. Bind off rem 10 sts.

LEFT HOOD AND BUTTONBAND
With larger needles, cast on 13 sts. Work in garter st until piece measures 21 (23)"/53 (58) cm from beg. Hood shaping **Next (inc) row (RS)** K1, M1, k to end. Rep inc row every other row 4 times more—18 sts. Cast on 8 (10) sts at beg of next RS row (place a marker at beg of this row), k to end— 26 (28) sts. Cont in garter st for 7"/ 18 cm more, end with a WS row. **Next (dec) row (RS)** K1, k2tog, k to end of row. Rep dec row every other row 4 times more—21 (23) sts. Bind off.

RIGHT HOOD AND BUTTONHOLE BAND
Work as for left hood and button band, reversing all shaping by working incs and decs at end of RS rows and work cast on sts at beg of a WS row, AT SAME TIME, when band measures 14½ (16)"/37 (40.5) cm and 19 (21)"/48.5 (52) cm from beg, end with a WS row, work buttonhole row as foll: K3, yo, k2tog, k3, yo, k2tog, k3.

LEFT POCKET
With smaller needles, cast on 15 sts.

P 1 row on WS. **Row 1 (RS)** K1, *k2tog, yo; rep from * to last 2 sts, k2. **Row 2 (WS)** Purl. Rep rows 1 and 2 once more. Keeping first and last st in St st for selvage, work 6 rows in rev St st. **Row 11 (RS)** K3, *p1, k2; rep from * to end. **Rows 12-14** K the knit sts and p the purl sts. **Rows 15 and 16** Rep rows 1 and 2. **Next row** K1, *k 1, p 1; rep from *, end k2. **Next 5 rows** K the knit sts and p the purl sts. Bind off.

RIGHT POCKET
With smaller needles, cast on 15 sts. **Row 1 (RS)** *K2, p1; rep from *, end k3. **Row 2** K the knit sts and p the purl sts. **Rows 3 and 4** Rep rows 1 and 2. **Row 5** K1, *k2tog, yo; rep from * to last 2 sts, k2. **Row 6** Purl. **Rows 7-10** Rep rows 5 and 6 twice. **Rows 11-14** Rep rows 1 and 2 twice. **Next row** K1, *k1, p1; rep from *, end k2. **Next 5 rows** K the knit sts and p the purl sts. Bind off.

FINISHING
Sew raglan sleeve caps to raglan armholes. With marked edge of left hood piece at center back neck, sew hood and button band along one half back neck, top of left sleeve and along left front edge. There will be approx 6"/15 cm at lower edge of front piece free. Sew right hood and band to other side to correspond. Join left and right hoods tog at center back. Sew side and sleeve seams. Sew pockets to front pieces using photo as guide and matching patterns. Sew on buttons opposite buttonholes.

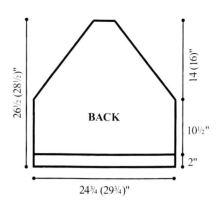

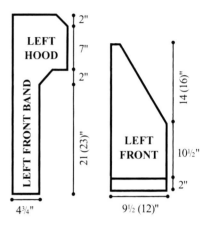

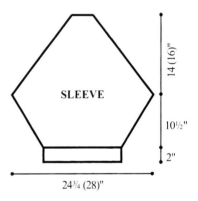

Medallion Coverup

EXPERIENCED

Loose-fitting poncho worked in lace medallions which are grafted together in finishing. One size.

KNITTED MEASUREMENTS
• Width 53¾"/136.5 cm
• Length 26¾"/68 cm

MATERIALS (3)
• 18 1¾oz/50g balls (each approx 136yd/125m) of Patons *Grace* in #62008 natural
• One set (5) size 4 (3.5mm) double-pointed needles OR SIZE TO OBTAIN GAUGE
• Size G/6 (4mm) crochet hook
• Stitch markers
• Stitch holders or scrap yarn
• Darning needle

GAUGE
1 square = 10¾ x 10¾"/27.5 x 27.5 cm (after blocking) using size 4 (3.5mm) needles. TAKE TIME TO CHECK GAUGE.

NOTES
1) Poncho is made of 24 squares which are grafted together to form a large square with an opening in the center. The back neck is one half-square grafted to the center, and the front neck is made up of 2 quarter-squares.
2) Full squares are worked in the round, half and quarter-squares are worked back and forth in rows.

SQUARE (make 24)
Cast on 8 sts leaving a long tail. K 1 row. Divide sts evenly on needles, join and place marker (pm), being careful not to twist sts. P 1 rnd.

Beg chart 1
Rnd 1 (RS) Reading chart from right to left, beg with the first st between red rep lines, work only the sts between rep lines 4 times around. Cont to work chart in this manner until rnd 43 is complete—46 sts in each rep, 184 sts total. Cut yarn. Place sts on holders or scrap yarn. With darning needle, weave cast-on tail through cast-on sts and pull tight. Block square to measure 10¾ x 10¾"/27.5 x 27.5 cm.

HALF-SQUARE (make 1)
Cast on 7 sts leaving a long tail, and k 2 rows.

Beg chart 1
Row 1 (RS) Reading RS row from right to left, beg with first st and work across entire row once. **Row 2 (WS)** Reading chart from left to right, beg with first st and work across entire row once. Cont to work chart in this manner until row 43 is complete—92 sts. Cut yarn. Place sts on holders or scrap yarn. With darning needle, weave cast-on tail through cast-on sts and pull tight. Block half-square to measure 10¾ x 5½"/27.5 x 14 cm.

Quarter-Square (make 2)
Cast on 5 sts leaving a long tail, and k 2 rows.

Beg chart 2
Row 1 (RS) Reading chart from right to left, beg with first st and work across entire row. **Row 2 (WS)** Reading chart from left to right, beg with first st and work across entire row. Cont to work chart in this manner until row 43 is complete—47 sts. Cut yarn. Place sts on holders or scrap yarn. With darning needle, weave cast-on tail through cast-on sts and pull tight. Block quarter-square to measure 5½ x 5½"/14 x 14 cm.

FINISHING
Foll assembly diagram, use Kitchener stitch or 3-needle bind-off to graft pieces together. Center stitch of quarter square can be joined with either side. With crochet hook, work 1 row hdc around entire edge of poncho, working 1 st into each open lp, and 3 sts in each open corner lp. Iron entire piece flat.

CHART 1

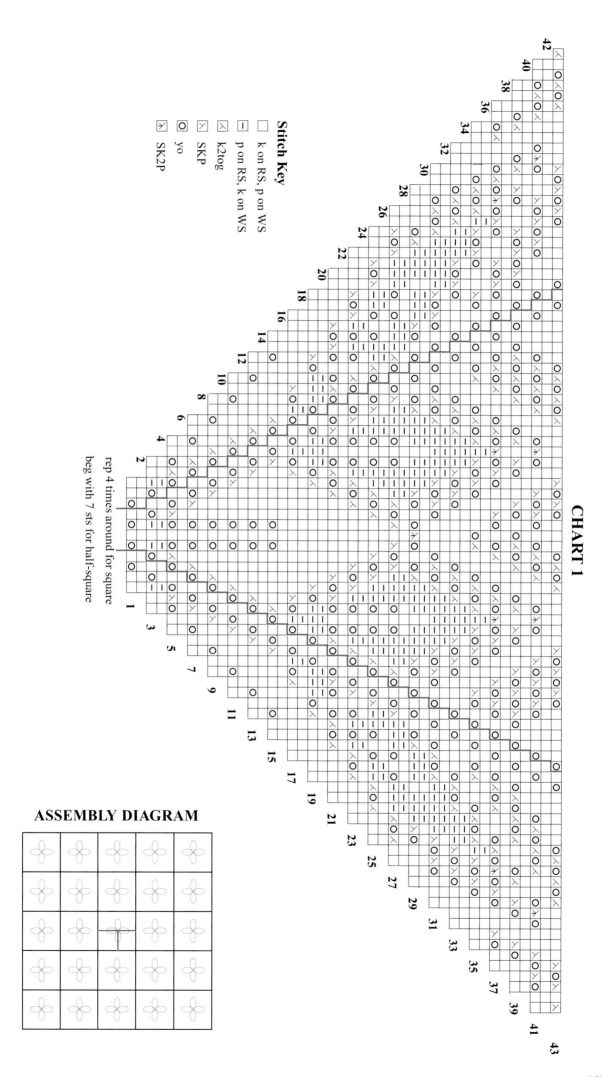

Stitch Key

☐ k on RS, p on WS

─ p on RS, k on WS

⊠ k2tog

⊠ yo

⊠ SKP

⊠ SK2P

rep 4 times around for square

beg with 7 sts for half-square

ASSEMBLY DIAGRAM

CHART 2

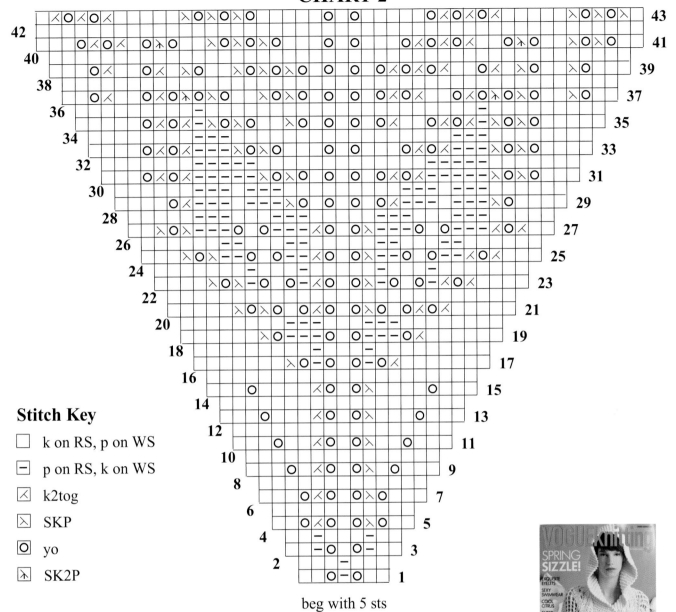

beg with 5 sts

Stitch Key

☐	k on RS, p on WS
▬	p on RS, k on WS
⟋	k2tog
⟍	SKP
⊙	yo
⋏	SK2P

Spring/Summer 2011 · No. 9

Gold-Tone Bikini

INTERMEDIATE

Standard-fitting bikini with side tie bottoms and side tie cups. Sized for X-Small, Small, and Medium. Directions are for smallest size with larger sizes in parentheses. If there is only one figure, it applies to all sizes.

KNITTED MEASUREMENTS
• Bust (adjustable) to 29 (31, 33)"/73.5 (78.5, 83.5) cm
• Hip (adjustable) to 28 (29, 30)"/71 (73.5, 76) cm

MATERIALS 🧶2
• 3 (4, 4) 1¾oz/50g balls (each approx 129yd/118m) of Katia/KFI *Gatsby* (viscose/nylon/metallic) in #20 gold

• Two size 1 (2.25mm) circular needles, 24"/60 cm long, OR SIZE TO OBTAIN GAUGE
• Two size 1 (2.25mm) double-pointed needles

GAUGE
33 sts and 50 rows = 4"/10 cm over St st using size 1 (2.25mm) needles. TAKE TIME TO CHECK GAUGE.

STITCH GLOSSARY
Short Row Wrap and Turn (w&t)
On RS row (on WS row)
1) Wyib (wyif), Sl next st purlwise.
2) Move yarn between the needles to the front (back).
3) Sl the same st back to LH needle. Turn work. One st is wrapped.
4) When working the wrapped st, insert RH needle under the wrap and work it tog with the corresponding st on needle.

TOP
Underbust strap
With dpn, cast on 6 sts. Work in St st for 46 (47, 48)"/117 (119, 122) cm. Bind off loosely. Sew long side edges tog.
Cup (make 2)
With circular needle, cast on 54 (58, 62) sts. Work in St st for 13 rows.
Form the hem
Next row (WS) Lay strap on wrong side of cup. Fold cast on edge of cup over the strap. **Next row (WS)** ★Pick up 1 st from cast-on edge of cup, sl to LH needle and p this st tog with next st on needle; rep from ★ until hem covers strap.
Short row shaping
Short rows 1 (RS) and 2 (WS) Work to the last 3 sts, w&t. **Short**

rows 3 and 4 Work to the last 6 sts, w&t. **Short rows 5 and 6** Work to the last 9 sts, w&t. **Short rows 7 and 8** Work to last 12 sts, w&t. **Next 2 rows** Work to the end of each row, closing up the wraps. Work 4 (6, 8) rows even on all sts. **Dec row 1 (RS)** K2, ssk, k19 (21, 23), k2tog, pm, k4, pm, ssk, k to the last 4 sts, k2tog, k2—4 sts dec'd. Work 3 rows even. **Dec row 2 (RS)** K2, ssk, k to 2 sts before marker, k2tog, k4, ssk, k to last 4 sts, k2tog, k2. Rep dec 2 every 4th row 6 (7, 8) times more—22 sts. Work 3 rows even. **Dec row 3 (RS)** K2, ssk, k to the last 4 sts, k2tog, k2. Rep dec row 3 every 4th row 5 times more—10 sts. **Next row** P2, p2tog, p2, p2tog tbl, p2. **Next row** K2, ssk, k2tog, k2—6 sts. **Last row** P1, (p2tog) twice, p1. Bind off loosely.
Rib trim
With RS facing and one circular needle, pick up and k 47 (51, 55) sts along one side of cup, 2 sts at top, then with 2nd circular needle, pick up and k 47 (51, 55) sts along other side of cup. Work in k1, p1 rib for 2 rows over all sts. Bind off loosely. Work 2nd cup in same manner.
Straps (make 2)
Work two 21"/53 cm straps as before for the shoulders. Sew securely to the tops of the cups.

BOTTOMS
With circular needle, cast on 62 (66, 70) sts for front edge. Work in St st for 13 rows.
Form the hem
Note Straps are not worked into the hem, but sewn to the 4 top corners in finishing.
Next row (WS) Fold and work hem as for cups. **Dec row 1 (RS)** K2, ssk, k to the last 4 sts, k2tog, k2. Work 2 rows even. **Dec row 2 (WS)** P2, p2tog, p to the last 4 sts, p2tog tbl, p2—58 (62, 66) sts. Work 2 rows even. Rep the last 6 rows 9 (9, 10) times more. Work 0 (2, 0) rows even. Rep dec row 1 for 0 (1, 0) time more—22 (24, 26) sts. Work even until piece measures 8½ (8¾, 9)"/21.5 (22, 23) cm from beg.

Then cont along the back edge, work as foll: **Inc row (RS)** K1, inc 1 st in next st, k to last 3 sts, inc 1 st, k2. Rep inc row every other row 19 (20, 21) times more—62 (66, 70) sts. Rep inc row every 4th row 13 times more—88 (92, 96) sts. Work even until piece measures 16½ (17, 17½)"/42 (43, 44.5) cm from beg. Bind off.
Hem
With RS facing pick up and k 88 (92, 96) sts in bound-off sts. Work in St st for 12 rows. Fold and work hem as before. Bind off loosely.

FINISHING
Pick up and k 126 (130, 134) sts along one side edge of the bottoms. Work in k2, p2 rib for 2 rows. Bind off. Work other side in same way.
Work four 16 (17, 18)"/40.5 (43, 45.5) cm straps as before. Sew securely to the 4 top corners of the bikini bottoms.

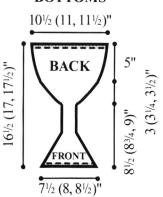

TOP

CUP

6 (6½, 7)"

6½ (7, 7½)"

BOTTOMS

10½ (11, 11½)"

BACK

16½ (17, 17½)"

5"

8½ (8¾, 9)"

3 (3¾, 3½)"

FRONT

7½ (8, 8½)"

"I have made many friends at *Vogue Knitting* over the years, including the dynamic, current Editor Trisha Malcolm, and have grown as a designer with *Vogue Knitting*'s support," says Nicky Epstein. "*Vogue Knitting* has also been instrumental in my success as a knitting author, publishing many of my books with Sixth&Spring. I value the combination of friendship and professionalism at *Vogue Knitting* and will keep designing, writing features, and hosting knitting tours for them as long as they want me. Our industry is lucky to have *Vogue Knitting*, and I wish them continued success."

Techniques & Abbreviations

KNITTING NEEDLES

U.S.	METRIC
0	2mm
1	2.25mm
2	2.75mm
3	3.25mm
4	3.5mm
5	3.75mm
6	4mm
7	4.5mm
8	5mm
9	5.5mm
10	6mm
10 ½	6.5mm
11	8mm
13	9mm
15	10mm
17	12.75mm
19	15mm
35	19mm

CROCHET HOOKS

U.S.	METRIC
B/1	2.25mm
C/2	2.75mm
D/3	3.25mm
E/4	3.5mm
F/5	3.75mm
G/6	4mm
7	4.5mm
H/8	5mm
I/9	5.5mm
J/10	6mm
K/10½	6.5mm
L/11	8mm
M/13	9mm
N/15	10mm

GLOSSARY

bind off Used to finish an edge or segment. Lift the first stitch over the second, the second over the third, etc. (U.K.: cast off)

bind off in ribbing Work in ribbing as you bind off. (Knit the knit stitches, purl the purl stitches.) (U.K.: cast off in ribbing)

3-needle bind-off With the right side of the two pieces facing and the needles parallel, insert a third needle into the first stitch on each needle and knit them together. Knit the next two stitches the same way. Slip the first stitch on the third needle over the second stitch and off the needle. Repeat for three-needle bind-off.

cast on Placing a foundation row of stitches upon the needle in order to begin knitting.

decrease Reduce the stitches in a row (that is, knit 2 together).

increase Add stitches in a row (that is, knit in front and back of stitch).

knitwise Insert the needle into the stitch as if you were going to knit it.

make one With the needle tip, lift the strand between the last stitch knit and the next stitch on the left-hand needle and knit into the back of it. One knit stitch has been added.

make one p-st With the needle tip, lift the strand between the last stitch worked and the next stitch on the left-hand needle and purl into back of it. One purl stitch has been added.

no stitch On some charts, "no stitch" is indicated with shaded spaces where stitches have been decreased or not yet made. In such cases, work the stitches of the chart, skipping over the "no stitch" spaces.

place markers Place or attach a loop of contrast yarn or purchased stitch marker as indicated.

pick up and knit (purl) Knit (or purl) into the loops along an edge.

purlwise Insert the needle into the stitch as if you were going to purl it.

selvage stitch Edge stitch that helps make seaming easier.

slip, slip, knit Slip next two stitches knitwise, one at a time, to right-hand needle. Insert tip of left-hand needle into fronts of these stitches, from left to right. Knit them together. One stitch has been decreased.

slip, slip, slip, knit Slip next three stitches knitwise, one at a time, to right-hand needle. Insert tip of left-hand needle into fronts of these stitches, from left to right. Knit them together. Two stitches have been decreased.

slip stitch An unworked stitch made by passing a stitch from the left-hand to the right-hand needle as if to purl.

work even Continue in pattern without increasing or decreasing. (U.K.: work straight)

yarn over Making a new stitch by wrapping the yarn over the right-hand needle. (U.K.: yfwd, yon, yrn)

GAUGE

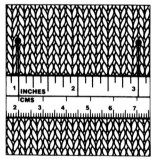 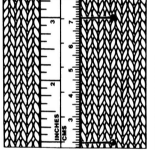

Stitches measured over 2"/5cm.   Rows measured over 2"/5cm.

Note: Gauge should be taken over at least 2"/5cm and preferably over 4"/10cm.

Make a test swatch at least 4"/10cm square. If the number of stitches and rows does not correspond to the gauge given, you must change the needle size. An easy rule to follow is: To get fewer stitches to the inch/cm, use a larger needle; to get more stitches to the inch/cm, use a smaller needle. Continue to try different needle sizes until you get the same number of stitches in the gauge.

SIZING

Directions are given for the smallest size, with the larger sizes in parentheses. If there is only one figure, it applies to all sizes.
SIZE+ listed under a pattern number indicates that a garment is sized XXL or larger.

BASIC STITCHES

Garter stitch Knit every row. Circular knitting: Knit one round, then purl one round.

Stockinette stitch Knit right-side rows and purl wrong-side rows. Circular knitting: knit all rounds. (U.K.: stocking stitch)

Reverse-stockinette stitch Purl right-side rows and knit wrong-side rows. Circular knitting: purl all rounds. (U.K.: reverse stocking stitch)

SKILL LEVELS FOR KNITTING

BEGINNER

Ideal first project.

EASY

VERY EASY listed under a pattern number indicates basic stitches, minimal shaping and simple finishing.

INTERMEDIATE

For knitters with some experience. More intricate stitches, shaping and finishing.

EXPERIENCED

For knitters able to work patterns with complicated shaping and finishing.

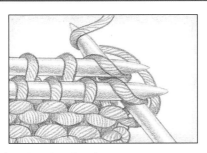

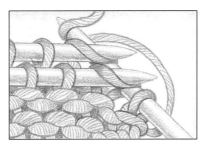

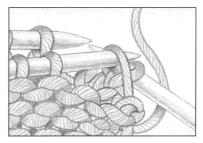

1. Hold right sides of pieces tog on two needles. Insert third needle knitwise into first stitch of each needle, and wrap yarn knitwise.

2. Knit these two stitches together, and slip them off the needles. ★Knit the next two stitches together in the same manner.

3. Slip first stitch on 3rd needle over 2nd stitch and off needle. Rep from ★ in step 2 across row until all stitches are bound off.

KNITTING ABBREVIATIONS

approx	approximately
beg	begin(ning)
CC	contrasting color
ch	chain
cm	centimeter(s)
cn	cable needle
cont	continu(e)(ing)
dec	decreas(e)(ing)
dpn	double-pointed needle(s)
foll	follow(s)(ing)
g	gram(s)
inc	increas(e)(ing)
k	knit
kfb	knit into front and back of stitch
LH	left-hand
lp(s)	loop(s)
m	meter(s)
mm	millimeter(s)
MC	main color
M1	make one (see glossary)
M1 p-st	make 1 purl stitch (see glossary)
oz	ounce(s)
p	purl
pat(s)	pattern(s)
pm	place marker (see glossary)
psso	pass slip stitch(es) over
rem	remain(s)(ing)
rep	repeat
RH	right-hand
RS	right side(s)
rnd(s)	round(s)
SKP	slip 1, knit 1, pass slip stitch over— 1 stitch has been decreased
SK2P	slip 1, knit 2 together, pass slip stitch over the knit 2 together— 2 stitches have been decreased
S2KP	slip 2 stitches together, knit 1, pass 2 slip stitches over knit 1
sl	slip
sl st	slip stitch (see glossary)
ssk	slip, slip, knit (see glossary)
st(s)	stitch(es)
St st	stockinette stitch
tbl	through back loop(s)
tog	together
WS	wrong side(s)
wyib	with yarn in back
wyif	with yarn in front
yd	yard(s)
yo	yarn over needle (U.K.: see glossary)
*	repeat directions following ★ as many times as indicated
[ ]	repeat directions inside brackets as many times as indicated

Standard Yarn Weight System

Categories of yarn, gauge ranges, and recommended needle and hook sizes

Yarn Weight Symbol & Category Names	**0** LACE	**1** SUPER FINE	**2** FINE	**3** LIGHT	**4** MEDIUM	**5** BULKY	**6** SUPER BULKY
Type of Yarns in Category	Fingering 10-count crochet thread	Sock, Fingering, Baby	Sport, Baby	DK, Light Worsted	Worsted, Afghan, Aran	Chunky, Craft, Rug	Bulky, Roving
Knit Gauge Range* in Stockinette Stitch to 4 inches	33–40★★ sts	27–32 sts	23–26 sts	21–24 st	16–20 sts	12–15 sts	6–11 sts
Recommended Needle in Metric Size Range	1.5–2.25 mm	2.25–3.25 mm	3.25–3.75 mm	3.75–4.5 mm	4.5–5.5 mm	5.5–8 mm	8 mm and larger
Recommended Needle U.S. Size Range	000–1	1 to 3	3 to 5	5 to 7	7 to 9	9 to 11	11 and larger
Crochet Gauge* Ranges in Single Crochet to 4 inch	32–42 double crochets★★	21–32 sts	16–20 sts	12–17 sts	11–14 sts	8–11 sts	5–9 sts
Recommended Hook in Metric Size Range	Steel★★★ 1.6–1.4 mm Regular Hook 2.25mm	2.25–3.5 mm	3.5–4.5 mm	4.5–5.5 mm	5.5–6.5 mm	6.5–9 mm	9 mm and larger
Recommended Hook U.S. Size Range	Steel★★★ 6, 7, 8 Regular hook B–1	B–1 to E–4	E–4 to 7	7 to I–9	I–9 to K–10 1/2	K–10 1/2 to M–13	M–13 and larger

★ GUIDELINES ONLY: The above reflect the most commonly used gauges and needle or hook sizes for specific yarn categories.

★★ Lace weight yarns are usually knitted or crocheted on larger needles and hooks to create lacy, openwork patterns. Accordingly, a gauge range is difficult to determine. Always follow the gauge stated in your pattern.

★★★ Steel crochet hooks are sized differently from regular hooks—the higher the number, the smaller the hook, which is the reverse of regular hook sizing

This Standards & Guidelines booklet and downloadable symbol artwork are available at: YarnStandaeds.com

Index

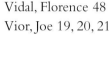

Acknowledgements

Vogue Knitting wouldn't be possible without the stellar team who puts each issue together. We'd like to give credit to all the resources involved with the magazine over the last thirty years: the careful and creative editors, the loyal designers, the tireless tech editing team, the visionary photographers, the skilled graphic designers, the dedicated web team, the numerous support staff—and, of course, all the beautiful yarn, which ties us all together.